P9-CTQ-522

Francis, Pope of Good Promise

Jimmy Burns

St. Martin's Press ❧ New York

www.stmartins.com

Library of Congress Cataloging-in-Publication Data

Burns, Jimmy, 1953–
    Francis, Pope of good promise / Jimmy Burns. — First U.S. Edition.
        p. cm.
    Includes bibliographical references and index.
    ISBN 978-1-250-07649-6 (hardcover)
    ISBN 978-1-4668-8792-3 (e-book)
    1. Francis, Pope, 1936– 2. Popes—Biography. I. Title.
    BX1378.7.B87 2015
    282.092—dc23
    [B]

                                                      2015017829

First published in Great Britain by Constable, an imprint of Constable & Robinson Ltd, a Hachette UK company

First U.S. Edition: September 2015

10 9 8 7 6 5 4 3 2 1

For Kidge, Julia & Miriam
And for Fr Nicholas King SJ

Contents

Prologue
First Engagement

From the moment Pope Francis stepped onto the balcony of St Peter's Basilica for the first time on 13 March 2013, a global audience caught a sense that not only the Catholic Church but the world at large could be entering a new spiritual as well as political and social age. Shunning the red shoes and *mozzetta* (shoulder cape) worn for the occasion by his predecessors, he was dressed only in the white papal cassock with a pewter cross around his neck. The sanctimonious pomp and circumstance that had characterized the Vatican for as long as most people could remember evaporated as Francis, with a simple gesture, bid everyone a peaceful '*Bona sera*' and asked the tens of thousands of people gathered in the square to 'pray over' him before he gave his first *Urbis et Orbi* blessing to the city.

His appearance surprised many. While the winning cardinal was widely believed to have come second in the 2005 conclave, he had barely figured in the predictions as to who would succeed Pope Benedict XVI. My knowledge of the elected Jorge Bergoglio, the only ordained Jesuit among the collegiate cardinals, was at the time too full of apparent contradictions to form a firm opinion as to whether the choice had been inspired. What I had reported of the Argentine Church's complicity in human rights violations and its support for the military junta's invasion of the Falklands Islands made me wary of the appointment of a cardinal of Buenos Aires as the new leader of the world's 1.2 billion Catholics. Yet, within hours of his election I found myself bombarded with enquiries and journalistic assignments from both sides of the Atlantic, which forced me to draw more fully on memories and sources from my Jesuit education and from my years as a journalist in Argentina. This book has its roots in those preliminary researches that shed light on the extent to which Bergoglio had been shaped by the politics and society of the country into which he was born, the holy order of which he had chosen to become a member, and the example of the radical and universally popular Francis of Assisi, the thirteenth-century saint whose name he adopted on becoming pope.

In the days following his election, there would be further signs of Bergoglio's simplicity that seemed to mirror the first apostles and the leader that inspired them. Francis chose as his home the Domus Sanctae Marthae, the hotel adjacent to St Peter's Basilica used by clergy and cardinals, rather than the privileged privacy of the Vatican's Apostolic Palace. He declared that the thirty papal rooms he had been assigned by right were an excessive luxury he was happy to do without. During his first Holy Week as pope, he washed the feet of young male prisoners and Muslim women, before heading into the crowds, made up of all cultures and ages, with the selfless engagement of a universal pilgrim. Not since Pope John XIII appeared on the scene half a century earlier had a new pope opened the windows of the Church in such a way as to let in some much needed fresh air. Nevertheless people could still only guess at where it all might be leading towards. The jury was out. More time would have to pass before a clearer picture could emerge of Bergoglio's life and the Francis papacy in action.

It was on a bright and mild Wednesday morning in early November 2013 in Rome – one of the last balmy days of autumn before the winter chill set in – that I caught up with Pope Francis in the early stages of his papacy. Armed with a ticket and advice provided by friends from the Catholic organization Opus Dei (for the record, I am not a member!), I turned up in a still relatively empty St Peter's Square and positioned myself in the front row of the papal route. Even if I stood no chance of talking to him properly, I would come face to face with my subject.

Within an hour the square was packed and I was barely holding my post, penned in between an Argentine family and a group of equally excitable young Italian students. On either side of the papal route, there was a huge multicultural and international crowd, with people waving their national colours or some emblem or poster identifying their college, school, seminary or association. Most seemed to be Catholic and either Spanish- or Italian-speaking but there were many exceptions judging by the other languages I heard and other faith groups I glimpsed. In the excited and cheerful crush, I noticed a young Italian couple, with the woman gently rocking a three- or four-month-old baby boy in her arms. They were several rows back and stood not a chance of getting anywhere near the papal route so I called out to them and suggested that, when the time came, they pass the baby along the rows and I would hold him.

And so it came to be that when the Pope's open-roof truck turned into the square and started moving in my direction I found a baby in my arms. He had been passed gently but purposefully from one row to the other, like a parcel on special delivery. I owe it to the baby that Pope Francis there and then gave me more time than I had otherwise expected. Seeing me with the child, he ordered his driver to stop so he could stoop over to kiss and bless the infant as I raised him up. In the seconds that followed, it was as if the whole square had disappeared and I was there, with the baby, alone with Pope Francis, enclosed in the moment. There seemed something providential, if not miraculous, that I of all people was holding somebody else's baby. You see, I was told from an early age

I could never father a child of my own – once a dark cloud in my life, but one that eventually lifted when my wife and I took a joint decision to adopt, bringing enduring delight into our lives. The Pope would not have known this, but his eyes and mine met, and in an instant I felt recognized and reassured, all stress and division dissipated. I was drawn to what I can only describe as the inner goodness of the man as he smiled and blessed me too, before he moved on across the square, where thousands awaited him.

When I had followed him that summer – on his first papal pilgrimage beyond Europe, to Brazil for World Youth Day – I had observed similar encounters in which Pope Francis seemed to touch an individual in the crowd with a sense of extraordinary personal engagement. My experience on that autumn day in Rome would chime with that of many others during his first years in office.

One of the phrases Pope Francis uses to explain transformative encounters is the Buenos Aires slang expression '*nos primerea*'. Literally translated it means: 'he prioritizes me'. It's a term that he picked up years ago from the terraces of his beloved San Lorenzo football club. It's often used by Argentine fans to talk of a good football move that ends in a goal – a move that 'anticipates you' or 'beats you to it'.

My own transformative encounter with the Pope provides a fitting image of the person Catholics are brought up to believe is Christ's Vicar on earth, but this portrait of Bergoglio and Francis's world – past and present – tells the story of a complex man. My subject is no picture-book saint but a very human priest who struggled to be a true witness of his faith in challenging times. In circumstances he neither sought nor foresaw he found himself handed the highest office at a time of institutional crisis, not just for the Church but for long-established institutions worldwide, from banks to political parties.

The book charts Bergoglio's formation as a priest and bishop against the dramatic backdrop of Argentina's turbulent politics and the challenging principles he adopted as a member of the Jesuit order. It examines the extent to which his social conscience was influenced by the legacy of the country's controversial populist president General Juan Perón and his wife Evita, and questions his moral standing during the Argentina military junta's 'Dirty War' against political dissidents, when thousands disappeared before being tortured and killed. At the time he stood accused of not having done enough on behalf of the victims, including fellow Jesuit priests.

Such accusations were made within the broader context of Church history, the exercise of political and religious power, of realpolitik, and the extent to which even the most spiritual of figures have sometimes been seemingly guided by the maxim that politics is always the art of the possible. Bergoglio's discreet refusal to condemn human rights violations publicly, and instead to intercede with the authorities to try and secure the release of political detainees, saved the lives of some individuals while avoiding his own martyrdom.

His survival paved the way for his transformation, following the end of military rule, into a strong advocate of social justice, earning the respect of his countrymen on account of his humility and denunciation of corruption, not least at government level. In challenging the ethics of successive presidents, bankers, corporations and fellow Church leaders, Bergoglio sent a signal to endemically failing systems around the world that the age in which we live demands spiritual and political renewal.

This is a big papacy that has already had a global impact but it is still in its early stages, marked by mixed expectations and contradictory acts that require explanation. Further testimony, investigation and reflection since the first wave of books that followed the papal election have brought Bergoglio's story into sharper perspective. I sympathize with one of the Pope's environmental advisers, the Brazilian theologian Leonardo Boff, who has stated that 'what matters isn't Bergoglio and his past, but Francis and his future'. However, I believe that the main protagonist cannot even begin to be understood without a detailed examination of the decades lived out when he was a Jesuit priest, and this demands close familiarity with Argentina's culture and history. To tell the ongoing story, I also examined the other dramatis personae within the Vatican impacting on the papacy, and the impact the papacy is having on the wider world – not least Catholics themselves.

This is a personal journey, as well as portrait. It draws on my own Catholic background – a Jesuit education open to diverse expressions and practice of faith from mysticism to popular religion, from ritual to social and political action. It also draws on my subsequent experience as a journalist in Latin America, based in Buenos Aires, and as an author investigating the life of Bergoglio in Rome and in other territories, leaning on a wide range of interviews with key protagonists, spanning decades and straddling continents.

I have written biographies of Diego Maradona and my late father, neither easy subjects. But this project poses its own particular challenge – as one friend put it, 'Jimmy, it must be quite difficult to write about God.' Catholic teaching defines the Pope as 'the perpetual and visible source and foundation of the unity both of the bishops and of the whole company of the faithful' who by reason of his office as Vicar of Christ, and as pastor of the entire Church, 'has full, supreme, and universal power over the whole Church, a power which he can always exercise unhindered'. Nonetheless, I see myself as an author who is a Catholic, rather than a Catholic author. Inevitably my Catholic faith has been a major influence on the writing of this book but it is not a hagiography.

I felt in conscience that if this book was to take shape in any meaningful and worthwhile form it had to involve sources of information and comment that together share my doubts as well as certainties. It is a search of truth through doubt, walking in the footsteps of the man who became pope, a term Francis himself eschews, preferring the more humble and collegiate term of Bishop of Rome. The prophecies of Malachy place the present pope as the last in line, but perhaps that will be solely because Francis's successors will also prefer the less ostentatious title of Bishop of Rome.

Nothing I have come across in the course of my researches has dissuaded me from the belief that the key to fully understanding Bergoglio and Francis lies in the fact that he is a Jesuit. For St Ignatius of Loyola, the founding father of the Jesuits, one of the great spiritual tenets was that true spirituality lies in 'finding God in all things'. For Ignatius, God cannot be confined within the walls of a Catholic church, but can be found in every moment of the day, in other people. Intrinsically linked to this concept is a positive awareness that anything we do, that is not evil, can be meritorious, regardless of faith, culture or background. Other aspects of Ignatian spirituality include the aim of 'contemplation in action' – in other words the capacity to listen with an open heart within a busy, demanding world. Along with this comes flexibility in words and deeds, and a recognition of the need to meet situations as they arise with a spirit of engagement and creativity, rather than dogmatic rejection and condemnation. This is why I have taken a calculated risk with the title: *Pope of Good Promise*.

Few Vatican elections have generated as much interest as that of Cardinal Jorge Bergoglio, the first pope from the Americas and the first from outside Europe in over 1,000 years. He will continue to command huge attention and controversy as he settles into office, knowing that his main challenge is that of being a truly global figure, transcending his own race and nationality, while assuming the role of teacher, prophet and preacher. Bergoglio will not need reminding that Francis of Assisi, the saint he evoked on his election as pope, was in the end forced to resign as head of his order, when his stark message of the need for humility and reform was neutralized by the actions of his own Church.

This book, while written by a cradle Catholic, is aimed at a broad constituency of believers and non-believers, giving readers a fresh insight into a key spiritual figure of our times whose political and social impact promises to be far reaching and widespread.

Part One

The Road to Conversion

Chapter One
Departure

To begin this journey through the life of Pope Francis, I should establish my own footing and explain why the pope – any living pope, but particularly one that is a Jesuit and from the Spanish-speaking world – has necessarily played an important part in my life.

I was born in Madrid in 1953 to a Spanish mother and a British Catholic father. My parents claim a variety of immigrant bloodlines in their ancestry straddling Latin America – Cuba on my mother's side, and Chile on my father's side – along with Celt (Scot) and Basque. My parents were both Catholics but each expressed their faith in different ways.

My mother was brought up in a country that drew its religious cultural heritage from the imperial feats of Catholics Kings – they reconquered Spain from Islam, and colonized the native Central and South American Indians – as well as mystical saints and the Virgin Mary. She was pious, devout and loyal to Church teaching.

My father was brought up in England, a country where to have remained a Catholic after the Reformation was to belong to a minority faith and thus to be considered somewhat eccentric if not entirely trustworthy by a majority of citizens. Had he been an Irish working-class immigrant his Catholicism would have ended up like that of my mother, smothered in holy water, rosaries, prayer cards and candle wax.

Instead, he was privileged enough to be educated in Stonyhurst, an English Jesuit (Society of Jesus) school founded in 'exile' at St Omer in 1593 but whose present site near Blackburn, Lancashire, was established in 1794. Later a leading publisher, my father became part of that generation of intellectual English Catholics – some of them 'converts' like two of his authors Graham Greene and Evelyn Waugh – who came to make of their faith a badge of intellectual worth and social prestige.

My father might have ended up a snob like Waugh, and not one of Greene's longest enduring friends, had he not been educated by the Jesuits or married my mother whose simple faith and instinctive humanity touched him. My father believed that the liberal spirit was as much a mark of the Roman Church as was its authoritarian structure, exemplified supremely by the Curia, the civil service of cardinals, bishops, priests and associated lay staff within the Vatican. He admired Cardinal Newman, followed his faith across continents, and embraced the reforms of the Second Vatican Council in a way that left him putting conscience before dogma on matters affecting his personal engagement with the secular world, and his God. My father and mother, each in their own way, had a very personal sense of their duties to their family, based on what each saw as a very human and forgiving God. My parents were no saints – nor did they pretend to be – but they taught me to put a high value on mercy and love.

Thus while I am a cradle Catholic I was brought up with a broad view of what it means to be human. I was not swaddled by orthodoxy on the one hand or led into cynicism about simple faith on the other. I grew up testing the multicultural influences of my elders against my own experience as a schoolboy and then as a journalist. I went to the same Jesuit school as my father but at a different point in history when the Jesuits, like much the whole

Catholic Church, struggled to keep up with the political movements and social changes of the late 1960s and 1970s. While my father's schooldays were characterized by conformity with the establishment, mine allowed for rebellion against it. My father's youth, inspired by Jesuits, was spent volunteering for General Franco in the Spanish Civil War. Mine, inspired by Jesuits, was spent campaigning against military coups in South America.

Simultaneously, my mother's heritage had me hugely in awe of the transcendence evoked by El Greco's paintings, happily attending Holy Week processions in Spain, dressed up as a monk and carrying a cross, and making pilgrimages to Marian shrines like Lourdes and Montserrat, while searching for other aspects of my faith among the indigenous people, missionaries and shanty towns of South America. Meanwhile, my Jesuit teachers encouraged me to think for myself.

I thank my parents that I was sent to boarding school at the age of thirteen, not at seven (the saying attributed to the Jesuits goes, 'Give me a boy at seven and he is mine for life'). My break from a family life that had protected me in my childhood years had a touch of liberation about it. When I boarded the school train at Euston, I experienced a tinge of excitement. Here for the first time I was travelling to an unknown place, on my own. Indeed, everything about my person hinted at a new found independence: the new tweed jacket and grey trousers, my personal trunk, my wash bag and rugby boots gave an expeditionary feel to the train journey, with all the other boys seemingly part of some great adventure.

Later less jubilant feelings crept in as I settled down for my first night in Stonyhurst. My sleeping quarters were in a long dormitory divided into cubicles. Like all the other first-year boys of Lower Grammar, my 'room' consisted of a bed and a chair divided from the corridor by a sliding curtain. It was separated from boys on either side by a wooden partition, leaving me with enough floor space for my slippers. And yet it was not the cramped conditions that saddened me, but the silence and the absence of a parental kiss. 'LIGHTS OUT!', 'NO TALKING!' were the last words I heard that day, before the excitement of the morning disintegrated amidst the coughs and whimpers of total strangers. Finally there was a sound that was to become only too familiar over the next five years: the swish of a Jesuit's 'wings' as he made his way purposefully along the cold and damp corridor.

The Jesuits insist that Sir Arthur Conan Doyle's description of the Hall in *The Hound of the Baskervilles* is really Stonyhurst, for the creator of Sherlock Holmes drew from his own schoolboy memories. Conan Doyle was there 100 years before I was, but I cannot improve on his portrait of the main building that housed both him and me: 'In the centre was a heavy block of building from which a porch projected . . . From this central block rose the twin towers, ancient, crenulated, and pierced with many loopholes. To right and left of the turrets were more modern wings of black granite. A dull light shone through heavy mullioned windows . . .'

There was of course much more to Stonyhurst than this central block. There was the imposing mountainous backdrop of Longridge Fell, like a giant's feet. There were the rapids and cascades of the River Hodder surrounded in spring by fields of buttercups and wild garlic. A long avenue, marked at its outset by a statue of the Virgin Mary and a block of stone, led to the school. There were sports fields and ponds on either side, and unspoilt countryside and woods that stretched for miles around. By my time, a complex of more modern outbuildings had sprouted alongside the church, the Boys' Chapel and the infirmary. It was in these new buildings, which lacked any grace, that we experimented with chemistry and modern languages.

Within the main building all manner of idiosyncrasies served as a reminder that after Stonyhurst the world would be a duller place. Our indoor swimming pool was the first such to be built in England. It dated from 1880 and was called the Plunge. It was lined with open changing cubicles, which together with the steam that hung over the water made us feel like Turks and Romans. Our indoor sports hall, the Ambulacrum, was also the first of its kind. It had been built in 1851 so that the seniors could play 'Bandy' (a Stonyhurst version of hockey) and the juniors 'Ambulacrum football' (a Stonyhurst version of football which consisted mainly of efforts to avoid kicking the ball into the nearby latrines).

There was a 'Stuart Parlour' hung with the portraits of England's Catholic kings and queens, a 'Long Room' containing all the birds and reptiles collected by an old Stonyhurst boy, Charles Waterton, when exploring South America, and the Observatory which, according to another former Stonyhurst resident, the poet Gerard Manley Hopkins, showed that we had 'the highest rain gauge in England'.

Parts of the buildings and outskirts had extraordinary names: the Jesuits lived in Shirk, ramshackle cramped quarters where the floorboards creaked and the bedclothes smelt of stale tobacco; the junior school could be observed from a piece of high ground called Paradise; one of the refectories, served by Spanish immigrant labour, lay beneath a storage room called Sewage Farm.

It seemed only natural that such a world should contain a wonderful diversity of characters. Those who do not really know the Jesuits have this idea of them as part of a regiment in which priests, like soldiers, lose all individuality. And yet I cannot remember two Jesuits who were ever quite the same. Among the more eccentric were those who had semi-retired. They wandered around the building like old wizards, reminding us of our history and the delights that lay hidden where we least expected. One of them was Fr Macklin. He used to recall the time when Stonyhurst was one big bird sanctuary. There was a great aviary filled with owls and hawks across the end of the Slave Garden, where we now played tennis. And long before the Jesuits leased the shooting rights, there were mallards, herons and black swans on the ponds. Fr Macklin was asked once whether he could see any continuity between the Stonyhurst of 1971 and the Stonyhurst of 1913. 'Only in the buildings – some of them – and the countryside,' he replied.

Among the younger 'working' Jesuits whom I remember fondly was Fr Tony Richmond. He came from a spell in America, carrying a guitar, and taught me that there did not have to be anything sanctimonious in one's attitude to the Mass. We could sing or say it in whatever way suited our moods. He allowed me to organize an evening once around a recording of the *Missa Luba* and some readings from Anne Frank's *Diary of a Young Girl* and Kahlil Gibran's *The Prophet*.

The traditional three-day retreat, which had for years ushered in the beginning of the Stonyhurst year with silence and meditation, was replaced in my time with a more flexible regime. Visiting Jesuits tested out more imaginative methods for bringing us closer to that hidden treasure – the better part of oneself – which the wounded St Ignatius (1491–1556) discovered on his hospital bed.

Religion was taught not in a vacuum but as part of our daily lives, sometimes with the aid of contemporary film documentaries. Those agnostics and stumblers among us who during Sunday Mass fell asleep were temporarily reawakened by these sessions in which few social or sexual dilemmas were left undiscussed.

Not all Jesuits, so it seemed to me at the time, were touched with such humanity at moments when we most needed it. I remember a harrowing assembly in the Ambulacrum after I and the other boys of my year, led by a courageous Jesuit scholastic, had protested about corporal punishment. The headmaster confronted us at the time by having us observe him whipping himself, after which he claimed that punishment was not worth complaining about. On another occasion I was sent for 'nine of the best' for some minor offence. Having been struck on my hand nine times with a piece of India rubber, I was given an extra one for good measure after I had sworn in response to the pain of the ninth.

Only many years later, as a journalist, would I discover how oblivious I had been to some of the darker forces of abuse that affected some of my peers. Towards the end of the 1990s nine teachers, among them Jesuits, were charged with alleged abuse of boys at Stonyhurst and its preparatory school, St Mary's Hall, following a police investigation into the years 1968–98.

The gut reaction of many old boys was hugely defensive. There was a sense of outrage directed at the police for engaging in an investigation of a scope and scale that had seemed to them quite disproportionate to what was alleged to have taken place, and verging on a conspiratorial vendetta. As things turned out subsequent trials resulted in two convictions, one of which was quashed on appeal. The police stood accused of wasting time and money. And yet I and other old boys – and some members of past and present staff – while understanding the sense of loyalty from which such outrage sprang, felt that the situation required a greater sense of humility.

As the Catholic Church itself has proven, it is instinctive in any institution to protect itself from outside scrutiny and criticism, but it is equally true that periodically institutions are forced by circumstance to explain themselves to an outside world that does not necessarily take certain things for granted, nor share the same basic loyalty. Stonyhurst's was just one of numerous sexual abuse scandals that were destined to shake the modern Catholic Church out of its complacency and force it to explain its conduct and lines of responsibility.

I recall the former nun Sister Lavinia Byrne commenting once that what had always impressed her about Stonyhurst was its sheer sense of space: its long avenue and the surrounding landscape of rolling fells, a perfect frame for the sweeping majesty of the building itself. Such space, she told us, was to be treasured, not in the negative sense of enforcing isolation from the rest of humankind, but in ensuring that its occupants remained receptive to and understanding of the challenges they faced.

Certainly, whenever I returned to the college, any initial reminder of just how remote Stonyhurst seemed from London was quickly superseded by the energizing feel of the air, and the sheer freedom to roam that is offered by the countryside. This explained why, on leaving university, so many of my contemporaries chose to travel. For many of us, England after Stonyhurst seemed simply too small. In my case, I went to live and work in South America.

Accordingly, I have always looked on the writings of an earlier old boy of Stonyhurst, Charles Waterton, as a reflection of my own feelings towards the Jesuits. Waterton entered Stonyhurst in 1796, aged fourteen, and stayed for four years before carrying out his celebrated wanderings in North and South America. Several of the specimens he brought home with him form part of a valuable collection that has survived to this day. Of Stonyhurst, Waterton wrote:

> The day I left the Jesuits' college was one of heart-felt sorrow to me. Under Almighty God and my parents I owe everything to the Fathers of the Order of St Ignatius. Their attention to my welfare was unceasing, whilst their solicitude for my advancement in virtue and literature knew no bounds. The permission which they granted me to work in my favourite vocation when it did not interfere with important duties of education, enabled me to commence a career which in after times afforded me a world of pleasure in the far-off regions of Brazil and Guiana.

From its early foundation at St Omers by a group of Jesuit fathers escaping the penal laws of Elizabeth I, Stonyhurst has survived and thrived through days of suppression and persecution. During the police investigation, there was a perception that the offensive by the outside world risked fuelling a sense of exclusiveness, of insularity, of misguided pride, of meanness of spirit within the community. And yet, as I wrote at the time, the greatest tribute to what old alumni remembered as best about the Jesuits was to allow justice to be done, and if necessary accept that the day might come when the Church would have to offer a collective apology for our omissions.

On balance, my good memories of the Jesuits far outweigh the bad ones, and this I believe has helped me approach writing about Pope Francis with a certain degree of respect as well as understanding of my subject, while reserving a necessary critical eye for his failings, as well as his achievements. I was extraordinarily fortunate that my Stonyhurst years coincided with a period of theological and social liberation, and that the majority of the Jesuits who taught me were well versed in the teachings of Vatican II. When I am asked what I learnt at Stonyhurst, I think not just of the gratitude I feel towards my parents for saving every penny to put towards my education, but of the lessons I took with me: the importance of justice and sacrifice for others, and the centrality of love in one's personal search for spiritual growth and truth.

My contemporaries at Stonyhurst went on to many professions in many parts of the world: bankers, soldiers, journalists, actors, social workers, barristers, priests, from Tyneside to Tierra del Fuego. I have kept in touch with many Jesuit old boys and priests, several of whom contributed to making this book possible. So much in common binds us, even the kind of women we love. The majority of us remain deeply troubled by the injustices of the world that surrounds us. In Establishment eyes, this is an unreliable asset. And yet it is the kind of value that lasts for life and which has been given fresh impetus by Francis, a Jesuit pope.

This background explains in part what motivated me to write a book about Jorge Bergoglio, a man of many parts not easy to pin down, but whose spiritual world as a Jesuit priest had aspects to it that echoed my own upbringing as a Jesuit boy. Later, my years as a journalist in Argentina and other parts of Latin America drew me closer to the experience of Bergoglio's politics and society, both as priest and bishop. When he was elected pope, my knowledge of him was not in any way detailed. But he was a Jesuit and an Argentine and this was something of which I had some close experience. This provided a point of departure for a journey in search of Bergoglio, Pope Francis, following in the footsteps of his faith and mine, among the Jesuits, and the other believers.

The journey was well underway, weeks after Pope Francis's election, in the summer of 2013 when I took a train from Montmartre, the Parisian neighbourhood where Ignatius and his small group of priests gathered to hear their first Mass together as members of the nascent Jesuit order. My next stop was Lourdes where I stayed a week with Fr Nick King, an inspirational Jesuit whom I had known from schooldays, and other old and current students of my former school helping the aged and infirm.

Lourdes is a mystery and you either believe in what happened there or you don't. It has been a place of pilgrimage since 1858 when, in the grotto of Massabielle, a young shepherd girl called Bernadette Soubirous claimed she saw a vision of the Virgin Mary. Today it's the Catholic Church's most popular Marian site, drawing millions of pilgrims every year from around the world. We prayed for the new pope, Francis, a great devotee of populist religion and the cult of the Virgin, mother of Jesus, and mother of us all. As Fr Nick told me once, those of us who are touched by Lourdes owe it to two things: the sense of real presence one feels before the candlelit grotto in the late hours of darkness, and the happiness and love generated by those you help as a volunteer.

After Lourdes, I took the train along the coastline bordering the Pyrenees, and picked up a car in Irun before venturing into the Basque country. On a rugged clifftop called Deba I watched the Biscay Sea crashing on the jagged black rocks and read about a legend of a doomed love affair between a young local lad and a

French aristocrat who was shipwrecked and washed ashore. He went back to France and died in battle, leaving his lady forever mourning her lost love. Such tales of chivalry had impacted on the young Ignatius until a cannonball hit him and changed his life.

I next visited Loyola, the palace where Ignatius was born and brought up to be a knight. Jesuits had turned it into a residence alongside a museum and a huge basilica. I had been told that there were Jesuits who weren't great fans of Jorge Bergoglio. Some recalled his time as head of the order in Argentina as a period of authoritarianism and absence of courage in the face of appalling human rights violations committed by the junta. Others mistrusted his belated populism.

I asked Fr Esteban, an elderly Basque priest, older than Bergoglio, who was in charge of the community at Loyola, what he thought about a Jesuit becoming pope. He answered: 'You have to remember that in Ignatius's time bishops and cardinals had a lot of political influence and Ignatius didn't want Jesuits to have ambition, power, money, fame . . . The Pope at the time wanted to make the Jesuit Francis Borja a cardinal but Borja was advised by Ignatius to leave Rome . . . so he came here to the Basque country to Ollate . . .'

So was he waiting for Bergoglio to leave Rome and head back to Argentina? I asked him.

'No. I don't see the same conflict of interest today. You can be a bishop and lead a humble life and we accept that a Jesuit can be pope not as a way of achieving power, but as a higher service to the Church although I have to say my first reaction when I heard Bergoglio had been elected was one of astonishment. But there is no one way of seeing the Church or seeing the future and now I think we need to go in the direction Pope Francis is going . . .'

Which is?

'The Pope wants to be a Church according to the Gospel, What do I mean by this? Well, a Church that is closer to the poor, that will not be bound by pomp and circumstance . . . more poverty, more humility, more simplicity, more communitarian, not a Church that orders and is obeyed, but that is engaged in problems of real life, a Church that is less centred on itself . . . like Fr Arrupe used to say – Faith and Justice – that is to say Faith that takes on a commitment to Justice, a committed defence of the poor and the most in need . . . and this is not politics. This is Faith. It is sacrifice and love . . . So here in the Basque country we have Jesuits working with prisoners, we have Jesuits helping immigrants . . . In India we have Jesuits who have studied law defending the poor from the unjust dictates of the State . . . and we have our martyrs, like those killed in El Salvador . . . The Society of Jesus has put into practice the option for the poor [i.e. preferential religious assistance for the poor and powerless in society].'

Fr Esteban was a fit eighty-five year old with broad shoulders and a strong Basque face. He was seventeen when he first came to Loyola to start his novitiate. Bergoglio was that age when he heard 'God calling'. So did he regret not having got married? I asked.

Fr Esteban smiled as he said: 'Some people think that marriage solves all problems – but then look at how many people are unfaithful and how many marriages end in divorce. Celibacy is not about sexuality. It is about the freedom for greater service. If I was married I would be worried about my child and would not have the liberty to serve others . . .'

So was he happy?

'All I can say is that from the moment I became a Jesuit to now – sixty-seven years – I have never doubted my vocation and I have always been happy . . . which is not to say I did not have some problems along the way . . .'

Fr Esteban had been a missionary, a teacher, a spiritual adviser and author, and had lived and worked in several countries. We sat in Loyola's grand hall for visitors. It was decorated with gold-plated chandeliers and antique Spanish wood furniture. Prominently hanging from one wall was a portrait of Saint Francis Borja, a sixteenth-century nobleman who after his wife died became a Jesuit and founded schools and universities.

I asked him which Jesuit he looked up to most.

'People come and go. I take the good along with the bad. It's all part of life,' he answered. 'But those who have taught me most are those who have taught me that God is to be found among the poor, to share in their humility, their hope, their generosity . . .'

Before I left he read me a short extract from his latest book. It recalled his childhood sitting around the dinner table with his Basque mother serving out the cod to her numerous family members. 'She always made sure we all got part of the fish first even if there was nothing left for her. I saw something blessed in that simple act with our family cod, which stayed with me all my life.'

I left Loyola and made my way to Arantzazu up in the Basque mountains where the Franciscans have a monastery. A plaque reminds visitors that Ignatius, founder of the Jesuit order, had prayed here in 1522. The monastery itself is a modernist structure of studded walls and a high-rise clock tower (most of the original was destroyed in a fire) impressively perched on some protruding rock. The crypt is full of bold artistic statement – a giant mural by Néstor Basterretxea juxtaposes the steps of creation with man's historic struggle of liberation, featuring broken prison-cell windows, blindfolded and gagged men with hands tied, and a giant bright red Christ, muscular and defiant, his fists clenched, breaking through the door of faith to life. Giant lettering covers a wall with the words of St Augustine: 'I threw myself on these beautiful things you created. You were with me, and I was not with you. I came to love you late – so old and yet new beauty . . . I loved you late . . .'

I met José Maria, a jovial Franciscan friar who wore a large Basque beret and had an unkempt white beard that covered most of his thick polo-neck jersey. He was a dynamo of a man, exuding inner energy and enlightenment. The community house where he and twelve other friars lived was a haven of peace, the silence broken only by the occasional marking of time by the monastery's bell tower. We met in the evening, with the monastery bathed in the fading light of dusk. The last of the day's pilgrims were entering the monastery to pray before the tiny doll-like Virgin. She looked down from high up, behind the main altar, framed by a huge modern mural of women in various phases of struggle from childbirth to slavery. José Maria reminded me that this had been a centre of positive energy, a healing sanctuary from the days of the Templars. 'Jesus was a healer. Whoever comes to him becomes a better person, more intuitively human,' he said.

We sat in a spartan room, facing each other, on two wooden chairs. 'Silence helps us disconnect with the world, helps provide us with the space to ask big questions,' he said. 'Thanks to it, one becomes more committed to creation. One sees everything more clearly: how plants regenerate, live and die and live again, hear birdsong, observe the sunrise and sunset . . . St Francis was a man who knew that the primary source of everything was God.'

I began to imagine Ignatius finding this place an important staging point for his onward journey, and to understand why the Jesuit Jorge Bergoglio had taken the name Francis on being elected pope. We talked, José Maria and I, about Marian shrines – he called them precious stones that God had touched, each unique in their own way. Thus Arantzazu was not commercialized like Lourdes – but nor was it much visited by the sick and dying. Was this because no one believed in miracles here? I asked.

'Each sanctuary has its own charisma,' José Maria replied. 'The positive energy here is the cure, it humanizes . . . one doesn't look for extraordinary manifestations or visions. Here everything is natural, it's evident . . . God is about finding me.'

So was he pleased that the new Pope had taken the name of Francis, the Francis of his order? I asked.

'We took it as a blessing. It was like him telling us we came from the same house,' José Maria replied, before adding, 'Remember, Ignatius chose to come here too – so it was a story foretold.'

I told him I was struggling, following in the Pope's footsteps. It was not just the challenge of trying to understand something of an Argentine Jesuit who had taken the name Francis, and who now was the most powerful spiritual leader in the world. It was the excruciating lower back pain I felt every step I took. I had heard that Pope Francis suffered from sciatica also. I prayed that this process of osmosis between biographer and subject, if that is what it was, might end soon.

José Maria said he would give me a 'prescription' for a certain cure. He took my notebook and drew a map, then told me to join him at the window. In the fading light of day, I could just make out a path he pointed to which led up into the hills. 'Take this map, and follow the trail. You will get to a forest and beyond that a mountain. It's a good walk.'

I woke next morning to find that, except for a lingering stiffness, my backache had receded. A mist was gradually lifting. Shafts of sunlight broke through my window; the only sound that of birdsong. The hostel where I had slept the night was built on a large bulbous limestone boulder partly covered in undergrowth. It resembled the chiselled bearded face of some giant. Beyond, the mist drifted and gradually cleared down in the valley revealing a seemingly infinite landscape of rolling hills and the sharp, jagged mountains of Navarra beyond, the barren heights turning golden in the first sunlight.

I looked across at the sanctuary – it was as I had left it the night before, silent, its streets emptied. Only the soft yellow lights from the Franciscan cells reminded me I was not alone. José Maria emerged looking a little wearier than at our last meeting. He told me that after our conversation he had seen a young couple who had come to him seeking help with their troubled marriage and that he had seen them again over breakfast. 'The confrontation turned into reconciliation,' he told me, his face lighting up with a smile.

So how did he break the cycle?

'I drew them both to God, by telling them that they each had his understanding. God became the common link – the ring.'

The founding Jesuit father Ignatius spent quite a lot of time, when not attending to the poor and sick, reconciling couples. He also asked for bells to be rung frequently. Today, the bell tower tolled from early light as I surveyed the varied contours and colours of the surrounding countryside – the Vizcaya Pyramid mountain, the Cordillera, the Picos de Álava, the Sierra de Aitzgorri . . .

I took the pilgrim's trail the Franciscan had mapped out for me, over the mountains, in the direction of Urbia. It began with a long, steady climb through a dense forest of oak, chestnuts, cedars, beech and pine. There was a scent of rosemary and lavender. Lichen and moss covered the occasional stricken tree. The climb got steeper, tightening my hamstrings. I prayed that my back would not start to give out on me. I was sweating, slowly dehydrating when I came across what I took for a young backpacker. He was covered in a waterproof which hid his face. He was drinking from a brook at the foot of a rock shaped like a grotto. He greeted me without looking up, and then told me this was where a shepherd had found a statue of the Virgin among the brambles before taking her down to the sanctuary. Then I heard some distant cowbells somewhere above me beyond where the path made its way through the thicket of trees. 'Keep going,' the stranger said, before turning away and walking on, down the path I had climbed.

Higher up, I became breathless, my heart beating, my head throbbing. I wondered how much longer I could keep going. The beautiful walk had turned into a test of endurance. Then, in a turn of the path as I faced the steepest gradient yet, the source of the cowbell came into view. It was a pony which had stopped to look at me. It then turned and started walking up the hill as if leading the way. Encouraged, I followed in his tracks. The pony led me on until it had joined up with two others. Following this equestrian trinity, I walked out of the forest onto an open landscape of highland pastures, beneath a blue sky. In that instance I had an extraordinary sense of God's beauty. As I stood there, hundreds of sheep appeared as if from nowhere, up along the side of the mountain and over the crest, walking bunched together towards me until I was submerged in their flock, as if I were part of it. Then as suddenly as they had appeared, the sheep overtook me and disappeared over the brow of the next hill, their bleating receding in the distance until all was silence again and the whole landscape stretched out before me, without a being in sight. I followed a sign that promised to lead me back to the sanctuary.

I walked on across meadows covered in gorse and wild flowers and odd stones laid out, like sarsens in lines and circles. Then the boulders I had seen on waking that morning came into view and I saw horses again, their bells tolling in welcome. Mankind before God is like that, I thought – never totally lost, but always found. I had remembered that the main altar of the monastery had been built facing the sunrise. I had walked keeping the sun behind me and now the monastery was silhouetted in the twilight, the landscape a patchwork of light and shadow. Swifts were reaching up into the sky, and then swooping down. The *eskino*, the local mountain parakeet, stood perched on a promontory, showing off his bright blue plumage, his occasional screech intruding on the silence.

Later that night, after evening Mass, I caught up with José Maria. When I told him about the route I had taken, he told me that I had walked twenty-seven kilometres (seventeen miles). 'Magnificent scenery. God's beauty in all things?' he asked.

'Yes,' I answered.

I told him how touched I felt by the enduring memory of the walk and the magnificence of nature as he had described it. It was where he found God and where I had come closest to finding him that day, as Ignatius must have done. I thanked him for the twenty-seven kilometres that I walked that day, in the steps of Bergoglio, Pope Francis, although all I had to show for it were two huge blisters on each of my feet.

'I saw something of what you told me helped us value our existence, father,' I told him. As I said that he held his arms out and placed his hands on my shoulders, his face breaking into a smile that seemed to radiate light and warmth. And he said, 'So you're going back to England, then? Remember me.' He then turned and silently followed his Franciscan brothers down the corridor.

The castle where that other Saint Francis – the Jesuit Francis Xavier – lived before becoming a priest lies in the province of Navarra beyond a river and at the end of a long avenue of ash trees, raised on a hill with a commanding view over the surrounding countryside. Bergoglio took the name of Saint Francis of Assisi because of his humility, dedication to the poor and love of the planet. But he also respected the Jesuit father Francis Xavier, a natural athlete who was also gifted with a good brain. While studying in Paris he won a long-jump championship, and then went on to lecture on Aristotle at Beauvais University. Francis Xavier was an early disciple of Ignatius who like the founder of the Jesuits gave up his privileges in search of God and became one of the order's most courageous missionaries, venturing in the sixteenth century to barely chartered territory in India and Japan and other islands of South East Asia. The Church of Bon Jesus in Goa, where he lies buried, is one of India's most popular places of Christian pilgrimage. It should have been a place of pilgrimage and prayer shared with Muslims and Hindus but that was a long time ago. Pope Francis prayed daily for such reconciliation between faiths, but fundamentalism was waging a brutal war.

The castle of Xavier has been extensively renovated. Among the few original contents, in the so-called Christ Tower is the fourteenth-century dark walnut crucifix known as 'The Smiling Christ'. Visitors have meditated long and hard over the meaning of this Christ, hanging from the Cross, head turned aside in a pose of rest not defeat, his eyes semi-closed and lips smiling, an image of blissful deliverance, of redemption and resurrection, of arrival. A loving Jesus content that he has saved himself and mankind, and having conquered suffering and death, found eternity. His ecstatic facial expression, against the background of a mural of skeletons dancing, is faith triumphant.

Tradition has it that the Smiling Christ sweated blood during the difficult moments of the life of St Francis Xavier, the last time on the day of his death. I can find no better reflection than written by the Jesuit Gerry Hughes and published on Good Friday 2005. Hughes begins by asking:

> Is there not a danger that such a portrayal can trivialise the cosmic importance of Christ's death, the severity of his suffering, physical and mental, the inhumanity and barbarity of his death? Even more serious: does this smile not trivialise the seriousness of our sins, the cause of his death? Could this smile be heretical, undermining the fundamentals of our faith? How must God the Father have felt, having willed the Son to die in punishment for all the sins of the world, on seeing him take it all with a smile?

Hughes celebrates what he saw before him in the Christ Tower of the Castle Xavier, in words that helped me connect many years later with the gesture and language of Pope Francis and his emphasis on mercy and reconciliation. 'Thank God for the sculptor of the smiling Christ!' wrote Hughes. 'He expresses spirituality with ancient roots, a spirituality which emphasises the extraordinary goodness, gentleness and attractiveness of God. In God's light, we see light and in God's Spirit we can glimpse the peace and love, the generosity and forgiveness which we are to become and, with God, to offer to all peoples.'

Another part of the castle had a special exhibition marking the 400th anniversary of the Jesuit missions in South America. Here was detailed the achievement of those seventeenth-century missionaries who challenged the brutality and economic injustices of the Spanish and Portuguese empires and the slave traders, and set up self-governing indigenous communities. The protected villages or so-called 'reductions' were built with the aim of preserving a true commonwealth, with houses laid out in uniform geometrical pattern round a central square, goods collectively stored, shared and exchanged, and everyone wearing the same clothes with distinction only for sex or marital status. Part of the day was devoted to communal work such as gardening or spinning, with each member of the community learning or developing a craft to which they felt best suited. The rest of the day was reserved for family and communal gatherings and education. Rather than impose the Catholic faith by brute force as the earlier *conquistadores* had done, the Jesuit missionaries allowed the Guaraní Indians to absorb its images and rituals by a gradual process of assimilation with their own deep-rooted beliefs.

This assimilation produced religious art and music of extraordinary beauty: carved wide-eyed Virgin Marys with kind expressions, similarly humanized Christ figures, melodic and harmonious hymns and operas in the Guaraní language, ritual and faith drawing the community together in an island of equality and happiness. Something like this had been imagined in an earlier century by Thomas More whose *Utopia* developed the notion of St Augustine's *City of God*, a congregation of believers ruled by the intervention of grace and divine law.

It was claimed by some that the Jesuit missions were Utopia, which was a contradiction in terms as Utopia could not be created by ordinary mortals. Moreover the Jesuit missions were, it seemed, destined to fail – the experiment was cut short after seventy years with the expulsion of the missionaries and the subjugation of the Guaraní to commercial exploitation. And yet the memory of those missions endured as something that could be done, and was done, and thus worth replicating when more benign circumstances arose. That seemed to be the message of the exhibition, an acknowledgement of the possibilities opened up now that a Latin American Jesuit, who had learnt Guaraní and lived and worked with the poor, had been elected pope.

And yet Fr Eduardo, the young Spanish head of the Jesuit spiritual centre near the castle, like several other Jesuits to whom I talked while researching this book, admitted to his lack of enthusiasm when he first heard of Jorge Bergoglio's election. 'He was not my choice. Bergoglio was a controversial figure when he was a Jesuit provincial in Argentina and Argentina is unlike the rest of Latin America. It has its own political and social idiosyncrasies,' said Fr Eduardo.

He also cautioned against expectations being raised that might prove difficult to meet within a relatively short time. 'The Church has a 2,000-year history. It's not going to move 90 degrees, still less 380 degrees in a few months. Change there will be but this is an institution which finds it very difficult to move forward. It is not a private company. Nevertheless I think we need to have a large dose of faith in this surprise election sprung by the Holy Spirit.'

And what of Bergoglio's record on human rights? I asked.

'He did what he could discreetly,' came back the reply.

If there was evidence one way or the other, this was not the place to find it I thought. This remained an unclear story and I felt I would have to probe further in Bergoglio's native Argentina if I was to reach some kind of valid judgement.

I was thinking on this as I drove away from Castle Xavier and onwards along the Ignatian way. I tried to imagine the humility and strength of faith of Francis Xavier as he rode out for the last time across his castle's drawbridge, and over the nearby River Aragon, and out into the open countryside, galloping over the hills and mountains of Navarra, in search of God in unconverted Asia. Perhaps, looking at the massive rock formation that confronted him across the plain served as a sign of the challenge that awaited him in Asia – or perhaps it was the enduring memory of the Smiling Christ that kept him going.

As for following in Bergoglio's footsteps, it was not proving to be an easy journey. But slowly I was discovering that apart from him being a Jesuit and looking rather like my Spanish grandfather, I had other things in common – not least our love of football.

I remember matches not because my team won or lost, but because I saw football played nobly and creatively, turned into art form – poetry in motion – and because of the solidarity that involves team, manager and fans. Football at its best: not as an expensive celebrity act, but a shared human endeavour – passionate, respectful of opponents and worthy of respect. At its best, football, like music, allows us to get in touch with our humanity, and in doing so, touch God's finger.

Chapter Two
The Rise and Resignation
of Benedict XVI

It sure felt that God's finger was trembling, and that my own faith and that of many others in the institution of the Church had been shaken to its roots, when on Good Friday 2005, a week before Pope John Paul II died, Joseph Ratzinger delivered a homily which the veteran Vatican reporter John Thavis believed probably earned him the papacy. During the annual *Via Crucis* procession in the Coliseum, Ratzinger stopped at the ninth station (where Catholics pray for their redemption from sin before Christ's third fall as he carries his cross to the crucifixtion) and prayed: 'How much filth there is in the Church, and even among those who, in the priesthood, ought to belong entirely to him [God] . . . Lord your Church often seems like a boat about to sink, a boat taking water on every side.'

Here was a man who had read the case files of the worst sexabuse cases, was outraged, and once elected was expected to take action. If his cardinal electors had agreed on anything it was that a vote for him was a vote for stability through unity and action. As pope, he did take action, but not enough and too late. As Thavis points out in his book *The Vatican Diaries*, Benedict's methodology was 'patience, and his primary objective was to protect the institutional church'. He was evidently ill-suited for tackling the avalanche of new sex disclosures that in 2010 surfaced in Ireland, Germany, Belgium, Austria, Switzerland and the Netherlands. Taken together, it seemed to suggest that nothing had changed since it emerged in 2002 that bishops in the US had shielded abusive priests, failed to act on allegations and rarely reported crimes to civil authorities.

During the papacy of Pope John Paul II, Ratzinger was head of the Congregation for the Doctrine of the Faith – the office supposed to be responsible for safeguarding the integrity of the Catholic faith and dealing with priests accused of paedophilia. However, controversy was fuelled by the Vatican's pedestrian handling of the investigation into the abuse of seminarians, fathering of children and bribery of officials by Fr Marcial Maciel, the Mexican founder of the clerical order Legionaries of Christ.

Allegations of Maciel's abuse, which began in the 1950s, first surfaced in 1998, but the priest continued to be defended by Curial officials and Pope John Paul II. Only in 2006, a year into the papacy of Benedict XVI, was Maciel removed by the Vatican from his priestly ministry. Maciel died two years later without ever having been brought to account in a civil or canonical court, despite his evident guilt.

Apologists for Benedict insist that he quietly strengthened the rules governing cases of alleged abuse, and showed himself sympathetic to the abuse victims, some of whom he met personally and out of the media spotlight. But his public stance on the issue disappointed many Catholics and failed to redress the enormous disrespect that much of the secular world felt towards the Catholic Church in an area that smacked not just of appalling misuse of authority but also of rank hypocrisy.

The particular evil that Cardinal Ratzinger had identified in his homily to the cardinals before the 2005 conclave opened was the 'dictatorship of relativism', which he warned was taking over the heartland of Christianity. Pope Benedict was to speak increasingly about moral relativism as the root cause of sexual abuse as if the Church had been undermined by modern society rather than because of deep problems within itself as an institution. Only belatedly in his papacy did he accept that a large part of the problem might lie in the rottenness of the prevailing structure – the inherent self-protection and secrecy of clericalism as exposed in Vatileaks. This was the scandal that broke in early 2012 when leaked Vatican documents exposed corruption, and it was followed by a claim that an internal Vatican investigation had uncovered the blackmailing of homosexual clergy. Benedict was also to face criticism that the problems facing the Catholic Church were aggravated by a lack of democratic accountability caused by his inability to follow a more collegial style of governance outside the walls of the Vatican. This left him adrift when he could have called his wiser and more ethical colleagues to his aid.

The sexual abuse scandal was so badly handled by the Vatican that at one point it threatened to undermine Benedict's most testing foreign trip, his visit to the United Kingdom in September 2010 – the first ever state visit by a pope to Britain (John Paul II's 1982 visit had been a 'pastoral' episode rather than an official state visit). Propagandists on both sides of the controversy were keenly aware of how much was at stake.

Days before the Pope's arrival, London's Conway Hall was packed for a debate that pitched Catholic journalist Austen Ivereigh and the Benedictine monk Christopher Jamison, founder and patron respectively of a project called Catholic Voices, against a panel made up of gay human rights activist Peter Tatchell and the atheist philosopher A. C. Grayling.

Catholic Voices was a project set up months before the papal visit with the aim of having 'authoritative' Catholic spokesmen and women. It featured a cadre of mainly young university students trained by a lecturer in broadcast media who had worked for the

BBC and by the communications experts of Opus Dei, the influential worldwide organization of Catholic laity and priests. Catholic Voices claimed it had the 'blessing' of the bishops of England and Wales in its defence of Pope Benedict.

Ivereigh had been deputy editor of the Catholic weekly the *Tablet* and a one-time spokesman for the Archbishop of Westminster, Cormac Murphy-O'Connor, and in 2014 published a book on Pope Francis. Fr Jamison was a charismatic former abbot of the private Benedictine boarding school Worth and had featured in a popular TV series, *The Monastery*. While not among the speakers, very much in evidence that night was another leading co-founder of Catholic Voices. He was Jack Valero, the clever and personable Spanish press officer of Opus Dei in the UK who had run a successful media campaign countering the distorted image of his organization projected in the book and film, *The Da Vinci Code*.

At Conway Hall, Valero led the applause of the pro-Pope team, somewhat in a minority, with passion. But this was no sixteenth-century Tyburn, with English Catholics, supported by Spaniards, professing their faith after being brutally tortured and before being hanged, drawn and quartered; nor was this 1780 when thousands heeded the call of Lord George Gordon, the head of the Protestant Association, and took to the streets of London in an outburst of anti-Catholic feeling. The so-called Gordon riots, prompted by the repeal of the more extreme laws discriminating against Roman Catholics in the UK, led to the ransacking of churches and Catholic homes. Over 280 rioters were shot dead when the Army intervened. It was the Age of Enlightenment, the age of tolerance and yet the Gordon riots went down in the history books as the most destructive uprising to take place in the English capital in the eighteenth century.

No, this was the Conway Hall, a centre of free speech and progressive thought, in the multi-faith, multicultural Britain of 2010, in an event organized by humanists to which Catholics had been cordially invited. It was days away from a visit – judged a waste of money by many secularists, and some Catholics – by the supreme leader of the Roman Catholic Church.

Tatchell's opening statement that the UK was about to receive a pope who pursued a 'hard line intolerant version of Catholicism which even many Catholics reject themselves' was objected to by Ivereigh, who cast him in a more benevolent light as a man of spiritual integrity. And yet no one in Catholic Voices could bring themselves to admit to institutional failure. By contrast Fr Michael Holman, the then Provincial Superior of the British Jesuits, had written only a few weeks earlier, in the *Tablet*: 'The [crisis] has spotlighted the inadequate way in which the [Catholic] Church has sometimes handled these cases and the damage that can be done when a culture of "don't rock the boat" prevails.' As Holman went on to point out, what was at issue was the Catholic Church's capacity to respond with effective protocols of conduct and control but also the need for action to address the underlying culture, including the way it exercised power and authority and went about making decisions.

In their unremitting campaign to defend the Pope from his detractors, Catholic Voices were certainly not in the business of rocking the boat of Church dogma and authority. They owed their existence to the belief that liberal Catholics, wracked by doubt like Graham Greene's whisky priest, were a liability in PR terms. And yet Benedict's visit showed that for all its divisions, the Catholic Church was broad enough to accommodate diverse perspectives on faith – something that Benedict's successor would keep very much in mind.

Benedict's first hours in the UK which began in Scotland, involved, on the one hand, pomp and circumstance as manifested in an official reception by the Queen, and on the other, the effervescent out-pouring of Scottish flags which undoubtedly did Alec Salmond the SNP chief minister no harm in his efforts to attract more Catholic voters away from Labour. But it was in London that political symbolism was at its most striking. In Westminster Benedict stood in the very hall where St Thomas More, a Roman Catholic victim of Henry VIII's Reformation, was condemned to death. The German Pope told those assembled that he wanted religion to provide the necessary ethical foundation for politics and business. His audience included 600 MPs and Lords, four former prime ministers and Nick Clegg, acting prime minister while David Cameron attended his father's funeral. No previous pontiff had addressed Britain's political elite in such a way, making an appeal for religion to have its place safeguarded 'in the public square'.

Whatever the controversies surrounding the papal visit to the UK, it was the beatification of John Henry Newman, the theologian and Church of England priest who became a Catholic cardinal, that played an important if not key moment during Benedict's state tour. And yet as his biographer John Cornwell recognized, anyone writing about the life and character of Newman faced a problem of scope and definition. Newman was a university don and preacher who spent much of his adult life in Victorian England, rarely stepping beyond the privileged circles of Oxford University life, and later his community of priests in Birmingham. Apart from a four-year interlude in Dublin as rector at the newly founded Catholic University of Ireland, Newman's trips abroad became increasingly focused on Rome during an extended process of conversion.

While the painted portraits of an older Newman confirm a certain intellectual gravitas, he lacked the mysticism of St John of the Cross, the simplicity of St Francis of Assisi, the missionary zeal of St Ignatius. His contemporary, Cardinal Manning, another convert to the Catholic faith, arguably can lay a greater claim than Newman as a major influence on Catholic social teaching. Manning famously bought land in central London but explicitly refused to build a cathedral on it on the grounds that the money could be better spent on the poor. His successor Cardinal Vaughan went ahead and built it anyway, and London's impressive Westminster Cathedral has endured as a symbol of Catholic self-confidence. In 2010, many of those who defended a liberating theological 'option for the poor' contrasted the willingness with which Pope Benedict agreed to beatify Newman with the Vatican's continuing reluctance to make a saint of Archbishop Óscar Romero – assassinated by a right-wing death squad in El Salvador and for many years venerated by Latin America's downtrodden.

Newman died peacefully in his bed after leading a comfortable life, much of it in later years secluded from the harsher realities of industrial Britain. In his lifetime, his occasional fasting included breaks for food. To those outside a closed intimate circle, his humanity was hard to dissect, not least because of his ambiguous sexuality. Newman disapproved of his male friends marrying while allowing a coterie of unquestioningly devotional, if occasionally hysterical women to build up around his celibate life. The priest Ambrose St John, Newman's close companion in adult life, was so inseparable that the Cardinal insisted that when they were both dead they should lie buried side by side.

Newman himself refused to be considered a saint – 'I have nothing of a saint about me as everyone knows', he wrote as he prepared for his ordination as a Catholic priest – and gave instructions for quicklime to be thrown on his coffin to accelerate the process of decomposition and thus the eradication of any future relics. Believing in Christianity, wrote Newman, was a process of 'heart speaking to heart', a deeply personal relationship with God which defied clever argument. Newman's conversion from Anglicanism to the Roman Catholic faith was slow moving, filled with doubt. It was a deeply thought out internal journey not without personal cost. In the bigoted, sectarian world in which he moved, Newman's path to Rome not only fuelled his rejection by family, friends and pupils, but also his exile from Oxford after he was obliged to resign his fellowship at Oriel College.

Newman enraged fellow Anglicans and not a few fellow Catholics both prior and after his conversion to Rome. Within the Vatican of his time, Newman fuelled suspicions as a priest who could come across as too independent. Even after being made a cardinal, Newman was accused by some Catholic priests of being too 'liberal'.

After his death in 1890, Newman's constituency broadened among new generations of Catholics and non-Catholics around the world. Had he lived today he would have clearly defended religious pluralism against all expressions of fundamentalism. He also came to be convinced that each individual encounters the divine presence in the voice of conscience. In his famous letter to the Catholic Duke of Norfolk, at a time when anti-popery, led by William Gladstone, was on the attack, Newman wrote: 'Certainly if I obliged to bring religion into after-dinner toasts . . . I shall drink – to the Pope, if you please, – still to Conscience first, and the Pope afterwards.'

For all these wise words, Newman was regarded as a major influence by the reformers at the Second Vatican Council, some of whose hopes for a more caring, more inclusive Church would be rekindled by Pope Francis. At the time of the papal visit to the UK in 2010, Cornwell feared that enough had been written by Newman for him to be ultimately 'hijacked' by Benedict and used to encourage the conversion of disaffected Anglicans, while discouraging doubt and dissent within the Catholic Church.

Some Newmanists objected to Cornwell's idea of 'hijacking'. The concept of a liberal Newman at odds with the present papacy sat uneasily with the fact that, at his investiture as cardinal, Newman stated that as an Anglican and as a Catholic, his life's work had been a struggle against 'liberalism in religion'. Newman warned of the danger inherent in liberalism as religious toleration and religious relativism: the idea that one religion may be as good as any other or indeed as no religion at all. This was Newman perfectly in sync with Pope Benedict. And yet in his lifetime Newman was not uncritical of the papacy, particularly an ageing one. 'It is an anomaly,' he wrote, 'and bears no good fruit. He [the Pope] becomes a god, has no one to contradict him, does not know facts, and does cruel things without meaning it.'

While judged a success by the Vatican, Her Majesty's ambassador to the Holy See and English Catholics, whatever comfort zone entered into by Benedict in the UK proved short lived. Within months his papacy had been rocked by further scandals, with unprecedented revelations of shady financial dealings and bitterly fought power struggles at the heart of the Vatican Curia. The Pope's personal butler who leaked dozens of incriminating documents to an Italian journalist was arrested and put on trial. However, the attempt to shoot the messenger (the butler got a reduced sentence after a quick trial) failed to hide the fact that Vatileaks had exposed a dysfunctional power structure with the papal authority seemingly unable to prevail among the intrigue and disarray.

On 11 February 2013, Benedict XVI surprised governments, Vatican-watchers and seemingly even some of his closest aides by his resignation after nearly eight years as the head of the Catholic Church, saying he was too old to continue at the age of eighty-five. According to a *Vatican Insider* digital news service report by the usually well-informed Andrea Tornielli – and later confirmed by official sources – Benedict had become aware of his frailty after suffering a fall during a trip to Mexico a year earlier. He had stumbled on the steps of the Cathedral of León and later that evening hit his head on the sink of his hotel room while trying to make his way to the bathroom. And yet the timing of the announcement – the first papal resignation in more than 700 years – fuelled media speculation that he had decided to quit after becoming utterly demoralized by the Vatican leaks affair. There was talk too of inner plottings within the Roman Curia, with the suggestion in a story carried by *La Repubblica*, Italy's largest circulation newspaper, that perhaps he had been brought down by a 'gay lobby' in the Vatican that felt it was losing its protection.

As one experienced ambassador put it to me in November 2013, there had been over the years an evident air of enduring preciousness among several priests and bishops working in and around the Vatican that suggested a certain repressed homosexuality. The source saw some parallels between the potential for blackmail in a clerical world characterized by a mix of careerism and doctrinal orthodoxy and the early cold war years, when homosexual acts between adults were still a prosecutable offence in certain Western countries. Western homosexual diplomats had been prone to fall into honeytraps set by the Soviets. I was also told by an experienced Vatican correspondent (himself gay) of a leading international Catholic weekly how he believed there were members of the clergy leading double lives after he had personally discovered priests in Roman saunas.

Stories that had received wide coverage in the press during the Benedict papacy included the suspension, in 2007, of Mgr Tomasso Stenico of the Vatican's Congregation for Clergy after he was caught on a hidden camera making contact with a young man posing as a potential 'date' in gay-oriented chatrooms, then taking him back to his Vatican apartment. In 2010, a 'Gentleman of the Pope', the job title given to volunteers who perform ceremonial duties in Vatican City, was alleged to have been caught on a wiretap trying to arrange a meeting for sex through a member of the Vatican choir. As John Allen wrote in the *National Catholic Reporter* during the last days of the Benedict era: 'Among many cardinals, it's become a fixed point of faith that the Vatican is long overdue for a serious housecleaning, and certainly the furore unleashed by the *La Repubblica* piece is likely to strengthen that conviction.'

Nevertheless the specific allegation that a commission of three cardinals created by Benedict XVI in response to the Vatileaks affair had investigated the presence of gay networks inside the Vatican was never substantiated; still less was any direct link established between the investigation and Benedict's resignation. Moreover, the speculation emanated from the Italian press, which had a long history of spinning and making money on unproven conspiracies.

A more credible narrative is that by early 2013, Benedict, a deeply thoughtful and prayerful man with a good grasp of Church history as well as canon law, had privately examined the past and his conscience. He had reached the conclusion that for the sake not just of the papacy but also of the future of the Catholic Church he needed to back down to make way for someone with the necessary energy and vision to not only clean up the Church but unify the faithful and reach out to the secular world in a transformative way.

Three years earlier, Germany's *Der Spiegel* had critically profiled Benedict as the 'failed Pope' for his alleged loss of command amidst mounting problems within the Church. Questioned by the prestigious magazine who he would like to see as the next pope, the president of the German Catholic Youth Association, Dirk Tänzler, had responded by saying that Benedict's successor should come from South America or some other area of the world that suffered poverty, so that he would bring a different vision of the world to the Vatican. While prophetic, there is no reason to suppose that Herr Tänzler was thinking of any cardinal in particular, nor did he name anyone.

However, at the time Bergoglio, who had rarely hitherto agreed to any on-the-record comments, had broken with his low-key media policy and given his blessing to the publication of a book about his life and beliefs which claimed to be the first ever authorized biography. Called simply, in its first Argentine edition, *El Jesuita* (The Jesuit), the book was based on a series of authorized interviews with two religious affairs correspondents, Sergio Rubin of *Clarín*, the Argentinian mass circulation daily, and Francesca Ambrogetti, who worked for the Italian news agency ANSA, and whom Bergoglio had entrusted to lead with the project as a long-term friend. The interviews were taped and transcribed before Bergoglio went through them and corrected them, 'removing anything he was unhappy with', according to a close aide.

Reporting on the book's publication, the anti-clerical Argentine journalist Horacio Verbitsky speculated in the left-wing newspaper *Página/12* that Bergoglio's launch into the public domain at a time when Pope Benedict's reputation had hit an all-time low was not coincidental. According to Verbitsky, it represented the conscious raising of the profile of a *papabile* (papal candidate) who had only been pipped at the post at the last conclave. However, Sergio Rubin, one of the co-authors of *El Jesuita*, gave a very different account of the project and why and how it was conceived, which suggests that if there was an element of journalistic opportunism involved there was nothing to suggest that Bergoglio himself consciously regarded it as a promotional tour on the way to his eventual election as pope.

According to Rubin, the idea for a book began to develop after a breakfast meeting of foreign correspondents based in Buenos Aires, which Ambrogetti, as president of their association, had organized with Bergoglio soon after his appointment as bishop in 2001. 'It was an informal meeting, not for quotation or reporting, but the journalists were really impressed by his humility and genuine spirituality,' recalled Rubin, 'among them a Russian who was particularly moved and who said afterwards, "We need priests like him [Bergoglio]."'

Rubin was approached by Ambrogetti soon afterwards with a proposal for co-authorship of a biography, and they both approached Bergoglio in the run-up to the conclave of 2005. 'When we went to see him he was very attentive while at the same making it quite clear he was not prepared to collaborate further on a book.'

Only in 2007, when Bergoglio was in the midst of a controversial battle of wills with the Argentinian Kirchner government did the two journalists find the breakthrough for which they had longed. Rubin recalled, 'One day Francesca was with him and asked him, "What do you mean when you say, 'One has to take it step by step, patiently'?"; and he said, "So you want to ask me these kind of questions in the book? Well, let's start, and see how it goes." And that's how we began. I looked on Bergoglio as a typical Jesuit who had a certain air of mystery about him, difficult to get to the bottom of. He was a Latin American who had nearly been elected pope in 2005. He was known for his confrontation with the government. I thought it worthwhile trying to find out more about his thinking and to share it with a wider public.'

El Jesuita was published in 2010 as a series of extended interviews linked by short passages of commentary by the authors. It was unreservedly sympathetic towards its subject, exonerating him of any blame for past failures – a hagiography which made no pretence to be forensic in its examination of Bergoglio's life as a Jesuit priest, bishop, and, at the time, recently appointed cardinal. Three years later, Bergoglio was elected pope, much to his official biographer's apparent surprise. 'Unlike the conclave of 2005 when I thought he was in with a chance, I didn't rate his chances of winning in 2013,' recalled Rubin, believing that Bergoglio, while ten years younger that Pope Benedict, was preparing to retire as a cardinal and withdraw from public duties. While the inner thought process of Bergoglio remained largely a mystery, the prime consideration that motivated Pope Benedict's decision to resign was certainly a very real sense of his physical frailty and the inherent fragility of his mental state as he approached the age of eighty-six. Having accompanied at close quarters the final stages of Pope John Paul II's reign, he had no wish to hang on to a similar point of having no control over events.

As a high level Curia source told me: 'Ratzinger knew more

than most people in the Curia about the extent to which John
Paul's frailty was affecting his ability to govern . . . I was there in
the secretariat of state right towards the end of the pontificate of
John Paul II. And I was aware that JP2 could no longer speak and
that our job was to prepare speeches for a pope who couldn't speak.
It was tragic.'

So what really lay behind Benedict's resignation? I asked the
source. Was he just tired of the job? Was he overwhelmed by the
problems he had uncovered and felt he needed a newer tougher
hand to deal with it? Did he feel that his secretary of state Cardinal
Bertone was out of control as Vatileaks had suggested . . . and
needed a stronger pope to push him? Or was there more to it . . .

My source came back: 'I was very surprised, and most people
were but then immediately it seemed to make perfect sense . . .
because we knew how frail he was . . . he was very frail. He was
getting to the stage when he might not be able to walk much
longer . . . I don't know what the specific medical condition was
but people close to him said he was having increasing difficulty in
walking and they were pretty confident that within months he
would be unable to walk . . . This was physical frailty not
accompanied by any life threatening condition . . . or mental . . .
so there was a problem of longevity and he had already outlived
most other popes . . .

'Plus you alluded to the difficulties that had surfaced of
administering a somewhat restive organization with lots of problems,
leaks etc. The pressures about the Vatican bank . . . I think he knew
that even in his prime he wouldn't have been any good at sorting
out that kind of thing, let alone in his old age because that is not
and never has been his gift. I think he sensed that a new pope was
needed that had other gifts . . . Benedict said it himself in *The Light
and the World* that if a pope felt he was no longer psychologically
or spiritually or humanly up to the demands of the role he
should resign.'

Not everyone was shocked when he resigned. Rumours that he might quit had been circulating for months in Rome although most Vatican watchers and cardinals couldn't quite bring themselves to believe in them. Not since 1294 had a pope, Celestine V, resigned voluntarily and it was always felt that any pope would remain in office until his death. A hermit monk, Celestine had only accepted the papacy reluctantly and he resigned after just five months. Benedict had laid flowers on the tomb of St Celestine when he visited Aquila in July 2010, although no one had made much if it at the time.

Whatever the motivations, the result of the resignation was to generally restore Benedict's reputation as a man who had always had the best interest of his Church at heart. There were conservative bishops, clergy and lay Catholics who objected to this break in tradition, fearing that it would in a sense undermine both the mystique and authority of the papacy. But Jorge Bergoglio was not among them, as he came to Benedict's defence, extolling him as a true visionary of the Church.

Bergoglio, the then Archbishop of Buenos Aires, said in an interview with the Italian news agency ANSA, on the day of Benedict's resignation: 'They speak of a conservative Pope, but what Benedict XVI did when he announced his resignation really represents a revolutionary gesture, a change to 700 years of history.' It was in such a context that Benedict's successor was elected, amidst huge expectation of transformative change.

Chapter Three
Habemus Papam Francisco

Late on the afternoon of 10 March 2013, one of Latin America's leading TV journalists – Gerson Camarotti of Brazil's Globo News – flew into Rome to join the massed media ranks that had gathered to cover the conclave due to begin two days later to elect Pope Benedict's successor.

While Camarotti seemed to be a rather belated arrival, he was ahead of most of the journalistic pack, having a key source among the Brazilian cardinals who was well informed about how opinion was panning out inside the preparatory pre-conclave meetings, known as congregations. Camarotti was told by his source that Cardinal Bergoglio of Argentina was emerging as an even stronger candidate than he had been in 2005 – which meant that he was likely to win.

On the eve of the conclave, Camarotti broadcast his tip on Brazil's TV's primetime news programme *Jornal des Dez* amid the scepticism of some of his colleagues who accused him of guesswork. Nor was the prediction given much credence by the Italian press and the hardcore Vatican specialists. Their list of runners and riders included the Argentine-born Vatican diplomat Cardinal Leonardo Sandri (the son of Italian parents), a conservative and long-term member of the Roman Curia, the Italian Cardinal Archbishop of

Milan Angelo Scola, a Filipino (Cardinal Tagle), an Austrian (Cardinal Schönborn) a Québécois Canadian Cardinal Ouellet, two Americans (Sean O'Malley of Boston and Timothy Dolan of New York) and Odilo Scherer, the Archbishop of São Paolo, Brazil. And yet, Camarotti had learnt through his source, Cardinal Scherer had lost his pole rating among the important Latin American lobby who had decided not to vote for him in the first round, but to rally round Bergoglio who, unlike his fellow countryman Cardinal Sandri, was not easily labelled politically or theologically. Not only did Bergoglio represent to them a potential bridge between conservatives and progressives, he was not seen as part of the Vatican machinery so was looked on as a potential breath of fresh air. The Latin Americans were not alone.

In an incisive analysis of what kind of pope the Church needed in its time of crisis, the *Tablet*'s Brendan McCarthy wrote ahead of the conclave that the key was choosing a pope that had a demonstrable administrative record and who could impose discipline, efficiency and business-like conduct in the Curia. But if Vatican II's desired collegiality was ever to have a chance, 'the new pope had to be guileful enough to overcome resistance in the Curia while preserving a creative tension between the Vatican and bishops around the world'.

Other qualities suggested by McCarthy were that of 'global fluency', an ability to engage comfortably with a great range of cultural experiences, as well as a healthy, resilient ego, and a charismatic personality. In the pre-conclave meetings, several cardinals had expressed a desire for someone who with his personal qualities could dramatize – and bring alive – the real essential: faith.

While he could have been inspired by a *Financial Times* management page profile, McCarthy was not just theorizing but placing the election of the pope in the real institutional context of the Church. The writer was also following his instinct as to which way the wind was blowing among the electors. Thus influencing the election would be the experience of the previous two popes. 'John Paul II's charisma was remembered for giving his papacy its dynamism, just as John Paul I and Benedict XVI cracked under the weight of office. Thus the College of Cardinals will want assurance that its chosen candidate is "up for the job" and unlikely to wilt under its strains,' speculated McCarthy.

Bergoglio came to the 2013 conclave ticking several of McCarthy's boxes as far as his fellow cardinals were concerned. Despite his advanced age (at seventy-six he was a year on from tendering his resignation from pastoral responsibilities as a bishop) and a health record that included having half a lung removed in his youth and suffering from sciatica, he had become a more dynamic public figure over the previous decade, gaining authority and respect as a deeply spiritual person with a simple personal lifestyle that still shied away from media exposure. His political and social skills, along with his theology, resonated well beyond the streets of Buenos Aires.

Since the last conclave, his reputation had grown in his native Argentina as an archbishop with missionary vigour and a readiness to engage with the secular world. He was seen to have a compassionate and practical attitude towards the poor and disadvantaged, and a critical and fearless attitude towards the abuse of power by government and other vested interest groups. He was also seen as a staunch defender of moral values.

However, the fact that his critics included within their ranks some religious conservatives, progressive Jesuits, and human rights activists reflected on the complex nature of Bergoglio's character. Writing for the international traditional Catholic website *Rorate Caeli* prior to the 2013 conclave, Argentine journalist Marcelo González wrote: 'Of all the unthinkable candidates, Bergoglio is perhaps the worst. Not because he openly professes doctrines against the faith and morals, but because, judging from his work as Archbishop of Buenos Aires, faith and morals seem to have been irrelevant to him.' González accused Bergoglio of making himself famous with 'coarse, demagogical, and ambiguous expression', surrounding himself with clergy of questionable moral credentials, and turning his back on Catholic orthodoxy and tradition by seeking 'impossible and unnecessary interreligious dialogue' with Protestants, Muslims and Jews. The blogger took particular issue with one event in which Bergoglio had shared a stage at Luna Park – one of Buenos Aires's most popular music venues – with evangelicals, allowing himself at one point to be 'blessed' by a Protestant TV pastor.

'This election is incomprehensible,' wrote González. 'He [Bergoglio] is not a polyglot, he has no Curial experience, he does not shine for his sanctity, he is loose in doctrine and liturgy, he has not fought against abortion and only very weakly against homosexual "marriage", he has no manners to honour the Pontifical Throne. He has never fought for anything else than to remain in positions of power.'

While he was carrying with him the legacy of controversy, within his own Jesuit order, concerning his authoritarianism over fellow priests and, within the human rights community, concerning his ambiguous role in his country's 'Dirty War', his standing within the wider international ecclesiastical world had been reinforced by the crucial role he played as a coordinator and emerging leader at a key summit at the popular Marian shrine of Aparecida, Brazil, in 2007 where Latin American bishops discussed evangelization and social justice.

During the decades following the Second Vatican Council, the continent of Latin America had become a controversial theological and doctrinal battlefield for the Catholic Church as conservatives and progressives, from the centre to the extremes, sharply divided in their response to the turbulence of modern politics and society. These divisions were accentuated in the aftermath of the Cuban Revolution in 1959 and the transformation of Latin America into one of the battlefields of the cold war.

While evidently opposed to the violent, continental Che Guevara-type revolution favoured by Argentine left-wing guerrillas in the 1970s, Bergoglio entered the post-cold war years of the twenty-first century with a deepening sense of the Church in Latin America's historic journey towards unity and the role it could play in the future of the world Church. In 2005, in a prologue to a book by Guzmán Carriquiry Lecour, a Uruguayan Roman Catholic activist and professor, Bergoglio predicted that Latin America would play a key role in the shaping of the 'great battles that are taking place in the twenty-first century'. These he identified as the search for new models of sustainable economic development to help eradicate poverty, and the reform of politics and the State to ensure they served the common good.

The concept of Latin American integration was rooted in Simón Bolívar's unsuccessful attempt to unify the continent after he had liberated several countries from the Spanish yoke in the nineteenth century. But the most vocal advocate of the continent's *patria grande* or great fatherland in the twentieth century had been the Argentine General Juan Perón, who during his presidency in the 1940s and 1950s, and right up to his death in 1974, frequently told fellow Latin Americans that the 'year 2000 will find us either united or enslaved'.

Bergoglio followed Perón, who saw a confederation of Latin states as the only road to development, free from domination by capitalism or communism, and then updated this vision as one of the tasks of a new evangelization. Bergoglio wrote that this would be pursued as a third way between a neo-liberal globalization that risked destroying particular identities and an 'adolescent progressivism' based on 'militant secularism'. This was a veiled reference to the radical populism of the kind that Venezuela's president Hugo Chávez had made emblematic, and which the government in Argentina at the time saw as a standard worth following. In his conviction that Latin America, drawing on its Christian beliefs, could become a source of inspiration for the whole Catholic Church, Bergoglio was also influenced by Alberto Methol Ferré, a Uruguayan philosopher, and Lucio Gera, an Argentine priest, who were critical of the Marxist elements of liberation theology.

By 2007, the majority of Latin American cardinals who had been appointed either by John Paul II or by Benedict XVI were Vatican loyalists in their respect for traditional teaching on issues ranging from contraception to homosexuality. They were nonetheless aware that the Church's most numerous supporters lay among the poor of Latin America.

Bergoglio came to the conference having already embraced Ferré and Gera's version of 'liberation theology' without Marxism or, as they preferred to call it, the *Teología del Pueblo* (the Theology of the People). Influenced by the pragmatic politics of Perón, founder of Argentina's most enduring and powerful political movement, Bergoglio from his early days as a seminarian had been opposed to the atheistic anti-clericalism of communism and its interpretation of history and political change through class warfare. Later, from the late 1960s, he similarly rejected the most radical elements of the emergent liberation theology that reinterpreted biblical texts to justify an engagement between Catholics and Marxism and the use of revolutionary political violence.

Bergoglio's *Teología del Pueblo* claimed to go deeper than simply anti-communism by concerning itself with the primacy of faith in judging reality and inspiring the consequent practice, rather than being dictated to by Marxist ideology and praxis. Doctrinally it appeared to be on a continuum with traditional Catholic social teaching dating back to the late nineteenth century, the papal teaching of Pius XI's encyclical *Quadragesimo Anno* (1932), which sought a third way between capitalism and communism, the reforming spirit of the Second Vatican Council, and now a cardinal that had the ability to convey the Gospel message in a manner with which Catholics and non-Catholics could empathize.

45

This was not so much a new theology, but one that had been redefined, drawing out aspects of the original liberation theology that had somehow been lost or overlooked because of its use of Marxism. An important part of liberation theology that was drawn on and given renewed importance was an acceptance of the centrality of religious popular belief among the poor, not least in Latin America where Catholicism, once brought to the continent by the early Spanish missionaries, drew on and adapted the iconography and mythology that was deeply imbedded in the native Indian cultures.

The conference's concluding document, of which Bergoglio was a principal author, did not use the term 'liberation theology', but its words about the 'building of a just and fraternal society' that ensures 'health, food, education, housing and work for all' gave fresh impetus to the orthodox version of the option for the poor, as articulated by the Peruvian theologian and Dominican priest Fr Gustavo Gutiérrez in his landmark book *A Theology of Liberation* (1971). Gutiérrez asserted that a preferential concern for the physical and spiritual welfare of the poor was an essential element of the Gospel.

The style of leadership Bergoglio showed at Aparecida in 2007 influenced, six years later, his election as pope of 'a Church that is poor and for the poor'. Working at his side on the final draft of the Aparecida document that year was the bishop of the Brazilian diocese of Petrópolis, Filippo Santoro. Of Italian descent, like Bergoglio, the bishop had arrived in Brazil in 1984 as a missionary '*Fidei Donum*' and the coordinator of *Comunione e Liberazione* or Communion and Liberation (CL).

The expression '*Fidei Donum*' in Latin means 'the Gift of Faith'. This is the name of the encyclical of Pius XII on 21 April 1957, which called on all bishops to share his vision 'to face the challenges of the universal mission of the Church'. This was not only by means of prayer and assisting each other but also by making priests available to other continents. After accomplishing their missions abroad, the priests still attached to their diocese are referred to as 'Fidei Donum priests'.

I owe to the US Catholic journalist John Allen the discovery that before Bergoglio became Francis, the Argentine cardinal 'became close to the Comunione e Liberazione movement' over the years, sometimes speaking at its massive annual gathering in Rimini, Italy, and presenting the books of CL's founder, Luigi Giussani, at literary fairs in Argentina. (It should be noted that Cardinal Angelo Scola, widely considered by many as the conclave's front-runner, was also a long-time CL collaborator.)

Giussani, a politically conservative Italian teacher, had started CL in Italy in 1969 as an evangelical Catholic movement loyal to the papacy in response to a period of rapid social and cultural change. The movement blossomed in high schools and universities where it opposed the growth of secularism and Marxism, remaining doctrinally entrenched on issues like same-sex unions.

The movement shared with evangelical Protestantism a belief that the central, saving event of one's life is a graced encounter with Christ. CL insisted in its founding principles on 'total fidelity and communion with the Succession of Peter', in other words the Church's authority as expressed by the Pope. After his appointment as a Catholic bishop in Buenos Aires, Bergoglio drew close to Protestant evangelicals as well as Catholic charismatics. In June 2006, by then already promoted to cardinal, Bergoglio chose to break with his discreet meetings with evangelicals and go public. He shared a stage with Mexican evangelical musician Marcos Witt at an effervescent, packed gathering at Buenos Aires's popular 8,000-capacity Luna Park arena, famous as the site where Perón met Evita for the first time on 22 January 1944. At one point Witt invited everyone to take the hand of whoever was next to them and pray for them. Bergoglio was caught on camera resting his head on the shoulder of an evangelical pastor. The moment is described by Austen Ivereigh in his book on Bergoglio, *The Great Reformer*, as one of 'intense prayer', and the gathering as a product of a 'unique ecumenical initiative' born in Argentina.

Drawing on an account by Bergoglio's authorized biographer, Evangelina Himitian, daughter of one of the evangelical organizers, Ivereigh described Bergoglio as 'on fire' at the event. According to Himitian, this event, which was organized, with the Cardinal's blessing, by an Argentine ecumenical group called the Communion of Renewed Evangelicals and Catholics in the Holy Spirit (CRECES), was a turning point in Bergoglio's spiritual development. 'He began to feel much freer. The key was his openness to the Spirit, his letting himself be guided by a new experience, even at his age.'

Members of CL are known as *ciellini*, and Bergoglio's relationship with them was another cause for consternation among his Jesuit brothers since, as John Allen noted, 'the *ciellini* once upon a time were seen as the main opposition to Bergoglio's fellow Jesuit in Milan, Cardinal Carlo Maria Martini'.

And yet there was much that Martini hoped for in a future papacy that Pope Francis came to personify. The influential and widely respected Martini proved prophetic when, just before he died in August 2012, he gave a subsequently widely disseminated interview to the Italian newspaper *Corriere della Sera* where he described the Church under Benedict as being '200 years behind' the times.

Martini, once tipped as a future pope, but who retired from his post in 2002 suffering from Parkinson's disease, gave his last interview to a fellow Jesuit priest, Georg Sporschill, and to a journalist when he knew his death was approaching. The sex abuse scandals obliged the Catholic Church to 'undertake a journey of transformation', he told them. Not just non-believers but Catholics themselves felt alienated by an excess of self-protective clericalism.

'Our culture has grown old, our churches are big and empty and the church bureaucracy rises up, our religious rites and the vestments we wear are pompous,' he said.

Martini also warned that unless the Church adopted a more generous attitude towards divorced persons, it risked losing the allegiance of future generations. The question, he said, is not whether divorced couples can receive Holy Communion, but how the Church can help complex family situations. Martini's final advice to the Catholic Church to conquer its tiredness and embark on a 'radical transformation, beginning with the Pope and his bishops', foreshadowed the papacy of Francis I.

All 151 cardinals of the Catholic Church gathered in Rome on Monday, 4 March 2013 for the first of the congregations that were scheduled to take place twice daily for a week prior to the conclave itself. They included those, like the retired Archbishop of Westminster Cormac Murphy-O'Connor, who were over eighty and would therefore not be entering the conclave to vote.

Had Murphy-O'Connor been present within the 2013 conclave there is no doubt that he would have been among the first Europeans to back Bergoglio as he had done in 2005. Following the conclave Murphy-O'Connor declared himself one of the few people who were not surprised by the election of Cardinal Jorge Bergoglio as pope.

The Archbishop Emeritus of Westminster said he had stood in the rain in St Peter's Square as white smoke billowed from the Sistine Chapel chimney and wondered whether Bergoglio had been chosen by the cardinal electors in the conclave. Even since then, Cardinal Murphy-O'Connor has made no secret of his delight at their decision. 'The General Congregations that took place before the conclave showed that all the cardinals were determined not only that there should be strong governance in the Church but something that was even more important, namely, a fresh spirit, and a different approach to the ministry of the Pope,' Murphy-O'Connor recalled later.

He had got to know Bergoglio, then Archbishop of Buenos Aires, when they were created cardinals on the same day in 2001 and often sat next to or near each other at meetings. 'I have had an opportunity to get to know him quite well and to understand the freedom, simplicity and dedication of the good man from Argentina,' he said.

On Sunday, 1 March, the evening before the first congress, Murphy-O'Connor and Bergoglio had an informal meal together, where the two discussed the kind of pope they felt should be elected. Both men shared a concern about a fall in the standards of competence and integrity in the last year of John Paul's papacy and during the eight years of Benedict's. They felt appointments approved by the Vatican had become susceptible to a culture of cronyism, with people chosen or promoted less on merit than on whom they knew. The two cardinals shared experiences of what they considered were ill-conceived and unjust interventions from some Vatican department or other. Bergoglio recalled how he had been prevented from appointing the rector of his choice to his diocesan seminary. But the Argentine was particularly upset by the letters of protest that had reached him because he had baptized a child whose parents had not married in church.

Murphy-O'Connor emerged from the supper with a feeling that Bergoglio feared the conclave would opt for a safe pair of hands. He also got the impression that Bergoglio 'genuinely did not think he was a potential candidate'. And yet as Murphy-O'Connor later wrote in his memoirs: 'There was a lot of talk amongst the cardinals of the need for someone with the vigour and energy that would be needed to take on the problems and challenges that faced the Church. Bergoglio was 76. Too old, he thought. I wasn't so sure.'

A week later, on 12 March 2013, the cardinals present in Rome, both voting and non-voting, gathered in St Peter's Basilica in the morning for the *Missa pro eligendo Romano Pontifice*, the traditional concelebrated Mass attended by all cardinals in spiritual preparation for the official start of the conclave later that afternoon.

Following the Mass, Bergoglio was walking alone across St Peter's Square on his way to lunch at the Domus Sanctae Marthae, when Murphy-O'Connor caught up with him. By then Murphy-O'Connor had heard enough during the week's meetings with other cardinals to intuitively feel that Bergoglio had at least a chance of being elected pope, and felt that his Argentine friend was by then prepared for whatever outcome. They talked for a few minutes and, as they went their separate ways, Murphy-O'Connor told Bergoglio: '*Sti dante*' ('Watch out!'). It was intended as support but also as a veiled warning of the challenge ahead. 'I understand,' replied Bergoglio with a look that suggested a man at peace with himself.

'He [Bergoglio] was calm. Did I know he was going to be Pope? No. There were other good candidates. But we both knew what might be coming,' Murphy-O'Connor recalled.

On 12 March 2013, 115 cardinals, in solemn procession, entered the conclave to elect Pope Emeritus Benedict XVI's successor. Of these sixty were European cardinals, twenty-eight of whom were Italians; fourteen were North Americans; nineteen from Latin America; eleven from Africa; ten from Asia and one from Oceania (Australia). Two cardinal electors could not participate: one, Cardinal Julius Riyadi Darmaatmadja, Archbishop of Jakarta and a Jesuit, for health reasons; the other, Cardinal Keith O'Brien, ex-Archbishop of Edinburgh, Scotland, for 'personal reasons'. O'Brien was in disgrace having admitted to allegations linking him to homosexual relations with priests. It meant that the conclave was to have no representation from the UK since Murphy-O'Connor had retired and his successor, the Archbishop of Westminster Vincent Nichols, had yet to be given his red hat.

At the 2013 conclave, early voting had Latin American, Asian and African cardinals (led by Óscar Rodríguez Maradiaga of Tegucigalpa of Honduras) forming an impressive Third World bloc of support for Bergoglio, with additional votes from several mainly non-Italian European cardinals. As president of the largest global Catholic charity, Caritas International, Maradiaga's influence and experience straddled continents, making him a key player as a cheerleader for Bergoglio, if not his effective campaign manager. Two other Latin American cardinals, both Brazilians, also played a key role in furthering Bergoglio's candidacy: Cardinal Hummes of São Paolo and Cardinal Damasceno of Aparecida.

A consensus had developed as to what the biggest challenges were facing the next papacy. According to one well-sourced account in the *Wall Street Journal* these were identified 'as the rise of secular trends in Europe and the U.S., the need to address a shift in Catholicism's demographics toward the Southern Hemisphere and the dysfunction of a Vatican bureaucracy that had become too mired in scandal to do anything about these problems'.

Veteran cardinals, who had cast ballots for Cardinal Bergoglio in 2005 and included those who could no longer vote, saw a chance to float his candidacy again. His earliest supporters viewed him as a consummate outsider. He had never worked in the Roman Curia and he was critical of Rome's apparent disconnect with far-flung dioceses. The challenge was getting Cardinal Bergoglio the seventy-seven votes he needed, representing two-thirds of the conclave, to become pope. He would need support from many different circles, including the so-called Ratzingerian bloc – men who were already lining up behind two candidates, Cardinal Scola and Cardinal Ouellet, closely associated with Benedict XVI. Whatever their misgivings, a majority of these cardinals had been promoted during the years that Ratzinger was at the heart of Vatican governance, first as Pope John II's enforcer, then as pope. More recently Ratzinger earned the respect of even his critics through what was perceived as an ethically selfless but politically sound gesture in his resignation.

In the years leading up to Pope Benedict's resignation, the pontiff had positioned Scola and Ouellet as possible successors. The highly intelligent and experienced Scola had the distinction of being put in charge, in succession, of two important archdioceses during the Benedict papacy. In 2011 he was moved from Venice to Milan, when he was almost seventy. A year earlier, in June 2010, Benedict transferred Canadian Cardinal Ouellet from the Archdiocese of Quebec to the Vatican in order to run the Congregation for Bishops, the Curia office that vets and advises the Pope on bishop appointments worldwide. The naming of bishops is among a pope's most important administrative powers. Bishops are his bridge to the rest of the world, tending to local flocks and implementing directives from Rome. Cardinal Ouellet's move, therefore, ensured that cardinals from every corner of the planet would be vying for his attention.

Scola's path to the papacy was destined to be blocked by the confluence of two geographically distinct groups: the non-European one (South America in particular) and other Italian diocesan cardinals – the so-called *curiali* who were themselves split between two factions, one in favour of the Dean of Cardinals, Cardinal Sodano, the other backing his successor as Vatican secretary of state, Cardinal Bertone. Both cardinals were inexorably hostile to Scola. The reason, reported *Vatican Insider*'s Giacomo Galeazzi, was a series of 'ancient envies and rivalries'.

As one of the influential Latin American electors put it: 'The Pope cannot be too closely identified with any one group within the Church, he needs to be representative of all of it. Groups like *Comunione et Liberazione* and *Opus Dei* are like political movements inside the Church. Each group wants to show that it is more faithful than the other to the Pope, truer Catholics than the other. That's dangerous.'

The 2013 conclave was quite unlike any other for the simple reason that none had ever taken place in modern times to elect the successor to a pope that was still alive and, although officially retired, in a position to influence matters. Indeed, it was the very act of Benedict's resignation that elevated the importance of the general congregation discussions before the voting started, in effect enhancing the quality of debate. Unlike previous conclaves, these deliberations were not taken up with sentiment and process surrounding the funeral of a dead pope, but transformed into honest, open discussions, at times verging on the confrontational.

At the same time, as the highly experienced Vatican-watcher John Wilkins has argued, the general unexpectedness of Benedict's resignation meant there had not been time to form settled blocs in favour of particular cardinals – hence a conclave that was characterized by the fluid and open discussion between electors despite their vow of secrecy to the outside world while their final deliberations in the Sistine Chapel were under way.

According to one of the most detailed records of the conclave, published subsequently by the *Wall Street Journal*, some of the most outspoken (and less discreet) about the desire for reform were the American cardinals, no doubt still smarting from a sense of collective responsibility for the sins of omission, if not complicity, of their predecessors. It was in the US that the modern-day sex abuse scandal had burst into headlines in the early 1990s, shattering the self-confidence of the richest Catholic Church in the world.

In the run-up to the conclave, the Americans brought 'some necessary fresh air to the byzantine enclosure of Vatican politics' – and to the somewhat incestuous relationship between some members of the Curia and Italian journalists, with a tradition of spinning conspiracies serving personal self-interest and power groups. The daily press conferences initially given by the Americans delighted in particular some of the journalists, less moulded by living too long in Rome, and who had flown in specifically to cover the papal election. But a papal election is quite unlike any other election, just as inner workings of the Vatican are quite unlike those of any other democratic governing system.

Both prior to and during the conclave, the cardinal electors spend a lot of their time in prayer, not politicking – or in the words of US Cardinal Timothy Dolan, 'You look for a man who reminds you of Jesus.' And yet the spiritual quest took place in a very idiosyncratic institutional context. As one senior European ambassador to the Holy See during this critical period told me: 'The basic fact is that the Vatican has a long history of functioning like a court . . . everything is a function of this being a court . . . On the one hand it leaks like a sieve, on the other hand it is utterly impenetrable . . . and it has its battles and feuds that go back a long time before this pope . . . generations and generations of priests being mentored by other priests as they rise to the top as cardinals . . . relationships of Italians to Italians . . . Europeans with other Europeans . . . the creation of nepotistic dynasties . . . links between high level to a low level . . . not just important in terms of policy but also in terms of presence, and access. It may turn out that a lift attendant is party to secrets because he has been around and his father has been there and his grandfather has been there.'

The American press conferences were short-lived. They were stopped by orders from above, on the instructions of the secretary of state Cardinal Bertone and his allies. The deliberate censorship served only to fuel Bertone's unpopularity and to strengthen the argument for reform. Moreover there appeared to be one rule for the foreign press and another for the coterie of Italian journalists who jealously guarded what they claimed were their unique sources.

On 5 March, after a long day of speeches at the Congregation, Cardinal Murphy-O'Connor joined a group of American cardinals for dinner at the Pontifical North American College. Sitting down at a long banquet table, they discussed a small number of papal candidates, including those of Scola and Ouellet. Then someone dropped Cardinal Bergoglio's name into the conversation. 'His name began to be thrown into the ring: Maybe this is the man?' recalled Cardinal Murphy-O'Connor.

As the evening wore on it became clear that, this time around, the Americans did not all share the English cardinal's enthusiasm for the Argentine. 'I thought the American cardinals were quite divided about where to go,' said Cardinal Murphy-O'Connor. Some of the US cardinals believed Cardinal Bergoglio, at seventy-six, was probably too old to become pope, especially after Benedict XVI had specifically cited his age and frailty as reasons for his resignation. 'We came into this whole process thinking: The next pope has to be vigorous and therefore probably younger,' Cardinal George was quoted in the *Wall Street Journal.* 'So there you have a man who isn't young. He's seventy-six years old. The question is: Does he still have vigour?'

Two days later, on 7 March, Bergoglio rallied the doubters to his cause in a four-minute speech delivered to a further meeting of cardinals prior to the conclave. Many cardinals had focused their speeches on specific issues, whether it was strategies for evangelization or progress reports on Vatican finances. Bergoglio, however, wanted to talk about the long-term future of the Church and its recent history of failure.

His speech notes were written in his native Spanish, but he spoke in the Italian he had learnt from his parents and grandmother, the language cardinals most commonly use inside Vatican City and the native tongue of Italy's twenty-eight voting-age cardinals, the most of any single nation. The leaders of the Catholic Church, Cardinal Bergoglio warned, had become too focused on its inner life. The Church was too self-referential. Bergoglio's speech made clear his desire for reforms against 'ignorance, self-reference and narcissism'. He continued:

Evangelizing pre-supposes a desire in the Church to come out of herself. The Church is called to come out of herself and to go to the peripheries, not only geographically, but also the existential peripheries: the mystery of sin, of pain, of injustice, of ignorance and indifference to religion, of intellectual currents, and of all misery. When the Church does not come out of herself to evangelize, she becomes self-referential and then gets sick. The evils that, over time, happen in ecclesiastical institutions have their root in self-reference and a kind of theological narcissism. In Revelation, Jesus says that he is at the door and knocks. Obviously, the text refers to his knocking from the outside in order to enter but I think about the times in which Jesus knocks from within so that we will let him come out.

The self-referential Church keeps Jesus Christ within herself and does not let him out. When the Church is self-referential, inadvertently, she believes she has her own light; she ceases to be the *mysterium lunae* and gives way to that very serious evil, spiritual worldliness. It lives to give glory only to one another. Put simply, there are two images of the Church: the Church which evangelizes and comes out of herself, the *Dei Verbum religiose audiens et fidente proclamans*; and the worldly Church, living within herself, of herself, for herself. This should shed light on the possible changes and reforms which must be done for the salvation of souls. Thinking of the next pope: He must be a man who, from the contemplation and adoration of Jesus Christ, helps the Church to go out to the existential peripheries, that helps her to be the fruitful mother, who gains life from 'the sweet and comforting joy of evangelizing'.

The word he used, *periferia* in Italian, literally translates into 'the periphery' or 'the edge' although it was a word that Jesuit missionaries have turned emblematic from the early days, meaning new frontiers of evangelization. To Italian- as well as Spanish-speaking ears, *periferia* was also a modern term describing the negative socioeconomic conditions provoked by an exploitative global free-market economy. It was on the periphery of cities that the poor lived, many of them immigrants. The core mission of the Church, Bergoglio told the congregated red hats, was getting in touch with the everyday problems of a global flock, most of whom were suffering the indignities of socioeconomic injustice.

The speech struck a chord among a large number of the assembled cardinals. Latin American cardinals and the German cardinals Reinhard Marx and Walter Kasper were among those who felt themselves listening to a fresh and simple voice talking about justice and human dignity, and the need to reform the Curia. 'This was the moment, I think, when some of them (many hesitant at first) began to wonder if they might not have heard the voice of the man who could lead the Church to find its true self again,' recalled Murphy-O'Connor. The North Americans in particular had spoken of the importance of having a pope with vigour and dynamism to shake up and lead the Church in unity.

At the end of the final meeting of all the cardinals, Murphy-O'Connor met the influential Archbishop of Chicago, Francis George. 'You know, this man you've been talking about,' George said. 'I think there might be something in it.' And yet there was nothing doctrinally to pose a potentially divisive split within the Church as disruptive as the divisions that had followed the Second Vatican Council.

Two cardinals, Juan Luis Cipriani Thorne of Lima and Jaime Lucas Ortega y Alamino of Havana, were so impressed that they promptly asked him for his notes in their original Spanish. For days they had heard speeches about 'new evangelization', a term from past popes that many cardinals used to honour their memory while disagreeing over what it meant. Suddenly, they were hearing someone speak about injustice and human dignity. And it was simple, clear, refreshing and authentic.

With the evidence of hindsight, Bergoglio's willingness to hand over his notes was not a casual gesture but a calculated move to ensure that his contribution was not simply passed over but mulled on as a manifesto that defined the new papacy. It was certainly considered as such by Cardinal Ortega y Alamino who considered he had Bergoglio's blessing to leak the notes more widely.

'He speaks in a very straightforward way,' Cardinal George of the US later commented. 'And so perhaps – more than the content – it was simply a reminder that here is someone who has authenticity in such a way that he's a wonderful witness to the discipleship.'

To Cardinal Cipriani Thorne, the address was vintage Bergoglio. For years, the Peruvian had heard his fellow Latin American cardinal deliver similar remarks. And like those earlier speeches, his message to the General Congregation walked a very fine line. Many cardinals, including Cipriani Thorne, were stern opponents of any rhetoric that appeared to invite class warfare. Popes John Paul II and Benedict XVI had reined in liberation theology, the teachings of Latin American priests who embraced Marxism, and churchmen like Cipriani Thorne had supported the crackdown. But Bergoglio's message to cardinals sidestepped those ideological pitfalls by grounding his message in a call to model the modern Church on the humility of its origins.

'He's not relating this to ideology, to, let's say, rich against poor,' Cardinal Cipriani Thorne said. 'No, no, nothing like that. He's saying that Jesus himself brought us to this world to be poor – to not have this excessive consumerism, this great difference between rich and poor.'

What many thought Cardinal Bergoglio was offering the Church – after a decade of struggling to overcome the sexual abuse crisis and years of internal bickering over issues like the liturgy – was a new narrative. He was telling a story of modern Catholicism that focused less on its complex inner workings and more on its outreach to those most in need.

By Sunday, 10 March, two days before the start of the conclave, a sense of rising expectation was taking hold among the cardinals. Cardinal Bergoglio was seen by many not only as a political contender, but one delivered by the Holy Spirit as a unifier who was nonetheless capable of restoring the embattled reputation of the Church.

Before voting got under way, Bergoglio shared a meal with Cardinal Antonio Cañizares Llovera, the Prefect of the Congregation for Divine Worship and the Discipline of the Sacraments. The former Archbishop of Toledo and Primate of Spain was widely regarded as one of the Curia heavyweights at the time. The physically small but powerful Spaniard was sometimes known by his nickname of 'Little Ratzinger', referring to the beliefs and opinions he shared with Benedict XVI. Nothing he heard from the Argentinian gave him grounds for concern. On the contrary it gave him grounds for hope that the Church was about to be strengthened.

'During our meal, our discussion focused on what kind of profile the next pope should have,' recalled Cañizares, 'and I told Bergoglio that the new pope should be like a new Saint Francis – a man of the beatitudes, a man of poverty, a man who could show us how to evangelize, a man capable of renewing the Church. And he said, "I totally agree with you."'

As described so vividly back in 1981 by the late Peter Nichols of *The Times*, who was a long-term resident of Rome and followed the Vatican closely for many years, 'a papal election remains a powerful mystery: dangerous and fascinating at the same time, with a strong touch of magic. It is carried out by a hundred or so members of the most exclusive caste to gather anywhere in the world to elect an international personality.'

As Nichols went on to describe in his evocative book on Catholicism, *The Pope's Divisions*, the cardinals sit in a chapel dominated by Michelangelo's imposing fresco, *The Last Judgement*. It is painted over the high altar in front of which the cardinals cast their vote. Nichols noted that Michelangelo, although from Tuscany, had a vision that was eminently Roman: 'monumental, authoritarian, weighty, full of assurance, strength and creativity, accustomed to decide and give the law'. His Jesus appears as judge and king, 'bereft now of all enigma, ambiguity, mystery . . . He is man's view of himself as God, which is likely to be less endearing than a man's day-dreams about what he would do if he suddenly became pope.'

Nichols continued: 'The Sistine Chapel Christ has nothing of the subtlety or ambivalence of the Gospel Christ, qualities also useful to a pope. He is immediately recognizable as a stern ruler, majestic, no longer likely to be mistaken for a gardener, or seen as a shadowy fellow-traveller on the road to Erasmus.'

Nichols leaves unanswered his question as to whether this was the proper atmosphere in which a man is chosen to be the Vicar of Christ. The 2013 conclave, once under way, followed election procedures almost unchanged for centuries. Essentially it involved all the eligible cardinals locked inside the Vatican and required by a law sanctioned in ancient times to find at least a two-thirds majority for the valid election of the supreme pontiff.

After Bergoglio's election, I asked the Spanish Cardinal Cañizares if the result had surprised him. 'I don't think a surprise in the end to anyone in the conclave . . . but for me it was clear that this was the Pope that God had elected. I was among the cardinals who felt he had been elected before we had even gathered. And for me the experience of the conclave and its outcome was proof that it had God's blessing.'

For Cañizares, this chronicle of a papal story foretold had a very clear sign: Benedict's resignation. 'That resignation meant that the Church's future was now in God's hands.'

Chapter Four
Immigrant Family

J orge Bergoglio's father Mario, and grandparents Giovanni
Bergoglio and Rosa Margarita Vassalo, arrived in the port of
Buenos Aires in January 1929, the year when the unbounded
optimism of the Jazz Age ended with the Wall Street Crash. To these
immigrants from northern Italy, Argentina was not only a Catholic
country. More importantly, it had temporarily replaced the United
States as the land of opportunity. This still relatively under-populated
new-found land in the southernmost reaches of South America
had seemingly infinite mineral and food resources, and enough
geographical space to accommodate a major increase to its
pioneering population. Argentina seemed graced by God even if
the ripples of the Great Depression were making their way across
the vast distances separating this southernmost country in Latin
America from the rest of the world.

Giovanni originated from Portacomaro, a quiet hamlet in the
Italian province of Asti, Piedmont, where he and his wife ran a
bakery. They later moved to Turin and owned a pastry shop which
doubled up as café in the evenings until the day Giovanni decided
it was time for himself, his wife and son to follow in the footsteps
of other Bergoglios who had emigrated to Argentina in the
aftermath of the First World War.

Bergoglio's great-grandfather, named Francesco or Francis, had bought a farmhouse in 1864 in Bricco Marmorito, which sits in the shadow of the snow-capped Alps in northwest Italy. Long-lost relatives dispersed around Piedmont were as excited as anyone when Bergoglio's name was announced as the new pope from the balcony of St Peter's Basilica 435 miles (700 kilometres) south in Rome in March 2013. 'When we heard the news we were really surprised because we never thought he could become pope,' Anna Bergoglio, a distant cousin of Pope Francis, said in the garden of her house in Asti, best known for its sparkling wines.

Pope Francis and the cardinals who elected him toasted his appointment on the day of his election with a glass of Asti spumante fizzy wine, a nod to his Italian roots and less expensive than the champagne sipped by Popes John Paul and Benedict. Francis was a man who was conscious of his roots and eschewed life's luxuries.

These days in Piedmont there is no shortage of locals claiming some relation – as third and fourth cousins – to Pope Francis, although the red-brick house where the new pope's grandparents lived was bought in 1993 by a businessman from Turin called Giuseppe Quattrocchio. In 2013, the year Jorge Bergoglio became Pope Francis, a seventy-five-year-old distant cousin, Delmo Bergoglio, was the last farmer left in Portacomaro, the original family village where many of the vineyards producing Barolo wines have now been abandoned and earning a living is tough. Delmo recalled the last time when the most famous Bergoglio had come to visit the village in 2003. The then Archbishop of Buenos Aires had scooped up a handful of earth and taken it back to Argentina.

It wasn't the first time that Jorge had flown over to meet with his extended family to better understand his identity and to keep up with his Italian, which is an Argentine derivative of a Piedmont dialect. On one such visit Fr Bergoglio played an impromptu game of football as if evoking his youth. He also always celebrated Mass in a region of enduring Catholic devotion with its many medieval churches and other older sanctuaries, some dating back to early Christian times. In 2006, 300 of his namesakes crossed the Atlantic from Italy and joined him for a reunion in the northern Argentine city of Córdoba, one of the first major towns of the early Jesuit missions in South America. Bergoglio's last visit to the village of his ancestors was in 2011, when no one could have imagined a pope resigning within two years and his replacement being a Latin American. 'He helped peel potatoes in the kitchen,' recalled Carla Bracchina, another cousin.

One of Bergoglio's enduring childhood memories was that of his mother, Regina Maria, peeling potatoes in the family kitchen in Buenos Aires. She had become housebound and restricted in her movements after being left semi-paralysed following a miscarried pregnancy. The election of Pope Francis meant that thirty Bergoglio Italian cousins made their way to an audience in St Peter's within weeks of the conclave. Most had travelled from Montferrat, a small number from Veneto. '*Il papa tra due mondi*', a pope between two worlds headlined the local newspaper *La Gazzetta d'Asti*.

The world Bergoglio's grandparents and father Mario left in the final days of 1928 was that of Mussolini's Italy. Many years later, in the aftermath of Bergoglio's election as pope, when critics suggested that Jorge had been complicit in Argentina's military junta, his sister Maria Elena testily pointed out that her family emigrated from Italy because their father was opposed to fascism, the clear suggestion being that Jorge Mario Bergoglio would never betray his father's memory by collaborating with dictators. On 23 March 1919, Mussolini and other war veterans founded in Milan a revolutionary, nationalistic group called the Fasci di Combattimento, named for the ancient Roman symbol of power, the *fasces*. His Fascist movement developed into a powerful 'radicalism of the right', gaining the support of many landowners in the lower Po Valley, industrialists and Army officers in the suppression of workers' rights by fascist blackshirt squads.

On 28 October 1922, after the Fascists had marched on Rome, Mussolini secured a mandate from King Victor Emmanuel III to form a coalition government. In 1925–6, after a lengthy crisis with parliament following the assassination of the Socialist leader Giacomo Matteotti, Mussolini imposed a single-party, totalitarian dictatorship.

Mussolini sought to move beyond contemporary party politics with his brand of fascism. He boasted a charismatic and dynamic leadership that would bring Italy away from the humiliation it had suffered since the late nineteenth century. There was no system or programme, just action for the sake of action, violence for the sake of violence. Mussolini wanted to destroy parliamentary democracy by substituting it with a strong, heroic elite. As a new religion, fascism was stamped on the mind of youth through control of education and similarly heavy-handed propaganda on the rest of Italian society. Il Duce's theatrical performance and pseudo-religious rituals secured a mass following and lingered in the minds of those who thought it better to escape from the lunacy of it all.

Toward the end of 1928, Bergoglio's father Mario, and grandparents Giovanni and Rosa, boarded the ship *Giulio Cesare* in Genoa with a sense that God was on their side. The administrative problems during the sale of their Italian assets, which took longer than expected, meant that the couple had delayed their voyage by over a year and cancelled an earlier booking they had made on other Italian transatlantic vessel, *Principessa Mafalda*. The luxury ocean liner had sunk off the coast of Brazil on 25 October 1927, with the loss of over 300 of the 1,252 on board, after a propeller shaft fractured and damaged the hull. The sinking was the greatest tragedy ever in Italian shipping. However, it failed to dissuade Italians emigrating to the New World to be reunited with relatives, in search of greater prosperity, the largest wave of Italian emigration ever in the southern hemisphere in peacetime.

On a hot morning in January 1929, after a long voyage across the

Mediterranean and the south Atlantic, the *Giulio Cesare* docked in the port of Buenos Aires, to the southeast of the city. Rosa stepped ashore wearing a fur coat lined with the proceeds of the sale of their house and business. The Bergoglios must have felt startled by the sight of the colourful, squat, corrugated-iron huts and wooden houses and bars of the neighbourhood that had grown up around the nearby trading centre and shipyard. It was known as La Boca, the city's first Little Italy and the main point of entry for Italians from the end of the nineteenth century. It was more evocative of Naples and disadvantaged southern Italy than Turin and the rolling hills, vineyards and sturdy stone villages – with a kaleidoscope of shades and tones – that characterized their native Piedmont.

And yet an Argentine, goes the well-known saying, is an Italian who speaks Spanish, thinks he's French and would secretly like to be British. With several waves of immigrants from Italy arriving since Argentina had won independence from Spain in the early nineteenth century, almost every second Argentine family had an Italian surname, a recent arrival or an ancestor hailing from some Italian region. These Italian descendants refer to themselves proudly as '*tanos*', Lunfardo slang for '*Italianos*'.

Argentina may have been colonized by the Spanish originally, and then by the British, but the Italians had ensured they had an equal if not even greater and more enduring influence over many areas of Argentine life, such as politics, food, fashion and language. By the end of the 1920s, Italians comprised about 42 per cent of the total influx of immigrants in Argentina; Buenos Aires was a city whose population spoke Spanish with an Italian intonation, and breathed a political, social and religious culture that was predominantly Italian in its intrigue, theatrics and corruption as well as spirituality.

But for the shock of that first sighting of La Boca, the Bergoglio family's new life in Argentina got off to an auspicious start. They settled in the thriving trading riverside town of Paraná, 200 miles north of Buenos Aires, in a spacious four-storey residence with the only elevator in the city. It had been built by three of Giovanni's brothers who had arrived from Italy in 1922 and set up a paving business. The extended Bergoglio family shared the house, with each family occupying one of the floors and contributing to the family business, which appeared to be thriving.

The crisis of 1929 was slow to hit prosperous Argentina, but in 1932 the Bergoglios had to sell the family home in Paraná and the elaborate family mausoleum in the local cemetery to cover their debts. Many years later, Bergoglio reflected on that period, not with regret for the lost family fortune, but for the money that had been wasted on camouflaging death. In a conversation with the journalists Sergio Rubin and Francesca Ambrogetti he referred to 'certain cemeteries that act as museums, works of art, and beautiful places, all to conceal the drama that lies beneath them'.

In 1932 one of his great-uncles emigrated to Brazil; another died of cancer; while Giovanni moved to Buenos Aires with Rosa and son Mario, where a 2,000-peso loan allowed him to open a small grocery store. The loan was arranged by Fr Enrico Pozzoli, a priest the family had befriended who belonged to the Salesians of Don Bosco, a teaching order of Italian origin that set up schools for the urban working class in various Latin American countries. Mario worked with his father, making deliveries, until moving to a job as an accountant in a local factory that manufactured socks. Mario was part of a circle of young male friends that regularly met up with Fr Enrico in the Salesian Church of San Antonio de Padua in the working-class district of Almagro. It was through this circle that Mario was introduced to Regina Sívori, whose family lived just a few blocks from the church. In 1935 he married Regina, a descendant of Italian immigrants from Genoa and Piedmont, of similar social background. By then, dark political clouds had begun to gather around the Bergoglio family, as ominous as those from which they had escaped in Italy.

Argentina during the 1920s had become the refuge for Italian dissidents fleeing the rise of fascism in the peninsula. A veneer of democracy endured with the elected government led by the moderate left Unión Cívica Radical (UCR) party, headed successively by Presidents Hipólito Yrigoyen and Marcelo Torcuato de Alvear. But the determined leader among an active group of Italian anarchists in Argentina, Severino Di Giovanni (born in Chieti in 1901), had nothing but contempt for the UCR, which he saw as a pale reflection of more right-wing and fascist elements in Argentine politics. The scene was set for confrontation politics. Much to the dismay of hard-working immigrant entrepreneurs like the Bergoglio family, Di Giovanni inaugurated a period of political violence in Buenos Aires, a precursor to the urban guerrilla warfare that was repeated on a much larger scale and under another ideological banner in Argentina during the 1970s.

Another leading figure of the Italian anarchist movement in Argentina was Aldo Aguzzi, born in 1902 in Voghera, Pavia, and who according to the local police 'fled clandestinely' Mussolini's Italy to Argentina in 1923. In December of that year, *L'Avennire*, a militant anarchist magazine with a communist tendency, began to circulate among the Italian community in Buenos Aires.

Aguzzi tried to bring together all of the Italian anarchist tendencies that came to the Río de la Plata region, in an active anti-fascist movement. On 6 June 1925 Aguzzi and his supporters were drawn into what was to become a dizzying cycle of violence that would mark Argentine politics for decades. On that day the small but influential Italian fascist colony in Buenos Aires celebrated the twenty-fifth anniversary of the start of Victor Emmanuel III's reign, which would eventually encompass the rise and fall of Mussolini. A massive party took place in the Teatro Colón; the president of Argentina, Marcelo T. de Alvear, and the Italian ambassador, Luigi Aldrovandi Marescotti (the count of Viano) were in attendance as were groups of blackshirts keeping security.

When the orchestra began the Italian national anthem, a group of anarchists, among them Severino Di Giovanni, interrupted the event by throwing leaflets and shouting 'Death to fascism!' and 'Assassins! Thieves!' The blackshirts managed to overcome them and hand them over to the police.

Days later, in protest at the executions in the US of the Italian anarchists Sacco and Vanzetti, the group around Di Giovanni began a bombing campaign against North American businesses in Argentina as well as their consulate. The series of violent actions in Buenos Aires and Rosario reached their highest point with a high-powered bomb explosion that destroyed the Italian General Consulate, killing nine and seriously injuring thirty-four more. This and other actions, such as various assaults on banks, resulted in the indiscriminate police repression of suspect anarchists in the Italian immigrant community.

Di Giovanni was executed by firing squad on 1 February 1931 under orders from General José Félix Uriburu's military dictatorship. Uriburu had taken power a year earlier with a coup and embarked on an anti-worker repression, the likes of which had never been seen before on the Río de la Plata. Di Giovanni was twenty-nine years old. He shouted *'Evviva l'Anarchia!'* ('Long live Anarchy!'), before being hit by at least eight 7.65 mm Mauser rifle bullets. Other captured anarchists of Italian origin were returned to face torture and execution in Mussolini's Italy. Several anarchists who had escaped arrest left in 1936 for the Spanish Civil War, among them Aldo Aguzzi, who in 1939, by way of Marseilles, was able to return to Argentina. There, in Buenos Aires, he committed suicide on 31 May 1939, seemingly despairing of the direction Argentine politics had taken, and the growing local sympathy towards Nazi Germany and Mussolini's Italy. Aguzzi's suicide can be taken as a symbol of the definitive end of militant Italian anarchism in Argentina. However, the violence the anarchists provoked would endure in the collective memory of the Bergoglio household, instilling a deep distrust of political aggression.

Three years before Aguzzi's suicide, on 17 December 1936 the future Pope Francis was born in Flores, a neighbourhood of Buenos Aires which the children and grandchildren of successive waves of Italian immigrants had helped develop into a colourful and commercially vibrant sector of the city. Carlos Gardel, the legendary tango singer, was among its most famous inhabitants. 'Neighbourhood of my soul, where I spent my youth and spent nights of love,' Gardel would sing in the 1930s.

Gardel was a popular idol who would have an enduring impact on Argentine culture despite his foreign origins. Born illegitimately in France, Gardel was shipped off to Argentina by his mother as a young baby and grew up in Buenos Aires, gaining a reputation for his good looks, charm and captivating voice; his rags-to-riches story became part of the popular myth that much endeared him to the Italian immigrant community long before he became an international star.

Argentine tango owed its idiosyncrasy to the early Neapolitan immigrants who brought their lyrical style of violin and dancing across the ocean in the late nineteenth and early twentieth centuries. The Neapolitans sang and played, danced and blended their traditions with the local population and, in so doing, altered the direction of an art form. Tango was initially only heard in portside brothels but gradually spread across Buenos Aires into the new immigrant neighbourhoods where Gardel romanticized it as the music of heartache and longing. Speaking of the Italian influence on tango, the maestro of the *bandoneon* concertina José Libertella, who arrived in Buenos Aires from Italy in 1934, observed, 'It's the music of immigrants. It's of emotional people going through emotional times.'

The development of a more choreographed dance form by the

late 1920s and 1930s showed an interplay of contrasts in the continual interweaving of slow and quick beats, smooth flowing motion and sharp turns, freedom and discipline, sensuality and control, a mirror of emerging Argentine society. At the heart of the tango was the interplay between man and woman. The male, as 'macho', struts, leads, imposes. And yet the female is responsive, not submissive. As dance critic Don Berry has written: 'It evokes the beauty, the grace, and the inner spirit of the woman, without which tango is only empty geometry.'

One can easily imagine the hugely popular Gardel, with his easy charm and handsome dark Latin looks immortalized in 1930s audio and film, becoming a pin-up in the Bergoglio household, and his music listened to as often as opera. However, few details have emerged about Bergoglio's father, other than that he met his future wife while attending Mass and later insisted that his son should get his first job working in a laboratory while studying chemistry. A domineering and dominating father-figure is absent from early biographies and other interviews suggest that his influence was limited. Jorge Bergoglio appears to have spent much of his family life with his grandmother, the undisputed matriarch of the family. She is remembered as a kind, down-to-earth, resourceful woman who touched her favourite grandson's feminine side with her devotion to the Virgin Mary and encouraged his vocation.

The neighbourhood of Flores is today an architectural mish-mash from palatial neo-colonial to art nouveau with apartment blocks encroaching on small European-style squares; corner shops have survived Buenos Aires's century-old transformation into Latin America's most sophisticated city. The days when the area was covered in prairie, dotted with isolated country houses owned by rich landowners, had long gone by the time the Bergoglios set up home in a house that once stood at 268 Varela Street.

Extraordinary as it may seem, it appears that due to a collective memory lapse by the Bergoglio family and friends, earlier biographers were given mistaken information that Jorge Mario was born elsewhere. More than a year-and-a-half after the election of Pope Francis details emerged of the mistake, which was caused by the urban landscape changing to the point that surviving older residents were confused about where they had lived as children. Local historian Daniel Vargas unearthed a key authenticated document, signed by Bergoglio's father Mario José Francisco Bergoglio, then twenty-eight years old, which stated that he had witnessed his wife Regina Sívori giving birth in the house on Varela Street in Flores to their son Jorge Mario at 21 hours on 17 December 1936. The historian's findings, accepted by the local authorities, the Argentina government and Pope Francis, dispelled the legend accepted by earlier biographers, and popularized by a local 'Pope' tour and a plaque, that Jorge had been born at 531 Membrillar Street.

What is known beyond doubt is this: the first of five children, Jorge Mario was born the year in which Buenos Aires marked the 400th anniversary of its foundation with the widening of its main avenue and the opening of the tallest building in Latin America. Such symbols underlined the people's aspiration to greatness that seemed destined, despite the potential wealth of natural resources, to never be fulfilled, except by its football stars and its first elected pope.

Jorge was born in the midst of the so-called *decada infama*, or 'infamous decade', marked by increasing political corruption, widening social divisions and a controversial trade deal that gave UK companies a monopolistic hold on Argentina's railways and lucrative meat business. In 1934 the tango 'Cambalache' (Spanish for bazaar or junkshop), written by Enrique Santos Discépolo and sung by Gardel, became hugely popular particularly among the poor immigrant classes as a radical denunciation of Argentina as a failed society without accountable institutions or a moral compass: 'that the world we live in was and is trash, I already know . . . It doesn't matter these days if you are an upright man or traitor, ignorant, wise, or a thief, generous or just a fraud.'

The year of Bergoglio's birth, 1936, was also the year of the military uprising in Spain of Franco and his generals against the democratically elected Republican government. The Spanish Civil War spawned stories of anarchists burning or desecrating churches, and executing bishops, priests and nuns. Such anti-clericalism contrasted with the military support that Franco secured from Hitler and Mussolini. Within the orthodox Catholic Bergoglio household such contrasts fuelled a predisposition towards authoritarian rule based around a nationalist corporate state as established by Franco in Spain once he had emerged victorious from the civil war in 1939.

In Argentina, the 1930s began with the toppling of the democratically elected Radical government by the armed forces, signalling the political direction of the next fifty years. Between 1930, the year of Argentina's first military coup, and 1982, the year of the Falklands War, the country had a succession of twenty-four presidents. Of these, only thirteen were civilian, and not one civilian government survived without having its constitutionally defined six-year term interrupted by the armed forces. The only elected government to have stayed the course during the early years of Francis's life was that of General Juan Perón, who ruled from 1946 to 1955 and for a year in 1973 before his death. With his military background and nationalist, redistributive agenda, no other figure in Argentinian political history has been more influential, even during his long years in exile.

As the oldest child, Bergoglio spent much of his early years in the company of his grandparents, who lived in a house nearby, while his father went out to work and his mother focused on bringing up his siblings. Although Bergoglio, as the firstborn male, was given a certain measure of authority as well as independence not extended to his siblings, it was, by all accounts, a closely knit and loving family, touched by the nostalgia and instinctive self-protection that characterized immigrant families.

We know very little about the childhood of his brothers and sister. But Bergoglio would later recall those early days, when all the siblings would have absorbed the conversation of their elders as a transformative rite of passage from childhood to manhood. The journalists Rubin and Ambrogetti asked what he thought about the suggestion that neighbourhoods like Flores faced away from the River Plate because they had been built by poor immigrants, who had suffered the wrench of being uprooted from their home, and who now looked out on the fertile prairies of the pampas as the best hope for the future. He replied, quoting from Homer's *Odyssey*, by describing the pampas 'lighting the way back to the bosom of the earth, the maternal bosom of the earth from which we sprang'.

He went on to compare the warmth of his own childhood with the alienation provoked in modern families. 'When we put our elders in nursing homes with a couple of mothballs in their pockets as if they were an overcoat,' Bergoglio told his interviewers, 'in a certain sense our nostalgic side has failed us, since being with our grandparents means coming face-to-face with our past.'

The young Bergoglio's closeness to his grandmother Rosa had him learning Piedmontese and developing a love of Italian literature. Among the books she read to him was the early nineteenth-century novel by Alessandro Manzoni, *I Promessi Sposi* (*The Betrothed*), an epic of love and redemption with good and bad clergy immersed in a turbulent world populated by God-fearing peasants, pious lovers and corrupt nobles. Piedmontese was the dialect with which his grandmother conversed with her husband and occasionally sang moving verses about the old country left behind and the new land of uncertainty as well as illusion.

Perhaps Rosa's biggest influence on Bergoglio was that she taught him to pray, instilling in him the pious devotion to popular saints as well as Marian shrines that would mark his faith. A Catholic activist in her youth, Rosa also often recalled seeing the thousands who had packed the streets of Buenos Aires when the Vatican secretary of state and future Pope Pius XII, Cardinal Eugenio Pacelli, officiated at the 1934 International Eucharist Congress. Such was the sense of religious fervour and Catholic revivalism during those days in the Argentine capital that the local Church hierarchy emerged from the Congress hugely empowered to defend its interests against any government that sought to challenge its moral teaching, riches and hold on education.

After spending time with his grandmother, Bergoglio reunited with his parents in the afternoons and evenings. He would listen to the opera on the radio, with his mother explaining the libretto when not showing him how to cook veal escalope and pasta. These were happy times of seemingly safe and harmonious family life, which contrasted with the violence and disfunctionality of the surrounding society.

Bergoglio learned to read and write and took his first Holy Communion in La Misercordia, a nursery run by nuns just a block away from his family home, before moving to a mixed state school in the neighbourhood. In those early days nothing really distinguished the young Jorge Mario Bergoglio from the other kids of his age who all began their day, dressed in similar white aprons, singing the Argentine patriotic song dating back to independence days with its exaltation of mythical military feats and sacrifice in defence of national sovereignty: 'The valiant Argentine to arms runs burning with determination and bravery, the war bugle, as thunder, in the fields of the South resounds. Buenos Aires opposes, and it's leading the people of the illustrious Union, and with robust arms they tear the arrogant Iberian lion . . .' The kids sang with their clerical teachers before the giant blue and white national flag permanently posted in the school courtyard.

The anthem, titled 'Oíd Mortales' ('Listen Mortals'), is one of the longest and most operatic known to man, and reaches a climactic statement of patriotic self-sacrifice: 'May the laurels be eternal, that we know how to win. Let us live crowned with glory . . . or swear to die gloriously!' Behind the mythology lay a cruder if more factual historical narrative, which might explain why Argentina squandered its huge potential as a nation. It might also tell us something about the politics that helped form a future pope.

'This is a country which is formed by Generals, liberated by Generals, led by Generals and today claimed by Generals,' General Juan Perón, the man who has cast a long influential shadow on the Bergoglio household, told the Buenos Aires Military Academy in 1950. And this was a sentiment that would move generations of Argentines in the run-up to the Falklands War in 1982.

The first record of military action on Argentine soil was that of a Spanish conquistador Don Diego de Mendoza, a leading nobleman of the Spanish imperial court who landed with 1,500 troops on the shores of the River Plate estuary in 1536. He had come in search of mineral bounty similar to that which his compatriots seized from the Aztecs and Mayans in Central America and the Incas in the Andes. Mendoza found only a vast expanse of fertile prairie partly inhabited by a hunting tribe of wild nomadic Indian horsemen, who decided to carry out some raiding parties. Besieged, outnumbered and demoralized, Mendoza's men were killed off one by one. Mendoza himself sailed back to Spain and died at sea, near the Canary Islands a year later.

Settlement there eventually was, but Argentina's emergence as a nation state would depend on belated immigration that concentrated its mass around the metropolis of Buenos Aires. Before then, military conquest had pushed the Indian tribes ever further south in Patagonia, making way for Argentina's equivalent of the robber barons – the large landowners or *estancieros*. In 1806 and 1807 the fuse was lit for Argentina's independence from Spanish colonial rule when two British expeditionary forces were routed in and around

Buenos Aires by local militias led by General Santiago de Liniers, a renegade Frenchman formerly in the pay of the Spanish Army.

But even more important in every Argentine child's first history book was General José San Martín, who abandoned service in the Spanish Army and led a revolutionary army of 5,000 men in an epic march of liberation from colonial rule across Argentina, over the Andes to Chile, and up the Pacific to Peru. To this day there is no government office without a poster or a statue to him, no town without a major street or square or schoolroom named in his honour.

Bergoglio's Catholic school outings included a mandatory visit to the reconstructed eighteenth-century cathedral in Buenos Aires's Playa de Mayo, where the great liberator General San Martín's permanently torchlit marble mausoleum – an impressive black sarcophagus guarded by three life-sized angelic female figures representing Argentina, Chile and Peru, the three liberated countries – dwarfed any Crucifix, Virgin Mary or saintly icon. San Martín endured not just as a Latin American military hero, but for most Argentines as a potent symbol of their nation's mythical military.

No matter that San Martín was a freemason, that he owed his military plans to the British and that he ended up dying in exile in France, increasingly disillusioned with his country's politics and the absence of solidarity between it and other Latin America nations. Such details were airbrushed from the history texts, enhancing the enduring reputation of the picture-book Argentine military heroes that had liberated the continent.

The next war to involve an Argentine army was with Brazil (1825–28) which led to the creation of Uruguay as a buffer state following British intersection. Argentina forged an alliance with Brazil and Uruguay (The Triple Alliance) that ended with the annexation of half of Paraguay and the killing of some 400,000 Paraguayans, an estimated 60 per cent of the population (proportionately the biggest military bloodbath in modern military history). It left most Argentine soldiers empty-handed while greatly enriching one landlord, former president General Justo José de Urquiza, who came to be the owner of 600,000 cattle, 500,000 sheep, 20,000 horses and more than two million acres of land. He was assassinated in April 1870 by followers of a rival leader, the soldier and politician Ricardo Ramón López Jordán. Eight years later another military hero General Julio Roca occupied Patagonia and wiped out most of the local Indian population in order to make their land available to white settlers. Roca's Campaign of the Desert became ingrained in the national consciousness as another major military feat. It would take more than a century before it was recognized as genocide.

To be an immigrant's grandson and son was to have the need to be more Argentine than the Argentines. One can imagine the young Bergoglio in his Catholic primary school run by nuns singing his heart out to 'Oíd Mortales' when not talking with the vibrant air of any Italian. He was occasionally rowdy, and seemed always running around with the other school kids, according to the legend passed from the older to the younger nuns. Two of his teachers from childhood, Sister Rosa who died in 2012 aged 101, and sister Dolores who died in her late nineties a year earlier, gave Bergoglio rudimentary religious instruction in the Catholic faith and encouraged him, with the support of his grandmother, to confess his sins and take his first Holy Communion.

'He was a devil, a little devil, naughty and very easily distracted at times,' commented Sister Martha Rabino, the seventy-one-year-old headmistress, hours after she had heard that Bergoglio had become Pope Francis in 2013.

Sister Martha was only a baby when Bergoglio was a seven-year-old schoolboy, two years away from taking his First Communion, learning his two-times table by jumping the school staircase two steps at a time, repeating as he did so, 'two, four, six'. But oral history had percolated through from one generation of nuns to the next.

Early photographs and reminiscences suggest that Bergoglio was relatively extroverted as a child although not physically very strong. He tended to read more than play sport. He was, however, unable to resist sharing in the passion his father and a majority of male Argentines felt for football. By the 1930s football in Argentina had developed into the country's most popular sport with its own creative style emerging from the poorer urban neighbourhoods populated by Italian, Iberian, Basque, Jewish, and Arab immigrants.

While kicking a ball about occasionally in the local square with his schoolmates and swapping stories with his father Mario, Bergoglio became a lifelong fan of the local club San Lorenzo, which claimed enduring links with the Catholic Church. The story has its beginnings in the early 1900s, when a street gang based in the nearby Almagro district would invite gangs from Flores to play street football by painting walls with the legend '*Los Forzosos de Almagro desafían*' ('Almagro's strongmen dare you'). Almagro was by then criss-crossed by tramway and bus lines so playing football was a risky business. When one day a young boy was run over by a tramway car, a local Catholic priest Lorenzo Massa took charge. To keep the kids off the streets and going to Mass, he hosted football games in the backyard of his parish church in the Avenida de Mexico.

Thus was born San Lorenzo football club. Either unwittingly or perhaps influenced by the advice of Catholic Scottish and Irish immigrants in Buenos Aires, Massa had followed in the steps of the Irish Marist Brother Walfrid, who in 1887 founded Celtic Football Club in the Glasgow immigrant neighbourhood of Calton with the purpose of alleviating poverty.

More questionable is the veracity of a story that, at the age of twelve, the young Bergoglio wrote a love letter to a childhood sweetheart: 'If I don't marry you, I will become a priest.'

The story was told by an elderly Buenos Aires pensioner called Amalia Damonte in the immediate aftermath of Bergoglio's election as pope. It later disappeared from the headlines just as quickly as it had surfaced. The story was never confirmed by Pope Francis himself, but according to a family member who had been close to him most of his life, his surviving sister Maria Elena, the letter was a figment of an old lady's harmless imagination. 'The sweetheart? The truth is she never existed. But if this lady says that she did, and is happy with it, why not let her tell her story?' said Maria Elena.

Chapter Five
Vocation

The Basilica of San José de Flores, built in the last quarter of the nineteenth century, was the Bergoglio family church. To walk inside this neoclassical eclectic church is to get a sense of the Byzantine world that immersed the young Bergoglio in his Catholic faith and where he eventually discovered his vocation for the priesthood.

Eight side altars and other sanctuaries line the walls, with their respective images of the Virgin, saints and Christ glowing in the light of candles. Among the venerated pantheon of saints, each figure provides an aspect of humanity at its most virtuous. All would find an enduring place in the faith of the future pope.

Among the most popular saints in the neighbourhood is the Italian Luis Gonzaga, one of the early sixteenth-century Jesuits who died aged twenty-three while selflessly caring for those who had contracted the plague. Other statues include those of the Jesuit missionary Francis Xavier and Saint Vincent de Paul who served the poor. Among the beatified women, St Teresa of Ávila takes pride of place in Bergoglio's parish church. Her legacy, he would have discovered from his book of prayers, was not just the convents she founded but her hugely influential writings with their detailed and painfully honest charting of mystical experience and the emphasis she placed on experience rather than dogmatic teaching.

Periodically the display of resplendent iconography is interrupted by elaborately carved, dark wooden confessional boxes, with a grill separating priest and penitent. Lines of marble columns and suspended chandeliers lead to the high altar, with giant frescoes depicting the life of Jesus from Holy Family to Crucifixion covering the domed ceiling. The high altar is inscribed with the words '*Altare Privilegiatum*', denoting this as a church whose special status was the granting of a plenary indulgence whenever Mass was celebrated.

Bergoglio's catechism lesson would have assured him that an indulgence reflected a God of mercy as the Almighty had agreed to withdraw from all those praying at the Mass the temporal punishment due to sins whose guilt had already been forgiven. Above the altar rises a crucifix and a statue figure of St Joseph, the church's patron saint, the simple carpenter called by God to be the Virgin Mary's husband.

Other Latin inscriptions are distributed around the church from a time before the vernacular and when the young Bergoglio read Latin like he read Spanish, as an integral part of his life, essential to understanding the core of his faith. For as the young Bergoglio knelt there, preparing to take Communion, he would have quietly looked up and read and whispered '*Christe exhaudi nos*' ('Christ graciously hear us'), before following the incantation repeated three times by the priest: '*Agnus Dei qui tollis peccata mundi*' ('Lamb of God who takes away the sins of the world').

The church, with its plaque commemorating its naming as a basilica by Pope Pius X in 1912, its altar overlooked by a papal crown donated by Pope Pius XII in 1956 and its gold plated baptismal crypt, exudes solemnity and authority as well as a keen awareness of the importance the revival of popular religion has played in modern Church history.

It was inaugurated in 1883, on the site of a previous church that had been erected when this neighbourhood was part of a large country estate owned by the controversial governor of Buenos Aires and ruler of Argentina, Juan Manuel de Rosas. A general of the Argentine Army, Rosas governed by decree in the 1830s and 1840s, created a cult of personality and persecuted his opponents. The Jesuits at the time were the only institution within Argentina's Catholic Church that spoke out against Rosas and were subsequently expelled from the country.

Prior to this the order's reputation for moral authority took a blow when one of its young priests eloped with Camila O'Gorman, the daughter of a reputable upper-class family of mixed Irish and Spanish descent. The twenty-three-year-old Camila was eight months pregnant with the child she conceived with Father Ladislao Gutiérrez, just a year older than her, when they were arrested and executed by orders of Rosas in 1848. He rejected a last-minute plea from his own daughter on the grounds that he needed to show his 'undisputed power, as the moral values and sacred religious norms of a whole society are at stake'. In the aftermath of their deaths, both friends and enemies of Rosas claimed to be appalled by the cruel and senseless execution. They wrote about it using terms such as 'the beautiful girl', 'the doomed couple' and 'the repression of love' – a perspective that informed María Luisa Bemberg's Oscar-nominated film *Camila*, which was released in 1984, to mark the end of military rule in Argentina.

Between catechism classes, Bergoglio studied Argentine literature and history, not an easy task given that both had fallen prey to political subjectivity over more than half a century. Rosas was demonized by his critics as a brutal dictator, while restored periodically by nationalist revisionist historians as a hero. Rosas's governor's mansion, a few blocks away from where Bergoglio was born and brought up, survived as a museum amidst the growing urbanization of the neighbourhood of Flores. But the church Rosas funded near his home was torn down after he lost power and went into exile. For any young Catholic brought up in Flores, the history of Rosas with its story of political repression and ecclesiastical scandal was not an easy one to digest. For the young Bergoglio, it was a story with mixed signals, as he struggled to interpret the call from God to a celibate life in a highly charged political environment.

Bergoglio visited the church regularly as a child and in his early youth, sometimes with his family, sometimes alone, and with his grandmother as his most enthusiastic companion. The richly decorated building provided the context for the faith she helped instil in him, lighting candles here and there, looking up to be reminded of the moving narrative of the Gospels, before being drawn into the mystery of the sacraments, with the priest, back turned to the congregation and in muffled tones of reverence, enacting the stages of Christ's death and resurrection. The ritual in 1930s and 1940s Argentina bound Catholics in orthodox piety, tradition, dogma and unwavering acceptance of papal authority.

Bergoglio was seventeen when on 21 September 1953 an unplanned visit to the church led to an encounter that would change his life forever. The most detailed record of the event is contained in a recorded conversation Bergoglio had in November 2012 with Fr Juan Isasmendi, from the small Caacupé parish in the Argentine capital's poorest neighbourhood. In the interview, Bergoglio spoke openly and in detail about the moment when he decided to enter the priesthood.

Bergoglio was at the time studying chemistry at a technical sixth-form college. This is his story as told to his fellow priest: 'It was September 21 – I always remember this – I went out for a walk with some friends and I passed the Iglesia de Flores. I went inside the church, I entered, I felt that I had to go in, there are things that you feel inside and you don't really know what they are. I looked and it was dark, a September morning, and I saw a priest coming towards me. I didn't know him, he wasn't from that church, and then he sat down in the last confessional, on the left, facing the altar, and then I don't know what happened to me.'

Bergoglio continued: 'I felt like somebody grabbed me from inside and took me to the confessional. I'm not sure what happened there, clearly I must have confessed, but I don't know what happened, and when I finished confessing, I asked the priest where he was from, because I didn't know him,' he recalled. 'He said "I'm from Corrientes [an Argentine city near the border with Paraguay], and I am living near here, in the rectory, and I am going to celebrate Mass here occasionally."'

The priest from Corrientes was suffering from leukaemia and died the following year. But it was a transcendent moment in more ways than one. Bergoglio found it difficult to describe in words. 'While I was there I felt that I had to become a priest, and I didn't doubt it,' he recalled.

Bergoglio's classmates recall his intense faith as one of his distinctive traits alongside his intelligence, displayed in an ability to grasp new ideas, which put him among the brightest in his year. By all accounts he was popular, engaging and selfless, often prepared to help others less bright than he in their studies. He also gained a reputation as being quite sociable, no introvert, and not a bad tango dancer, which helped him break out of his shyness. He grew up at a time when small, friendly groups of teenagers from good, hard-working, Catholic immigrant families enjoyed themselves on Saturday nights with parties at each other's homes in the company of parents. The boys, in suits and ties, brought the soft drinks, the girls, in suitably modest dresses, the *masitas* (cakes) and *empanadas* (pasties). They would all be at Mass the next morning.

The young Bergoglio, nonetheless, was no picture-book saint, assuming pious airs and claiming a visitation from God from an early age. Even his authorized biography does not claim a damascene conversion from anti-God to sainthood. Based on loose conversations the authors Rubin and Ambrogetti had with Bergoglio when he was Archbishop of Buenos Aires, the future pope described that event on 21 September 1953 as 'a great gift that sneaked up on me unnoticed'.

The day marked the first day of spring in Argentina, one traditionally celebrated as the 'Day of the Student' in Argentina for it was on that date in 1888 that the body of the country's enlightened nineteenth-century president Domingo Faustino Sarmiento was repatriated to be buried with state honours in a huge mausoleum in the city's Recoleta Cemetery. Sarmiento, who was president in 1868–74, was a highly cultured and liberal-minded individual who built 800 new schools as part of his dream project of transforming Argentina's troubled post-colonial society – dominated by powerful landowners and their rough and ready workforce of gauchos or Argentine cowboys – into a prosperous nation based on law-abiding and educated new immigrants from Europe.

But it was *Facundo*, a book written by this exiled author and journalist prior to becoming president, that turned Sarmiento into an important figure not just in Latin American literature but also in Argentina's search for a true identity. Subtitled *Civilization and Barbarism, Facundo* contrasted the cruder aspects of a populist Latin American leader's culture of brutality and demagoguery with the enlightened ideas of European and classical origin. *Facundo* described the life of Juan Facundo Quiroga, a gaucho who had terrorized provincial Argentina in the 1820s and 1830s, in a thinly veiled critique of the tyranny of the Argentine dictator Juan Manuel de Rosas, whom General Perón would later resurrect as a national hero.

That September in 1953, Sarmiento was celebrated as he had been for many years, but the celebration was far from universal. Perón and his followers had reluctantly accepted Sarmiento as a patriot after reinventing him as a general despite his lack of any real military status, for only as a soldier was he accepted by the regime. In fact Sarmiento's *Facundo* provided ammunition for those who saw Perón as nothing but a militarist, a twentieth-century version of the barbaric Rosas.

Bergoglio was ten years old when Perón came to power in 1946. His adolescence and early vocation to the priesthood were lived out against the background of Perón's rule and the huge influence the populist general had on moulding the nation's political culture and sense of identity. As Perón's biographer Joseph Page puts it, 'Juan Perón was a distinctly Argentine phenomenon, incomprehensible except in the context in which he emerged . . . indeed the relationship between the man and the country often seemed symbiotic. It may not be far from the mark to suggest that Perón was Argentina and Argentina was Perón.' No life of Jorge Bergoglio, the first ever Argentine pope can make sense without an acknowledgement of Perón's influence on his political and spiritual formation.

Like Stephen Dedalus in James Joyce's *Portrait of the Artist as a Young Man*, Bergoglio grew up grappling with his nationality, religion, family and morality. But whereas Stephen – educated by disciplinarian Irish Jesuits – finally decides to reject all socially imposed bonds and instead live freely as an artist, Bergoglio chose to become a priest. This was just at the time that the bishops and clergy who had collaborated with the Perón regime broke with it and were headed for confrontation.

In 1929, the year Jorge Bergoglio's father and grandfather arrived in Argentina from Italy, Perón, the son of a minor public functionary and tenant farmer with family roots reaching back to Sardinia, graduated from the military war academy and became embroiled in General Uriburu's military uprising against the democratically elected Radical government. The coup was supported by large numbers of civilians, instilling in the young Perón an enduring respect for mass mobilization as a way of pursuing and maintaining political power.

Perón had been on various military assignments attached to the chief of staff. He went on to teach at the military academy – a post that guaranteed the loyalty of new recruits – before serving as a military attaché in Chile, a key intelligence post given the historic suspicion Argentina had of its Andean neighbour.

During the Second World War, when Argentina officially remained neutral, Perón was posted to Italy and was openly sympathetic to the Axis powers. He was impressed by the organization and mobilization of the German and Italian people under Hitler and Mussolini and their use of a mass spectacle as a political tool. He viewed Nazi Germany and Fascist Italy through the prism of his military background and believed they were developing an alternative to capitalism and communism. By contrast, his populist instinct blamed imperial ambition for the hold British commerce had, in alliance with the rich landed elites of the late nineteenth and early twentieth centuries, on strategic areas of the Argentine economy such as the railways, shipping, engineering and the meat trade. His ideology adhered to a third position that took the middle ground between free-market capitalism, in which big business called the tune, and the dictatorship of the proletariat favoured by communism.

In elections in 1946 Perón was propelled to power with a working-class powerbase and the support of the military. His advocacy of political, social and economic justice and his brand of nationalism based on his defiance of British and US 'imperial' interests won him the political support of the middle classes as well as organized labour. His anti-communism and initial respect for Catholic teaching on abortion and divorce, and the Church's hold on areas of education from primary to university level, secured the support of the Catholic hierarchy and a whole new generation of priests, many of whom were trained in Franco's Spain. Perón's particular genius lay in his pragmatism and the way he seized the opportunity for statesmanship after the turmoil of the 1930s, as his biographer writes, 'transferring the essence of military leadership to the game of Argentine politics and in comprehending his fellow citizens far better than any of his contemporaries'.

The legacy of Perón and his charismatic, radical second wife, Evita, was a hybrid political movement with a nationalist leadership predisposed towards authoritarian rule, and with support that included sectors of the armed forces, non-foreign businessmen, trade unions and the poor. The notion Perón championed, that social justice can be reached by a balancing of the interests of capital and labour, touched the hearts of lower-middle-class immigrant Catholic families like the Bergoglios, echoing as they did the papal encyclicals of the late nineteenth and twentieth centuries which defined official Catholic social teaching.

But Perón brought into Argentine political culture not just a convergence of ideology, but also a claim to a distinct formula for the exercise of political power over the masses, which borrowed a concept learnt from the military and translated it into civilian life – this was the need for centralized control in the hands of a *conductor*, or powerful charismatic leader. What Perón and his apologists claimed set him apart from a tyrant or dictator was the elasticity of his following even though democracy remained illusory. Thus, as his biographer Joseph Page notes, while no one whoever watched Perón perform in front of a mass audience could miss the symbiotic relationship between them, an essential component of his leadership was the availability of a citizenry not only willing but ready to be led, as unquestioning as soldiers behind their general.

Thus did Peronism produce its famous anthem titled the 'Marcha Peronista' ('The Peronist March') with its most memorable and enduring phrase uniting the leader with the masses:

Perón, Perón, que grande sòs, mi General cuanto vales
Perón, Perón, gran conductor, sos el primer trabajador.
(Perón, Perón, how great you are, my General, how much
    we value you
Perón, Perón, great conductor, the first among workers.)

In the early years, during which the future Pope Francis received his first education and made his first Holy Communion at his local Misericordia parish school, run by nuns, Perón and the Catholic hierarchy preserved an atmosphere of reciprocal benevolence, mirroring Franco's Spain. The Church kept its silence in the face of the deterioration of civil liberties such as the intimidation of free-thinking journalists, or the imprisonment of independent trade unionists or professional officers who refused to obey orders because they felt that the general who was also president had become an ideological demagogue. The regime, for its part, respected the privileged position of the Church, especially in the area of education. Unless you were rich and landed or in exile, there was no incompatibility between being Catholic and being a *Peronista*. The modest Bergoglio family, raised on an abhorrence of the anti-clericalism of the early immigrant Italian anarchists, was both.

Of those days, contemporaries remember Jorge Bergoglio as an energetic boy with no major incident impacting on his transition from childhood to youth, although the family dinners ingrained a respect for Perón that first manifested itself during his adolescence and would endure into old age. With the passage of time, some other memories contradict each other. Thus, one of Bergoglio's early unauthorized biographers drew on an account by one of his contemporaries that in his early days in secondary school, the future pope gained a certain notoriety among his peers after turning up for lessons sporting a large brooch with Perón's insignia on his lapel. The display of political symbols was officially banned by the school, but Bergoglio went on wearing his badge of loyalty until his teacher forced him to take it off. Pope Francis later denied this specific story.

Instead, in one of the authorized books on him – *Aquel Francisco* by the Argentine journalists Javier Cámara and Sebastián Pfaffen – he recalls an occasion when he went as his school's representative to a mass Perón meeting in the early 1950s (Pope Francis gives no precise date) at the Teatro Colón, one of the capital's emblematic centres of culture. He also recalled that he came face-to-face with Eva Perón in a Peronist party office in central Buenos Aires on another occasion while collecting leaflets. Pope Francis has never disclosed publicly what impact Perón or Evita had on him, although he has drawn parallels between Peronist doctrine and the Catholic Church's social teaching.

Bergoglio's call from God after his confession in San José de Flores in 21 September 1953 coincided with a sinister development in Perón's determination to have his movement control all aspects of Argentine society: the creation of the Union of Secondary Students to organize, control and ultimately indoctrinate Argentine teenagers in Peronism. The brainchild of Armando Méndez San Martín, Perón's education minister, it was embraced enthusiastically by Perón himself who had pledged to win a third term with youth votes. While the universities still bred dissent against the regime, Perón believed the hearts of adolescents could be won before they went to university.

The new union set out to foster sports-orientated recreation with boys' and girls' branches, and the government providing facilities for both. Such moves won supporters among the high-school students, including no doubt some of Bergoglio's classmates, but caused tensions with the Catholic Church, which saw it as interference with family life. Indeed, by September 1953, it seemed only a matter of time before the reciprocal benevolence and collaboration preserved by Perón and the Catholic hierarchy since he had come to power would collapse.

Perón's relations with the higher echelons of the Catholic Church in Argentina, and its allies in the military and the landed classes, had been deteriorating since the death from cancer the previous July of the President's thirty-three-year-old wife, Evita. She was hugely popular with the poor and sectors of the unionized workforce. But moves by Perón to have her canonized were blocked by the bishops and the Vatican. Determined to make her mythology endure in the popular imagination, Perón had Evita's body embalmed while unveiling plans for a gigantic mausoleum, standing taller than the Statue of Liberty and with sixteen marble statues, depicting aspects of his life together with her, lining the circular base.

Without Evita, Perón seemed to lose both his political instinct as well as the little moral authority he might once have claimed. He broke the de facto political pact with the Catholic Church while laying himself open to rumours of sexual scandals, including one involving an alleged affair with a teenage member of the student union he had set up to bolster the youth vote.

Perón had on numerous occasions publicly manifested his loyalty to the Catholic faith, encouraging the building of Catholic schools and churches, and showing off his veneration of the popular cult of the Virgin of Luján, that had for years drawn millions of pilgrims to her site near Buenos Aires. But on 10 November 1954 he launched into a public attack against what he claimed was a conspiracy to undermine his regime involving reactionary bishops, priests and lay Catholics.

By then he had succeeded in antagonizing his previous ecclesiastical collaborators by threatening the separation of Church and State, scrapping from the list of government holidays a number of Catholic feast days and ending religious instruction in state schools. He also announced plans to legalize divorce and prostitution, and give equal legal rights to illegitimate children.

Meanwhile, reports reached Perón by the summer of that year that a group of Catholics had formed a Christian Democrat party in opposition to his movement, and that Catholic Action, a lay society sponsored by the bishops, was competing openly with the regime's student unions.

Little if any contemporary account or reminiscences have emerged to shed light on how these events may have impacted on the future pope. But it is not hard to imagine the confusion this political backdrop must have provoked in the young Bergoglio as he turned eighteen. He had been brought up in a family that not only saw no contradiction between their Peronist affiliation and their Catholic faith but saw Perón and Evita as personifying Catholic social teaching as spelt out by the papacy.

We know that despite the 'gift that sneaked up on him', as he described his call to the priesthood, Bergoglio did not immediately enter a seminary at an early age as several of his contemporaries did. In his early days at school his father Mario found him a job as a cleaner in the office of the railway company where he worked as an accountant. Later, after that first illuminating encounter with the anonymous priest, he went on to finish his schooling while working part-time at a nutrition analysis laboratory.

Late in November 1955, two months after Perón had been deposed in a military coup, Bergoglio told his parents that he had been accepted by the Buenos Aires diocesan seminary of Villa Devoto, which he intended to enter as soon as possible without pursuing a university degree as a layman. The news shocked his mother Regina. With an eye on him eventually becoming the main family breadwinner after her husband retired, Regina had banked on her oldest son going on to study medicine, as he had once hinted was his ambition. There followed days of tension in the close-knit Bergoglio family circle with Regina accusing her son Jorge of lying to her, and he replying, so his young sister Maria Elena later recalled, that he was being consistent with his conscience. 'I'm going to study medicine of the soul,' Bergoglio told his mother. A more serious family bust-up was averted thanks to the mediation of the old family friend, the Salesian Fr Pozzoli just before Christmas that year, after he celebrated Mass on the occasion of Mario and Regina's twentieth wedding anniversary. Bergoglio entered the seminary the following March in 1956.

The seminary of Villa Devoto was set in a leafy residential

suburb, known as the 'Garden of the City', of early nineteenth-century palatial houses, landscaped with large manicured lawns and a variety of trees. The seminary's large, thick stone building with grilled windows occupied a block and was owned by the Jesuits. It was also at the time taking in boys as young as twelve for early religious-based schooling prior to formal training as priests. Bergoglio was one of the older students who had yet to progress to a major seminary. He still lacked a solid basis in Latin and Greek before advancing to philosophy and theology studies. No evidence has emerged to substantiate claims made by some of his early biographers that, both prior to and during his early days at the seminary, Bergoglio struggled to put behind him worldly thoughts that briefly challenged his ideal of pursuing a celibate life.

But two years after entering the seminary, Bergoglio suffered an experience that would have a more enduring impact on his life. In August (midwinter in the southern hemisphere) 1957 he developed pleurisy, an inflammation of the membrane surrounding one of his lungs. Bergoglio's condition deteriorated to the point that he was struggling to breathe and suffering terrible chest pain. He might have died had the superior of the seminary, Fr Humberto Bellone, not recognized the symptoms and rushed him to a hospital where he worked part-time as chaplain. There Bergoglio underwent an emergency operation to have three non-malignant cysts and a small part of his upper right lung removed. Fr Bellone, who was present throughout, recalled many years later: 'When he first got ill, he was in such a bad way that I thought he was going to die. It was really serious although the operation, carried out by a specialist surgeon, went well and he recovered after spending several days in an oxygen tent.'

The near-death experience – bringing him close to the suffering of Christ and through it the thought of redemption – impacted on Bergoglio, as did the several weeks he spent convalescing in a hillside retreat house owned by the Salesians near Tandil, 220 miles south of Buenos Aires. The relative solitude he experienced and conversations he had with some of the priests there strengthened his spiritual resolve while seemingly setting aside – at least temporarily – any political concerns he might have otherwise felt in the aftermath of Perón's abrupt toppling from power.

Bergoglio later recalled this period as a crisis of maturity that led him to spend more time in solitude. It was a 'passive solitude', the kind one suffers for no apparent reason as opposed to an 'active solitude which one experiences when facing transcendental experiences'. Of his politics at the time, we know that Bergoglio was no radical activist. Nevertheless his sympathy towards Peronism seems to have made him open to other ideologies that claimed to stand up for the rights of the working classes and against the kind of privilege personified by the large landowners and company executives who had made fortunes through Argentina's meat and wheat trade.

In an interview prior to becoming pope, he revealed his 'political concerns' were at the time intellectual and that, although never a communist, he owed part of his political education to the writings of Leónidas Barletta, one of the best-known members of the Argentine Communist party as well as a renowned figure in the world of culture. He was introduced to Barletta's articles in the party's journal, *Our Word and People*, by Esther Ballestrino de Careaga, one of his supervisors when he worked in the laboratory while completing his high-school studies. Ballestrino, who was of Paraguayan origin and was an active member of the Paraguayan left-wing opposition Partido Revolucionario Febrerista (PRF), also taught him to speak the dialect of the indigenous Guaraní, a tribe that owed its conversion to Christianity to the early Jesuit missionaries.

The Guaraní language would be useful to the future Archbishop of Buenos Aires in his engagement with poor migrants who populated the shanty towns of the capital. The extent to which

Ballestrino contributed to Bergoglio's political formation is more difficult to discern, largely because of the shifting politics of the Communist party in so far as its relationship with Peronism was concerned. Ballestrino's descendants claim that she was not a communist but belonged to a Paraguayan movement that defined itself as social democratic. When Perón first stood for election in 1946, the Argentine Communist party opposed him as part of the broad Democratic Union coalition whose campaign slogan was 'For Liberty, Against Nazism'. This was a reference to a growing number of escaping Nazis who were finding post-war refuge in Argentina with the complicity of Perón and other pro-Axis officers.

Once in power, Perón was duplicitous in his dealing with the communists. On the one hand, he boasted in his relations with the United States that his political philosophy provided an effective vaccine against the spread of Marxism, while for internal purposes he stressed that his movement was the only viable and truly Latin American alternative to international socialism. The Argentine Communist party, loyal to Moscow, adopted a pragmatic line towards Perón, abandoning the accusation that he was a Nazi-Fascist while at the same time arguing that his reforms did not go far enough.

Many years later Bergoglio's communist supervisor Esther Ballestrino Careaga would return and occupy a place in his life when she, together with her daughter, son-in-law and two French nuns – Alice Domon and Léonie Duquet – joined the ranks of the disappeared following the military coup of 1976; this challenged the future pope to account for his own role in defence of the human rights of thousands of victims, some of whom he knew personally and owed favours. But in the mid-1950s Bergoglio's crisis of conscience was of a far less dramatic kind, if still one whose resolution, through becoming a Jesuit priest, would be a crossing of the Rubicon.

Certainly his illness, by taking him away from the workplace and student life and putting him at a distance from Buenos Aires, effectively separated him from the fast-moving political story surrounding the aftermath of Perón's fall and flight into exile. He might have become involved had he continued as a student or indeed joined the Communist party.

Perón's first government began to unravel rapidly in June 1955 when he had two Catholic priests deported to Italy; the Vatican promptly responded by excommunicating 'those responsible', i.e. Perón, without specifying exactly who. Then elements of the Navy and Air Force rebelled and planes dropped bombs on Buenos Aires, killing some 350 people. The rising was put down, but gangs of young thugs started looting and desecrating churches. One group of Peronist loyalists set fire to the main offices of the Archbishop of Buenos Aires before smashing through the main portals of the cathedral and pillaging the altars and sacristies. With parishioners looking on helplessly, Perón's stormtroopers dressed up in priest vestments and danced in a sacrilegious parody of the Mass. Elsewhere an eighty-year-old parish priest who tried to resist the marauders was beaten to death.

Such scenes profoundly shocked the capital's Catholic immigrant families like the Bergoglios, echoing as they did the violent anti-clericalism of anarchists during the Spanish Civil War. Peronist violence provoked an enduring revulsion among conservative bishops and clergy who formed the majority of the Argentine Church, with the horror of it all no doubt reaching the retreat house where Bergoglio convalesced. And yet as shocking for many poor Argentines – those who had seen their living standards and access to state support improve thanks to Perón's redistributive policies – was the eventual coup that toppled Perón and forced him into exile.

At the end of August 1955 a report that a sector of the armed forces was plotting Perón's overthrow provoked a general strike in solidarity with him and a carefully organized protest demonstration in Buenos Aires, at which Perón made a violently inflammatory speech, encouraging his supporters to kill their opponents. But within a month Perón had fled to neighbouring Paraguay on a gunboat after military units, led by General Eduardo Lonardi, seized the northern city of Córdoba and Buenos Aires, and stormed the Peronist headquarters where 500 civilian loyalists had barricaded themselves in. Lonardi was himself replaced that November in a further coup led by his former anti-Peronist plotter General Pedro Aramburu.

Being torn between his instinctive Peronist sympathies and loyalty to the Catholic faith he had been brought up in must have proved an increasing dilemma for the young Bergoglio. He found solace with the Salesians, before entering a seminary and the Jesuit order.

Chapter Six
Jesuit Roots

On 11 March 1958 [Bergoglio] entered the novitiate of the Society of Jesus. He completed his studies of the humanities in Chile and returned to Argentina in 1963 to graduate with a degree in philosophy from the Colegio de San José in San Miguel. From 1964 to 1965 he taught literature and psychology at Immaculate Conception College in Santa Fé and in 1966 he taught the same subject at the Colegio del Salvador in Buenos Aires. From 1967–70 he studied theology and obtained a degree from the Colegio of San José.

On 13 December 1969 he was ordained a priest by Archbishop Ramón José Castellano. He continued his training between 1970 and 1971 at the University of Alcalá de Henares, Spain, and on 22 April 1973 made his final profession with the Jesuits. Back in Argentina, he was novice master at Villa Barilari, San Miguel; professor at the Faculty of Theology of San Miguel; consulter to the Province of the Society of Jesus and also Rector of the Colegio Máximo of the Faculty of Philosophy and Theology.

On 31 July 1973 he was appointed Provincial of the Jesuits in Argentina, an office he held for six years. He then resumed his work in the university sector and from 1980 to 1986 served once again as Rector of the Colegio de San José, as well as parish priest, again in San Miguel. In March 1986 he went to Germany to finish his doctoral thesis; his superiors then sent him to the Colegio del Salvador in Buenos Aires and next to the Jesuit Church in the city of Córdoba as spiritual director and confessor.

L'Osservatore Romano, Year LXIII, no. 12

By his own admission, Bergoglio was attracted to the Jesuits because of their character as 'an advance force of the Church, speaking military language, developed with obedience and discipline'. But who were these Jesuits? Where had they come from? What was it that had fuelled a passionate following while turning them into one of the most mistrusted and, in extreme cases, hated defenders of the Catholic faith? What parts of their controversial history influenced the choice of the young Argentine seminarian and help us understand his subsequent spiritual and political evolution?

The essential encyclopaedia for any serious student of the Jesuits is *Monumenta Historica Societatis Iesu*, an authorized collection of edited scholarly documents on the origins and early years of the Society of Jesus. The collection was prompted by the Jesuit General Congregation XXIV of 1892, which recommended to the Superior General – the head of the order – that writing the Society of Jesus's history be resumed after a turbulent political period lasting three centuries during which the order had suffered expulsion from various countries and at one point suppression by papal decree (Pope Clement XIV in 1773).

The initiative, entrusted to a group of Spanish Jesuits, was stimulated by the renewal of historical research which characterized the late nineteenth century with its emphasis on primary oral and documentary sources. A first volume was published in Madrid in

1894, with the work carried on by researchers attached to the Jesuit Historical Institute set up in Rome in 1930.

By 1958, the year Bergoglio decided to train for the Jesuit priesthood, the finely edited volumes of the *MHSI* numbered seventy-five. He would have been hard pressed to absorb even a fraction of the monumental work. However, there were enough more erudite Jesuit scholars around the globe who had studied the material in depth and used it as their own source material for making the narrative more accessible to a contemporary colleague with less time on his hands.

What follows is in part drawn from *Saint Ignatius Loyola: Pilgrim Years* by James Brodrick, a book written by a widely respected English Jesuit historian with the help of Spanish-speaking colleagues in the early 1950s, which Bergoglio would have found easy to absorb in translation as part of his education.

The book focused sympathetically on the sixteenth-century founder of the Jesuit order in the political and social context in which he lived, while underlining the important role played by Ignatius and the early missionaries in setting an example to subsequent generations of priests.

Ignatius's life periodically transposed would have an influence, straddling centuries, on wide sectors of society across the globe from schoolchildren and university students to a range of historic figures in public life. Those educated in institutions owned by the Jesuits have included, to name just a sample, writers (Cervantes, García Márquez, Clancy, Joyce, Conan Doyle, Lorca), actors and movie directors (Peter O'Toole, Denzel Washington, Buñuel, Hitchcock), politicians (Richelieu, Robespierre, Pierre Trudeau, de Gaulle, the Castro brothers, Bill Clinton, John Kerry), businessmen (John Paul Getty, Donald Trump), rock stars (Freddie Mercury), priests and missionaries, bishops and cardinals, and ultimately Jorge Bergoglio, the man destined to be the first Jesuit pope.

The mosaic of personalities suggests that to be educated by the Jesuits or to be one did not guarantee sainthood. It also suggests that Ignatius produced not so much a regimented army, pre-packed and uniform, but individuals with an acute sense of their own personal freedom to do their best for God and mankind even if many may have failed to reach that ideal.

Although the modern Jesuit order is wary of being identified as an army, Ignatius had indeed used a military metaphor – writing of soldiers of God and the defence of the faith – when forming his order partly because his previous life had been that of a nobleman who bore arms, but largely in response to the circumstances in which the Catholic Church found itself after having its legitimacy and power challenged by the Reformation.

The life of Ignatius began in deceptively encouraging times for cradle Catholics – at least those, like Ignatius, who owed their allegiance to the Spanish crown. The son of a Basque nobleman who fought in the reconquest of Spain from Moorish domination, the baby Inigo, who later Latinized his name to Ignatius (after Ignatius of Antioch), was baptized in 1491 just as, in the words of Brodrick, the 'long dream, not only of Spain, but of all Christendom was about to be fulfilled and the banner of the Cross float triumphantly above the turrets of the fabulous Alhambra'.

The conquest of Granada was followed by Christopher Columbus's discovery of the New World, causing an extraordinary upsurge of energy and exaltation at the royal Spanish court of King Ferdinand and Queen Isabella and amidst a generation of military entrepreneurs and missionary priests.

In 1517, less than a quarter century later, and before Ignatius had turned twenty-five, Martin Luther nailed his ninety-five theses to the door of the castle church at Wittenberg in Germany, ushering in the beginning of the Protestant Reformation. Luther denounced a Catholic Church that had become complacent and corrupted and separated from the Gospel. His theses were primarily an attack on the granting of indulgences in return for money for the rebuilding of St Peter's in Rome.

However, he soon broadened his attack to include the papacy and other aspects of church organization, the sacraments, and much of Catholic piety and devotional life including religious orders. At root was his attack on centralized and hierarchical Church authority and clericalism, which he claimed had moved Christian practice away from its essential faith based on scripture.

The Catholic Church was thus under pressure to respond to Protestantism with a missionary effort that was both vigorous and strategic. It took a battlefield injury to produce the person called by destiny to be a key figure in the Catholic Counter-Reformation.

Jesuit scholars like Fr Nicholas King are not convinced that Ignatius was consciously reacting to Luther. What does seem clearer is that Ignatius grew up, amid tales of chivalry, to serve as a gentleman soldier until 20 May 1521, the day at Pamplona when a French cannonball struck one of his legs and shattered it completely. While recovering from his wounds, Ignatius passed the time reading *The Life of Christ* by Ludolph of Saxony and the *Flos Sanctorum* of Alfonso Villegas, a popular history of saints. None impressed him as much as the life of St Francis of Assisi, the thirteenth-century, high-spirited and wealthy merchant's son who after going off to war and falling ill had a vision that converted him to live in poverty.

'He was a merchant up to the twentieth year and he spent that period living in vanity. But God chastised him with infirmity, and changed him from the hour into another man,' wrote Villegas in a passage that would be noted by Ignatius and resonated through subsequent centuries. Ignatius never made any claim to originality, but he tried to set the benchmark for his order, by practising in his lifetime poverty just as radically as Francis of Assisi. And yet the extent to which, as Brodrick puts it, 'the grace of God insinuates itself into a man's life', is never as simple as suggested by some picture-book stories. The history of the Jesuit order would show that just as there would be Jesuit priests of a high moral calibre, there would also be those who would opt for economic and political security and be seduced into spiritual complacency by ecclesiastical promotion – Jesuits who would fall well short of the ideal of the founding fathers.

Ignatius's spiritual journey drew its inspiration from popular religion of a kind that later Lutheran reformers would try their best to discredit. Thus in Ignatius's memoirs, which Bergoglio studied as part of his Jesuit training, the founding father recalls lying awake one night and clearly seeing an image of the Virgin Mary with the child Jesus – an image that filled him with a sense of remorse for his past life of indulgence from which he subsequently felt liberated.

Following this apparition, Ignatius bid farewell to those he loved at Loyola and his palatial family home, and set out on a long journey he hoped would take him to Jerusalem. His only companion was a mule – the offspring between a mare and a donkey, perhaps a conscious compromise or rites of passage for the noble horseman turned humble pilgrim. Man and beast travelled for weeks across four kingdoms of Spain (Navarre, Old Castile, Aragon and Catalonia), heading first up into the mountains of southern Guipúzcoa, to the sanctuary of Aranzazu.

There, he again paid homage to the Virgin, this time at a locally venerated statue that had appeared miraculously to a shepherd. He then travelled across a land of vast solitudes along the banks of the Ebro river and via Tudela to Zaragoza, crossing the old Roman bridge, and continuing along the old Royal Route or Camino Real to Lérida, the *llerda* of Caesar's *Commentaries*. He headed north across the Catalan hinterland, via Igualada to the sanctuary and Benedictine monastery of Montserrat near Barcelona. He had travelled for three weeks and covered some 400 miles.

Ignatius would have needed a good head for heights and a capacity for endurance as he made his way up the steep mountain tracks on foot. He was amply rewarded for his efforts, sharing in the sense of awe on arrival at the Benedictine sanctuary clinging to a rocky outcrop. There can be few more wondrous approaches to a place of pilgrimage than that which takes you to the Virgin of Montserrat and, doing it on mule and on foot, Ignatius would have appreciated the extraordinary human achievement and religious devotion of the first Benedictines who settled there.

While in Montserrat, Ignatius, so he later related, made a long confession to a kindly monk who alone knew that his closely guarded secret was of renouncing the world and assuming the life of a mendicant at the service of others, like St Francis. That night Ignatius approached one of the hundreds of beggars who hung around the monastery and exchanged his suit for a sackcloth robe.

He then walked to the nearby town of Manresa. It was there that he begged alms, while staying in a hospital for the poor sick, when not in a cell run by Dominican monks, and when ill and exhausted physically recovering in the houses of generous people who counted it a privilege to nurse him. Periodically he would retire to a nearby rocky outcrop whenever he felt the need for solitude to pray.

Four months into his time in Manresa, Ignatius experienced his severest spiritual test – that 'Dark Night of the Soul' in which the mystic feels abandoned by God and loses all joy only to find the dark cloud lift as suddenly as it had gathered to encounter ecstatically a heavenly beauty. It happened when he was sitting one day on the banks of the nearby River Cardoner. His chronicler Luis González takes up the story as related to him by Ignatius. 'As he sat there, the eyes of his understanding began to open and, without seeing any vision, he understood and knew many things, as well as spiritual as those appertaining to the faith and to the realm of letters, and that with such clarity that they seemed to him completely knew.'

Unspecific and intangible as seemed this experience, it proved decisive for from it would eventually flow Ignatius's handbook for followers – the *Spiritual Exercises*: the practice of methodical meditation and prayer, of self-analysis, and discernment or detached examination of the action of good and evil influences affecting the soul, which is at the heart of every Jesuit's formation.

Of his first visit to Rome, little was recorded other than that he arrived anonymously on Palm Sunday 1523, dressed still in beggar clothes, having travelled on foot from Gaeta. He obtained a blessing from Pope Adrian VI along with other prospective pilgrims in a public benediction, and then departed for Venice from where he sailed to the Holy Land in *The Pilgrim Galley*, reaching Jaffa in late August, after the pilot had misread his bearings and taken the ship fifty miles off course, until the 'minarets of Gaza loomed into view'.

Ignatius was armed with letters of recommendation to the provincial of the Franciscans who had papal authority over visiting pilgrims and their right to stay. He was allowed to stay long enough to follow the traditional itinerary of Holy Places while being given lodgings led by monks and closely guarded by the occupying Turkish Army.

He was moved profoundly by the experience of following the various 'stations' involved in the memory of Jesus's death and resurrection, spending the entire night in the Church of the Holy Sepulchre, following the Via Dolorosa 'from the house of Pilate unto the place of his crucifying' on Mount Calvary where he took Holy Communion, then visiting the Mount of Olives where he wept before 'the stone upon which our Saviour standing ascended into Heaven'.

Ignatius next rode to Bethlehem, spending a day and a night in the church built on the site of the stable were Jesus was born, before trekking through the hot and dusty valley of Jehoshaphat to the Garden of Gethsemane, where Ignatius's tears flowed once again for his Lord in his agony. There followed an all-night vigil in the Church of the Holy Sepulchre back in Jerusalem before another long trek by donkey, this time to Jericho and the River Jordan. He and the other pilgrims returned to Jerusalem by night only to learn the next morning that some 500 janissaries, the fiercest anti-Christians in the Ottoman army, had come to the city from Damascus. After seeking protection from a local Franciscan monastery on Mount Zion, Ignatius managed one more expedition, alone, to the Mount of Olives but he was prevented from visiting Galilee as it was considered too dangerous and he never set eyes on Nazareth. So, after just less than three weeks since their arrival, Ignatius and his pilgrims left Jerusalem and reached Jaffa again, after being attacked and robbed by Bedouins along the way.

By Lent of 1524, Ignatius was back in Barcelona where he stayed for two years and began to recruit his first disciples – a Frenchman, a Portuguese and two Spaniards – who in March 1526 followed him to the university town of Alcalá de Henares, near Madrid.

The city was then throbbing with intellectual vitality as it had become the focus of enlightened humanism in Spain. However, Ignatius preaching to growing crowds on aspects of Christian doctrine and his training in the Spiritual Exercises drew the suspicion of orthodox Catholics, not least those serving as watchdogs for the Holy Inquisition. Ignatius was thrown into a local prison, after rumours spread about his friendship with a married woman.

Investigated by the ecclesiastical authorities, Ignatius was cleared of having engaged in witchcraft, having Jewish blood and of being a concealed Lutheran, but was charged with having exercised undue influence over wives and daughters he had instructed in the Christian faith. Together with his disciples Ignatius was banned, under pain of instant excommunication and perpetual banishment from Spain, to discuss religion with anybody except after three completed years of officially vetted study.

Ignatius felt he had no choice but to move out of the town and seek pastures less guarded by the bastions of orthodoxy so he travelled to Salamanca and from there back to Barcelona from where he ventured, across the Pyrenees, into France. The year was 1526. Henry VIII was in love with Anne Boleyn and wanted to divorce his Spanish wife Catherine. England and France were at war with Spain. Ignatius was warned by friends that the French had developed the habit of spitting and roasting any Spaniard that fell into their hands. Undeterred, Ignatius loaded a donkey with scholastic books and headed towards Paris in the winter of 1528.

He entered the French capital through the Porte of Saint-Jacques on 2 February 1528, a feast of the Virgin Mary. He took lodgings in the Latin Quarter and embarked on a course in Latin grammar at the Collège de Montaigu, before furthering his theological studies at Collège Sainte-Barbe where he met two of his most influential followers – the Frenchman Pierre Favre and the Spaniard of noble blood Francis Xavier.

These were testing times for Ignatius and his first disciples. The anti-Catholic propaganda of the Reformation was rampant in Paris and other French towns. On 21 May 1530 during the night a group of Lutherans defaced one of the many images of the Virgin Mary painted in the houses of Paris. Ignatius responded by writing an update to his *Spiritual Exercises* which he called 'Rules for fostering the true spirit which ought to be ours as members of the Church Militant'.

These rules included a firm adherence to the traditional Catholic rituals of regular Communion, Mass, pilgrimages, lighting of candles, veneration of images, fasting and abstinence, and works of penance both interior and external, along with a sturdy and resolute defence of the commandments. Inigo wanted to lead by example, reinvigorate the Catholic Church not by toppling her in a revolution but by restoring her essence of faith and spirituality so that mankind could be transformed for the better. His rules were a battle order for his disciples to come to the defence, with their hearts and minds, of Holy Mother Church.

Ignatius was a loyal Catholic soldier but not an uncritical one.

Thus he responded to the criticism of the reformers by urging fellow Catholics not to spread scandal when 'speaking to ordinary folk' but at the same time to have the courage to reveal the faults and failures of priests, monks and bishops to their superiors, i.e. cardinals and even the Pope.

Ignatius in his writings lets the reader into the empathy he felt for the suffering of others. He relates how on one occasion he visited a house whose occupants were afflicted with the plague and, finding a sick man, consoled him by taking his ulcerated hand. After comforting the sufferer, Ignatius came away and his hand became painful: he felt he had contracted the disease himself. With a sudden impulse he put it into his mouth. Thereupon, the strong impression in his mind and pain in his hand disappeared together.

And yet Ignatius continued to suffer periodically and would do so for the rest of his life from acute stomach pains, a condition that remained undiagnosed until an autopsy performed on him after his death discovered numerous stones in the kidneys.

Both his illness and his pecuniary circumstances failed to undermine Ignatius's sense of mission and in Paris he persevered in building up his close circle of friends into a formidable following of professors and students who were profoundly influenced by his charisma and evident holiness.

In August 1534, Ignatius gathered Pierre Favre – the only ordained priest among them – Francis Xavier and four other companions in the chapel known as the Sanctum Martyrium, belonging to the Benedictine nuns that crowned the summit of Montmartre. After Favre had celebrated Mass, each in turn, beginning with Ignatius, pronounced a vow of chastity because of their intention to also become a priest, and of poverty.

Ignatius's own life crossed a Rubicon in early April 1535 when after seven years in Paris he left the city, and set out to pursue his spiritual journey and sense of mission in other lands. Mounted on a pony he covered a distance of 460 miles via Chartres, Tours,

Poitiers, Angoulême and Bordeaux before heading towards Bayonne and entering his native Basque country. Rather than head for the assured comfort of his family estate in Loyola, he left the main road at Irun and headed towards Azpeitia where he spent three months in the Magdalen Hospital, a local poorhouse.

When once his brother Martín reproached him for living like a beggar, Ignatius answered that he had not come back to Spain to live in a palace. Days later Ignatius persuaded the local authorities to have the bells of the parish church and of the rural sanctuaries rung at morning, noon and evening so that people might be reminded to pray for mortal sinners.

Those who had sinned included local priests who were living with their mistresses. By the early sixteenth century this had become such a common practice that the priests' women would openly wear a veil, as was the custom of young local girls who got married. Ignatius got the governor to enact a law that any woman who veiled for a man not her husband would be brought to justice and punished.

Ignatius was remembered, however, not as a fundamentalist but for more benign activities such as acting as a marriage counsellor, caring for the sick and dying, and persuading the local authorities to provide relief to the genuine poor.

His kidney stones were once again playing up with excruciating pain. But Ignatius endured, as he set off again, this time criss-crossing northern and central Spain via Sigüenza, Madrid and the imperial capital of Toledo, before reaching the port of Valencia from where to took a ship to Genoa and then overland via Bologna and Venice to Rome, accompanied by two of his disciples, Frs Favre and Laynez.

Before arriving in Rome the three men stopped to pray in a chapel in the village of La Storta. There Ignatius had a vision which he felt so suffused with spiritual feeling that he saw Christ crucified on the Cross and beside him God telling him, 'My will is that you should serve US.' It was late November 1537.

Before Easter of the following year Ignatius was well settled in Rome and gathering around him a growing number of followers. As they met in conference they had much to report: enthusiastic crowds listening to their sermons, a growing number of faithful attending confessions, young priests offering to join them.

The conference was cut short when Agostino Pierinteses, an influential Lutheran preacher posing as an Augustinian monk, aided by powerful friends, spread a rumour that Ignatius was a condemned heretic and that his followers were fugitives from Spain, France and Venice. Ignatius cleared his name before three judges and got Pope Paul II to publish the verdict proclaiming his complete innocence.

On 27 September 1540, Pope Paul II promulgated the Bull 'Regimini militantis Ecclesia', canonically establishing as a religious order the new Society of Jesus. In April 1541, Ignatius was elected the first Jesuit General.

Four hundred and seventy years separated that moment from the election in March 2013 of the first ever Jesuit pope. There are many orders in the Church far older than the Jesuits; there are also orders that have shown as much if not more vigour; but the history of the Society of Jesus throws up an array of talent and inspiration that has laid an enduring mark on very different societies and cultures. The individual lives of Ignatius's successors, to quote from the Jesuit historian Nicholas King, showed not so much that they were extraordinary people but they were perfectly ordinary people, like you and me, 'who were able to do extraordinary things because they let God into their lives'. Their example provides a measure by which to judge Jorge Bergoglio in his progress from young seminarian to pope.

One of the best known of Ignatius's early disciples, the impetuous Basque Francis Xavier, ended up as one of the great missionaries of the sixteenth century. In the eleven years he spent in Asia, his missionary journeys took him to India, Sri Lanka, Malaysia,

Indonesia and Japan, where he concentrated on the poor and marginalized, lepers and pearl fishermen, and converted an estimated 700,000 to Christianity. In the words of the Jesuit historian Norman Tanner, Francis Xavier was a 'vigorous preacher, inventive in the methods of evangelization, and his organization of new converts into Christian communities produced lasting results'. In southern India he converted thousands of Goanese to the Catholic faith. He was less successful in Japan and on his way to China he was badly let down by a Chinese pirate and he died, with a Chinese Christian looking after him.

Francis Xavier's selfless service to the underprivileged left its mark, as did the missionary work of Peter Claver, 'the slave of slaves', among the African slaves in Latin America. A native Catalan, Claver spent most of his adult life dedicated to helping alleviate the terrible suffering of the thousands of Africans who were traded every year through the Colombian port of Cartagena.

The sixteenth century produced other notable Jesuits, facing up to very different challenges in a time of mounting, visceral, religiously motivated distrust, intolerance and hatred, no more so than in England where the separation of the Church of England (or Anglican Church) from Rome under Henry VIII, beginning in 1529 and completed in 1537, brought England alongside the broad anti-Catholic Reformation movement.

In 1585 Queen Elizabeth I enacted a new law identifying Jesuits as traitors and spies. The defeat of the Spanish Armada three years later was the defining moment when Catholics were turned into *unnatural* Englishmen and Jesuits into declared enemies of the English State to be hunted down whenever they set foot on English soil.

Several Jesuits were subsequently executed. They included the Oxford 'don' Edmund Campion, his one-time servant Nicholas Owen, the Cambridge-educated lawyer Henry Walpole, the poet Robert Southwell and the ex-Calvinist Scot John Ogilvie. They all considered themselves God's agents and actively sought martyrdom. They were all hanged, drawn and quartered after being brutally tortured.

Five years after Campion's execution in England in 1581, Jesuit missionaries in parts of Asia were facing similar persecution. In Japan Jesuits who had followed Francis Xavier and his colleagues Cosme de Torrès and João Fernandes were forced to go underground after local warlords clamped down on the growing Catholic community, which had sprung up under the protection of the Portuguese. One of the Jesuits was Paul Miki, whose prosperous Japanese family had converted to Christianity from Buddhism when he was a small boy. He and two other Japanese Jesuits, Joan Soan and James Kisai, were crucified before spears were plunged into their sides. 'Into your hands I commend my spirit,' the thirty-three-year-old Miki is reputed to have said, just before his death, imitating Christ.

Other Jesuit martyrs through history include the Portuguese Joan de Brito, beheaded in India in 1693; the Spanish missionaries in Paraguay and Brazil Roque González, Alonso Rodriguez and Juan de Castillo; eight men (the North American Martyrs) who were killed in the mid-seventeenth century in the wars between rival India tribes in Canada; and six priests shot dead in El Salvador on 6 November 1989 after being dragged out of their beds by a detachment of soldiers. Those who died for their faith were promised a martyr's crown and everlasting glory, but not all aggressively sought martyrdom, and many were victims of circumstances beyond their control. And there were cases where half the struggle was in those who, rather than hurry to their death, had time to reflect on what the true call of their Jesuit faith was in extremely challenging political circumstances. Such was the life of the German Jesuit Alfred Delp.

He joined the Jesuits in 1926, ten years before Bergoglio was born. In the next decade he continued his studies and worked with

German youth, made more difficult after 1933 with the interference of the Nazi regime. Ordained a priest in 1937, Delp worked on the editorial staff of the Jesuit publication *Stimmen der Zeit* (*Voice of the Times*), until it was suppressed in 1941. He then was assigned as rector of St Georg Church in Munich. Delp secretly used his position to help Jews escape to Switzerland.

Concerned with the future of Germany, Delp joined the Kreisau Circle, a group that worked to design a new democratic social order. He was arrested with other members of the circle after the attempted assassination of Hitler in 1944. After suffering brutal treatment and torture, Delp was brought to trial. While he knew nothing of the attempted assassination, the Gestapo decided to hang him for high treason. Delp was offered his freedom if he would renounce the Jesuits. He refused and was hanged on 2 February 1945.

While his physical remains disappeared, Alfred Delp left behind letters smuggled out of prison. They reveal a man of courage who told the prison chaplain accompanying him to his death, 'In half an hour, I'll know more than you do.' During his six-month incarceration prior to his execution, he wrote of his fear, sadness, and anger, and then his transformation from an 'unholy character into a saint'. In the end he did not seek his martyrdom aggressively, but reflected on his love of God, sense of peace and surrender. As Thomas Merton, the monk and poet, has observed about Father Delp's prison writings: 'In these pages we meet a stern, recurrent foreboding that the "voice in the wilderness" is growing fainter and fainter, and that it will soon not be heard at all. The world may sink into godless despair.' And yet through the doubt, Delp's faith in God ultimately prevails.

Delp's writings testify to the fact that Christian opposition to National Socialism was not sporadically whispered by timid souls but boldly proclaimed by men and women who paid for their acts with imprisonment, torture and death. As he reminded his Munich congregation on the slips of paper he smuggled out of his Gestapo prison cell, true freedom is not merely the ability to make one choice rather than another, but – as Ignatius insisted – to contribute to that freedom through simple acts of honest humility, a readiness to serve and the praise of God.

When he was ordained a priest, Bergoglio did so conscious that he would be serving in a largely loyally Catholic if politically unstable country. Radical dissent to the established order, not least to the conservative politics and theological orthodoxy many Jesuits had opted for, were stirring in Europe and the Americas. However, he could have scarcely imagined the challenges that awaited him.

Chapter Seven
Perón's Return

Jesuits, at the end of their training, make promises not to 'strive or have ambition' for high office in the Church and the Society of Jesus. The founding father Ignatius was adamantly opposed to the clerical careerism that he saw in the Renaissance and so he built into the final vows a safeguard against this kind of climbing. But there is also freedom built into Ignatian spirituality for a Jesuit to be available to serve the Church in whatever way he might be called to do so. The Constitutions of the Society of Jesus prohibit Jesuits from seeking to become bishops – but over time Jesuits have become bishops and cardinals, with the blessing of the Vatican, and we now have a Jesuit pope.

Apart from Ignatius, it was Pierre Favre to whom Bergoglio looked as his iconic example among the early Jesuit founders, and he canonized Favre when he became Pope Francis. Favre was the only one of Ignatius's companions who did not come from an aristocratic background. He was also among the least controversial or indeed memorable of the early Ignatian missionaries. Favre, wrote Fr Nicholas King in his book on exemplary Jesuits, was 'a gentle shepherd from the High Savoy in the mountains of south-eastern France who went on to be one of Ignatius' roommates at the University of the Sorbonne where he focused on developing the fledging order's spirituality'. Another of Favre's biographers, Michel de Certeau, described him simply as a 'reformed priest' for whom 'spirituality, dogma, and structural reform were inseparable realities'.

So what was it that most impressed Bergoglio about this self-made and contemplative theologian whom Ignatius considered the best director of the Spiritual Exercises he knew?

'His dialogue with everyone, even those who seemed most distant, and including adversaries; his simple piety, his certain probable ingenuity, his immediate disposition, his attentive internal discernment, the fact that he was a man capable of making great and strong decisions which were compatible with being gentle,' Bergoglio told fellow Jesuit Antonio Spadaro in a series of reflective conversations the two Jesuits had after the papal election.

Bergoglio began his prescribed period of training in the Jesuit order – as a novice – in March 1958. The setting: a novitiate some 400 miles north of Buenos Aires, in Córdoba, Argentina's second largest city. Set amidst fertile forested hills and higher, more rugged sierras, Córdoba has a historic urban landscape marked by the Catholic Church, particularly the Jesuits who established an important presence in early colonial times. Founded seven years before Buenos Aires by the Spanish *conquistador* Jerónimo Luis de Cabrera, it was one of the first colonial towns in the region that became Argentina (the oldest being Santiago del Estero).

With the start of the reforming Second Vatican Council still four years away, and the majority of Argentine clergy and bishops among the more conservative in South America, Bergoglio's experience of Jesuit life was characterized by tradition, discipline and orthodoxy. As conceived by Ignatius of Loyola, and based on his experience and that of the early Jesuit fathers, Bergoglio underwent a series of 'experiments' designed to test his vocation and obedience. This included a month-long retreat, then doing menial tasks such as washing bedpans, sweeping floors and kitchen duties in a hospital and in the Jesuit house where he lived, and teaching religious doctrine and reading to local school kids. Bergoglio has not shared his memories of this period, perhaps because the experience was of a too intimate nature, one of which he might have struggled to make sense with the evidence of hindsight. The 'experiments' are supposed to help novices discern the presence of God and help identify whether or not they are committed to become Jesuit priests.

The first two years Bergoglio spent in Córdoba ended with him taking his vows of poverty, chastity and obedience, confirming him as a member of the Jesuit order. A rare memoir of this period by a Jesuit novice, Jorge González Manent, recalls that Bergoglio came across as bookish and pious, rather different to the football-loving tango dancer of his adolescence. It suggested that, in his early days with the Jesuits, Bergoglio willingly surrendered to the demands of authority and suppressed his emotions.

Early on in his priestly training, following the seminary at Villa Devoto in Buenos Aires and his noviceship in Córdoba, Bergoglio spent just over a year, from early in 1960, with the Jesuits in Chile in a small rural retreat fifteen miles outside the capital, Santiago. This period of the protracted formation of a Jesuit is a largely academic and spiritual one, taken up with the study of the humanities and extensive prayer and meditation. However, it was in Chile that Bergoglio's social conscience began to stir in parallel with the strict rules and discipline that still prevailed inside seminaries with practices long assumed to be normative and unchangeable – even if their destabilization by Vatican II was on the not too distant horizon.

The Jesuit communal life into which Bergoglio entered in Chile included a strict separation between young novitiates and older students; the younger ones were not allowed to read newspapers and were made to take baths in cold water, while much of the rest of the official twelve-hour day, which began at six, was taken up in classes, prayer and reflection. At meal times silence was imposed except for a reading from a lectern. Nevertheless novitiates were encouraged to think for themselves about the subjects they were taught, and to talk and debate with each other outside the lecture rooms, with a special corridor assigned to conversations in Latin. The students were also allowed to use an open-air swimming pool in their leisure time.

Chile of the late 1950s and early 1960s was influenced, like much of Latin America, by the Cuban revolution and had entered a period of political turbulence. The right-wing civilian government of Jorge Alessandri was facing increasing calls from socialists, communists and the Christian Democrat party for radical income redistribution and agrarian reform amidst a widening gap between rich and poor. Surrounded by large, privately owned country estates and just a short bus ride from the poor neighbourhoods of the capital, Bergoglio was acutely aware of the politics of Chile even before he set foot in the community – and would not remain unaffected.

The community with which he studied was named after and aimed to follow the enduring example of Alberto Hurtado, a priest who devoted his life to improving the social condition of the marginalized poor, but not on the basis of the Marxism-Leninism of the increasingly popular Chilean communist and allied socialist parties. Rather, he followed the Church's social doctrine that sought a third way between the extremes of unfettered capitalism and the dictatorship of the proletariat. Whereas in Argentina this third way had been appropriated by the populist Peronist movement, in Chile it had its champion in the centre-left Christian Democrat party.

In 1947, Hurtado founded the Chilean Trade Union Association as an alternative to the communist-controlled trade unions. The association aimed to instil Christian values and loyalty to the Church at a time when surveys showed a crisis of vocations and low church attendance. Hurtado later served as confessor to the

Chilean Falange Nacional, a precursor of the Christian Democrat party which countered communist influence on national politics. A deeply spiritual man, Hurtado combined theological reflection with an untiring dedication to low-paid workers and young people, which he showed right up to the moment of his sudden death in 1952 from belatedly diagnosed acute pancreatic cancer.

Among Hurtado's numerous writings that were to have an enduring impact on Bergoglio was this one proclaiming Christ's living presence among the poor and marginalized:

> I hold that every poor man, every vagrant, every beggar is Christ carrying his cross. And as Christ, we must love and help him. We must treat him as a brother, a human being like ourselves. If we were to start a campaign of love for the poor and homeless, we would, in a short time, do away with depressing scenes of begging, children sleeping in doorways and women with babies in their arms fainting in our streets.

Father Hurtado was beatified on 16 October 1994 by Pope John Paul II and canonized by Pope Benedict XVI on 23 October 2005. St Alberto was one of the first people to be elevated to sainthood during the papacy of Pope Benedict XVI; he was also the second Chilean saint, after Saint Teresa of the Andes.

Long before then, Bergoglio had found his own sense of vocation when confronted with the plight of the poor. Those who studied alongside him in Chile suggest that the experience of being drawn out of Argentina for the first time in his life had a liberating impact on him. They recall him as studious but not introverted, participating actively in discussions on politics and theology, and enjoying his swimming, a sport he was encouraged to pursue by his doctors to help strengthen his weaker lung. Bergoglio was one of a number of Argentine students whose political arguments identified them as Peronist (radical) or anti-Peronist (conservative/reactionary). He fell clearly into the former camp, defending Peronism as the Argentine exponent of Catholic social teaching, and speaking out on behalf of the poor. As he wrote from Chile to his sister Maria Elena on 5 May 1960 after giving a religious doctrine class to a group of young children:

> Much of the time, they haven't got anything to eat and many of them have no shoes and in winter they really suffer the cold . . . I am telling you because you never go hungry and when you are cold you just get up close to the stove . . . I am telling you this so you can think that when you are happy, there are many children who are crying . . . when you sit at the table, there are children who have only a small piece of bread to eat and when it rains and it's cold can only seek shelter in tin shacks . . . And the worst thing of all is that they don't know Jesus, they don't know him because there is no one to teach them.

In 1963, after his time in Chile, Bergoglio returned to Argentina and took up a succession of teaching and study posts at the Colegio Máximo de San José in San Miguel, Buenos Aires Province, his base for twenty-three of the next twenty-six years. It was while studying for the Jesuit priesthood in Buenos Aires that Bergoglio came under the influence of his spiritual director, Fr Miguel Ángel Fiorito SJ (Society of Jesus), a pious and right-wing Jesuit who steered his young charge away from the more radical aspects of liberation theology, by emphasizing the spirituality of Argentine popular culture with great emphasis on devotion to the Virgin and gaucho icons, as immortalized in the nineteenth-century epic poem *Martín Fierro* – one of the most widely read books of Bergoglio's childhood.

The saga of *Martín Fierro*, much admired by General Perón and his followers, depicts the Argentine cowboy's struggle for survival and self-respect against the repressive, corrupting constraints of a colonial-style authority claiming to represent progress and civilization. Fiorito saw *Martín Fierro* as a heroic figure in Argentine culture, helping romanticize the Argentine national character and giving it a Catholic dimension.

Martín Fierro was one of the books that Bergoglio enjoyed most when teaching literature and psychology during the 1960s in secondary schools run by the Jesuits, first at the Colegio de la Inmaculada Concepción in the Argentine City of Santa Fe and later at the Colegio del Salvador in Buenos Aires. One of Bergoglio's favourite authors was the Argentine Leopoldo Marechal, in particular his novel *Megafón, o la guerra* (*Megaphone, or War*), in which the author imagines a successful popular uprising against the right-wing military officers who toppled Perón in 1955. The future pope was later to develop a strong empathy with the works of the great Russian novelist Fyodor Dostoyevsky with their examination of the human soul. For the Argentine Jesuit searching for ultimate good, Dostoyevsky provided a profound insight into faith and associated doubt, the mental suffering and questioning inherent in the step of realizing the 'truth' of Jesus Christ, a mirror of Bergoglio's own spiritual exercises.

One of Bergoglio's earlier biographers, Elisabetta Piqué, suggests that after studying chemistry in his teens, it came as a surprise to him to have found himself teaching very different subjects to a similar age group. But Jesuits are expected to defer to the wisdom of their superiors and accept all their assignments, however contrary to their initial preferences, as a call to duty, to better serve the glory of God.

It was not just the subjects that tested Bergoglio's vocation but the fact that the boys he would teach came from privileged backgrounds, very different to the young Chileans he had written about to his sister with such concern. The two Jesuit schools in which he taught have long traditions dating back to early colonial times, with their current impressive buildings built in the nineteenth century when Jesuit private education began to attract the country's political and social elites after the interlude of the order's suppression.

Some of his old alumni recall the young teacher Bergoglio, in his late twenties, cutting a gaunt, sombre figure discreetly pacing the long corridors of the school with his rubber-soled black shoes and his musty, somewhat crumpled, black Jesuit soutane or cassock. His almost silent, swishing passage contrasted with the rowdy bustle of the boys echoing along the broad staircases and seemingly endless corridors.

But once inside the classroom, a more engaging personality would unfold – one capable, with one phrase and with a disarming sense of humour, of enthusing even the most recalcitrant student. Bergoglio had a back-to-basics Ignatian attitude to human psychology, which was that the best way for someone to feel good about himself was to feel good about others – to find God in all things. Not for him Freud's navel gazing and obsession with sexuality – so popular with Argentine psychology students in the 1960s. He believed in the good news of the Gospel. He thought in positives. A former Argentine ambassador to the UK after the Falklands War, Rogelio Pfirter was among the boys he taught who went on to take on important posts in public life. He recalled that Bergoglio had the gift of encouraging his pupils to think for themselves and to ask questions. His religious doctrine classes conveyed a sense of joy as well as security. He was popular without courting sentimentality.

Thus, remembers Pfirter, when at the end of his final school term one of the boys began to cry, Bergoglio cut him short, took him to one side and said: 'Quit those tears, take strength from what you've learnt, but don't get stuck in the past but rather throw yourself with a sense of happiness and commitment into the future.' Those who took his advice also remember how Bergoglio livened up his literature courses by bringing in outside speakers, including occasional well-known authors he befriended like Jorge Luis

Borges, who subsequently agreed to write a prologue to a collection of short stories written by the Jesuit's schoolboys.

It was during his school-teaching days that Bergoglio met for the first time the newly elected head of the Jesuit order, the Spaniard Fr Pedro Arrupe, during a visit he made to Argentina in 1965. The two seem to have got on well although neither left a detailed record of their encounter, nor is any reference made to it in the most authoritative biography of Arrupe by the Spanish Jesuit Pedro Lamet.

According to a contemporary account by Fr Michael Campbell-Johnston, Arrupe was a charismatic figure who had no need of the conventional props and trappings of authority. 'He assumed no airs and graces, and was devoid of affectation . . . he bubbled with high spirits, laughed a lot, loved jokes against himself.'

Arrupe, at that first meeting, would have been impressed by Bergoglio's evident humility and the positive impact he had on some of his students. For his part Bergoglio had every reason to be in awe, initially at least, of his new Superior General. Arrupe was already something of a legend in his own lifetime within the worldwide Jesuit community for having survived the atomic bomb on Hiroshima in 1945. Still a novice master, aged thirty-eight, he dedicated himself to helping the sick and the dying in the immediate aftermath of the bomb being dropped.

And yet when Bergoglio subsequently wrote to him, asking that he be sent as missionary to Japan, he was turned down on health grounds, with Arrupe citing the fact that the Argentine had lost half of a lung because of pulmonary difficulties. While initially hugely disappointed by this early snub to a perceived calling, Bergoglio later came round to concluding that 'we are not all made up to be saints' while thanking Arrupe for making what he believed was a providential decision. As he later recalled, 'What Arrupe told me made me want to try harder to be a missionary which is why

I had joined the Jesuits in the first place: to go out into the world and proclaim Jesus Christ, and not get stuck in a rut.'

And yet when, on 13 December 1969, Bergoglio was ordained a priest, for all the emotion of family, friends and his own surrounding the occasion, he knew that his spiritual journey was only just beginning, with several crossroads to come. The following year, having embarked on the final stages of his spiritual formation as a Jesuit, the tertianship, Bergoglio travelled to Spain and installed himself in a Jesuit house in the university city of Alcalá de Henares.

After three decades of the Franco dictatorship, the Spanish political and social landscape was on shifting sands, with senior bishops of the Catholic Church joining in the growing campaign for democracy. The campaign involved an increasing number of young idealistic priests working in the poor *barrios* and liaising with the political opposition. The Spanish extreme right accused them of being communists and dubbed them *curas rojos* ('red priests'). One of them was Father José María de Llanos, a Jesuit from a wealthy family, who went to work among the poverty-stricken rural migrants from Andalusia who had crammed into a shanty town on the outskirts of Madrid. Shocked by what he saw, he soon took up the cause of the poor and dispossessed to such an extent that he admitted that they had redeemed him more than he had redeemed them.

Spanish Jesuits closely involved in supporting Spain's transition to democracy at the time have no recollection that Bergoglio was actively involved politically in any way while in the country. 'We felt at the time that Argentina because of its politics also had Jesuits who had a different perspective of what their mission should be,' recalled Fr José María Martín Patino, the private secretary of the Cardinal Archbishop of Madrid Vicente Enrique y Tarancón. Both Spaniards were vocal in their criticism of General Franco's dictatorship and played an important role in helping Spain's transition to democratic rule.

Bergoglio, as a visiting foreign Jesuit, used his time in Alcalá de Henares to pursue the Jesuit equivalent of an extended retreat, submitting himself to a supervised course of the Ignatian Spiritual Exercises. Those who were with him at the time describe him as a good student, somewhat reserved and austere, and far from outspoken in his views. Nor is it the case, as claimed by one of the first published books on the Francis papacy, that Bergoglio was asked by his superior Fr Arrupe to help rein in a group of ultra-conservative Spanish Jesuits who threatened to form a breakaway order.

According to Pedro Lamet, Arrupe's biographer, that role was entrusted not to Bergoglio, but to Fr Jesús Corella, a widely respected Spanish Jesuit who straddled the Hispanic world, was extensively involved in Jesuit government and formation, and for a time was a director of novices. After avoiding a damaging split in the Jesuit community Corella moved to Buenos Aires where he died in 2004 while teaching spirituality at the University of Salvador after moving there from the Pontifical Comillas University in Madrid.

If Arrupe had plans for Bergoglio, it was in his native Argentina. In 1971 – his Jesuit 'formation' or training complete – Bergoglio returned to Argentina and was put in charge of supervising young entrants into the Jesuit order at Villa Barilali in San Miguel, before being appointed Rector of the Jesuit Colegio Máximo and lecturer in the Faculty of Theology, all positions that made him keenly aware of political tensions in Argentina of a far greater complexity and violence than anything he had experienced in Spain.

Months earlier the terrorist group Montoneros had dramatically raised the political stakes by killing former president General Pedro Aramburu, leader of the coup that had deposed Perón in 1955. The Montoneros had arrived on the Argentine political scene in 1968 following the usurpation of power by General Juan Onganía, the latest regime change involving the armed forces. Several founding members of the Montoneros, including Aramburu's assassins, came originally from conservative Catholic university lay groups like Catholic Action before becoming radicalized in the aftermath of the Second Vatican Council. They were followers of a synthesis of Peronist nationalism and Third World revolution as propagated by Che Guevara,

The decision to opt for a violent path to force political change was born from the frustration of any semblance of democratic process being blown away by a succession of military coups. Another influence was a romanticized notion of the first Peronist government as the only one in Argentine history to serve the interests of the popular majority. But as Richard Gillespie points out in his seminal history of the Montoneros movement, 'acceptance of armed struggle and the flourishing of left-wing and popular expressions of nationalism could never have occurred on the scale which they did without the wind of change which blew so forcefully through the Catholic Church during the same decade'.

The Second Vatican Council condemned poverty, injustice and exploitation as caused by man's greed for power and wealth, and urged Christians to struggle for equality, and priests to commit themselves to working more closely among the poor. In 1967, two years after the council had ended, Pope Paul VI's encyclical *Populorum progressio* was categorical in its condemnation of social injustice and human rights violation but was less clear about the remedy. Thus it ruled out violence, 'save where there is manifest long standing tyranny which could do damage to the fundamental personal rights and dangerous harm to the common good of the country'.

Such was the enthusiasm of the many priests attending Vatican II or reading the documents that emanated from it that they formed the Third World Priests Movement. In Argentina a growing number of priests took to working in factories or in the shanty towns, developing contacts with radical middle-class students, and implanting in the Montoneros embryo a radical theology of liberation. However, the Third World Priests Movement struggled from the outset to maintain a coherent ideological and tactical framework in which to operate, with its membership representing different strands of Peronism or socialism, and with sharply divergent positions on issues like their own involvement in violent action and whether membership should be extended to married priests.

One of the early influences on the Montoneros was Carlos Mugica. Charismatic and well educated, the good-looking Mugica put behind him the privileged family environment into which he was born and sought work as an ordained activist in some of the poorest neighbourhoods of Buenos Aires. Mugica continued to sleep in his parents' house where he had been brought up, but insisted on sleeping rough in a rooftop storage room rather than return to the comforts of his childhood bed. Although never officially a member of their organization, Mugica had maintained friendships with several Montoneros from childhood, taught some of the founders at university and celebrated Masses for those who were killed by the security forces.

In the shanty town, Mugica was venerated by the poor and marginalized of his parish. Those who worked alongside him never doubted his sincerity. But it was not just his sworn enemies on the right that failed to be positively impressed by Mugica. On a visit to Argentina in the early 1970s, the novelist V. S. Naipaul, who was writing a series of articles for the *New York Review of Books*, was introduced to Mugica by Bob Cox, the veteran editor of the English language newspaper the *Buenos Aires Herald*. As Cox later recalled, there was little chemistry between Naipaul, the Trinidadian born of Indian ancestry, and the fair-skinned Jesuit preacher of noble Basque ancestry. Naipaul was unimpressed by what he regarded as the naive but dangerous politics of a rich kid who had found his social conscience.

In his sermons Mugica insisted that the priest had a defined political role in confronting a system 'where the rich get richer and the poor poorer', while rejecting his direct involvement in violent action: 'I am prepared to be killed but I am not prepared to kill.' But Mugica failed to dissuade Naipaul from his overriding sense that Argentina was a failed state, and that Peronism in whatever guise had much to answer for this.

A founding member of the Third World Priests Movement, Mugica had officially affiliated himself to Peronism in 1956, at the age of twenty-six. He later claimed that the key to his conversion was a feeling of intense guilt at the Church's support for the 1955 overthrow of Perón. As far as Mugica was concerned the overthrow had interrupted Argentina's liberation from capitalism and colonialism, a process which, Mugica believed, Perón had instigated in 1945.

Mugica was open about his socialist sympathies in the sermons while showing enduring respect for Perón as a 'man of the people', a true man of the Gospel, who had the best interests of the poor and downtrodden of the Latin American continent in his heart and mind. Mugica's sermons were published many years later in a collection called *Peronism and Christianity*, which became popular among Catholic lay workers and priests working in the shanty towns. 'I personally am convinced that Argentina has only one way out and this is through a revolution, a true revolution, one that involves a change of structures within and without. As the French students said in May 68, we have to kill the policeman we carry within us, the oppressor. The Christian must be prepared to give his life for this.'

Mugica was murdered in May 1974 by an unidentified assassin thought to work for the Triple A, an anti-communist, right-wing, Peronista hit squad controlled by José López Rega. The one-time police officer had been promoted by General Perón to his trusted inner circle, naming him as his wife Isabelita's private secretary while they were in exile in Spain. López Rega later returned to Buenos Aires and established a powerful political base for himself, ahead of Perón's return, as head of the Social Welfare Ministry.

On 31 July 1973, a year before Mugica's death, Bergoglio, aged thirty-six, had been made the new head of the Argentine Jesuits, the youngest provincial ever to be appointed in the history of the order. He replaced Ricardo 'Dicky' O'Farrell – an Argentine of Irish descent who had struggled to hold his order together in the aftermath of Vatican II and his country's divisive politics. O'Farrell had hoped at one stage to have his able and widely respected deputy, Fr Joaquin Ruiz Escribano, succeed him, but he was killed in a car crash. Bergoglio's appointment came as a complete surprise to O'Farrell because of his youth.

Bergoglio's name was recommended to the head of the order, Fr Arrupe, by a committee of influential Jesuits in Argentina led by Bergoglio's spiritual mentor, Fr Fiorito. They argued that youth, piety and theological orthodoxy were the qualities to help pilot the Argentine Jesuit ship through increasingly stormy waters. The Jesuit community in Argentina was not only divided politically but also undergoing something of a vocational crisis, with a growing number of departures from the priesthood.

Not everyone agreed with the appointment. Among the sceptics was Fr Ignacio Pérez del Viso, at thirty-eight just two years older than Bergoglio and one of his former theology teachers who claimed to have a better insight into human psychology.

'I argued that Bergoglio was too young to be appointed to such a position, that he would be burnt out by the experience. One thing was to be in charge of young novices that look up to you and are under your control. Quite another matter is to head up an entire Jesuit community in a country like Argentina which requires real leadership, the ability to deal with neurotics, unhealthy individuals requiring patient care, and alcoholics. I felt Bergoglio lacked this experience . . . There were others who recognized the force of my argument, but who felt that we were in a very special moment that required a pilot with the imagination and energy of a young person, and the decisiveness of a mature man – and that was Bergoglio.'

Fr Arrupe fell into the second camp. He was no conservative, and had shown himself a considerable risk taker as well as a progressive in fully embracing the reforms of the Second Vatican Council. The year O'Farrell's succession was decided, Arrupe was preparing for a major conference of all the heads of his order – known as the 32nd Congregation – to update the Jesuits' mission statement.

Despite his early concerns about Bergoglio's health, Arrupe was persuaded by Fiorito that it was time for serenity and order to prevail among Argentine Jesuits, in the midst of the country's evident spiral into political violence, and the risk that this posed to any bishops or priests who might become embroiled.

The risk was made evident only too clearly less than two weeks after the appointment, when Bergoglio hosted Arrupe for another visit that had been previously planned by O'Farrell. On 12 August 1973 the two Jesuits travelled to the northern province of La Rioja for a meeting with Enrique Angelelli, the local bishop whose reputation had grown because of his public denunciations of local government corruption and the repression of local rural workers by big landowners. Angelelli told the visiting Jesuits that he and his priests were facing daily death threats and he had narrowly escaped being stoned by an organized mob who invaded a local church while he was saying Mass. He and his visitors faced further hostility from a group of right-wing militants at the local airport before Bergoglio and Arrupe flew back, deeply shaken by the experience, to Buenos Aires. The experience left Bergoglio with a real sense that Argentina was spiralling out of political control, and fearing the consequences for any priest, including himself, who put their head above the parapet, as Mugica and Angelelli had done.

But Argentina was only one country in a continent where the Jesuits were having to ask themselves hard questions about their role in society and how they should react to a turbulent political landscape. Three years earlier, the heads of Jesuit social institutes in

Latin America, meeting in Mexico, had examined a country-by-country survey, which showed that a growing sector of the Church in several countries was taking a lead in promoting radical revolutionary reform. This brought the Church into conflict with civil and ecclesiastical authorities and sometimes led to violence. The question of how to react to this was proving increasingly divisive during the late 1960s and 1970s.

In 1968 a conference of the Latin American hierarchy in Medellín, Colombia, aimed to give the Church on the South American continent a more distinctive voice in the aftermath of Vatican II, with an emphasis on what it called the preferential option for the poor. It also denounced State-sanctioned violence and unjust social structures. A year later, Argentina's bishops, concerned that the Medellín directives were too radical, brought out their own declaration calling for greater respect for authority, criticizing the mounting social protest and lamenting a collapse in priestly vocations.

While lay Catholics felt empowered by Vatican II's definition of the Church as 'the People of God', the status of ordinary priests remained largely unchanged, which was one of the reasons why so many left the Church and why many of those that remained were confused. Not so the conservative wing of the Argentine hierarchy and their Jesuit followers. A key part of the Argentine bishops' document was written by Fr Lucio Gera, one of the widely recognized influences on Bergoglio. While deploring oppression and exploitation, it came out strongly against Marxism as 'alien not only to Christianity but also to the spirit of our people'. Gera drew a clear line in the sand in opposition to the Marxist element in liberation theology. Thus he described the 'option for the poor' as a radical identification with ordinary people as subjects of their own history, rather than a 'class' engaged in a social and political struggle with other classes.

Gera formed part of a wider debate about the future of the

Catholic Church fuelled by Vatican II, where the Europeans had taken the lead but, as the four sessions continued, the perspective steadily widened with important contributions of Latin Americans like Dom Hélder Câmara, the Archbishop of Recife, Brazil, and other missionary bishops on the progressive side. As the influential German Jesuit theologian Karl Rahner put it, the Vatican Council saw the birth of the world Church. Of course the Catholic Church had always been a Church in and for the world – but on the basis of its European heartland. Rahner meant that with the Council's rediscovery of the local Church in the developing world, this basis no longer applied.

Rahner, who was hugely respected by Arrupe, wrote that the Church had to embrace change if it wasn't to continue being just being made up 'mainly of the rural class and small bourgeoisie, typical of the old Europe'.

Arrupe's overview of the Latin American continent was that the situation required a clear statement from the Jesuits in defence of social and political justice, while he was less clear about how they should behave when confronted with a situation of violence when perpetrated by either a repressive military regime or their opponents, be they demonstrators or full-trained guerrillas.

Such ambiguity had provoked a growing campaign against Arrupe led by a group of right-wing and theologically conservative Jesuits, who were mainly from his native Spain but had a strong following in Argentina (where many Jesuits were of Spanish origin), France and the US. The group, called Jesuitas en Fidelidad (Jesuits in Fidelity) wanted Arrupe sacked on account of his liberal theology and what they claimed was his inefficient management of the order. Their aim was the restoration of the Jesuit order under papal control and closely identified with the Catholic political establishment in whichever country it operated.

The campaign was gathering momentum when, in December 1974, Bergoglio was one of the 237 delegates from ninety Jesuit provinces across five continents summoned to Rome by Arrupe for the 32nd General Congregation (GC32). Unlike previous gatherings similar to this, this was not to choose a new head of the order but to have Arrupe, as 'general', rally his troops around the reforming spirit and progressive theologies that had emerged from the Second Vatican Council and Medellin. In particular, Arrupe wished the GC32 to endorse an unequivocal commitment to social justice and human rights. It has been claimed in some of the earlier books on the Francis papacy that Bergoglio was enlisted by Arrupe to help rein in Nicolás Puyadas, the ringleader of the ultra conservative Spanish Jesuits who threatened to form a breakaway order.

Puyadas, who wrote under a pseudonym Javier Pignatelli, by all accounts was a Walter Mitty character – Arrupe's biographer Pedro Lamet describes him generously as an 'eccentric'. Puyadas, on the eve of the GC32 Jesuit gathering, circulated an extended pamphlet entitled 'La Verdad sobre La Compañía de Jesus' ('The Truth about the Society of Jesus') in which he attacked Arrupe with a series of wild allegations, all never proven.

These ranged from claims that he had rigged votes in his election, had kept Jesuits in the dark about what the Vatican had to say about them, and had a secret plan to turn the Society of Jesus into an order of laymen.

Those who claim Bergoglio played a key role in successfully heading off Puyadas's intended coup too easily ignore the fact that Puyadas had been living unopposed or undisciplined by his fellow Jesuits in Argentina since the mid-1960s. As soon as Bergoglio became provincial, he sent Puyadas to Spain, from where he stepped up his anti-Arrupe campaign. While there is no suggestion that Bergoglio was part of the anti-Arrupe plot, his role as heroic defender at the gates in this instance sits uneasily with the absence of any previous disciplining of Puyadas. Moreover, Austen Ivereigh's claim that at the time of the GC32 , Bergoglio had 'as little patience with restorationists as he had with Marxists' must be judged against the attitude the Argentine struck regarding the specific proposal submitted by Arrupe and approved by a clear majority of delegates. The controversial Decree Four stated that the purpose of the Society of Jesus was the 'service of faith, of which the promotion of justice is an absolute requirement'. To its critics, it appeared to radically politicize religion by incorporating social justice as a key part of every Jesuit activity. Bergoglio considered that this put the order at risk of takeover by a movement or government, and blurred the distinction between evangelization and political action, and between priests and social activists.

Bergoglio was so at odds with Decree Four that in his remaining time as a provincial and teacher he never quoted it when speaking to novices. Moreover, in an address he gave after GC34 he again made no reference to Decree Four but instead supported Pope Paul VI's thinly veiled warning to Arrupe that the Church was becoming too politically radical by reducing its mission to a mere 'temporal project' left open to 'manipulation by ideological systems and political parties'. Bergoglio encouraged the Jesuits under his command to focus on the devotional life of 'true believers', eschewing any Marxist dialectic in favour of a simple distinction between true workers and layabouts.

One of Bergoglio's first major initiatives in his new post as head of the Argentine Jesuits was to carry out a sweeping purge of left-wing students and radical teachers, among them several Jesuits who had taken control of the Jesuit University of Salvador, in Buenos Aires. He also reasserted his authority at other Jesuit schools and institutions, particularly the seminary of San Miguel where he had built up a strong following among young novitiates who felt more secure in their spirituality thanks to the authority and discipline he imposed. Jesuit students were required to wear the traditional clerical cassock and stiff collars, focus on their vows of chastity and obedience, and live in the community rather than in separate civilian living quarters. Soon into his appointment as provincial, Bergoglio was to take other measures that offended the sensibilities of some Argentine Jesuits.

On 25 May 1973, just a few months prior to Bergoglio's appointment, Montoneros and other left-wing groups, along with the trade unions, had celebrated the election of the radical Peronist candidate Héctor Cámpora as president. But with Perón planning his return from exile in Madrid, Cámpora was on borrowed time, and struggled to contain the different ideological forces that competed for power. While right-wing and trade-union representatives became increasingly dominant in government, the leftists were encouraged to give up their arms and obtained as their treasured trophy the control of the state-owned University of Buenos Aires. The new rector was a one-time leading Communist party member who had converted to Peronism: Rodolfo Puiggrós. He set out to transform a traditionally liberal institution into a 'national and popular university'. University staff not judged radical enough were sacked, police were ordered off the campus, and students were encouraged to become involved in the running of their courses with suitably inflammatory titles evoking the benefits of revolutionary change.

The capital's well-funded and academically prestigious private university, the Jesuit-run Salvador, was officially guided by its own internal governance and had for years managed to maintain its independence from state intervention by remaining politically non-controversial. But within weeks of Cámpora's election victory, the winds of revolution had begun to stir within Salvador's lecture halls, much to the horror of some of its staff.

Rafael Braun, an ordained priest who had been appointed head of the political science department at Salvador, entered his lecture room one day to find its walls covered with graffiti in support of the radical Peronist and other left-wing youth groups along with painted personal insults that depicted him as a right-wing reactionary who should immediately relinquish his teaching post. His class was later interrupted by a group of Montoneros chanting slogans. They were led by a Jesuit priest in civilian clothes. Far from an isolated incident, the demonstration set the pattern for what followed, as more classrooms were occupied by radical Jesuits and their student companions, many of whom were not even registered in the university.

Braun recalled, 'I spoke to the university rector, Fr Ismael Quilmes, and to the head of the Argentine Jesuits, S. O'Farrell, but they didn't seem to want to do anything as if they had surrendered to a political situation that seemed to be Argentina's equivalent of the Cultural Revolution. It seemed to me and many others as if the authorities had lost control.'

Just days after Cámpora's election victory, the soon-to-depart head of the Jesuits O'Farrell received an eighteen-page dossier prepared by the Jesuit adviser to the university's board of trustees, Fr Pérez del Viso, warning that the political agitation at Salvador risked undermining the university's financial position: delays on the payment of fees were compounded by the withdrawal of charitable donations by politically conservative benefactors who paid the salaries of some of the teachers.

Two months later Bergoglio was appointed as the new Provincial General of the Argentine Jesuits and almost immediately took the series of steps that were to make him as many enemies as friends within the Jesuit community. Early action included the sale of various buildings owned by the Jesuits in Córdoba, Argentina's second largest city and the one time centre of the order's main missionary effort in the region. The Archbishop of the city at the time, the politically influential Cardinal Primatesta, was among those who tried but failed to stop Bergoglio ordering that a Jesuit church in the final stages of construction be dynamited in order to realize the full value of the land.

Further asset sales followed in Buenos Aires including apartments where some Jesuits shared living quarters with laymen and -women – an engagement with the secular world they claimed was in the reforming spirit of the Second Vatican Council. Bergoglio not only saw these Jesuit private apartments as a waste of money, but as theologically, politically and psychologically misguided, raising the risk to those involved of embracing terrorist organizations, as well as breaching their vows of celibacy.

'When Bergoglio took over, it was a time of huge disorientation among certain Jesuits with this mania among some of the younger ones that their true mission was to live in small communities and away from religious houses and seminaries as part of their involvement in civilian society. But Bergoglio felt the Jesuits had become too secularized, hanging up their vestments, and had separated religion from their private lives, in effect sacrificing their spirituality,' recalled Fr Pérez del Viso.

'We were in the aftermath of the Second Vatican Council, where everyone had his own way of interpreting the signs of the times and each Jesuit claiming his only guide was the Holy Spirit. But in Argentina the Jesuits needed to study more closely what the Vatican Council was really trying to say, and have a figure with sufficient authority to guide them along the right path.'

In Buenos Aires, Bergoglio decided that the University of Salvador was worth saving but on terms that were politically controversial. Having cleared the university of its debt, he withdrew all the Jesuit teachers and replaced them with a new teaching and administrative staff structure that could be trusted to stem the revolutionary tide. All senior posts, including that of the rector of the university, went to anti-Marxist militant Catholics who belonged to a Peronist faction called Guardia de Hierro (Guard of Iron). The origins of the name remain a subject of dispute within the Peronist movement to this day. Some of its senior figures interviewed for this book insist they took their name from Puerta Hierro (Door of Iron), the gated rich residential neighbourhood in Madrid where Perón had lived in his exile years, turning increasingly to the right politically. However, journalist Horacio Verbitsky, a supporter of the left wing of the Peronist movement who accompanied Perón on his plane back from exile, claims the origin of the name lies in the Romanian fascist group the Guard of Iron, also known as the Legion of Archangel Michael, founded in the 1920s by Corneliu Codreanu.

The purge of the Jesuit University of Salvador was completed after the ailing Perón returned to Argentina and took over the presidency in October 1973. Within months Perón had died, aged seventy-nine, leaving government in the hands of his politically inept widow Isabelita and her sinister adviser, López Rega. In his essay published in the *New York Review of Books* in September 1974, V. S. Naipaul reflected on his earlier visit to Argentina in which he identified Perón as both the symptom and the cause of Argentina's failure as a state. He concluded that the task of reorganization was perhaps beyond the capacities of any leader, however creative. 'Politics reflects a society and a land. Argentina is a land of plunder, a new land, virtually peopled in this century. It remains a land to be plundered; and its politics can only be the politics of plunder,' he wrote.

Chapter Eight
The Dirty War

On 25 November 1977 in the Buenos Aires neighbourhood of
Almagro some 400 guests, mostly cadets and non-
commissioned officers dressed neatly in the white and dark colours
of the Argentine Navy, marched up a wide marbled staircase lined
with religious images before entering and taking their seats in a
neatly furnished private theatre.

This was no ordinary official night out. The venue doubled up
as one of the main conference halls of the Jesuit University of
Salvador in a building founded as a convent school in the nineteenth
century. The main focus of interest that evening was its special guest
and conference speaker, Admiral Emilio Massera, the head of the
Argentine Navy and member of the junta that had seized power
in a military coup in March 1976.

The occasion was the granting to Massera of an honorary
professorship by the lay university board, which had been put in
place by Bergoglio on his appointment as head of the Jesuits in
Argentina four years earlier. The hosts on the day included the
rector Francisco José Piñón, a member of the staunchly Catholic
right-wing Peronist group Guardia de Hierro, and Fr Victor Zorzin,
the second most senior Jesuit in the country.

The precise reasons why Bergoglio chose to be absent are not clear. When asked by his authorized biographers Sergio Rubin and Francesca Ambrogetti if he had been involved in awarding Massera the 'honorary doctorate', Bergoglio replied: 'I believe it was a professorship, not a doctorate. I was not a sponsor. I was invited to the venue but I did not attend. And when I found that a group had politicized the university [an apparent reference to the Peronist Guardia de Hierro] I went to the Asociacion Civil [trustees meeting] and asked them to leave, despite the fact that the university no longer belonged to the Society of Jesus and that I had no authority other than as a priest.'

While administered by lay staff and overseen by a largely secular board of trustees, the university was still owned by the Jesuit order and as such it is unlikely that Bergoglio would not have had prior notice of such an event involving the highest profile member of the ruling three-man military junta. Those members of the university management who had helped organize the event, including leading members of Guardia de Hierro, remained in post despite Bergoglio's alleged reprimand. Curiously there is no mention of the event in the university's official fiftieth anniversary commemorative history, subsequently published in 2006, as if it had been airbrushed out. However, the limited circulation history does include, along with several photographs of Bergoglio attending functions at the university, a mission statement signed by him as Jesuit provincial on 27 August 1974, a year after his appointment, showing that his politics and theology were far from radical in the run-up to the coup in 1976.

The statement stresses that the university's priorities should be the fight against atheism, and the return to the Jesuits' missionary roots, respecting the contribution of indigenous people to national culture, respecting diversity within a vision of universality, and, in a selective reference to the Jesuits' 32nd Congregation (where the main message was an option for justice and for the poor), adapting education to local needs. But 'for the fight against atheism' there is little here that would justify any kind of honour being given to Massera.

The gap that had opened up between the Argentine 'province' under Bergoglio and other Jesuits, not just in South America, but in other key areas of the order became evident during a visit to Argentina in April 1977, seven months before the Massera event, by Fr Michael Campbell-Johnston. He was one of the Jesuits' Provincial General Fr Arrupe's key advisers at the time on social and political issues in the developing world.

Fr Campbell-Johnston, from the Jesuit headquarters' Social Secretariat in Rome, had been impressed by the courage shown by Jesuits and other priests in Chile, Brazil and Argentina while on a tour of Latin American countries, then under repressive military regimes. These priests faced intimidation and persecution for standing up for social justice and human rights issues. Some were forced into exile or paid with their lives, others survived clandestinely. When Campbell-Johnston reached Buenos Aires, he spent a week divided between visiting priests, including Jesuits, who were working in poor neighbourhoods, and inspecting another key area of local Jesuit activity – a social institute and think-tank called Comisión Interprovincial de Accion Social (CIAS) dedicated to communications and publications. He discovered that in contrast to the stand against the military regime's injustices taken by other priests, CIAS had adopted a policy of non-confrontation with the junta, under orders from Bergoglio.

'I was visiting our Jesuit social institutes throughout Latin America, where, in many of the countries, they were facing opposition and even persecution . . . in some forced to act underground and in secrecy,' Campbell-Johnston later recalled. 'But this was not the situation of our institute in Buenos Aires which was able to function freely because it never criticized or opposed the government. As a result, there were justice issues it could not address or even mention.'

It would later emerge that the Jesuit institute in Buenos Aires, as part of its policy, would go on to turn down an approach by human rights activists, including the Nobel Prize-winner Adolfo Pérez Esquivel, to join forces in a more active campaign of denunciation against the regime. Pérez Esquivel, a Catholic sculptor and professor of architecture, had left the teaching profession in 1974 to campaign using non-violent means on behalf of the poor and politically repressed in Latin America, co-founding SERPAJ (Service, Peace and Justice Foundation), a nongovernmental organization (NGO). He was subsequently imprisoned as a political dissident in Brazil and Ecuador, and in 1977 was detained and tortured by the Argentine security services for a period of several months. He was released after an international campaign on his behalf and awarded the Pope John XXIII Peace Memorial Prize, followed by the Nobel Peace Prize in 1980.

Pérez Esquivel used his raised international profile to continue to campaign actively on human rights issues, not least in his own country, supporting organizations like the Mothers and Grand-mothers of May. When he was awarded his Nobel Prize, the journal published by the Jesuit CIAS gave him a glowing tribute. But when days later Pérez Esquivel approached CIAS and suggested firmer support for his human rights campaigns, he was turned down. As Fr Ignacio del Viso, one of the Jesuits who worked at CIAS at the time, recalled: 'Esquivel wanted to work together with us – but we told him we couldn't because SERPAJ had strongly criticized the alleged complicity of the Argentine hierarchy with the military and we were partly financed by the hierarchy and we didn't have the freedom we thought he had to operate.'

The topic of how far Jesuits should go in promoting justice as an essential condition for their service of faith was one that Campbell-Johnston had discussed at length with Bergoglio in the protracted and sometimes fraught conversation they had had in 1977, three years before Pérez Esquivel's approach to the Jesuits. 'He

[Bergoglio] naturally defended the existing situation though I tried to show him how it was out of step with our other social institutes on the continent. The discussion was lengthy and inconclusive since we never reached an agreement,' reported Campbell-Johnston later to his superiors in Rome.

In later years Campbell-Johnston, or C. J. as he was more popularly known, would publicly defend Pope Francis as an enlightened reformer, exonerating him of any blame on the human rights front. Privately, however, C. J. harboured an enduring belief that Bergoglio had fallen short of the standards set by other more courageous members of the Church in the era of military government in Latin America, with Archbishop Romero and the Jesuit martyrs of El Salvador among the continent's most honoured martyrs.

While some Jesuits, including C. J., felt that their duty of loyalty to the Pope meant they had to rally round Francis, and draw a line in the sand regarding the past, back in 1977 there was no hiding the cultural, political and theological divide that had opened up between Arrupe's special emissary and Bergoglio. From an upper-crust Catholic Scottish family, Campbell-Johnston was a former English private-school teacher (he had taught at Stonyhurst) who had been radicalized by his experience of the Third World, and the liberation theology emerging from Vatican II.

From 1966 to 1975 (formative years for the Jesuits and the Church as a whole in the Third World) he had worked among the poor in Guyana, a country from which he was expelled by the government of Forbes Burnham for his alleged political activities. As an old friend and colleague Peter Hardwick noted some years later, C. J. was never principally political. Rather, as Hardwick noted, 'he cared for the wretched of the earth and wished to live with them and to teach them to care for each other, but if this brought him into conflict with those whose ultimate purpose was to preserve the power and wealth of their own family class, or state, then he was prepared to accept their enmity until they could change their heart'.

C. J.'s superiors were the first to recognize this. Far from being hidden away after Guyana, he was based in Rome in the Borgo Santo Spirito as the secretary of the Jesuits' social apostolate. There he worked closely with the liberal Fr Arrupe, becoming in effect his close political adviser and 'ambassador at large'. It was, as Hardwick put it, 'work in the front line, with the Jesuits drawing the fire of many of those regimes, generally military, whose poor they were trying to help, and of all those people who held simply that the Church should stay out of politics'.

When he returned to Rome after his visit to Buenos Aires, C. J. reported that there were at least 6,000 political prisoners and another 20,000 'disappeared' in Argentina, together with numerous cases of torture and assassination. He also received a copy of a letter addressed to then pontiff Pope Paul VI signed by more than 400 Argentinian mothers and grandmothers who had 'lost' children or other relatives, and who were begging the Vatican to exert some pressure on the military junta. C. J. took it into the Vatican's Secretariat of State. He never received any acknowledgement. But C. J. himself agreed to meet a delegation of four mothers of the group that weekly braved the authorities and demonstrated between the cathedral and the presidential palace in Buenos Aires's Plaza de Mayo. As one of them told C. J. in tears: 'When you have lost your two children, what else can they take from you?'

Weeks after Pope Francis's election, C. J. had not forgotten his encounter with Bergoglio in 1977 but was reluctant to be drawn into controversy. 'Although certainly not accepting the human rights issue, there seems to be little he or our social institute could do to change it. For himself, Bergoglio led a poor and simple life and was well respected by his fellow Jesuits,' C. J. wrote in the *Tablet*.

This still leaves the question as to why an event took place, months after C. J.'s visit to Buenos Aires, at the Jesuit university which was clearly against the institution's founding principles of respect for meritocracy, human dignity and academic freedom, and why Bergoglio – according to his own account – waited until it was over to lodge his complaint.

Interviews I conducted with several key individuals connected with the university at the time suggest that Massera's university 'title' appears to have been part of secret negotiations that had been going on between Bergoglio and the military junta since the coup of March 1976. Conceding the 'title' was considered a necessity as it might help not only protect the university from greater military intervention but also save the lives of some of those who had been kidnapped and held without trial by members of the armed forces and police. I learnt that young Argentine Jews in fact came to consider the University of Salvador a safe haven during a time when the repression showed distinctive anti-Semitic characteristics. I am indebted for this observation to the journalist and historian Hernán Dobry, who together with Daniel Goldman investigated the repression of the Jews in Argentina during the1970s for their book *Ser Judio en Los Años Setenta*.

Earlier that year, Massera has sent word to the rector José Piñón via a key intermediary between the Navy and the Guardia de Hierro – a retired naval officer and friend of Massera called Captain Bruzzone – that he would be open to the offer of an honourable title at Salvador, one of the country's most prestigious private universities. Massera was motivated by political ambition. As the head of the Jesuits in Argentina, Bergoglio appears to have been prepared to comply with the request, as long as it was slightly modified to minimize the embarrassment of such a blatant violation of academic ethics, not to mention collaboration with the military.

The compromise accepted by Massera was that he would settle for a token and largely ceremonial honorary professorship rather than the more elevated *honoris causa*, the granting of which was traditionally subjected to tougher internal rules – the recipient would usually have institutional ties as a current or one-time senior lecturer or donor, neither of which appears to have been the case.

Nonetheless the arrangements still breached other principles such as the university's ethical code, which insisted on the moral qualities of the recipient as a pre-condition for the granting of any titles. Massera's notorious philandering and misuse of public funds and private assets seized following the coup, and his responsibility for widespread human rights violations ranging from torture to the 'disappearances' of thousands, should have disqualified him for a high academic accolade in a university that officially remained Catholic.

Even the lesser title set Massera apart from many other officers of his rank, establishing a symbolic link with an important area of civilian life and academic respectability. It pretended he was a man of culture and education even though the reality was that he was a torturer and murderer. His 'honour' was a politically expedient illusion that played to the vanity of a psychopath and lacked any moral foundation, other than it might help save lives – as some believed.

As for the ceremony, it did not take place in the main University of Salvador building but in one of its outlying faculties. This again was intended to downplay the suggestion of formal institutional links between the Jesuit university and the military authorities, although such nuances did not stop those attending from considering that such ties were evidently existing, nor Massera from using the occasion to make a politically highly charged acceptance speech justifying the military and its Guardia de Hierro allies' intervention in university life.

Massera spoke in a building belonging to the faculty of psychology, a one-time hotbed of student radicalism from which numerous Montoneros had emerged. Condemning Marx and Freud, both sacred icons along with Perón of many of Argentina's middle-class revolutionaries, Massera urged the surviving university students not to follow the 'decadent example of those who get into rock music, promiscuous sex and hallucinogenic drugs before pursuing death because in the end their own destruction is justified as social redemption by those who manipulate them ideologically'.

As commented by Marguerite Feitlowitz in her book *A Lexicon of Terror*: 'it says something for the moral decadence, intellectually vacuity, and ideological bankruptcy of the junta, that Massera emerged as its most forceful and populist component'. Massera was not only 'brutal, sadistic and predatory' but also the 'grand orator' of the Process of National Reorganization – the junta's manifesto – under which the regime tried to justify its existence. 'Massera was the master of the majestic rhythm of seemingly cultured speech which even at its most confusing, could captivate those that listened,' noted Feitlowitz.

While the pious Army chief Jorge Videla's religious hypocrisy and lack of statesmanship took time to reveal itself, and the Air Force's Brigadier-General Orlando Agosti maintained a relatively low profile in the junta that removed Isabelita Perón in 1976, the charismatic Massera made a name for himself as the main architect of the regime's notorious crimes against humanity. His single-minded pursuit of power through a dark and complex tapestry of insidious conspiratorial alliances involved sectors of the Peronist party – Guardia de Hierro and recalcitrant Montoneros – collaborators in the Catholic Church, and the international Masonic lodge Propaganda Due (P2), led by Licio Gelli, whose influence during the 1970s penetrated deep into the Vatican and Italian political parties. Among the conspiracies circulating at the time was a suggestion that Gelli – worried about a political breakdown in an Italy fought over by the Mafia and the Red Brigades as it faced the prospect of the Communist party coming to power – had dreamt up an idea of moving the Pope and key Curia staff to the Argentina of the juntas. No evidence has ever emerged that such a plot actually existed, still less that Gelli and Bergoglio ever met, but when it came to Gelli any conspiracy seemed possible.

What is reliably known about Gelli is that he fought as a young volunteer for Franco during the Spanish Civil War, before fighting the Allies in the Second World War. In 1945, he saved his skin by changing sides and joining the Italian partisans before they captured and summarily lynched Il Duce and his mistress Clara Petacci. After the war, Gelli spent much of his life in Latin America where he met and befriended Perón during his first presidency, while all the time developing his business interests in Italy.

In Rome, one of Gelli's key friends was the lawyer Umberto Ortolani whose banking interests extended from Milan to Montevideo, where he served under the title of honorary ambassador to Uruguay of the order of the Knights of Malta, a network of influential and rich Catholic laymen dedicated to financing the protection of worldwide Catholicism since the days of the Crusades. Ortolani became Gelli's most trusted lieutenant in P2, a key into the murky world of Roman politics, particularly where its financial interests crossed into the Vatican, as was exposed during the notorious case of Italian banker Roberto Calvi, the head of Banco Ambrosiano. At the time the biggest collapse of a bank anywhere since the Second World War, Ambrosiano's downfall exposed years of reckless financial behaviour by the Vatican bank, calling into question the judgement of Pope Paul VI who reigned in 1963–78.

The broad slant of P2's extensive network was anti-communist and right wing; the Latin American dimension involved regimes sharing similar philosophies based on power and greed, and bolstered by a large apparatus of repression. During the 1970s Gelli appears to have judged Massera to be a potential successor to Perón, when he served the president's widow Isabelita as head of the Navy. Gelli enlisted Massera as a member of P2, and negotiated secret arms deals on his behalf.

A year after the military coup of 1976, and around the time of the 'doctor honoris' award at the Jesuit university, Gelli mediated secretly in the negotiation of several major Italian arms contracts with Massera. The admiral acted without the official approval of his junta partners or the knowledge of the Argentine civilian economy minister at the time, José Martínez de Hoz. It was not the first time, nor certainly the last, that Massera involved himself in such deals through which he personally enriched himself. He initiated a major arms procurement programme during the last Perón government in preparation for an increasingly militant stance over Argentina's disputed territorial claims with Chile over the Beagle Channel, and with Britain over the Falklands.

Massera was the most corrupt and ruthless of the members of the junta that had overthrown the discredited government of Perón's widow Isabelita but he was also a pragmatist who had seen the hard lessons that Perón had learnt about the need to keep powerful sectors of the Church and other groups happy. Bergoglio, as head of the Jesuits, was not someone that Massera considered worth risking a public fight with. He saw Bergoglio as a reasonable if politically cautious individual with whom he could deal discreetly, unlike others who threatened to confront him publicly.

During 1974, a year in which Massera had initiated his links with the Catholic Church, Bergoglio brought some of the leading supporters of the Guardia de Hierro into the new administration of the University of Salvador. This was his attempt to counter the anarchic conduct of students and Jesuit priests who were pursuing liberation theology through the perspective of Marxist revolution. Bergoglio appears to have been drawn unwittingly to strike deals with Massera by his determination to keep not just his university but his Jesuit fathers generally out of the political violence that preceded his 1976 coup and the brutal military repression in its aftermath.

In 2010, Bergoglio, then Archbishop of Buenos Aires, told a judge investigating human rights violations at the Escuela de

Mecánica de la Armada (ESMA, Navy School of Mechanics) in Buenos Aires that his concern for the safety of fellow Jesuits in Argentina had increased after the gunning down of the shanty-town priest Fr Mugica in 1974 and the assault by stoning of the radical Bishop Angelelli in 1973. Angelelli continued to be the recipient of regular death threats and in August 1976, just a few weeks after the military coup, he was killed – or assassinated – in a car crash.

Compared to the bombast and improvisation that had characterized previous military interventions in Argentina, that of 24 March 1976, led by Massera, Videli and Agosti, was initially a clinical affair – bloodless, serene and quickly executed, with a majority of the population breathing a sigh of relief with the end of Peronist government. But within weeks a growing number of people identified as political dissidents were being taken from their homes, or kidnapped from the streets and taken to clandestine detention camps. In the first three years of the military regime, thousands 'disappeared', many were tortured, and a majority were summarily executed and buried in unmarked locations or dumped in rivers or the sea. They included priests and other religious figures accused of being politically subversive because of their support for liberation theology and their links with members of the Peronist paramilitary groups. Working in the shanty towns, as many of them did, was enough to raise suspicion, even though only a small minority actually took up arms themselves.

Among those who were victimized within weeks of the coup were two Jesuit priests, Orlando Yorio and Francisco Jalics, who were arrested by security forces on 23 May 1976. Their fate was sealed ten days earlier, when a special unit of Navy personnel, under the orders of Massera and camouflaged in Army fatigues, raided a series of private homes and kidnapped four young female Catholic women and the husbands of two of them. The group included Monica Mignone, the twenty-four-year-old daughter of a widely respected Catholic lawyer, Emilio Mignone. A psychology graduate and socially committed Catholic, Monica had worked closely with Catholic nuns and priests as a social worker and teacher with the small surviving Mapuche Indian community in Patagonia; she also worked in the shanty town of Bajo Flores in Buenos Aires where she was openly supportive of the more radical left-wing elements of Peronism.

Emilio Mignone in his youth had been a right-wing political activist with the militant lay group Catholic Action before serving as a minister of education during Perón's first post-war government. Subsequently, during the early 1960s, he served in Washington, DC as an official of the Organization of American States before returning and working as a legal adviser to the presidential office and becoming founding rector of the state university of Luján – whose local Virgin is venerated throughout Argentina – during the military government of General Ongania. By 1976, the year of Argentina's last military coup, Mignone had retired and was writing textbooks about civic education.

Deeply committed to his Catholic faith, and after a long, hard-working life dedicated to upholding the rule of law, when not sympathizing with anti-communist nationalist politicians, Mignone saw the world he had trusted turned upside down in an instant when the group of armed men raided his family flat in Buenos Aires's smart Barrio Norte neighbourhood and took away Monica, the third of his five children.

When first confronted by the armed men, Mignone felt reassured when they showed identification as Army personnel. He told the terrified Monica to cooperate and go quietly with the men, reassuring her as they left that he would secure her release in court within hours. At the time the scale of 'disappearances' was not widely known, and Mignone, who had served under civilian and military governments, had never lost his faith in due process. He never saw his daughter again. He spent the last two decades of his life, politically radicalized by her abduction by the military, campaigning on her behalf and that of thousands of other 'disappeared'.

In the immediate aftermath of Monica's disappearance, Mignone and his wife, Angelica, spent weeks approaching courts and ministries and meeting senior military officers they had known over the years. Each meeting was meticulously recorded by Mignone who would then circulate the statements among his network of friends and former colleagues. Despite endless writs of habeas corpus, the Mignones learnt nothing initially about Monica's whereabouts or fate. The Mignones contacted Church officials, but they found them unhelpful and, in some cases, deliberately obstructive. Years later Mr Mignone wrote *Dictatorship and Church*, in which he criticized the inaction and open collaboration of the Church in Argentina in that period while identifying a minority of bishops and priests who were tortured, killed or forced into exile because of their opposition to the regime.

By then his personal crusade had helped unravel the terrible circumstances of Monica's torture and subsequent murder. He discovered she had been taken to the ESMA naval school, a military barracks near Buenos Aires's River Plate football stadium, which had been turned into a notorious death camp by Massera following the coup. Diligently pursuing every possible contact that might provide a useful clue, and following up every lead, Mignone spent days and nights forensically reconstructing the terrible details of what had happened, establishing a connection between the kidnap of his daughter and her friends and that of the two Jesuit priests ten days later. Doused when not submerged in water, detainees were subjected to high electric currents – a method of torture similar to that practised in Pinochet's Chile on British doctor Sheila Cassidy following her arrest for treating a wounded guerrilla.

During torture sessions, the names of Yorio and Jalics were mentioned by the interrogators, who alleged that they were linked to subversive activity undertaken by the Montoneros. Soon after the Jesuits were arrested, they were shown photographs of Monica Quinteros, the oldest woman in the group of catechists in which Monica Mignone had worked among the slum dwellers. Yorio admitted that he had known Quinteros for ten years and that they had worked together among the poor and destitute of the shanty town. Their heads hooded to prevent them identifying their captors or the location of their detention, the priests were held in dark isolated cells with their feet chained. Only later would they discover they were being held at the ESMA. 'Now and again someone would come in and insult and threaten me,' Yorio recalled. 'I couldn't sleep or go to the bathroom. I had to relieve myself where I was and I had no change of clothes. One day they gave me an injection and started asking me questions about Monica Mignone.'

Yorio endured his interrogations in a half-sleep or suffering from hallucinations, during which he sometimes imagined hearing Massera preaching from the Gospels or accusing Yorio of being an ideological priest who had erred by interpreting what the scriptures had to say about the poor in Marxist revolutionary terms, not in the spiritual terms of Christ.

On 1 July 1976, while Yorio and Jalics and hundreds of others remained detained at the ESMA, Mignone was granted a meeting with Admiral Oscar Montes, the head of Navy operations who owed his promotion to Massera. During the meeting Montes denied the Navy had had anything to do with his daughter's arrest, but admitted they had arrested the priests.

Mignone learnt that, days before Yorio was arrested, the Jesuit's priestly licence had been removed by the then Cardinal Archbishop of Buenos Aires, Juan Carlos Aramburu. This convinced Mignone that there was not only growing collaboration but outright complicity between the military and high-level representatives of the Catholic Church. The supposed joint goal was to rid Argentine society of wayward liberation theology priests whose politics led them to sympathize with if not directly support the actions of armed revolutionary groups like the Montoneros.

In early October 1976 Mignone met Colonel Ricardo Flouret, a member of President Videla's staff, who was destined to be given a senior command during the Falklands War in 1982. Flouret told Mignone that Pope Paul VI had expressed concern via the papal nuncio in Buenos Aires, Pio Laghi, about the fate of the two Jesuit priests, but gave no further details. A few days later, on 26 October, Yorio and Jalics, heavily sedated, were transported by helicopter from the ESMA and released into freedom on a piece of industrial wasteland in Canales, a suburb of Buenos Aires. They were thus saved from the fate that befell hundreds of other detainees of the ESMA, including, it is believed, the 'disappeared' Monica Mignone, who were dumped – naked, drugged but alive – from military aeroplanes and helicopters in flight to let the ocean and sharks make identification impossible. No mass graves, no evidence – and what complicit Catholic priests, according to direct witnesses, thought a 'less violent, more Christian method' to deal with 'subversives'.

To his dying day in 1998, Mignone always believed that the release of the two Jesuits came about as a result of pressure from the Vatican, and not from their superior Jorge Bergoglio. Yorio, who died in 2000, went to his grave believing that Bergoglio had been complicit in his detention. On 17 April 2013, less than a month after Bergoglio's election as pope, Yorio sister's Graciela testified in open court, during the trial of a group of Navy officers accused of human rights offences in the ESMA, that Bergoglio had turned his back on Yorio before and after he was detained. She said both Yorio and Jalics had felt abandoned by Bergoglio, and by the Church hierarchy as a whole.

'My brother was abandoned, expelled, without a bishop, without the support of the Jesuits to protect him, and that's why he was kidnapped. He was practically abandoned by the Church,' she said.

Even before the March 1976 coup, her brother and Jalics were turned away by Bergoglio after being accused of being 'subversive and extremists' for their work with the poor, Graciela reported. She said they pleaded with Bergoglio to do something to stop 'the rumours, because with these rumours their life was in danger'. But Bergoglio told them he was under too much pressure from Church officials, and urged them to find a bishop who might help. None would, she said. She and her mother went to Bergoglio seeking help. 'We had three interviews, and he never told us anything. Yes, I do remember that he told us, "I made good reports." He also told me to be very careful, because a sister of another person who didn't have anything to do with this was detained.'

Other witnesses, by contrast, support Bergoglio's own claims that far from collaborating with the military, he helped intervene not only on behalf of the two Jesuits but also of several other priests and lay people whose lives were in danger. In 1999, the year after Mignone died, Bergoglio, by then Archbishop of Buenos Aires, told the Argentine journalist Horacio Verbitsky that he had tried to meet Mignone before he died to explain his side of the story, but that the lawyer 'appeared to have his mind made up, and didn't want to listen'.

One of the witnesses for Bergoglio's defence was the late Alicia Olivera, a human rights lawyer who had worked with Mignone, and whose sister worked alongside Monica Mignone and Fr Yorio in the Bajo Flores slum. Olivera told Verbitsky that Bergoglio had warned Yorio and Jalics to leave the slum because they were on a military hit list, and he feared for their lives, but his advice had been ignored, as was a personal letter Bergoglio had obtained from the head of the Jesuit order, Fr Arrupe in Rome, in February 1976 ordering them to abandon their slum work for their own safety. After their arrest, Bergoglio secured a meeting with Massera and pleaded for their release.

'So what has Bergoglio got to say?' Massera said, greeting him with the kind of relaxed charm that the Navy chief displayed with people he felt he could cooperate with, or owed him a favour. Quite what promoted such familiarity remains unclear to this day. But Massera appeared to feel confident that Bergoglio was on side. The junta had received a discreet blessing from several Catholic bishops on the eve of the 1976 coup, and Massera liked to boast that the papal nuncio, Pio Laghi, was among his regular tennis partners.

Laghi later claimed that he agreed to his tennis games with the Navy chief as a way of keeping open an informal line from the Vatican to the junta, along which he would elicit intelligence on the disappeared. No evidence has been uncovered to suggest that the Navy chief had developed a warm personal friendship with Bergoglio that might have compromised the head of the Jesuits.

According to Olivera's account – based on what she had been told of the conversation by her friend Bergoglio – the Jesuit was in no mood to humour Massera, and got straight to the point. 'What does Massera say? I have come to tell you that if the two Jesuits [Yorio and Jalics] are not released, I will, as their provincial, denounce their detention.'

The two Jesuits were released the next day, five months after their arrest, according to Olivera. The chronology raises serious question marks over why it had taken so long for Bergoglio to intercede on their behalf. Bergoglio himself told Verbitsky in May 1999 that he worked behind the scenes to secure the release of Yorio and Jalics soon after their abduction and against great administrative difficulties managed to secure not just one but two meetings with Massera, and two separate ones with President Videla. 'I have no reason to believe that Bergoglio did anything to secure our freedom, if anything quite the opposite,' said Yorio, who claimed that while in detention Bergoglio had visited the ESMA, a claim that was never substantiated.

Verbitsky was one of Argentina's best-known journalists with a professional career spanning over three decades and steeped in controversy. His early days in journalism during the 1960s were spent working as a reporter and sub-editor for three Argentine newspapers *Noticias Graficas*, *El Siglo* and *El Mundo* before he joined the culture section of *Confirmado*. This was edited by one of the country's most dynamic and influential media moguls, Jacobo Timerman. The newspaper supported the military coup that toppled the centre-left Radical government of Arturo Illia in 1966. Timerman went on to launch a new politically independent broadsheet newspaper *La Opinion* in 1971, with Verbitsky on his staff, known popularly by now as '*El Perro*', the dog, because of his reputation as an obsessively driven news editor who was ruthless in his pursuit of a story, and also for his reputation for being unwavering in his loyalty to his friends.

Verbitsky was sacked by Timerman within months of his appointment because of political differences. In 1972 Verbitsky joined the Montoneros, the left-wing Peronist urban guerrilla group. His former newspaper went on to editorially initially support the 1976 coup, only to subsequently fall foul of the military regime as the repression intensified. Timerman was detained without trial and tortured before being released and allowed to go into temporary exile in the US following a strong international human rights campaign in his support.

Several Argentine journalists 'disappeared'. One of the most famous among them, Rodolfo Walsh, was shot dead by a task force from the ESMA a year after the 1976 coup. His friend Verbitsky escaped arrest and helped coordinate the anti-junta propaganda organized by the Montoneros in the run-up to the World Cup in Argentina in 1978. Verbitsky lived clandestinely for long periods in Argentina, writing under a pseudonym before returning to public life as an investigative reporter and a human rights activist after the end of the Falklands War.

His detractors included the US journalist Martin Andersen, the former *Washington Post* and *Newsweek* Buenos Aires special correspondent. Andersen took issue with the fact that, during the military regime, Verbitsky collaborated with a high-ranking military officer by ghost-writing his book. Verbitsky admitted to having collaborated on the book written by retired Air Force officer Juan José Güiraldes and published in May 1979 at the height of the military repression. Verbitsky told me: 'The officer in question retired twenty-five years before the military coup of 1976 and was an old friend of my family. My father wrote an essay on Güiraldes's uncle, the famous Argentine author Ricardo Güiraldes. The book in question was on commercial aviation, the author's speciality because he was a former president of the national airline Aerolineas Argentinas, and makes no reference to the military government or national politics.'

I shared an office with Andersen, known by his colleagues as 'Mick', in central Buenos Aires during the 1980s. I remember him as a fearless if occasionally reckless reporter, who was passionately focused on uncovering human rights abuses. For several years Andersen regarded himself as a good friend of Verbitsky and collaborated with him professionally. The Argentine, Andersen later recalled, used to joke that he was his 'first and only' American friend. After leaving Argentina and returning to the US to work on the professional staff of the Senate Foreign Relations Committee, Andersen spent 'considerable time trying to help a supposedly crusading Verbitsky in his various scrapes with the corrupt government of Carlos Menem'.

Verbitsky's book *The Silence*, published before the papal conclave of 2005, alleged that Bergoglio had not done enough to protect his own priests. Related articles began to circulate in Rome in the run-up to the conclave called to appoint a successor to John Paul II. Verbitsky's detractors, including Fr Marco, Bergoglio's spokesman when he was Archbishop of Buenos Aires, claimed he was the spearhead of a deliberate campaign to undermine Bergoglio morally and politically as his name began to emerge as a *papabile*. Like so many conspiracies, the Verbitsky plot against Bergoglio lacked any evident motive. Despite claims from some right-wing Catholic sources that Verbitsky was an atheistic Jew who hated the Catholic Church, his reports, which drew source material from minutes and documents archived by Emilio Mignone, were the result of diligent, painstaking investigation of documents that were either overlooked or kept deliberately classified during the high-profile and historic trials of military junta members in 1985.

In *Offnews.info*, Martin Andersen made a visceral attack on Verbitsky's reputation soon after the papal election of 2013. He quoted Julio Strassera, the former federal prosecutor who successfully presided over the trials against the military juntas. Strassera claimed that Verbitsky's attempts to link Bergoglio to the atrocities were 'a dirty trick'. 'It is absolutely false – during the entire trial [of the juntas] there was not a single mention' of Bergoglio, Strassera pointed out. He also noted that Bergoglio's name did not surface in the Raúl Alfonsín government's official and much praised (but nonetheless incomplete) *Never Again* (*Nunca Más*) study of the period, published in 1984.

Andersen went on to proclaim:

How is it that the *Washington Post*, the *New Republic*, *Reuters*, the *Associated Press*, and others extensively quote allegations made by this Argentine against the spiritual leader of world Christianity [Pope Francis], without also explaining who this purported human rights advocate is? Why are their stories missing critical information about what the accuser of the Pope himself did as some 25,000 of his countrymen were detained and secretly tortured and murdered in concentration camps which in their horror and number imitated the practices of the Nazis, so admired by many of the Argentine generals of that time?

The truth be told, perhaps the Pope's accuser and the

self-proclaimed campaigner against 'ethical betrayal', the Argentine journalist Horacio Verbitsky – should stand among the accused, once the course of his own career is appropriately addressed.

The phrase 'ethical betrayal' was used by Verbitsky to describe the human rights policy pursued by the first civilian government of Raúl Alfonsín on the alleged grounds that the trials of the juntas which it had ordered had not gone far enough in bringing to account all those responsible in some way for the 'disappeared'.

The Silence is one of more than twenty investigative and historical books authored by Verbitsky, seven of which are on the Catholic Church, and were published between 1995 and 2010. Verbitsky's interest in Bergoglio and the first articles he wrote about his involvement with the Yorio and Jalics case were sparked off by a detailed interview he conducted in 1999, six years before the papal conclave in which Bergoglio came a close second. The interview was with Adolfo Scilingo, a former Navy captain who had been closely involved in operations against alleged political dissidents during the so-called Dirty War. Scilingo, the first officer to detail human rights violations at the ESMA, made serious allegations of complicity between the Catholic Church and the junta. Verbitsky later also discovered classified Argentine government documents which suggested that some elements in the military regime considered Bergoglio a fairly compliant cleric who could be counted on not to confront them publicly over human rights violations, still less someone so determined to live up to his faith as to seek martyrdom.

The regime by then was aware of the speed with which Bergoglio had removed radical Jesuit priests from the University of Salvador in Buenos Aires. One of the documents Verbitsky published was a secret Army intelligence report on the Jesuit order following the military coup of 1976, and at the time of Yorio and Jalics's detention. 'Despite the good will of Fr Bergoglio the Society of Jesus has yet to be fully purged,' an official of the military government noted. Another classified Argentine Foreign Ministry document discovered by Verbitsky was a memo by an official reporting on a request for a passport extension for Jalics made by Bergoglio, in which there is an allusion to the priest's alleged links with armed activity. In *The Silence*, Verbitsky describes the document as 'devastating', a further indication of Bergoglio's complicity.

But Bergoglio could still count on reasoned and influential counsels for the defence. Thus in the widely respected US newspaper the *National Catholic Reporter*, the Jesuit Fr Thomas Reese wrote about the Foreign Ministry document:

> Not only did this take place after they [Jalics and Yorio] were arrested and after they were released, it was after they were safely out of the country. Nothing Bergoglio could say would endanger them, nor was he telling the government anything it did not already know. He was simply trying to convince a bureaucrat that it was a good idea to extend the passport of this man so he could stay in Germany and not have to return to Argentina.

When asked about the Yorio and Jalics case by his authorized biographers Rubin and Ambrogetti, Bergoglio responded:

> I never believed that Yorio and Jalics were involved in 'subversive activities' as their persecutors claimed, and the reality was that they were not. But because of their relationship to other priests in the slums, they were exposed to a paranoid witch hunt. When they stayed in the slums, they were abducted during a raid, when several people (suspected subversives) were rounded up by the security forces.

Bergoglio continued: 'Fortunately, sometime later they were released, firstly because they couldn't find anything to substantiate their allegations, and second because on the very night I heard they had been arrested, I started seeing what I could do on their behalf.'

On the day Yorio and Jalics were released, Bergoglio received advance warning via the papal nuncio. He told his second-in-command in the Jesuit order at the time, Fr Victor Zorzin, to go and pick them up. Zorzin recalled: 'On the day of their release, I got a call from Bergoglio: "Victor, go to such and such a place, you will find Yorio and Jalics. Pick them up and take them to the papal nuncio." So I followed the instructions, driving a grey Ford Falcon that belonged to the order. I prayed all along the journey that nothing would happen to them as they had no ID, and they were on a death list.' Zorzin insisted that his superior did everything he could to save the lives of the two Jesuit priests. But Yorio continued to claim that he had been betrayed by the Church.

In 2010, Bergoglio told a judge investigating human rights abuses during the military regime that as the head of the Jesuit order in Argentina he had no real power to protect other priests from being kidnapped by the junta, but insisted on saying that he had worked behind the scenes to win their freedom. In the same year, he was quoted in a book by his authorized biographers that he did everything in his limited powers to appeal to the military junta and, separately, to unnamed Church officials with more authority than him, to help free the men. He also testified before the judge that he tried to protect Yorio and Jalics, offering them shelter and protection at a time when any slum priest was in danger.

Yorio died in 2000 convinced he had been badly let down if not betrayed by his superior. But Jalics, who, after Argentina, went to live in a German monastery, in March 2013, a week after the papal election, issued a statement exonerating Bergoglio of any blame, after earlier holding him partly responsible for his detainment. Jalics said he was addressing reports that he and Yorio were imprisoned because Bergoglio had passed on information about them to the authorities. 'I myself was once inclined to believe that we were the victims of a denunciation,' Jalics said. '[But] at the end of the 90s, after numerous conversations, it became clear to me that this suspicion was unfounded. It is therefore wrong to assert that our capture took place at the initiative of Father Bergoglio.'

His comments followed a less categorical statement that he made soon after Pope Francis was elected. In that earlier comment, he said he and Bergoglio had reconciled and 'hugged solemnly' in 2000. But he also noted that he 'could not comment on the role played by Father Bergoglio in these events'. In his later statement, published on the official website of the Jesuit order in Germany, the eighty-six-year-old priest said that his earlier statements on 15 March 2013 had been misinterpreted by the media. He adamantly denied then that Bergoglio played any role in causing his five-month-long captivity alongside Yorio.

'As I made clear in my previous statement, we were arrested because of a catechist who worked with us first and later joined the guerrillas,' he explained. 'For nine months we never saw her again, but two or three days after she was detained, we were detained as well,' he continued. 'The official who interrogated me asked for my papers. When he saw that I was born in Budapest, he thought I was a Russian spy.' He explained his thoughts about Bergoglio's involvement:

In the Argentinean Jesuit congregation and in Catholic circles, false information spread in the years prior that claimed we had moved to the poor *barrios* because we belonged to the guerrillas. But that was not the case. I suppose these rumours were motivated by the fact that we were not immediately released. I was once inclined to think that we were the victims of a betrayal. But at the end of the 1990s, I realized after many conversations that this assumption was baseless. For this reason, it is wrong to assert that our capture happened because of Father Bergoglio.

Jesuits who knew Jalics underlined the critical importance of the encounter he had with Bergoglio in 2000, two years after his former Jesuit superior had been promoted to Archbishop of Buenos Aires. Exactly what was said has never been revealed, but the word 'reconciliation' gives rise to a plausible explanation that the Argentine asked for forgiveness from the Hungarian–born Jesuit for any harm perceived to have been done. Jalics, meanwhile, may have apologized for any unintended slander while pledging to forgive, if not to forget. The two may have accepted that the greater glory to God, to which all Jesuits sign up, could be served better by putting the past behind them for the sake of the unity of the Church.

One of the fullest early biographies of Bergoglio, by Paul Vallely, suggests that something of a conversion experience intervened between the Argentine's time as Jesuit superior and his appointment as bishop. However, further evidence that has come to light suggests that Bergoglio struggled over how best to put his faith into action throughout his time as a Jesuit priest – and that only when he became a bishop, and in particular Archbishop of Buenos Aires, did he begin to come to terms with his own self and reconcile himself with others. The more authority he was given the humbler he became, and the easier he found it to conquer fear.

The year 2000 proved an important crossing of the Rubicon for Bergoglio, as he followed his meeting with Jalics with other gestures of similar symbolic significance. Bergoglio was the only Church official to reconcile himself with Jerónimo Podestá, a former bishop known for his outspoken political views against the military as a priest and whose marriage to his former secretary had him strongly criticized by the Vatican. That same year, Bergoglio hoped to help draw a line in the sand by saying the Argentine Catholic Church needed 'to put on garments of public penance for the sins committed during the years of the dictatorship' in the 1970s.

Nevertheless the controversy over the Argentine Church's alleged complicity returned to cast a shadow over Bergoglio when he was elected pope, with the Jalics and Yorio story resurfacing courtesy of Verbitsky. Among those who lined up in Bergoglio's defence was the Jesuit historian Fr Jeff Klaiber. He told the US *National Catholic Reporter* that he interviewed fellow Jesuit Fr Juan Luis Moyano, who had also been imprisoned and deported by the Argentine military. According to *National Catholic Reporter*, Moyano told Klaiber that Bergoglio intervened on behalf of imprisoned Jesuits. Disagreements have continued to this day, not least within the Jesuit order, as to whether Bergoglio did as much as he should have for them and for others persecuted by the military.

According to Moyano, who died in 2006, and other witnesses who came forward after Pope Francis was elected, during the worst period of the military repression Bergoglio's main concern was to protect as best he could the Jesuit community in Argentina, by intervening, more belatedly in some cases than in others, on behalf of those priests who might be at risk and either sheltering them or getting them out of the country. Nello Scavo, an Italian journalist employed by the Italian Episcopal Conference, published a book called *Bergoglio's List* on the first anniversary of Pope Francis's election, claiming that an estimated 100 individuals were helped by Bergoglio to escape torture and certain death. Among those offered shelter in the main Jesuit seminary of San Miguel were three seminarians from the diocese of La Rioja following the suspected assassination of their bishop, Angelelli. At San Miguel they joined other escapees who used attendance of an extended course of Jesuit Spiritual Exercises as a 'screen behind which to hide' from those pursuing them.

One witness told Scavo: 'I saw [Bergoglio] helping many to leave the country. Quite a few came to San Miguel: they had come either as individuals or in groups. They would stay a few days and then they would disappear. They said they were there to do Spiritual Exercises. They were laymen that Bergoglio helped escape as best he could, risking a great deal.'

One case involved an individual who had a physical resemblance to Bergoglio. The Jesuit leader gave him his ID card and a priest's cassock, which allowed him to cross the frontier into Brazil. There were other cases such as that of the Jesuit priest, Julio Merediz, who was warned he was on the military's death list, but unlike Yorio and Jalics, followed Bergoglio's advice and left the slums, finding shelter in another Jesuit house. Another slum volunteer was Sergio Gubulin, a former student of Bergoglio from the University of Salvador. He was arrested on 11 October 1976 when the military raided the slum. His wife alerted Bergoglio who brought pressure on the authorities and had him released after eighteen days of detention, during which he was tortured.

Unlike Oscar Schindler, the German industrialist who helped mainly Polish Jews escape the concentration camps in the Second World War by offering them factory work, Bergoglio did not follow a premeditated plan. Those who were helped did not belong to any specific racial or political group, but were a small minority of threatened individuals who were lucky enough to benefit from the occasions when Bergoglio felt he could do something to help them. While there is no documentary evidence supporting the estimate that he saved 100, even this is a small number compared to more than 1,000 saved by Schindler, and the estimate of between 9,000 and 30,000 Argentines who 'disappeared' between 1976 and 1982.

In fairness, while authors like Scavo, writer of *Bergoglio's List*, saw themselves on a mission to exonerate the elected Pope Francis from accusations of collaboration, and engaged in a kind of retroactive whitewash, Bergoglio himself never claimed to have had a 'list'. Referring to the three seminarians from La Rioja, he played down his alleged heroism: 'They weren't hidden, but they were looked after, protected,' he told his authorized biographers. It took many years before Bergoglio said anything about his role in Argentina's Dirty War. In the same interview conducted a year before he became pope, which was carefully vetted before its publication, he was asked why he had taken such a long time to speak out. 'If I said nothing at the time, it was so as not to dance to anyone's tune, not because I had anything to hide,' he said.

One of his spiritual mentors, Juan Manuel Scannone, offered Scavo a different explanation: 'Scannone told me that his friend Jorge [Bergoglio] never liked talking about that period, because he didn't want to look as if he was whitewashing his name. Moreover he realized that what he had done was small compared to the magnitude of the disaster that Argentina lived through in those years, and against which the Church did not do enough.'

It is important to reach a judgement, in the context of what happened to the Catholic Church in Argentina at the time, about Bergoglio's own actions not just as a Jesuit priest, but as the head of his order, and the extent to which these stand up to moral scrutiny. An appraisal of Bergoglio not just as a Jesuit but as pope turns on what happened in these crucial years.

On 23 March 1976, before the coup, Mgr Adolfo Tortola, Vicar-General of the armed forces and the president of the Argentine Episcopal Conference, the main body of bishops, held a private meeting with the leading plotters, General Videla and Admiral Massera. He gave his veiled blessing to the overthrow of the elected if deeply flawed civilian government of Isabelita Perón, widow of the legendary populist General. The next day the military coup that was to unravel into the most brutal repression carried out in modern Latin American history was under way. Two months later on 15 May the Argentine bishops issued a public letter stating that while murder or abduction for political ends (a practice carried out by guerrillas, right-wing hit squads and state agents) could be considered a sin, the coup had been carried out for the 'common good'.

'Moreover, we should remember that it would be a mistake to believe,' the bishops continued, 'that the security forces can act with the purity of action of peacetime when there is already blood on the streets. It is necessary to accept some constraints on our liberties as demanded by the circumstances.'

Between 1976 and 1981, the Episcopal Conference issued four more pastoral letters that, while condemning the violation of human rights, at the same time implicitly accepted that there was a moral and social justification for the regime. During the same period the bishops sent four unpublicized messages to the junta. The messages were more specific in their concern about the 'disappeared', but nevertheless still erred on the side of compromise, if not collaboration.

After the collapse of the military regime in 1983, bishops defended their approach to the issue of human rights. Private messages and diplomatic language, they argued, were more effective in saving lives than outright confrontation with the authorities. At the same time they pointed to the particular political circumstances. The Catholic Church as an institution would not allow itself to be identified in any way with the left-wing guerrilla groups. The military was always quick to remind a demurring bishop that the 'terrorists' of the 1960s and 1970s had exercised their early militancy affiliated to university groups like Catholic Action and had received the formal blessing of priests linked to the Third World Priest Movement. Some bishops were even shown videos of interrogation sessions, during which prisoners confessed their links with certain priests.

However numerous the doctrinal and tactical reasons for the attitude of the Argentine Catholic hierarchy, the Church can only be really judged on results rather than motives. Numerous human rights activists insisted that many more lives would have been saved had the Church as an institution taken a more forceful and public stand during the period when journalists, trade unionists, judges, lawyers and politicians along with priests, nuns and some courageous individual bishops were silenced by intimidation, proscription and, in many cases, murder.

At no time during the military regime did the Argentine Church as an institution assume effective leadership of those who felt persecuted, as its equivalents did, for example, in Chile during the 1970s, or in El Salvador during the 1980s, where the Jesuit order took a particularly courageous stand against social injustice and human rights violations. In El Salvador, on 18 November 1989, six Jesuits, their housekeeper and her daughter were brutally murdered by government soldiers. The Jesuits were all teachers at the Central American University José Simeón Cañas (UCA) based in San Salvador, the capital city.

For several years UCA had been calling for economic and social reforms in order to bring an end to the bitter civil war between left and right that had claimed more than 70,000 lives, but it was seen as a hotbed of political militancy by the regime. The killings took place during a major offensive by left-wing guerrillas opposed to the government. The soldiers were ordered to shoot in cold blood by Lieutenant José Ricardo Espinosa, a former student of one of the priests at the local Jesuit school, the Externado San José. After shooting dead one of the Jesuits, the university rector Ignacio Ellacuría, they cut out his brains and spread them on the grass. While he served as rector, Ellacuría had often spoken out for the rights of the poor, insisting that the main mission of the university should be outside, not within its walls, alongside 'the majority who suffer inhumane conditions'.

In Argentina back in the 1970s, the Church as an institution, including the leadership of the Jesuit order, seemed to have no intention of seriously questioning the regime beyond a token intervention on behalf of some individuals. The human rights groups formed by the female relatives of the 'disappeared', the mothers, *Madres de La Plaza de Mayo*, and grandmothers, the *Abuelas*, had copious files of letters which distraught relatives had written to the Argentine Episcopal Conference asking for help and which were never answered. The *Madres* remember with bitterness how the doors of the cathedral in Buenos Aires were nearly always barred to them, particularly when they tried to escape from the baton charges of the riot police or the kidnap attempts of the death squads.

By contrast, leading members of the Argentina Church like the Cardinal Primate of Buenos Aires, Juan Carlos Aramburu, always accepted invitations from the military to attend public functions ranging from marches to *Te Deums* in which the unity of the militarized State achieved its ultimate religious endorsement. In 1980 Aramburu was invited to London along with two Chilean bishops. The latter took cheap lodgings in the Paddington area and spent much of their time visiting refugees. Aramburu, however, immersed himself in the pomp and security of the lavish Argentine ambassador's residence in Belgrave Square and made a point of avoiding all contact with fellow Argentines who had fled to England for political reasons.

The most blatant collaboration with the military regime was practised by military chaplains. They not only provided a theological context for the use of torture against alleged antichrists but actively acquiesced in the military's actions. One former detainee recalled the visit of a military chaplain during which a fellow prisoner cried out: 'Father, they are torturing me terribly during interrogations and I beg you to intercede to stop them from torturing me any more.' The priest replied: 'Well, my son, but what do you expect if you don't cooperate with the authorities interrogating you?'

Perhaps the most notorious case involved Fr Christian von Wernich, as recounted by a repentant former police officer who belonged to one of the task forces responsible for the 'disappeared'. The officer recalled how on one occasion he and his colleagues used the butts of their guns to beat two women and a man whom they had taken prisoner. The torture sessions and the subsequent killings – the three were given lethal injections by a police doctor – were witnessed by Fr von Wernich.

'The priest saw what had happened had shocked me and spoke to me telling me that what we had done was necessary; it was a patriotic act and God knew it was for the good of the country,' the policeman remembered.

Within the Argentine Catholic Church there was a minority of bishops, priests and nuns who were prepared to lay their lives on the line in defence of social and political justice during the military regime. Nuns and priests and other religious figures were kidnapped, tortured and killed. Others were forced into exile as were many Catholic lay volunteers. A bishop died in suspicious circumstances. The survivors included three outspoken bishops – Jaime Nevares of Neuquén, Miguel Hesayne of Viedma and Jorge Novak of Quilmes; and the Catholic laymen led by Adolfo Pérez Esquivel who in 1980 was given the Nobel Peace Prize for his stand on human rights.

The military regime had long since collapsed following the Falklands War of 1982, when in 2005 Pérez Esquivel appeared alongside Horacio Verbitsky and one of the *Madres de La Plaza de Mayo*, Marta Ocampo de Vazquez, as guests on an Argentine current affairs programme. A new pope was to be elected and Pérez Esquivel was asked about one of the cardinals whose name was beginning to circulate – the then Archbishop of Buenos Aires, Jorge Bergoglio. In his commentary Pérez Esquivel recalled the duplicity of many bishops who, when told about a detainee, would reassure a close relative that they would do everything on his or her behalf when in fact they did not do anything.

When asked about Bergoglio, without hesitation Pérez Esquivel answered: 'The attitude of Bergoglio is that of thinking that all those who worked alongside the poor were communists, subversives, and terrorists.' He then went on: 'A pope has to have very clear and concrete definitions. Bergoglio is intelligent, he is capable, but he is an ambiguous person. I hope the Holy Spirit is awake on the day of the election, and doesn't make a mistake.'

As things turned out, Bergoglio did not win the election. He came runner-up to Cardinal Ratzinger, who took the name of Benedict XVI, and succeeded him eight years later. Pérez Esquivel's view about Bergoglio appeared to have changed with the passage of time. 'The Pope had nothing to do with the dictatorship . . . he was not an accomplice,' he told the BBC in March 2013. The new pope, who served as Jesuit provincial from 1973 to 1979, 'was not among the bishops who were in the front line of the defence of human rights because he preferred a silent diplomacy to ask about the missing, about the oppressed'.

From the early Christians of the Roman Empire through to those today persecuted by Islamic fundamentalism, Church history is populated by individuals who have invoked their God-given right to kill others. But there are also many examples of those who have laid their lives passively on the line on account of their faith. In the words of the American Jesuit Fr Thomas Reese: 'In the face of tyranny, there are those who take a prophetic stance and die martyrs. There are those who collaborate with the regime. And there are others who do what they can while keeping their heads low.'

During Argentina's Dirty War, Jorge Bergoglio fell into the final category. It would take him years for his conscience to tell him it was not enough.

Chapter Nine
Bishop of Buenos Aires

Early one afternoon in October 1998, the serene and seemingly secure premises of the Argentine Catholic Church's most senior bishop, situated next to Buenos Aires Cathedral, had a surprising and not entirely welcome visitation from an investigating judge accompanied by a posse of officials and police.

The raid's timing – 2.30 p.m. – assured maximum coverage by the media as well as the attention of the public close to the scene. The nearby Plaza de Mayo was filled with employees who had just finished their lunch break. Its high-profile nature seemed a calculated attempt to gain maximum publicity for an ambitious judge bent on challenging the immunity and integrity of the highest figure in the Argentine Church.

The fact that the new Archbishop of Buenos Aires was the former head of the Argentine Jesuits, Jorge Bergoglio, and that his predecessor and mentor Antonio Quarracino had died six months earlier under a cloud of criminal suspicion, required urgent damage limitation. The raid, after all, was the result of the embroilment of the Church in what had become a major banking scandal. But Bergoglio was nowhere to be seen when the raid took place.

It seems likely that the then still media-shy Bergoglio had been tipped off, and had chosen wisely, not for the first or last time, not to be caught in the headlights of controversy. He was away, elsewhere in the capital, seemingly on a pastoral visit. However, his youthful and media-savvy spokesman Father Guillermo Marco, alerted by phone by his boss, was quickly on the scene and put on a robust show in his Archdiocese's defence. Marco told the gathered pack of journalists that they were witnessing the worst unwarranted assault on Church property since the mid-1950s when a group of anti-clerical supporters of General Perón had tried to torch the cathedral, claiming they were defending the President against an attempted coup by right-wing Catholics linked to the military.

The analogy may not have been quite to the liking of Bergoglio, who had always respected the memory of Perón as a 'man of the people', but the more politically conservative Marco – a diocesan priest from an upper-class Buenos Aires family who was not afraid to speak his own mind – performed like a master of spin, choosing a statement that painted an image of almost sacrilegious intrusion.

He went on to tell the gathered media that Bergoglio had acted with a great sense of transparency and accountability in the case and could not possibly be accused of breaking the law. Bergoglio had offered the investigating judge full cooperation including access to all pertinent financial records belonging to the Archbishopric – an offer, Marco claimed, the judge had ignored, choosing instead to fuel the publicity that was guaranteed by the raid. Marco suspected the dark hand of politically motivated anti-clericalism. For not only was there no suggestion that his new boss Bergoglio was under suspicion, but Bergoglio's mentor Archbishop Antonio Quarracino had also professed his innocence and had not been charged prior to his death.

'Bergoglio succeeded Quarracino in the middle of the storm . . . It was not an issue of institutional corruption involving the

Church but a crooked deal between the Trussos [the family who owned Banco de Crédito Provincial, BCP, the bank at the centre of the scandal] and a member of the clergy,' insisted Marco. 'We confronted the problem and proved that the Archdiocese had nothing to answer for . . . moreover the Archdiocese ended up a plaintiff together with the military insurance company Sociedad Militar Seguro de Vida (SMSV) against the Trussos and their bank.'

That is how, indeed, things turned out. However, long before the raid on his offices, Bergoglio would have been in no doubt about the seriousness of the case that was being investigated and was keenly aware that not only his own reputation but also that of the Church in Argentina would be severely damaged if he did not act quickly to calm the storm. So on the basis that the best line of defence is attack, no sooner had he been installed as Archbishop than Bergoglio had commissioned an independent audit of the Archdiocese's accounts by the international accountancy firm Price Waterhouse, which suggested that at worst Quarracino had been duped by a less than honest priest who happened to be employed as his private secretary.

The Price Waterhouse report had been completed and handed over to the investigating judge when the raid took place. The judge justified the action as part of an ongoing investigation into an alleged financial fraud involving the medium-sized Banco de Crédito Provincial, which had been declared bankrupt after making millions of dollars in bogus loans. The Archbishopric, a major client, had become embroiled along with the two main shareholders of the bank, close friends of the then Peronist President and the former governor of the Argentine province of La Rioja, Carlos Menem, who also had links to the Vatican.

Details of the scandal had hit local headlines a year earlier when it emerged that the BCP had defrauded thousands of clients, including a life assurance company that covered the savings of military personnel. Investigators had discovered that a money transaction involving $10 million supposedly handled by the bank between SMSV, the insurance company, and the Archbishop of Buenos Aires had been diverted to a mysterious third party and had not been accounted for.

The bank's principal shareholders, and from the outset prime suspects in the scam, were two brothers, Francisco and Pablo Trusso. The first had served as Argentine ambassador to the Holy See and adviser to a commission of cardinals, and was a known benefactor of Opus Dei, the politically influential international Catholic lay organization. The second was a former treasurer of Cáritas Argentina, the major charity run by the Argentina Catholic Church. A third brother, Juan Miguel, was the only one of three not to be a board member but he acted as a legal adviser to the bank as well as serving as vice-president of Cáritas.

Over the years the Trusso family had managed to win the friendship and trust of Quarracino, who had become a client of the bank as well as an unwitting facilitator of some of its more dubious transactions. Quarracino died of a heart attack on 28 February 1998 as the investigation into BCP was gathering pace. Four months earlier, on 1 November 1997, Pablo Trusso and nine directors of the bank had been arrested on suspicion of 'illegal association, multiple frauds, and falsification of documents'. Meanwhile, an international arrest warrant was issued for Francisco Trusso after he had reportedly fled Argentina to an unknown foreign location.

It later emerged that the Trusso brothers' father, Francisco Eduardo Trusso, had been involved with two other notorious bank failures in the 1980s. Trusso senior had been an adviser to the Banco de Intercambio Regional, whose liquidation in March 1980 provoked a financial crisis in Argentina leading to other bank runs that severely damaged the reputation of the Argentine banking sector. The conspiratorial web was fuelled still further by the fact that the patriarch of the Trusso family had also been a director of the Buenos

Aires branch of Banco Ambrosiano, the Italian bank linked to political and financial corruption involving Vatican funds during the 1970s.

The Trusso brothers were among a handful of prime suspects in the BCP case. They included Quarracino's private secretary, a priest called Roberto Toledo who had direct access to the accounts held on behalf of the Archbishopric and was also arrested on suspicion of 'fraudulent administration'.

Quarracino was devastated when the scandal broke and the stress of having to explain the Church's role and his own alleged innocence in the affair ended up killing him, recalled someone with close knowledge of the case. As investigators closed in on him, Quarracino issued a statement admitting that the Trussos had paid his expenses, but defending his role in the affair and denying any criminal impropriety:

> If having an account in a bank, trusting in its management, accepting an occasional gift, and billing expenses for occasional trips, while believing in friendship is a sin, then I accept, I sinned. But to go on to accuse me of complicity in dark transactions, involvement in a fraud that damages others, is to falsely submerge me in a quagmire which is causing me inexplicable and terrible pain.

Fr Marco, Quarracino's press spokesman whom Bergoglio inherited, did not doubt his sincerity, when interviewed for this book: 'The Trussos had a personal relationship with Quarracino and paid for a lot of his expenses. It was ridiculous to suggest, as early reports suggested, that the Archdiocese needed to borrow money when it actually had quite a lot of money. To suggest that the Archbishop needed to get a loan from an insurance company via a bank just didn't make sense.'

It was nonetheless a murky business into which the Archbishop had allegedly stumbled. Quarracino had told investigators that his signature on a document approving the fraudulent £10 million transaction – part of some $200 million of suspect transactions – was forged. Certainly Quarracino's death after being severely disabled by a heart attack left many unanswered questions. It handed his successor and protégé, Bergoglio, a potential poisoned chalice which threatened to challenge the exemplary reputation he had begun to build up since being appointed the most favoured of Quarracino's auxiliary bishops.

Pablo Trusso was acquitted after serving six months in jail. Mgr Roberto Toledo spent a day in jail but was never charged. While he lost his job at the Archdiocese of Buenos Aires, he eventually resumed lower profile duties elsewhere within the Argentine Church. In 2010, he was appointed parish priest of a church in Sarandí, a Buenos Aires suburb, with a court order on December 2013, ending all further criminal proceedings against him related to the BCP case.

Bergoglio's promotion to the highest ecclesiastical office in Argentina followed a period of mixed fortunes within his own order. Having been made the youngest ever head of the Jesuits in Argentina, on 31 July 1973, Bergoglio served for six years as provincial or head Jesuit in Argentina. His conservative theology and administrative authoritarianism – in contrast to the more liberal if ineffectual management of his predecessor O'Farrell – made him as many detractors as friends among other more progressive Latin American Jesuits. They felt that Bergoglio was too ambiguous in his attitude to issues of social justice and had not stood up sufficiently to the Argentine military regime.

Another close adviser to Fr Arrupe, the Provincial General or head of the Jesuit order, at the time was Fr Francisco Ivern, a native Spaniard who served many years both in Rome and as a priest in South America. Four years older than Bergoglio, the Catalan-born

Ivern was party to the reports that reached head office of the tensions provoked by Bergoglio's leadership.

'Bergoglio's time as provincial was marked by ambiguities and silences and the perception that he didn't take a clear stand against the military regime,' recalled Fr Ivern, before adding, 'He might have saved the lives of some Jesuits, but he wanted them to leave Argentina.' And yet, as Fr Ivern also remembered, those were turbulent times throughout Latin America for the order, with Arrupe at times more worried about the extreme political radicalism of some members of his order than the conservatism of Bergoglio. The latter's main priority was to remain loyal to the Pope, save some of his colleagues from unnecessary martyrdom and in the process impose some discipline within the organization.

Far from entering a period of exile from his own community, Bergoglio's influence and power within the Jesuit order in his own country endured. Bergoglio had developed a strong friendship with his immediate successor as provincial, Fr Andrés Swinnen. The two shared a respect for theological orthodoxy and supported the purge of radical elements within the order who had occupied key university posts and embraced liberation theology during a time of political and clerical upheaval. Both Bergoglio and Swinnen insisted that novitiates and priests wear traditional cassocks. They also were in favour of having students demonstrate their patriotism by daily singing the national anthem before the Argentine flag. Such was the empathy between the two men that Swinnen allowed Bergoglio to retain the keys to the provincial's office, and regularly sought his advice on key decisions.

In January 1980, Bergoglio flew to Dublin on what turned out to be a bleak beginning to a new decade in Ireland. Recession as well as the deep frost of winter gripped the streets. The euphoria surrounding the visit of Pope John Paul II a few months earlier had largely dissipated with Taoiseach Charlie Haughey making his infamous television address to the nation warning that the country was living 'way beyond our means'. Haughey's reputation was destined to be tarnished with revelations of corruption, embezzlement, tax evasion and a twenty-seven-year extramarital affair.

But neither the economic anguish faced by the nation nor the shortcomings of its prime minister would have been immediately evident to Bergoglio as the car transporting him from the airport took him into the fine Victorian residential area of Ranelagh, otherwise known as Dublin 6, the Irish capital's affluent suburb, before delivering him to the prestigious Jesuit Centre in the Milltown Institute. At the time, the college of philosophy on the rambling Sandford Road campus was a hive of academic activity, with Jesuit students coming from all corners of the earth to attend courses. It was there that Bergoglio settled into an English language course that was to prove very useful in his future years as pontiff.

Nobody who lives there today remembers meeting their Argentine colleague, and Bergoglio's official biographies and interviews omit any reference to this visit. But the July 1980 edition of the Jesuit bulletin, the *Irish Province News*, notes that among the 'constant stream of visitors who found hospitality with us we may mention Fr Jorge Bergoglio, ex Provincial of Argentina and Rector of our Theologate in Buenos Aires'. An old ledger belonging to the community reveals that on 21 January he went to the bursar and borrowed £14 to buy language tapes. The *Irish Independent* reported after the papal election in March 2013: 'At the time, Pope Francis was 43 and had just completed a seven-year spell as provincial (head) of the Jesuit order in Argentina. He left for Ireland at a time of profound danger in his home country, during the brutal military dictatorship.'

After the three-month study course, Bergoglio returned to Argentina in 1980 as the rector of the Philosophical and Theological Faculty of San Miguel, where he retained control and influence over a new generation of Jesuits. Despite the first stirrings of political opposition within the Peronist-controlled trade union movement and a continuing campaign from human rights groups, the junta had made militant dissidents 'disappear' either by summary execution or exile; the terrorist Dirty War was effectively at an end, with most key figures responsible for the worst brutality no longer in government. Jesuit life in Argentina was certainly very different to what it had been when Bergoglio was provincial in the 1970s when involvement in the slums or speaking out against the military regime risked a potential death sentence.

At San Miguel, Bergoglio earned the respect and loyalty of the young seminarians by insisting that they balance their studies with an experience of the outside world as long as they did not engage in radical politics. This had the young Jesuits regularly being sent out to the nearby poor neighbourhoods to celebrate Mass and participate in communal festivities of a religious nature. And in a recognition of the debt his spirituality owed to St Francis of Assisi, as well as to St Ignatius, Bergoglio transformed part of the extensive grounds of the Colegio Máximo into a dairy farm and vegetable garden. While conceived partly as an aid to contemplation, the project, which included breeding rabbits, also responded to a socio-economic consideration. Self-sufficiency helped the Jesuit community cope with Argentina's endemic inflation and, in particular, high food prices. But it also acted as a further bridge to the poor, helping to feed surrounding neighbourhoods, as part of a learning curve that Bergoglio felt some of his young charges from higher income families should follow in the course of their priestly formation.

Meanwhile, soon after becoming rector, Bergoglio obtained his friend Swinnen's approval for an extension of San Miguel's already impressive facilities to include a new lecture hall and library, financed by funds raised by the Jesuits among rich Catholic benefactors in Germany.

Bergoglio was much taken up and enthused with the new project when the Argentine forces surprised the world and invaded the British colonized Falklands Islands in April 1982. The Falklands or Las Malvinas, as they were known in Spanish, were a thinly populated archipelago in the South Atlantic, 300 miles from the Argentine mainland. Despite their small population of just over 1,200, the Falklands were of strategic interest as a staging post to the Antarctic. The sea surrounding the islands was also rich in fish and had potential oil reserves that had never been exploited. The subject of divergent claims of discovery and early colonization, sovereignty over the islands had been claimed by Argentina ever since Britain reasserted its rule in 1833.

However much the invasion shocked the British, its NATO partners and Latin American democrats, it was 'sold' by the junta to the Argentine public as a patriotic crusade blessed by God and the Virgin Mary. The junta's propagandists named the invasion Operation Rosario. The feast of the Virgin del Rosario (Virgin of the Rosary) was established in 1573 by Pope Gregory XIII to commemorate the crushing naval defeat of the Turks by the Catholic troops led by Don John of Austria at the Battle of Lepanto. The Argentine military commanders had convinced themselves that the infidel, personified by the colonial British, was about to suffer an equally heaven-sent defeat.

The equation between Argentine sovereignty and holy conversion had its precedent, and was deeply ingrained in the Argentine national consciousness. Argentine nationalist historians, whom Bergoglio read and much admired, devoted many pages to the first Spanish missionaries to Las Malvinas; the priests are portrayed as picture-book saints laying their sacramental rock in the heathen land. What was perceived as a subsequent decline of civilized life on the islands was blamed on the spiritual emptiness of British colonialism. Meanwhile, much was made of the fact that Jesuit priests had been among the inhabitants of Buenos Aires who had frustrated British attempts to seize control of the then Spanish colonies around the River Plate basin in 1806 and 1807.

During the Falklands War, just as Argentine bishops and priests had lent their tacit blessing to defence of 'Western Christian values' during the repression of political dissidence, they now established the theological validity of the claim to Las Malvinas in their veneration of popular religious culture, which Bergoglio felt very much part of his theology.

'The gaucho Virgin Mother is Mother of all men, but in a very special way the Mother of all Argentines, and has come to take possession of this land, which is also our land,' said the military's chaplain general, Mgr Desiderio Elso Colino, as he blessed a statue of the Virgin of Luján, along with eight crucifixes, generals, politicians, trade unionists and an estimated 10,000 troops on 7 April 1982 when General Mario Benjamín Menéndez was sworn in as the new military governor of the islands after a group of British marines and their governor Sir Rex Hunt had surrendered.

From that moment on, and as the British fought back to regain the islands, Argentine pilots hung rosaries round their sights before firing their Exocets at Royal Navy ships, and dedicated the shooting down of RAF planes to the Virgin of Luján; Argentine soldiers carried Bibles to protect themselves from the bullets; and military chaplains broadcast regularly, proclaiming their troops as heroes and saints. Bishops and priests, in their sermons to their flocks, defended Argentina from the charge that the military invasion on 2 April was a flagrant violation of the pro-British inhabitants' right to self-determination and international rules of law. The Argentine Church not only blessed the occupation of the islands but refused to acknowledge that human rights were an issue. 'All Argentines, in church and out, believe our cause is just. I think that the good God is content with this faith of ours,' commented Fr Augustin Luchía Puíg, the editor of *Esquiú*, a Catholic newspaper, to which every seminary subscribed and which throughout the war was sold aggressively outside Catholic churches all over Argentina.

During Sunday Masses, priests dedicated their sermons to a call for generous contributions to the 'Patriotic Fund', which was collected by the military for their war efforts but was never publicly accounted for. In their only major joint statement during the war, the bishops expressed their fear of a 'war of unforeseeable consequences' and referred to a papal condemnation of military conflict. However, by defending the legitimacy of Argentina's sovereignty claims, the bishops encouraged the military junta to prolong its military occupation of the islands.

The few churchmen who refused to toe the official line were censored by the military authorities and isolated by their peers, just as they had been during the years of the repression following the 1976 coup. Bishops Novak and Nevares, both of whom had been outspoken critics of the junta's human rights record, wrote their own position papers prior to a bishops' meeting, recommending that the Church adopt a more explicitly pacifist line while at the same time maintaining its political distance from the regime. Novak warned that the moral, cultural and economic costs of the invasion could be irreparable. However courageous the military action, he wrote, it lacked 'wisdom and prudence'. The papers were discarded by the other bishops and were never included in the agenda for discussion at their meeting.

Bergoglio refrained from making any public comments and has left no apparent paper trail as to his views expressed within his order or to others. However, he strongly supported his country's claim of sovereignty over the islands. His feelings on the subject surfaced ten years later, on April 2012, when as Archbishop of Buenos Aires he celebrated Mass on behalf of dead and surviving Argentine war veterans, many of whom were represented by an association of ex-combatants led by a former Army intelligence officer who had served under the juntas. 'Let us pray for those who have fallen, sons of the fatherland who went out to defend the fatherland, to claim as theirs what had been usurped [by the British],' Bergoglio said, speaking at a special service for the veterans held in the cathedral.

Not acknowledged at the ceremony was the contribution that Britain's victory in the Falklands War had made to the collapse of military rule and the transition to democratically elected government.

Bergoglio's time as rector of San Miguel continued through the Falklands War. The Jesuit watched the rapidly shifting political landscape beyond the seminary gates without becoming directly part of it even if he, like millions of Argentines, felt emotionally behind the cause of Las Malvinas. But the historic visit by Pope John Paul II in the final days of the war, prior to Argentina's surrender, would have an enduring impact on the future Pope Francis when, in later years, he reflected on the Vatican's role as peacemaker and its challenges, not least when it came to dealing with the nationalistic rulers of his own country and other governments who fought over disputed territory.

Pope John Paul II arrived in Argentina on 11 June 1982. He kissed the ground at Buenos Aires's Ezeiza airport and was greeted by General Leopoldo Galtieri, the then head of the military junta. 'At this moment, humanity should question itself once again about the absurd and always unjust phenomenon of war, on whose stage of death and pain still stands the negotiating table which could and should have prevented it,' Pope John Paul II told the Argentine nation in his first broadcast speech. He went on to stress that his visit, like the one he had just made to Britain, had no political overtones. 'It is simply a meeting between the father of the faith and his suffering sons . . . I shall pray that the governments of both sides and the international community will find ways of avoiding damage, heal the wounds of war, and find the necessary solutions for peace.'

It was a clear message of papal authority in a Catholic country. It was also a plea from the Polish Pope of the cold war for reconciliation between an instinctively anti-communist regime and a leading member of NATO as part of one of the most challenging diplomatic initiatives of the modern papacy. Just four years earlier, in the run-up to Christmas 1978, Vatican mediation authorized by Pope John Paul II had brought Argentina and Chile back from the brink of war over a separate sovereignty dispute involving the Beagle Channel.

The Falklands War presented the Vatican diplomacy with an unusual diplomatic scenario. The Pope's visit to Argentina – described as a pilgrimage – had been hastily arranged at the last minute to dampen Argentine anger at Pope John Paul II's visit to the UK. Because of the Pope's sensitivity to the generally pro-Argentina feelings of the Italian immigrant community in particular, he had sent word to the Catholic Archbishop of Westminster, Basil Hume, that because of the Falklands War he had been left with no option but to postpone a long-planned trip to England. The Cardinal was bitterly disappointed. He regarded the papal visit – the culmination of years of preparation – as of historic ecumenical importance, aimed, as it was, at building bridges with the Church of England. Rather than accept the decision to postpone the visit as final, the Cardinal had a select group of influential English Catholics, led by Derek Worlock, the dynamic Archbishop of Liverpool, discreetly negotiate with the Vatican for the Pope to visit Britain and Argentina. Arrangements were also made for a Mass in Rome jointly celebrated by Argentine and British bishops.

Following his arrival at Buenos Aires airport, Pope John Paul II's motorcade travelled along the main highway into the capital, flanked by large enthusiastic crowds, and arrived at the cathedral. There, at a service for priests, nuns and bishops of the Latin American Church, Bergoglio heard the Pope talk again about reconciliation and the difference between patriotism and nationalism, with the former based on feelings of love, while the latter provoked a need to conquer and suppress the other. 'Genuine love of your nation may lead some of you to sacrifice, but at the same time it must take into account the patriotism of others, so that both can peaceably communicate with each other and enrich each other in a spirit of humanism and Catholicism,' he said.

Later the Pope joined the members of the military junta in the presidential palace, the Casa Rosada, just across the square. Such was the enthusiasm shown for him by the crowds outside that the Pope acceded to popular demand and stepped out onto the balcony to wave to them, pointedly alone. But what followed demonstrated the military regime's determination to exploit the situation for political ends. The crowd could only see the Pope, a striking symbol of peace as well as personal authority, but the state-controlled TV cameras, which were giving live coverage, filmed from the inside looking out, deliberately distorting the perspective. The viewer saw a large enthusiastic crowd and the three members of the ruling junta – General Galtieri, Admiral Jorge Anaya and Brigadier-General Basilio Lami Dozo – standing just behind him, as if they too were on the balcony being cheered by the crowds.

Later that day the Pope was taken through the suburbs of the city to the sanctuary of the Virgin of Luján, which Bergoglio in common with millions of Argentines had venerated since childhood. It is the Lourdes of Argentina. The official TV commentator lost little time in spinning the occasion in propaganda terms. He reminded televiewers that the Virgin of Luján was a very special miracle worker who was credited with having helped local forces repel British troops when, twice in the early nineteenth century, they tried to seize Buenos Aires. The Virgin was also Captain-General of the Argentine armed forces. Throughout the Falklands War, Argentine air force pilots had offered her bits of Harrier jets in thanksgiving.

However, John Paul II ignored every attempt to exploit his visit for the junta's narrow political aims, seemingly finding synchronicity with the large crowds at Luján who, far from jingoistic warmongers, seemed in their majority transformed into faithful Catholics on an anti-war pilgrimage with their spiritual father. 'How beautiful it is to watch . . . the messenger of peace come down from the mountain,' sang an estimated one million Argentines gathered there. 'We want peace, we want peace,' they chanted.

The next day, 12 June, Bergoglio went with the staff and students of the Máximo to an open-air Mass near Palermo Park in a northern neighbourhood of Buenos Aires, again before vast crowds (two and a half million) as well as officialdom and clergy, where Pope John Paul II dedicated his sermon to the youth of Argentina. He did so conscious there were fewer younger men in their twenties and thirties there than would have been usual. There was a generation languishing in trenches, or behind barbed wire, or in unmarked graves, many 'disappeared'.

On the Falklands Islands, British troops on Mount Tumbledown and Wireless Ridge prepared for their final assault on the young Argentine conscripts huddled in defensive positions round the capital, Port Stanley. In Palermo Park, the Pope's words were a message of peace and renewal in a country traumatized by its recent history: 'Do not let hope wither your generous energy, and your capacity for understanding.' In Argentina, at that moment in history, to understand was to realize that the war was over, and with it the military regime. Like the vast majority of his fellow countrymen, Bergoglio believed that the Malvinas were part of Argentina – but by then the disillusion with the junta's conduct of the war had become widespread and Bergoglio held the authority of John Paul II in huge respect.

A year earlier the Pope, while convalescing from an attempt on his life by Turkish national Mehmet Ali Ağca in St Peter's Square, had imposed his own personal delegate, the Italian Jesuit Paulo Dezza, on the Jesuit order after Arrupe, who had been Provincial General since 1965, suffered a cerebral thrombosis that left him partly paralysed and increasingly without speech. The papal intervention angered many Jesuits who felt it was a breach of their constitutional right to elect their own general – but there is no evidence that Bergoglio was among them. In fact, while a few Jesuits quit, the order as a whole exhibited exemplary obedience. Nor did Bergoglio raise any objections when in February 1982 John Paul II told a meeting of leading Jesuits in Rome that the order needed to ensure a distinctly 'priestly' engagement in the quest for social justice as well as a rigorous formation that was 'spiritual, doctrinal, disciplinary, and pastoral'.

In 1983, the Pope finally allowed a General Congregation to be held, the thirty-third in the order's history, which duly elected a mild, less controversial figure, Dutch-born Fr Pere-Hans Kolvenbach, as the new Superior General. Fr Kolvenbach was to remain in office for the next twenty-five years, during which, according to the Jesuit historian Norman Tanner, 'the Holy See's confidence in the society was much improved', even if the number of Jesuits, which had gone on a downward curve after Vatican II, continued to decline.

Argentina's humiliating military defeat in the Falklands War initiated a period of political and economic instability as one military junta gave way to another and an attempt to delay a return to civilian rule fuelled growing strikes and demonstrations. But among the politicians was a charismatic lawyer, Raúl Alfonsín, who was convinced he could change Argentina for the good.

In 1972, the year before Bergoglio was elected Jesuit provincial, Alfonsín had formed Renovación y Cambio (Renovation and Change) – a social democratic faction within the centrist Radical party, one of whose earlier presidents, Arturo Illia, had been toppled by a military coup in 1966. Elected as a young congressman for the provincial capital of La Plata in 1958, Alfonsín watched with increasing despair as Argentine politics lurched through a seemingly endless cycle of repression and economic crisis.

But by the end of military rule, Alfonsín was one of the few major party figures to emerge with integrity, having defended victims of human rights violations and refusing to back the military invasion of the Falklands on the grounds that it diverted attention from the real political and economic challenges facing the country. Alfonsín's personal prestige and the activities of what in effect became a 'shadow' government in waiting gave Renovación y Cambio a strategic advantage, strengthening their hold on the Radical party and widening the gap with the traditionally powerful Peronist party once the opportunity to make a bid for power arose.

On 5 December 1982, five months after the Argentine military collapse in the Falklands War, Alfonsín was among the most popular politicians that joined a mass pro-democracy demonstration, which included human rights groups, trade unionists, students and the few churchmen – bishops and priests – who had put their head above the parapet and openly denounced the repression at its height. Bergoglio was not among them.

The resounding chants of 'Liberty, liberty' and 'Dictatorship is going to end' underlined the essentially political nature of the 'march for life', which included support for an investigation into the 'disappeared' and for those responsible to be brought to justice. With sectors of the military determined to hang onto power, the apparatus of the repressive State still intact, and publicly exposed collaborators of the regime, including priests and bishops, worried about how they too might be held accountable, these were tense times and the Jesuit community was not immune.

Old divisions among Jesuits provoked by Bergoglio's authoritarian style of leadership and perceived theological conservatism resurfaced. One of the most unresolved conflicts was that between Bergoglio and a progressive Argentine Jesuit called Fernando Storni, who was rector of the Catholic University in Córdoba when its departments in the main Jesuit novitiate were closed down by order of Bergoglio when he was provincial in the mid-1970s.

Bergoglio subsequently had Storni removed from his post as publishing editor and director of CIAS, the key think tank, magazine publisher and study group the Jesuits ran in Buenos Aires. Storni was transferred far from the capital to the remote frontier city of Posadas, near the border with Paraguay and Brazil, and the region where the first Jesuit mission to the Guaraní Indians had been established in 1609.

The conflict between the two Jesuits remained unresolved when Alfonsín was swept to power as leader of a reformed Radical party in the presidential election of 30 October 1983 after an impressively organized campaign. The defeated Peronist candidate, Ítalo Lúder, a former head, during Perón's time, of the country's penitentiary system, proved lacklustre, and his party struggled to contain its internal divisions.

Alfonsín's victory showed Bergoglio – with his mixed record during the military regime, theological orthodoxy and reputation within his own order as an authoritarian – to be out of step with the times, while providing his nemesis Storni with an opportunity to come in from the cold and into the mainstream of political life.

As a Jesuit contemporary of both, Fr Ignacio Pérez del Viso recalled: 'While Bergoglio, like many Argentine Jesuits of his generation and younger ones, was Peronist in his sympathies . . . Storni was not. Instead he supported the Radical party which under Alfonsín seemed to him to represent more universal values.'

From the early months of Alfonsín's government, Storni advised the newly elected president on ethical questions and relations with the Church, and raised no objections to a new divorce law in a country where the Church had turned a blind eye to the separation of thousands of Catholic couples. Storni was evidently out of step with the Argentine hierarchy. But what particularly angered some of the bishops were other Alfonsín appointments, which they suspected sprang from an anti-clerical tendency within his party.

'Broadly speaking, and with a few exceptions, the bishops were more in favour of Peronism and couldn't stomach Alfonsín as president for appointing a woman to lead relations with the Church, and a Jew in charge of cultural affairs. The Jew they put up with, but they found having to deal with a woman offensive,' recalled Fr Ignacio.

In his pre-election manifesto Alfonsín devoted several pages to analysing the phenomenon of Perón's rise to power. Although adamant that Perón's governance smacked of authoritarian corporatism that emulated traits of European fascism, Alfonsín paid tribute to his ability to engage with nationalist sentiment and to communicate with the poor and disenfranchised. 'Perón knew how to convey to his people a message of hope in the language they understood,' Alfonsín wrote. The assessment could well apply to Alfonsín's own emergence on the political stage following Argentina's Falklands defeat.

In 1985, during Alfonsín's first year in power, Bergoglio kept a discreet if cordial distance from the President with whom he struggled to see eye to eye politically. Instead Bergoglio focused on organizing and chairing a well-attended conference at San Miguel where there was evidence of the growing influence in Argentine Jesuit circles of what came to be known as the 'theology of the people'. This emphasized the importance of pastoral activity focused on the poor, not least in the shanty towns, and celebrated popular Catholic culture, but disengaged from the Marxist analysis and call for revolutionary change of liberation theology.

With the so-called theology of the people, which he drew from the writings of other Argentine and Uruguayan theologians, Bergoglio hoped to relegate to history the turbulent times around the 1976 coup during which Jesuits were among priests who felt it their moral duty to ally themselves with those involved in political action.

In 1986, the Superior General of the Jesuits, Fr Kolvenbach, appointed a new head of the Jesuits in Argentina. Fr Swinnen was replaced by Fr Victor Zorzin, who had loyally served as Bergoglio's deputy when he was provincial but who now sensed certain disquiet within the Jesuit HQ in Rome with Bergoglio's divisive legacy. Rather than deal with the issue straight away, he agreed to Bergoglio's request for a break from his duties at San Miguel and a short study leave abroad so he could improve his language skills and deepen his theology.

In 1986 Bergoglio spent several months at the Sankt Georgen Graduate School of Philosophy and Theology near Frankfurt, Germany, while considering possible dissertation topics. Also living in Germany at the time was Fr Francisco or Franz Jalics, one of the two Jesuit priests who had been arrested in Argentina during the Dirty War and subsequently released in controversial circumstances that raised questions about Bergoglio's role. While the other Jesuit Orlando Yorio had left the order, with little resistance from his superiors, Jalics was persuaded to remain a Jesuit by his colleagues in Germany where he had originally studied. No record has come to light that Bergoglio met Jalics at this stage, which suggests that one or the other or both felt it too early to seek the reconciliation that would occur several years later.

What is known is that among the subjects Bergoglio investigated while studying in Germany was the work of the priest Romano Guardini, the twentieth-century German Catholic philosopher. Guardini wrote on the importance of recognizing God as the authority of human life in defining the true self in modern society. This influenced several major Catholic writers and theologians including Flannery O'Connor, Thomas Merton, Walter Kasper and Karl Rahner. After the rise to power of Hitler's National Socialists, Guardini famously criticized Nazi anti-Semitism and the religious justification of violence. His thoughts would influence Bergoglio in his later constructive engagement with the Jewish community in Argentina and helped strengthen his opposition to violent political action.

There are some interesting parallels between Guardini and

Bergoglio: they came from Italian immigrant families, studied chemistry, and pursued their Catholic faith in challenging political and social circumstances. The focus of Bergoglio's studies while in Germany was meant to be *Der Gergansatz* (Contrast), a study of Marx and Hegels's theory of dialectics – a method of argument as a way of resolving disagreement – as applied to Church reform. In his book *The Great Reformer*, Austen Ivereigh suggests that Guardini's text was 'of a piece with [Bergoglio's] core underlying interest in politics and institutional reform, and helped to shape what as cardinal he would promote as a "culture of encounter"'.

And yet Bergoglio cut short his studies, returning to Buenos Aires without seeing out his first year in Frankfurt. The precise reasons why Bergoglio acted thus are unclear. This remains one of several key episodes in his life that authorized biographies and interviews have blurred or left unanswered. What is known about the circumstances suggests the decision sprung from practical as much as spiritual reasons.

While in Germany, Bergoglio visited the Jesuit church of Sankt Peter am Perlach in the Bavarian city of Augsburg, where he saw *Maria Krotenloserin* (*Mary, Untier of Knots*), an early eighteenth-century painting of the Virgin Mary. The painting, by a relatively unknown artist named Johann Georg Melchior Schmidtner, measures six feet in height and almost four feet in width. It depicts Mary suspended between heaven and earth, resplendent with light. The Holy Spirit in the form of a dove is above her head while her feet crush the head of a serpent, representing the devil. The most striking image is that of the Virgin untying a thread full of knots passed to her by one angel, while giving the unknotted thread to another angel.

The painting was informed by a locally popular story, dating from the early seventeenth century, about a nobleman, Wolfgang Langenmantel, who was suffering a marriage crisis with his wife Sophia and had sought the counsel of Fr Jakob Rem, a Jesuit priest.

Rem asked Langenmantel to bring the white ribbon used in his wedding ceremony and prayed over it for the couple's reconciliation. His prayer was inspired by what had been written by the second-century saint, Irenaeus: 'The knot of Eve's disobedience (in the Garden of Eden) was loosened by the obedience of Mary (as the Mother of God).' Wolfgang and Sophia subsequently reconciled and their marriage survived.

After praying before the painting, Bergoglio picked up a pile of *Maria Krotenloserin* prayer cards, which he later took back to Argentina and periodically distributed to friends and followers, usually men or women in some kind of emotional distress. 'Cast your eyes of compassion upon me, and see the snarl of knots that exist in my life,' went the prayer. 'Mary, my mother, I entrust to your loving hands the entire ribbon of my life. In your hands there is a knot which cannot be undone.'

While the devotion was initially localized to Germany, it took on new life – and publicity – during Ukraine's Chernobyl nuclear power plant disaster in 1986 when victims were reported to have sought help through the intercession of Mary, Untier of Knots. The first chapel outside Germany to be named in her honour was constructed in 1989 in Styria, Austria. (These observations I owe to a Jesuit priest, Fr Hedwig Lewis, who is an author of psycho-spiritual books and is a devoted follower of Mary, Untier of Knots.)

During the 1990s a replica of the painting, known in Spanish as *Maria Desatanudos*, was hung in San José del Talar, a church in Buenos Aires. It became a place of pilgrimage, which in turn fuelled an international cult of devotion with special prayers calling for Mary, Untier of Knots's intercession in cases of mental or physical suffering or spiritual doubt.

I owe a debt to British journalist and author Paul Vallely who was the first to draw attention to the link between the Marian painting and Bergoglio's spirituality, making *Untying the Knots* the title of his book on Pope Francis, published within weeks of his election. Austen Ivereigh would develop the theme, asserting that Bergoglio's prayers in the chapel in Augsburg were directed towards trying to work out how best he could pursue his vocation as a priest. Despite the divisions he had caused as provincial, and the doubts he felt about his role as a Jesuit, he now prayed that his faith in God's authority would see him through.

'During those hours in the bare stone church chilled by the coming Bavarian winter,' Ivereigh wrote in *The Great Reformer*, 'he passed his prayer, his knot to the angel, who passed it to the Virgin, who gently untied it and passed it to the other angel, who took it to Buenos Aires, where Bergoglio followed.'

There is no evidence provided by Ivereigh of cause and effect here – simply the subjective supposition of a Catholic author who holds his subject in unwavering reverence. From a non-religious perspective, I think it is equally fair to speculate that Bergoglio was at this stage feeling some of the psychological pressures that other Jesuits have experienced in trying to keep to the strict training and discipline of the order. For example, in his book *The Other Side of the Mountain*, the English Jesuit Gerald O'Mahoney described how his 'search for God' involved him coming through five nervous breakdowns. One period of 'darkness' was the 'lack of joy' he felt when studying philosophy compared to reading literature, and how he suffered, during a period of relatively isolated study, the absence of familiar colleagues and people. Add to this a rather sudden displacement from a position of authority to anonymous status in a foreign land, and perhaps one begins to understand more of what Bergoglio might have been going through.

Certainly Bergoglio has never revealed exactly what went through his mind when he was in Germany, still less while he was in private prayer, beyond confessing that at one point he felt homesick. While in Frankfurt, working on his thesis, he would take a stroll in the evenings to the nearest cemetery, from where he could see the international airport. As Bergoglio told the authors Rubin and Ambrogetti in *The Jesuit*: 'One time I bumped into a friend who asked what I was doing, and I replied, "Waving to the planes. I'm waving to the planes bound for Argentina."'

Rather than spend the minimum three years researching and writing his PhD thesis as required by his assigned university, Bergoglio quit his studies in Germany in December 1986 and returned to Buenos Aires, having spent less than a year away from Argentina. Some Argentine Jesuits who were critical of Bergoglio were not best pleased to see him back and were genuinely surprised. But far from being a spur-of-the-moment decision, Bergoglio had been in discreet communication with his allies among the Jesuits to ensure a soft rather than a crash landing back in familiar territory.

On his return, according to arrangements discussed in advance with his friend, the former deputy and now provincial Victor Zorzin, he found a room waiting for him in the Colegio del Salvador, the prestigious private school the Jesuits ran in central Buenos Aires. Treated as a special guest by its rector Luis Ignacio De Maussion, Bergoglio was invited to take a teaching post while finding time, if he so wished, to pursue his doctorate (although there is no evidence that he ever completed his PhD). Fr Ernesto López Rosas, another friend who was the superior at the Colegio Máximo in San Miguel and shared Bergoglio's theological ideas at the time, re-established Bergoglio's links with the training seminary. He was given a job in the Faculty of Theology, teaching pastoral work to a new generation of Jesuit priests.

Then, within three months of his return from his German academic 'exile', in March 1987 Bergoglio accepted another influential appointment, this time as the Argentine province's procurator general. This made him in effect a special adviser to the Jesuit Provincial General Kolvenbach, with the task of collecting intelligence from Jesuits houses, schools, seminaries and universities around Argentina and feeding it directly to the Jesuit HQ in Rome.

The information provided by the so-called 'procurator general' in each country was meant to supplement the reports that the provincials periodically also had to send in. It was supposed to flag up any pressing issues that might require the calling of a special deliberative congregation or conference.

A month later, in April 1987, Pope John Paul II flew into Buenos Aires to celebrate the first World Youth Day to be held outside Rome. The biannual event was instigated by Pope John Paul II in 1985 as a way of giving fresh impetus to the Catholic faith's reach to young people internationally as the attractions of Marxism faded along with the cold war. In the same year, Mikhail Gorbachev became leader of the USSR and began to reform the Soviet system by allowing *perestroika* (competition in business) and *glasnost* (freedom). In terms of internal Argentine politics, the visit did not carry the same potential as the Pope's previous visit towards the end of the Falklands War. However, the charismatic pontiff cut an impressive figure – almost like an ageing rockstar – as his Popemobile motored through the crowds formed by thousands of enthusiastic youths from all corners of the world, and with a particularly strong local contingent of Latin Americans, not least Argentines.

The event was organized by the Vatican-based Argentine cardinal Eduardo Pironio, who ensured that his friend Bergoglio met the Pope for the first time at a meeting with Christians of different denominations. Of his brief meeting with Pope John Paul II, Bergoglio would many years later tell those in the Vatican considering making the Polish pontiff a saint that what most struck him then was his gaze, that of a 'good man'. As Bergoglio immersed himself among the huge crowds of young people, he may have recalled the enthusiasm his grandmother Rosa had for the International Eucharist Congress in 1934, and he must have hoped that a Catholic revival, based on popular Christianity, was well underway.

No one could have imagined, least alone himself at that stage, that it would take another three decades for the papacy to touch young people with anything like such enthusiasm.

For a while Bergoglio seemed restored to a privileged status at the centre of Argentine Jesuit life, a position almost as influential as his appointment as provincial in 1973–9. He moved quickly to re-establish his network of contacts with Jesuit novitiates, priests and rectors scattered around Argentina, with total freedom to meet and engage with them. The process, however, turned into a double-edged sword. While still popular among the Jesuits he had helped form and promoted, he stirred long-standing resentments among those who felt they had been censored or passed over in some way during his years as provincial and at the Colegio Máximo de San Miguel during which he had exercised his authority.

It was during this period, while giving a retreat in Ignatian spirituality at the Colegio Máximo that Bergoglio first caught the attention of Mgr Quarracino, who was by then being fast-tracked up the Argentine clerical ladder by Pope John Paul II – as a bishop he was well in line with the Vatican's doctrinal teachings and an able communicator.

Quarracino attended one of Bergoglio's retreats and was impressed not only by the Jesuit's spirituality but his record of imposing discipline. Such impressions would play in Bergoglio's favour eventually. But in 1990, such was the growing rumour of internal dissent provoked by Bergoglio's restoration, that two former close collaborators withdrew their support. In April 1990 López Rosas, the rector of the Máximo, removed him from his teaching post, while Zorzin, who was provincial from 1986 to 1991, thought it best to remove him from Buenos Aires altogether for a while and send him to the northern city of Córdoba. This broke the effective duopoly of power that Bergoglio and his friend Fr Swinnen had enjoyed over the Colegio Máximo de San Miguel and the capital for two decades.

Zorzin and Ignacio García Mata, his successor as Argentine provincial in 1991–7, considered it their mission to try to ensure greater unity across generations in the Jesuit order. This meant appeasing some of the less conservative Jesuits who had fallen foul of Bergoglio and Swinnen's authoritarian rule. During their governance, a whispering campaign questioning Bergoglio's personality and conduct spread across the Jesuit communities in South America and filtered into the order's HQ in Rome.

Bergoglio's enemies followed him to Córdoba, as did his friends. One of Bergoglio's disciples, a young Jesuit called Fr Angel Rossi, recalled how rumours began to spread that the reason Bergoglio had been removed from Buenos Aires was that he was mentally unstable. Rossi told the journalists Javier Cámara and Sebastián Pfaffen, who investigated the Córdoba period, that during the funeral of Rossi's grandmother a Catholic layman with close connections with the Jesuit community approached him and pointed to Bergoglio, who was then praying silently by her coffin. 'What a shame that that man is mad!' the layman said. Rossi looked at him and said: 'If that man is mad, what is there left for me?'

However, Bergoglio's eventual 'exile' from Buenos Aires was not as dramatic or damaging as some writers have portrayed it. Bergoglio himself as Pope Francis told Cámara and Pfaffen in a private audience in September 2014: 'I would not use the "dark night" to describe my experience; it wasn't as bad as that. The "dark night" (of the soul) is for saints. I am just a poor guy. You could say I went through a period of purification.'

While celebrated initially by his antagonists as representing a demotion, Bergoglio's transfer to Córdoba did not exactly send him into purdah. Córdoba, 400 miles north of Buenos Aires and linked by regular train and flights with the capital, was not a depopulated outback like some of the starker northern regions of Jujuy or Salta, or of Tierra del Fuego in the southernmost tip of the continent, where Bergoglio would have found himself cut off and forgotten within a relatively short period. Córdoba was Argentina's second largest city with a strong clerical tradition, not least as the foundation city for the early Jesuit missionary activity in Paraguay and one of the bulwarks in the country of the Catholic Church since the days of the Spanish Empire, where the Jesuit presence and influence over education and local politics had endured. Throughout history the city had also proved a good template for national politics, anticipating some of its more dramatic developments, as when in 1970 a violent clash between students and security forces foretold the future guerrilla warfare between Argentina's radicalized Peronist youth and the armed forces.

Bergoglio's time in the main Jesuit residence in Córdoba was characterized by a life of spirituality. He had an increasing engagement with active pastoral work involving visitors who felt marginalized by society in a far more extreme way than Bergoglio felt ostracized by some of his former Jesuit colleagues in Buenos Aires. Years later, Bergoglio recalled how his dark mood would lift whenever he listened and forgave the prostitutes who asked him to hear their confession. He said he found in those women 'humble hearts damaged by the circumstances of life', and that his attitude towards them 'was always one of understanding not condemnation'.

Bergoglio recalled his period in Córdoba hearing confessions and helping out in parish work as one of a 'great internal crisis'. Word had reached his Jesuit superiors in Rome that the influence he had exercised over his fellow priests in Argentina had caused internal tensions and that the Jesuit order in Argentina was facing a deep split between his supporters and those he had alienated. In the Jesuit Curia in Rome, it was felt only belatedly that perhaps the best solution might be to bring in an outsider as provincial to break with the closely knit power relationships that governed the order internally in Argentina.

The man chosen as firefighter was Fr Álvaro Restrepo, an

amiable as well as intelligent Colombian Jesuit who was widely respected within the Jesuit order in Latin America. While based in Rome at the Jesuit HQ as a younger priest, he had proved himself a popular and effective adviser on Latin America when Fr Arrupe was Provincial General, and had gone on to manage with skill and sensitivity the extensive Jesuit presence in Colombia, one of the most politically and social challenging countries on the continent.

Of the same generation as Bergoglio, the Colombian came without his Argentine political baggage, and was seemingly more reconciled to the suggested reforms emanating from Vatican II, not least an unambiguous commitment to social justice and greater internal democracy within Church institutions.

'When I arrived in Argentina,' Restrepo recalled later, 'I expected to find a division between modernists and reactionaries. But I discovered that the problem was one of leadership. The Argentine gets very easily attached to, and needs a leader, and at some point there seemed to be different kinds of leadership. Some followed Jorge Mario [Bergoglio], others, the younger Jesuits, wanted a generational change at the top.'

Bergoglio's leadership, in other words, had proved as divisive as that of that other 'conductor' Perón, whose ideology and conduct he had much admired in his youth. It had taken an outsider to identify a very Argentine problem.

By 1997, when Restrepo was appointed as García Mata's replacement as Jesuit provincial in Argentina, Bergoglio had already been thrown a lifeline that lifted him from the depression he had periodically sunk into during his two-year stint in Córdoba. His rescuers were not fellow Jesuits, but the higher echelons of the institutional Church. On 27 June 1992, he was ordained Auxiliary Bishop of Buenos Aires by the capital's Archbishop Quarracino, with the blessing of John Paul II. He also had the strong support of Mgr Ubaldo Calabresi, the papal nuncio in Buenos Aires who had known Bergoglio for some years and held him in high regard, valuing his spirituality, loyalty to the authority of the Vatican and administrative experience.

Thus while Bergoglio may have been thrown into bouts of depression and felt betrayed, as he had once been alleged to have betrayed his own Jesuit brothers, his stay in Córdoba proved relatively short term. As a key auxiliary bishop, he would be entrusted with the task of managing the pastoral work of the diocesan priests spread out across the parishes and shanty towns of the capital.

A theological liberal in his early days as a young priest, Quarracino had become increasingly conservative during the papacy of John Paul II and in 1983 was elected as a safe pair of hands as the president of the Latin American Bishops Conference (CELAM), with the Vatican's blessing. John Paul II promoted him to the Archdiocese of La Plata, and then in 1990 to the Archdiocese of Buenos Aires as Primate of Argentina. Quarracino became head of the Argentine bishops' conference the following year.

Quarracino, like Bergoglio, had never hidden his sympathies for the Peronist movement and, from an early stage following his election, harboured a strong dislike for Alfonsín, the first democratically elected Argentine president to seriously challenge the Peronist political dominance and power of the military since 1930. Promoted to Archbishop of La Plata in December 1985, Quarracino openly opposed Alfonsín's policy of putting on trial high-ranking military officers who had previously ruled the country, rallying other Peronist-leaning fellow bishops behind a call for immunity from prosecution of all military officers under the questionable banner of 'national reconciliation'. He also opposed other areas of government policy such as moves to liberalize Argentina's divorce laws and the creation of a new ministry of culture that sought to liberate education and the arts from interference by the Catholic hierarchy.

In May 1989, Carlos Menem, a Peronist candidate who was the flamboyant governor of the province of La Rioja, defeated Alfonsín's Radical party in a general election with a substantial margin in the midst of growing domestic economic problems. A crestfallen Alfonsín handed power back to the Peronist movement five months before the official expiry of a term in office that had initially raised hopes of a genuine reform of Argentina's endemically corrupt political culture but floundered when confronted with deeply entrenched vested interests.

Menem had manoeuvred himself into the leadership of the country's most nationalist, populist and powerful party through a series of tactical alliances both with rebel Army officers and some of the most corrupt members of the Peronist movement. The son of Syrian Muslim immigrants, Menem had spent his adolescence immersed in the picture-book heroes of Argentine history: the charismatic *caudillos* who backed by cowboys – the gauchos of the prairie pampas – had fought against the imported liberal Western values of the nineteenth century. He went on to model himself on them physically, growing his hair and sideburns and wearing the poncho or rough woollen tunic of the gaucho, deliberately resurrecting the memory of the most famous of all Argentine *caudillos*, Facundo Quiroga.

While the landed and professional classes regarded the early version of Menem – like Quiroga – as a barbarian, the poor of the suburbs and the rural labour force saw him as the enduring spirit of true nationhood. Peronism provided Menem with the perfect vehicle to pursue his political ambitions. His election campaign in 1989 nevertheless conjured up all the populist tricks of Perón; he claimed to speak a language with which ordinary Argentines could understand and empathize. He told thousands who flocked to one of his major election rallies: 'For the hunger of poor children, for the sadness of rich children, for the young and the old, with the flag of God which is faith, and the flag of the fatherland, for God,

I ask you: follow me and I will not deceive you.' A majority of Argentine voters believed him.

Within weeks of the new government being sworn in, the director of the National Health Administration, Luis Barrionuevo, casually disclosed in a radio interview that he had routinely taken kickbacks for government health contracts. Then a newspaper report written by Horacio Verbitsky revealed that the new US ambassador, Terence Todman, had protested privately to the Menem government that the US meat packing company, Swift Armour, had been solicited for a bribe by at least one Argentine official. After 'Swiftgate', as the widely disseminated story was called, came Yomagate, when Amira Yoma, a younger sister of Zulema Yoma, Carlos Menem's ex-wife, and Amira's husband, Ibrahim il Ibrahim were alleged to have links to international drug trafficking. Yet no incriminating evidence was found against Menem himself in these particular cases, and a majority of the population seemed quite happy to ignore the air of pervasive corruption; instead they enjoyed during a honeymoon period the fruits of the economic upturn which made the country one of the top performers of the developing countries. Argentina's GDP (below 1973 levels when Menem took office) increased 35 per cent from 1990 to 1994.

By the mid-1990s a series of bank failures suggested that the bubble – which had seen a widening disparity between rich and poor – could be close to bursting. Few scandals exposed the questionable network of interest groups created by the Menem government more sarkly than that involving the Banco de Crédito Provincial, straddling Church and State in an alleged conspiracy of financial corruption.

Quite apart from its links with the Menem government the BCP also acted as the representative bank in Argentina of the Bank del Monte di Paschi di Siena (Italia), one of the oldest of Italy's banks whose own dubious reputation included close links to the controversial Vatican bank and the seamier side of Italian politics.

When Bergoglio succeeded his mentor Quarracino as Archbishop of Buenos Aires, the investigation into the shady dealings of the bankrupt bank were at an advanced stage, having surfaced in an exposé in Argentina's biggest selling daily, *Clarín*. Initially, there was no suggestion that Bergoglio, first as Quarracino's most trusted bishop and later as his successor, himself was involved in any impropriety.

Indeed, while Quarracino developed close political ties with Menem, this was not emulated by Bergoglio, who increasingly distanced himself from the regime, its philosophy of economic liberalism and endemic corruption. Bergoglio focused on developing a network of priests to work among the poor of the shanty towns, while ensuring the loyalty of priests he assigned to parish and other duties in the richer neighbourhoods.

In his style as a bishop Bergoglio stood out from the other members of the hierarchy, and acted as if he had been cut from entirely different cloth from most of them. While Quarracino was an outspoken media communicator, openly embraced the luxuries that came with office, and kept aloof from his priests, Bergoglio did not like giving interviews, but showed himself personable and approachable to ordinary laymen and -women he felt he could trust and those of lower clerical rank.

Fr Guillermo Marco, a priest who worked closely with Bergoglio and Quarracino recalls: 'Quarracino brought Bergoglio back to Buenos Aires when he was in Córdoba, relegated by the Jesuits, doing penance and underused . . . After a short time as a bishop Bergoglio began to distinguish himself from the rest . . . he didn't use a chauffeur driven car, he walked, and travelled in public transport . . . we were all pretty amazed at the time . . . if not shocked . . . He would go and visit individual priests . . . .develop a personal relationship . . . listen to their problems, something that other bishops didn't do as they settled comfortably into their elevated roles. Quarracino would go round Rome in a Mercedes limousine and he wouldn't stop at a priest's house. He acted as prince of the church, aloof from ordinary mortals. But he had a sufficient human instinct to see Bergoglio as a man who was profoundly religious and who had a way of managing things that set him apart from the others.'

Quarracino claimed to be impressed by Bergoglio's spirituality and humility. But the Archbishop had also calculated that the Jesuit's political acumen would act as a necessary counterbalance to the power of other bishops, not least his most powerful rival, the future Archbishop of La Plata, Mgr Héctor Aguero. A notorious *ultramontane* (theologically extremely conservative) Catholic strongly opposed to the new spirit of engagement with the modern world emanating from Vatican II, Aguero had developed close links with two key Vatican insiders. One was Cardinal Leonardo Sandri, an Argentine of Italian immigrant roots who had left for Rome twenty-five years earlier to run the day-to-day operations of the global Church's vast bureaucracy and roam the world as a papal diplomat. The other was the Italian Cardinal Angelo Sodano, the one-time papal nuncio to Pinochet's Chile whom Pope John Paul II had promoted to be his secretary of state. Quarracino, however, had his own direct line to Pope John Paul II through his friendship with the papal nuncio in Buenos Aires in 1981–2000, Mgr Calabresi, which prevailed with the appointment of Bergoglio.

The Argentine hierarchy, with Bergoglio at this stage a simple pawn, was thus maintained in a tense political balance under the Vatican's control. Moreover Quarracino found in Bergoglio a bishop who did what was expected, defending his mentor and his Church's reputation. In 1994, for example, during his regular TV commentary slot, Quarracino spoke against homosexuality saying that lesbians and gay men should be 'locked up in a ghetto'. He also described homosexuality as 'a deviation of human nature, like bestiality'. While there were Catholics and non-Catholics who disapproved of Quarracino's bigoted views as well as extravagant living, there is no record of Bergoglio having said a word against him. As his auxiliary bishop, Bergoglio professed total loyalty to Quarracino and never expressed – publicly at least – the slightest doubt that the Archbishop was innocent of the allegation of corruption against him and that he was the victim, not the perpetrator, of a financial fraud.

Following initial hearings into the Banco de Crédito Provincial case, one of the original plaintiffs, the military insurance company SMSV, dropped a claim against the archdiocese and both issued a statement claiming they had been defrauded. One of the defendants, Francisco Javier Trusso was arrested after two years on the run, part of which he had spent hiding in a house in the Argentine seaside resort of Pinamar belonging to a senior Vatican official, Archbishop Leonardo Sandri. Trusso was sentenced to eight years but was freed following a personal guarantee by Hector Aguero, who in 1998 was made Archbishop of La Plata when Bergoglio succeeded Quarracino as Archbishop of Buenos Aires.

Others alleged to have been involved in the Banco de Crédito Provincial case were either acquitted or never charged. In 2000, Sandri was promoted to the post of Substitute for General Affairs, the third most important position within the Vatican, serving as the chief of staff of the secretary of state Cardinal Archbishop Angelo Sodano, with both men playing an increasing influential role during the declining health of Pope John Paul II. Sandri was one of the front-runners tipped by the Italian media to succeed Benedict XVI in the 2013 conclave that Bergoglio won. The inquiry into the collapse of the bank officially continues (although it is semi-dormant and effectively shelved) seventeen years after the first police raid on the archdiocese in December 1998.

Chapter Ten
Political Broker

On 21 December 2001, the Argentine president Fernando de la Rúa was forced to resign after thousands took to the streets of the capital to protest at his centrist Radical party government's handling of Argentina's worsening economic crisis. At least twenty-two people were killed in riots and looting around the country in the worst civil unrest for a decade.

De la Rúa had been elected just three years earlier having campaigned on promises to rescue the country from a deepening recession and end corruption after the ten-year rule of the Peronist Carlos Menem. But de la Rúa had squandered his own support by his mismanagement of the economy, provoking a run on bank deposits and bringing Argentina to the edge of default on a massive debt. When his economy minister Domingo Cavallo tried to impose controls on cash withdrawals, he only succeeded in fuelling uncertainty and anger, sparking off a wave of protests. On 19 December, the government declared a state of siege, giving it special powers to stop the worst looting and riots in a decade. Five thousand protestors gathered outside Cavallo's apartment building, banging on pots and pans, and after an hour of that he resigned, taking the whole Cabinet with him overnight.

For a few days Argentina teetered on the brink of institutional collapse. The Radical party was in tatters; Argentina's traditionally most powerful political grouping the Peronist party was divided between warring factions; and the military was lacking any civilian support after its humiliating defeat in the Falklands War and yet to be brought fully to account for human rights violations on a major scale. Those turbulent days in the run-up to the first Christmas of the new millennium were to mark a watershed in Argentine history, providing an opportunity for the entrance into national politics of the most radically populist government since the last days of Perón, and the more discreet, if no less important entrance of Jorge Bergoglio as a key political player.

Bergoglio had been appointed the new Archbishop of Buenos Aires following the death in March 1998 of Quarracino, his predecessor and mentor. One of the first challenges faced by Bergoglio was dealing with the allegations of financial impropriety surrounding Quarracino and his dealings with the failed bank. But the new Archbishop was also acutely aware that the Church as an institution could not sit idly by while the country started to show signs of being gripped by an unprecedented financial and social crisis that questioned the survival of the nascent democratic state.

Bergoglio began by marking his distance from the extravagant style of office favoured by his predecessor, moving his living quarters from the palatial archbishop's official residence and grounds in the leafy Buenos Aires neighbourhood of Olivos to more discreet living quarters above the main administrative office of the archdiocese next to the cathedral. The gesture was largely symbolic and stopped short of being revolutionary. The Olivos residence, which had been donated to the Argentine Church by one of the country's richest families, was left unsold and put to no other more charitable use. The maintenance of the building and gardens was left in the hands of its long-term household staff on full salary.

Moreover, there was method as well as gesture behind Bergoglio's decision to have his living quarters next to the cathedral. It meant that his official home, overlooking Plaza de Mayo just across the square from the presidential palace, the Casa Rosada, in the midst of the capital's financial and administrative centre, put him just a few steps away from the cut and thrust of those running the country.

But much more than mere political opportunism was beginning to show in the biographical narrative of Bergoglio. He was a man who listened to his conscience, and who now felt that as Archbishop he had a moral obligation to make up for the shortcomings he had shown as a leader while serving as Jesuit provincial. Not since the collapse of the military regime in 1983 had Argentina demanded such redemptive leadership from those in a position to exercise it. Because Bergoglio had been named as his successor by Quarracino when he was still alive, with the Vatican's blessing, there was no need for his succession to be marked by any pomp and ceremony – and he made it clear that he had no intention of having any organized for him. On the news of Quarracino's death in March 1998, Bergoglio shied away from the sudden local media interest in him, and temporarily withdrew himself from any public appearance for a spiritual retreat lasting several days.

His first public appearance was at a ceremony given in the presidential palace honouring Bergoglio's friend and ally, the long-serving and influential papal nuncio Ubaldo Calabresi on the occasion of the fiftieth anniversary of his ordination as a priest. As Bergoglio took his seat on one side of President Menem, with Calabresi the other, a civil servant sitting in the front line of facing VIP seats whispered to his colleague: 'Who is that sombre looking monsignor next to Menem, on the other side to Calabresi?' He didn't get an immediate answer. On that date, 18 March 1998, Bergoglio was still a largely relatively unknown part of the Argentine political and social landscape who had never given a press interview nor been identified as a significant spokesman for the Catholic Church – such was the Jesuit's determination to keep out of the public limelight beyond discreet meetings with fellow clerics, friends in the Peronist movement and, during the times of the juntas, senior officers with blood on their hands. This was now about to change.

One of Bergoglio's first staff appointments was that of Guillermo Marco, a young, well-educated and affable secular priest whose self-confidence and training in communications made him a necessary shield for the new Archbishop, when necessary, as well as tactical adviser. It was Marco who set about helping the new Archbishop develop a public relations strategy that, with its emphasis on transparency and acts of humility, was aimed at drawing a clear line in the sand with the Argentine Church's – and Bergoglio's – troubled past. Less than a month after stepping for the first time into the presidential palace, Bergoglio chose a far less formal setting for the traditional Maundy Thursday washing of the feet ceremony in commemoration of Jesus's Last Supper with his disciples prior to his crucifixion. Instead of marking the occasion as his predecessors had done in the cathedral, he delegated the service there to one of his junior bishops, and he went to a state-run hospital where he washed the feet of twelve Aids patients. The following year he caught public bus no. 109 to the capital's main prison, Villa Devoto, dressed again in simple vestments, and washed the feet of twelve inmates.

Such symbolic gestures, far from becoming a token public relations exercise, came to define Bergoglio's pastoral mission as that of religious leader who felt that it was his moral duty to speak out on behalf of those who felt most impoverished and abandoned materially, physically and socially as a result of the failings of government and the established economic order. As Archbishop, Bergoglio did not want the Church simply converted into a charitable NGO administering to a passive population. He also saw it as his duty to increasingly speak out and act in defence of the common good. He wanted engagement with those who believed and did not believe, between rich and poor.

He was driven by an evangelical sense that harked back to the early days of Christianity, committed as he was to a plan of redemption for those prepared to trust in and be reconciled with a just and forgiving God. Bergoglio's political as well as spiritual manifesto became that of the Beatitudes, with the poor in spirit, the merciful, those who thirst after justice, the pure in conscience and the peacemakers deserving of blessing or conversion.

On 12 October 1998, Bergoglio, with his bishops and priests, drew close to 100,000 people to two open-air Masses in Palermo, the residential northern quarter of the city. Those attending reflected a cross-section of society – from the higher income residents of the immediate neighbourhood to equal numbers drawn from the outlying '*villas*' or shanty towns in a shared display of faith. The crowds included some 21,000 Argentines and immigrants of all ages and social backgrounds who were being baptized for the first time.

In numerical terms this was equivalent to the traditional annual pilgrimage to the Virgin of Luján but with a contemporary relevance: the demonstration, in the heart of the capital, showed a Church emerging out of the shadows and making its presence felt, as the deteriorating political and social circumstances demanded.

Five months earlier, on 25 May 1998, Argentina's national day – marking independence from Spain – the increasingly unpopular President Menem and his government entourage attended the *Te Deum* or religious thanksgiving service in the cathedral. In his sermon, Bergoglio distanced himself from a government that under his predecessor Quarracino had enjoyed a mutually beneficial relationship with the Church authorities. Bergoglio warned that Argentine society was threatened by increasing political and social tension because of the increasing perception that power was being monopolized and exploited by the failure of a self-interested political class in tackling urgent social problems affecting the population as a whole.

'A few are sitting at the table and enriching themselves, the social fabric is being destroyed, the social divide is increasing, and everyone is suffering; as a result our society is on a road to confrontation,' he said.

In another sermon, delivered two months later, Bergoglio was even blunter, focusing his attack on the recklessness of the Menem government's free-market policies. 'The Church can't just sit sucking its finger when faced with a frivolous, cold, and calculating market economy.'

The condemnation of the Menem presidency was a story foretold given Bergoglio's early political idealism forged in his youth by a strong regard for the socially distributive policies of the first post-war Perón government. But it had been a long time coming, with Menem only belatedly identified as a false *Peronista*, the latest personification of Argentina's failed state. Bergoglio's political coming of age was not a response to a particular event but a protracted process which began in his early days studying for the priesthood against the background of Perón and Evita's coming to power, and developed as expectations were raised and dashed by a succession of failed military and civilian governments, all of them with Peronism still the unrivalled political, cultural and indeed spiritual force in the country.

Nevertheless, if there was a defining moment it was the social and political collapse surrounding de la Rúa's forced resignation from the presidency in 2001. The two most influential Argentine Church leaders of the previous decade – Cardinals Primatesta and Quarracino – had both died three years earlier within months of each other, leaving Bergoglio as the most senior Church figure, no longer able, in conscience, to keep his head below the parapet. As Fr Marco, his spokesman, recalled: 'This was a detonating moment when Bergoglio felt he had no choice but to get actively involved in the political and social life of his country.'

After de la Rúa was forced to resign, Argentina entered a period of political limbo as a series of interim presidents struggled to maintain control. Protestors and sectors of the media publicly blamed the political class, using the slogan '*que se vayan todos*' ('away with them all'). In January 2002, a new interim president, Eduardo Duhalde, the former Peronist governor of Buenos Aires, abolished a fixed exchange rate, allowing the Argentine peso to devalue by more than two-thirds of its value and throwing half of the population into poverty.

At this point a broad agreement involving key Peronist and Radical politicians and other smaller party groupings, trade union figures, business representatives and grassroots organizations representing the hardest hit neighbourhoods agreed on a consensual emergency economic and social plan aimed at defusing the growing unrest. The Argentine Church took on the role of a key peace broker.

Formal talks between all the parties were carried out in committees which included Argentine bishops and were subjected to the full glare of the media. But the more substantial negotiations occurred in secret bilateral talks between Bergoglio and key political players who had the ability to forge a broader consensus. Among the politicians involved was Miguel Ángel Toma, Jesuit educated and one of Bergoglio's former students. An influential figure in the Peronist party, Toma had befriended Bergoglio, as had several other Peronists, while studying theology at San Miguel. Elected to the Argentine Chamber of Deputies for the City of Buenos Aires in 1985, Toma had served in the Menem government as Secretary of State for Security. During the political crisis that exploded in December 2001, Toma was promoted briefly to Minister of Justice, Interior Defence and Human Rights, before becoming involved in the multi-party negotiations as president of the Peronist party in the province of Buenos Aires.

In 2002–3 Toma was head of Secretaría de Inteligencia de Estado (SIDE), the Argentine secret intelligence service, and led an investigation into the bombing of the Israeli Embassy in Buenos

Aires in 1992 and the Jewish community centre AMIA in 1994, which led to the deaths of over a hundred people and the injury of many more. The investigation into the attacks was subsequently drawn into a web of conspiracy as to who might have been involved. Suspects included corrupt Argentine policemen, right-wing Falklands War veterans and Middle East terrorists working together in a sinister plot against Israeli interests. Although those implicated included Iranian diplomats based in Buenos Aires during the Menem government, the official investigation failed to identify the full organization behind the attacks and suspicion remained that high-level members of the Menem administration were deeply implicated because of their links with Middle East arms and drug dealers.

Many members of Argentina's immigrant society had Jewish ancestry, and there was a smaller proportion of citizens of Middle Eastern Arab extraction, making the bombings potentially hugely destabilizing in the midst of an already highly charged political landscape. But they led to Bergoglio becoming increasingly involved in inter-religious dialogue as part of his growing participation in nation building. As Abraham Skorka, a leading Argentine rabbi involved in the process, recalled: 'After the Buenos Aires bombings, the dialogue began from a very low point but it was Bergoglio who took the initiative in the second half of the 1990s. He wanted to forge a new relationship between the Catholic and Jewish faith in the spirit of *Nostra Aetate*, the Declaration on the Relation of the Church with Non-Christian Religions of Vatican II promulgated on 28 October 1965 by Pope Paul VI. This was very important because it marked a turning point in the traditional Catholic view holding the Jewish people responsible for the crucifixion of Christ, the people who killed God.'

When I interviewed him in Buenos Aires following Bergoglio's election as pope, Skorka told me, 'I myself considered this dialogue very important . . . I saw that Bergoglio's virtue as Archbishop of

Buenos Aires lay in defining the depth of the dialogue and it went deep . . . I would propose ways forward to him. He would always go a step further . . . he showed huge commitment, opened doors . . .'

It was in May 1998, at the first *Te Deum* service celebrated by Bergoglio as Archbishop to which the rabbi was invited, that Skorka realized that behind the seemingly self-effacing, deeply spiritual and politically untested Catholic leader lay a personable interlocutor he could trust as a friend.

'When Bergoglio approached the various invited delegations, he came up to me and asked me what football team I supported; somewhat taken aback I said, "River Plate of course." He said, "Well I support San Lorenzo." River Plate hadn't won a championship for twenty-four years . . . the fans were called "chickens" by rival fans on the grounds that their team didn't have enough power to win a championship,' Skorka recalled. He went on: 'Later at this *Te Deum* in May 1998 Bergoglio stood alongside the papal nuncio, shaking hands with the invitees. We had been advised by the protocol people not to say anything, just to make a salutation. But I could not stop myself from complimenting Bergoglio on the service and quoted two biblical verses he had quoted. He then looked me straight in the eyes, and came out with a non-theological response I shall never forget. "I believe that this season we are going to eat chicken soup!" he joked. By that he meant that San Lorenzo was going to wipe us out. The nuncio, who was not familiar with football jargon, looked very nervous and tried to move Bergoglio on. But the Archbishop of Buenos Aires turned to the man from the Vatican and said, with a mischievous smile, "Don't worry. We are only talking about football."'

Skorka concluded: 'This was one of the episodes that marked the start of our relationship. What this was telling me was this: he was a person who is open with me and joked with me. This is someone I can build up a special relationship with, which is exactly what we did.'

The higher echelons of the country's political and diplomatic class included Catholic Peronists, including the former Argentine spy chief Toma, who had been educated by the Jesuits. Some of them witnessed Bergoglio the politician developing within his clerical clothes. 'When Bergoglio became Jesuit provincial,' Toma told me, 'he had a big impact on the Jesuit University of Salvador where there was a big fight going on between left and right. He relied on the support of the Guardia de Hierro to sort things out. But it is completely false to suggest that he subsequently collaborated with the military regime. He protected several Peronists who were being pursued as political dissidents and used his contacts within the military to secure intelligence that helped him help others.'

Toma recalled meeting Bergoglio for the first time in the late 1960s in the seminary at San Miguel where, despite a twelve-year age difference, they studied theology together for a year. Toma was thinking of joining the priesthood at the time while Bergoglio was already ordained. 'I remember Bergoglio being very focused on his studies, rigorous, and demanding of himself. At one point he started working in the *villas* with groups of four of five seminarians. His contact with poverty was there from a very early stage in his adult life as a seminarian. In the seminary there was a big quadrangle with galleries. All our reflection was done walking. We would coincide on some of the courses. I remember him with hair swept back, wearing moccasin shoes, dark sweater, and an untreated leather belt. In 1977 I met him again when we were both involved with Salvador university. At that time Bergoglio began to have a very strong relationship with Peronism. He was very linked to Guardia de Hierro. He was opposed to the Montoneros on the left, and had links to Army officers (including Julian Licastro and José Luis Fernández Valoni who had organized the student repression during *El Córdobazo* [the civil uprising in Córdoba in 1969]) but they were less violent than the more reactionary forces on the right who answered to López Rega . . .'

Toma is adamant that Bergoglio from his early days as a Jesuit identified with the Catholic Church's social teaching which 'questioned power against the backdrop of poverty and the marginalized'. However, he concedes that it was not until he became Archbishop, coinciding with a major institutional crisis, that he became more proactively involved politically (while maintaining himself orthodox in other areas of traditional Catholic teaching such as opposing abortion and gay rights).

Toma also told me: 'In 2001–2 Bergoglio became very involved in promoting the *Mesa de Diálogo* [round-table discussions]. Duhalde and other Peronists were among those who wanted the Catholic Church to promote political dialogue and social engagement, to contain the situation, to avert disintegration. Bergoglio accepted and offered to have the Church facilitate constructive encounters. I and other leading Peronists (Umberto Rogero, Jorge Maskim, Oscar Lamberti, Miguel Pocheto, Díaz Bancalari, Leopodo Moro), among others, had meetings with him. Bergoglio was very committed to helping restore the credibility of the institutions of the State, including Congress, so that democracy could be consolidated in the context of diversity.'

Some encounters were more public than others, and Bergoglio throughout the process focused on making progress in secret meetings, thereby avoiding the pressure of the media pre-empting outcomes. Rumours, difficult to substantiate, would later circulate that senior government officials used a secret tunnel that links the presidential Casa Rosada to the cathedral. The tunnel, originally used by nineteenth-century smugglers, was reactivated to guarantee the secrecy of those attending certain meetings. Meanwhile, two bishops – Jorge Casaretto of San Isidro and Justo Laguna of Morón – attended the widely publicized multi-party talks which came to be known as the *Diálogo Argentino* in different locations around the capital.

The talks drew on the advice of officials linked to the UN

Programme for Development, and the participation of party officials, businessmen, trade unionists, and health, education and housing officials. They lasted just short of two months. According to Fr Marco, Bergoglio's spokesman at the time, Laguna and Casaretto were not on the same party political and doctrinal wavelength as the Archbishop of Buenos Aires. Bergoglio considered Laguna – a close ally of the anti-Peronist Raúl Alfonsín when he was President – as too progressive and out of step with the Vatican of Pope John Paul II. For their part, Marco told me, both bishops thought Bergoglio 'something of a conservative and too cautious politically who wasn't as good as they were in reaching deals'.

Whatever the feeling of mutual mistrust that might have existed within the Argentine Catholic hierarchy at the time, it did not lead to any public rift capable of undermining the talks, which were inaugurated in a public ceremony held in the Church of Santa Catalina. All three bishops said they were committed to working towards a consensual position that would pave the way for stable government and effective action for those most affected by the economic crisis. Bergoglio was not present in Santa Catalina and kept away from the main talks. Marco recalled: 'Bergoglio played his own part in the process but on his own terms – he presided over his own *Mesa de Diálogo*, meeting politicians and government officials he had direct access to. Bergoglio managed power as Archbishop of Buenos Aires . . . They all lined up to see him, from the President to leading opposition congressmen. The only condition was discretion, no publicity . . .'

So what motivated Bergoglio at the time, and why the secrecy? I asked Marco.

'Bergoglio was thinking about the future of his country. He was worried about the deepening crisis and how this was affecting people. He wasn't seeking personal advantage which is why he shied away from publicity.'

Many of those involved with the *Diálogo Argentino* believed they were part of a genuine effort to re-establish the foundations of a viable social and political coexistence that would benefit all those thrown into abject poverty and despair by the 2001 crisis. An agreed document emerging from the talks, entitled *Constructing the Transition*, was published on 28 February 2002 with further documents in the following weeks.

The paperwork, which ran into thousands of pages, pledged a bold programme which aspired to the transformation of Argentina from a failed State to a functioning social democratic society. It committed the State, with the support of the private sector, NGOs and trade unions, to a range of measures from fiscal and financial reform aimed at guaranteeing equitable and sustainable growth to improved public health, education and social housing action programmes to alleviate those worst hit by the crisis. It also pledged reforms of the discredited judiciary, including the police, and of the political parties to ensure transparency, accountability and the rule of law, along with a free and truthful media, and the 'institutionalization of dialogue' – as opposed to confrontation – as a way of delivering policy. It committed Argentina to putting behind it once and for all its pariah status as an unreliable debtor, illegal arms trader and an inconstant member of the United Nations. 'Argentina, as a true democracy, will engage with the world,' went one of the pledges.

Days after Bergoglio was elected pope, Eduardo Duhalde, the Argentine Peronist president who presided over the *Mesa de Diálogo*, recalled Bergoglio's key role in saving his country from political and social collapse: 'In the midst of the crisis of 2001, Bergoglio assumed a key role in the *Diálogo*,' he wrote in an article in *La Nación*. 'It was an epic collective effort by all Argentines. There were providential figures in the rescue, giant personalities who, while modestly avoiding sitting at the main table of negotiations, played a crucial role in saving the country from social disintegration which at that time was a clear and present danger. Jorge Bergoglio was one of them.'

Duhalde wrote on: 'When no one gave a cent for the possibility of a positive outcome, the Argentine Church and its bishops insisted on the possibility that we might find a way out together . . . Bergoglio was not politically indifferent; like millions of Argentines, although with a clearer head than a majority of them, he felt completely identified with the cause of social justice.'

A somewhat different perspective was provided by Bergoglio's close aide at the time, Fr Marco. His view was that the two bishops involved in the official talks, notably Laguna and Casaretto, were led down the proverbial garden path by Duhalde who, behind all the political spin about social justice, exploited them as mere political pawns. While the *Mesa* initially helped defuse social tensions and provided some necessary political breathing space, this eventually was undermined by deeply entrenched interests in the Peronist party. With the help of Duhalde and other party barons, they ensured the continuance of a revolving door of access into the presidential palace of a political movement that had overshadowed Argentine politics since the 1940s.

As Marco recalled: 'Bergoglio told me: "Why am I going to get involved with the *Mesa* when this is something that should involve party leaders and Congress? Won't the Church's involvement risk its credibility by identifying with discredited politicians? Why should we save their necks?"'

Marco added: 'The reality is that Duhalde never delivered on the reforms promised by the *Mesa*. The Church put its prestige on the line to save Duhalde from following de la Rúa into the political abyss only to see all the pledges mothballed once the crisis had been temporarily defused. I think Bergoglio was proved right for not getting involved more directly and publicly.'

Certainly Bergoglio neither predicted, still less influenced, what came next: the coming to power of a new political regime that came to see him as a key political opponent. Bergoglio now entered a period in public life that was to enhance his reputation not just as a spiritual leader but one with considerable political courage, attributes that would accelerate his path to the papacy.

Chapter Eleven
Battle Lines

Not even the main actors involved could say with any certainty the precise moment when the engagement between the Argentine president Néstor Kirchner and Archbishop Bergoglio turned from coexistence to confrontation.

However, the *Te Deum* service in the Cathedral of Buenos Aires on 25 May 2004, a traditional service marking the anniversary of Argentina's independence as a nation state, attended by the newly elected Peronist Kirchner and celebrated by Bergoglio, marked a turning point. During it, Bergoglio made a thinly veiled attack on the falsehoods emanating from the propaganda machinery of the new Peronist government. He criticized a strategy of 'exhibitionism and strident announcements' before adding: 'The people are not taken in by dishonest and mediocre strategies. They have hopes, but they won't be deceived by magical solutions emanating from obscure deals and vested political interests.'

Just two years after his discreet efforts to rescue Argentina's discredited political class from oblivion by brokering a cross-party consensus around a root-and-branch package of social reforms, Bergoglio felt badly let down by the re-emergence of bad government. It was the last significant State event at which President Kirchner and Bergoglio the Archbishop, soon to be designated

Cardinal of Buenos Aires, would stand side by side, after which a growing political chasm opened up between them.

A year earlier Kirchner had been sworn in as the new president. He inherited an exhausted nation and a people disillusioned with politics after the record debt default in 2001, the collapse of the peso and the biggest financial crisis in Argentina's history. Of mixed Croatian and Swiss descent, Kirchner was born in Río Gallegos, a small coastal city in southern Argentina. He joined the Peronist party there as a fledgling lawyer. In 1975 he married Cristina Fernández, a fellow lawyer and political activist. Soon Fernández allowed her own career to be subsumed by that of her husband.

Initially, Fernández balanced her family life – she gave birth to a son, Máximo, and a daughter, Florencia – with political ambition, helping her husband run a successful private practice and helping him climb the ladder of the Peronist party machinery. Her official biographer rather vaguely refers to Néstor Kirchner gradually building up a local power base by working discreetly among Peronists sympathizers from 'neighbourhood to neighbourhood'. Other less hagiographic accounts, including a detailed unauthorized political history of Kirchner, written by three political opponents – Julio Barbaro, Oscar Muiño and Omar Pintos – provide a more sinister narrative. This is that in its network of personal favours, graft and intimidation, the rise and rise of Néstor Kirchner owed more to the tactics usually associated with the Mafia than with a Western democratic political party.

Meanwhile, his wife's days as a law student in La Plata, the city where she was born, were overshadowed by the growing conflict between left and right armed groups which intensified after Perón died in 1974. The extent to which Fernández, like her husband, dabbled in the radical politics then being pursued by those who had supported Perón on the left remains a subject of dispute, although in government the Kirchners were to increasingly assume the rhetoric of the revolutionary 1960s and early 1970s, and encouraged more trials of military officers and their alleged collaborators for human rights violations.

When Isabelita Perón was toppled by the military coup in 1976, Kirchner left La Plata and resettled in the far-away Patagonian town of Río Gallegos, in the province of Santa Cruz. 'I am going to be governor of Santa Cruz one day,' Kirchner told Fernández. She followed him.

Fernández was elected a deputy in the Santa Cruz provincial legislature after Kirchner became governor of the province of Santa Cruz in 1991. Four years later, when her husband was re-elected to office, Fernández became a representative of Santa Cruz in the national Senate where she gained a reputation as a hard-working conviction politician, with an ability to absorb a detailed brief and to speak movingly without notes, as well as embarrass her opponents with aggressive questioning. By contrast Kirchner was a political dark horse nationally outside his native province of Santa Cruz, where he served as governor until assuming the presidency. His performance in the 2003 election campaign was lacklustre, and he actually lost by a slim margin to his Peronist rival, the ageing Carlos Menem, but finally took the presidency by default when Menem bowed out of a second round of voting following a sequence of opaque internal wheeling and dealing within the country's most powerful political movement.

By mutual agreement with her husband, and the endorsement of key Peronist male barons, it was Néstor Kirchner who bid successfully for the Argentine presidency in 2003. The move was timed to take maximum advantage of the confused political fallout from the economic meltdown in 2001. During her husband's first term, Fernández was First Lady, a title that understated her own political role in supporting her husband in power. Inevitably the Kirchners based their popular appeal on memories of the legendary General Perón and his second wife, the charismatic Evita, who

when in power during the late 1940s and early 1950s were loved as
much as they were hated. Such was the shadow Evita cast over her
own sex, that she became a measure by which all female Argentine
politicians became judged, her legacy in Latin America an obstacle
to some women coming to power, an encouragement to others.
While her husband set about consolidating his personal ties in
business and the trade union movement, Fernández's highly
combative discourse fuelled a militant core of additional support
among young students and lower income groups. It was textbook
Peronism, with Fernández famously telling one interviewer she
identified herself with the Evita 'of the hair in the bun and clenched
fist before a microphone'.

One of the areas in which the Kirchner presidency broke with
the politics of previously elected governments since the end of
the military regime was in not seeking from the outset to ingratiate
itself with the Catholic Church. 'I am not interested in the
Church,' Kirchner privately confided to a senior aide. By this he
meant to underline his agnosticism. Certainly Kirchner did not
ignore the Church in political terms. Judging it by its history of
complicity with the ruling landed elites and right-wing military
regimes, Kirchner regarded the Catholic hierarchy as politically
reactionary and potentially destabilizing of any radical project that
aimed to challenge its claim to represent the common good. As
such Kirchner came to see the increasingly popular and outspoken
Archbishop Jorge Bergoglio as an obstacle, if not a potential
enemy.

According to close friends of the President, the distrust Kirchner
felt towards the Catholic Church dated back to his early days as a
schoolboy when he suffered physical abuse in a Salesian college. In
adulthood, this made him actively hostile whenever he saw the
Church exercising its authority. His wife Cristina, by all accounts,
had gone through a relatively trouble-free school education at the
hands of benevolent nuns and retained her faith. However, her

political ambition and loyalty to her husband while he was alive took precedence over anything else.

Whatever the psychology involved, it was evident from the early days of the Kirchner presidency that he and Bergoglio were on a collision course. Both men got off to a bad start with each other by failing to even agree the terms of protocol. Days after taking office, Kirchner sent word to Bergoglio via his most senior official Oscar Parrilli that the Archbishop was expected to visit the Casa Rosada to pay his formal respects.

'Well that's not the way it's going to be,' Bergoglio told his spokesman, Fr Marco. 'If the president wants to see me, he has to come to my office; if I want to see him then I go and see him.'

The stand-off was in sharp contrast to the warm collaboration between Bergoglio's predecessor Quarracino and the former Peronist President Carlos Menem. The *bon vivant* and overtly political Quarracino used to take his guitar along to the presidential residence in Olivos, and stay up until late drinking and socializing with the hedonistic Menem and his entourage.

Julio Bárbaro, an influential politician and an old Peronist friend of Bergoglio, claimed that the lack of engagement between the Jesuit Archbishop and the President was not through lack of trying on his behalf. Early on in the presidency, Bárbaro tried to broker a deal between the two rival leaders but failed. 'It was one of my biggest political failures; spirituality was not something that my friend Néstor was moved by,' Bárbaro later recalled.

One year into the first Kirchner government, opinion polls showed confidence in the government plummeting. People had been spending money assuming their wages were going to go up, but for many they had not, and inflation was rising. The biggest worry expressed in the poll was the perceived erosion of law and order. There had been an increase in marches by *piqueteros*, groups of aggressive unemployed protesters demanding bigger benefit handouts from the government. The marches, which often involved masked demonstrators armed with wooden clubs, cut off main roads and caused traffic chaos in Buenos Aires. Nevertheless favourable international prices for Argentine commodities like wheat and soya boosted State reserves, some of which were channelled into subsidies for the low paid and unemployed. Initially the Church, which counted on substantial donations to its charity, Cáritas, and the State found common ground over how to share out some of their resources.

Bergoglio's vanguard group of priests, the *curas villeros*, who had been sent into the shanty towns, found themselves working side by side with representatives of the State and NGOs in areas like health and housing – but such cooperation came to be undermined partly by the corruption of local officials and partly by the lack of an understanding between the Kirchners and Bergoglio in other areas of government policy that the Archbishop saw as contrary to Catholic social and moral teaching.

It was the *villas* or shanty towns that Bergoglio came to identify as the target of his main missionary and evangelical effort, and yet it was in the *villas* that the shortcomings of the State were most exposed. They housed a growing population of social outcasts that included immigrants, drug addicts and drug traffickers, the homeless, abused housewives, abandoned children, prostitutes and others who eluded taxation and defied the so-called forces of law and order because they had long ceased to be beneficiaries of transparent and accountable welfare and security.

Meanwhile, Kirchner aimed to consolidate his grip on power by ruling through an inner circle of trusted friends and a network of mutual interests across the public and private sector, fuelled by bribery and selective access to government contracts. An increasingly authoritarian, populist, sycophantic and intolerant style of government began to take shape behind the public facade of radical democratic initiatives of the Kirchner set. Just over a year into his presidency, Kirchner sacked his justice minister Gustavo Béliz for no ostensible reason other than that Béliz was showing his frustration with the prevalent cronyism. Béliz bemoaned the lack of collegiate government.

One person who did not feel intimidated by Kirchner was Bergoglio. When I asked Fr Marco when he thought matters moved towards confrontation between the two leaders, he told me: 'It began with the realization that you have in front of you a government that tries to seduce, and if it can't do that, to confront openly and harass, which is how Kirchner dealt with friends and enemies. Bergoglio didn't allow himself to be either seduced or intimidated. The person who thinks that because he has got to know Bergoglio he can influence him doesn't really know him. Bergoglio is not a person that can be manipulated. He is the least easily manipulated person in the world, he is not easily influenced, and he keeps his own diary, scribbled in a small notebook.'

In May 2005, the year after Bergoglio used the *Te Deum* as an opportunity to criticize Kirchner's government, the President seemed to be on the back foot. Rather than risk being humiliated politically at the same event, Kirchner chose not to join Bergoglio in the Cathedral of Buenos Aires and instead marked independence day in the poor northern province of Santiago del Estero, where his political supporters included the local bishop Juan Carlos Maccarone. The diversion proved a disaster in government propaganda terms, suggesting that Kirchner could not face up to Bergoglio. But matters got worse for the President. And for his friendly bishop.

On 25 August 2005, in what Colin McMahon of the *Chicago Tribune* described as 'Part morality play, part conspiracy tale and part soap opera', sixty-four year-old Bishop Maccarone resigned amid newspaper reports that the Vatican had received a copy of a videotape showing the bishop having 'intimate relations' with a twenty-three-year-old chauffeur. Church officials, including Bergoglio's own spokesman, rather than focus on Maccarone's political links with Kirchner, jumped to the bishop's defence claiming he had been set up. They suspected Maccarone was targeted for his work on behalf of the poor and his opposition to local political clans and as part of a broader attempt to discredit the Church.

'Everything points to . . . political revenge,' Marco told the media at the time. The chauffeur, a youth called Alfredo Serrano, said he had made the video to get back at Maccarone for failing to help his family and find him a good job. At first Serrano said he was not paid for the cassette but then he said a television station had paid for it. He wouldn't say for how much. In various interviews with the Argentine media, Serrano's evidence also varied as to how long he and Maccarone had been sexually involved, from a few years to as many as five. 'Sounds like it was put together by some secret intelligence agency,' Marco told a radio station. Then to underline the sensitivity of the topic, Marco added that despite his role as the official spokesman for Cardinal Jorge Mario Bergoglio, in this case he was giving his personal opinion.

However, the scandal was a strong blow to the Church's credibility, according to Fortunato Mallimaci, a Buenos Aires sociologist who has written extensively about religion and Catholicism in Argentina. 'This means that the idea of the Catholic Church as the moral reference of the Catholic nation is very strongly put in doubt,' Mallimaci commented at the time. 'It shows that a double standard exists within the Church itself. This is not a Church that speaks only on religion. It has a strong public presence . . . So I hope this is going to open a debate about what is the political sphere of the Catholic Church.'

Such comments were music to the ears of Néstor Kirchner. The alleged scandal at the very least had served to expose the mutual mistrust between government and Church.

Less than a year later, in May 2006, another attempt by some government aides and Church officials to bring about a reconciliation between Kirchner and Bergoglio ran into the ground. The occasion was a service in Buenos Aires commemorating the murder of five priests from the Irish Pallottine order by a government-sanctioned death squad in July 1976, during the early days of the military regime. Months prior to the commemoration, during a visit to Rome, Kirchner had laid some flowers at a plaque dedicated to the priests in the Pallottines' Church of San Silvestro. He was then advised by his officials that his self-proclaimed image as a human rights crusader would benefit if he attended a similar service that was planned to take place in the Church of San Patricio in Buenos Aires, the scene of the original massacre.

Among those invited to the service was the British-born Anglican bishop and Primate of the Southern Cone in Buenos Aires, Gregory Venables, who found himself sitting next to Bergoglio, for whom he professed great respect. Venables recalled what happened next: 'We were sitting in front of the altar waiting for the celebration to begin when Kirchner's head of protocol came in and said: "The President would like to join you on the same bench." But Bergoglio told him, "No, this bench is for bishops," and made him sit on the other side of the aisle. I got the feeling that the President was not best pleased with the snub.'

Venables continued with his story: 'Later we went into a side room, where a plaque had been placed near the area where the priests were murdered. Bergoglio and I stood there in silent prayer, heads bowed, side by side. We were like that, when Kirchner barged in followed by his retinue. We did not move. For a moment Kirchner looked from side to side, seemingly at a loss as to why he was not at the centre of things, and why no one had greeted him. Kirchner was distracted by power, by protocol, by his own ego. It was obvious to us he did not see the need to recognize that a human tragedy was being commemorated and what was needed was not politics but humble reverence.'

By then further battle lines were being drawn between Kirchner and Bergoglio. Such was the distrust that Bergoglio on occasions took to switching on a radio and putting up the volume in order to disrupt what he suspected might be an attempt by the President's secret services to secretly record the Archbishop's private meetings. Publicly there were important issues of government policy over which the President and the Archbishop were fundamentally opposed to each other. One involved public morality, an issue over which Kirchner's libertarianism clashed with Bergoglio's sense of ecclesiastical responsibility.

An early testing ground was in April 2004 when the Ministry of Culture sponsored an exhibition by the Argentine artist León Ferrari which included an image of Christ on a US fighter aircraft and a bottle with the image of Pope Benedict XVI covered in condoms. Bergoglio published an open letter accusing Ferrari's works of being blasphemous and criticizing the holding of the exhibition in a public space that 'is funded by money that Christians and people of good will pay through their taxes'. The Archbishop asked for the capital's Catholics to mark their collective disquiet with a day of prayer and fasting. The appeal was not widely adhered to but did provoke a protest march through the city centre and a bomb threat against the cultural centre where the exhibition was being staged.

'The difference between me and Bergoglio,' responded Ferrari in a statement to the media, 'is that he thinks that people who don't think like him should be punished, condemned, while I think not even he should be punished.' Bergoglio did not say another word in public on the matter, not wishing to fuel the polemic in a way that would simply publicize the artist even more. With the evidence of hindsight, it was not the Archbishop's finest hour. His actions sat awkwardly with his later image of tolerance towards the imperfect human condition even if, in Vatican eyes, it confirmed him as a safe pair of hands doctrinally.

Nevertheless Bergoglio touched a more popular chord among

a growing body of voters, worried by the lack of transparency and accountability in government, with his denunciation of drug and human trafficking and his opposition to the rapidly expanding gambling industry, which he saw as exploitative and dehumanizing.

With the suggestion of government complicity, these were not the only issues that rattled political nerves in the Casa Rosada, turning Bergoglio, during Néstor Kirchner's first term, into the government's 'main leader of the opposition', to quote one of his own aides. Bergoglio's outspoken attacks on the corruption of the State came as he became increasingly involved, together with his priests, with the poor and marginalized of the *villas*, an area a populist Peronist government saw as its political reservation. Bergoglio also believed that the Kirchners were manipulating the human rights agenda for their own political purposes, falsely exaggerating the Church's and Bergoglio's alleged past collaboration with the military so as to discredit his moral and political authority.

As Archbishop, on issues relating to the family and sexuality Bergoglio showed himself initially less openly critical of gay partnerships than some more conservative bishops like the Archbishop of La Plata Aguero, but nevertheless took a much firmer line against Argentina becoming the first Latin American nation to legalize gay marriage. A week before the legislation was due to be voted on by the country's lawmakers, Bergoglio wrote a letter to a group of nuns, later widely leaked, in which he described gay marriage as 'something that the Devil himself was envious of, because it brings sin into the world by trying to destroy the image of God: men and women with their God-given mandate to grow, multiply, and exercise their dominion over the earth'.

Bergoglio had already urged Catholic schools and parishes around the country to oppose the new law, focusing on the sacred nature of the family unit – 'the right of every child to be raised and educated by a mother and father'. He also supported a protest to Congress by outraged orthodox Catholics and evangelists, although he did not participate in it, seemingly drawing back at the eleventh hour from turning the issue into a personal crusade. It was a wise move politically, and one that seemed to restore a sense of equilibrium in Bergoglio's social baggage, after his near-homophobic letter to the nuns. The demonstration drew just over 20,000 – 40,000 less than organizers had hoped for. The law allowing same-sex marriage was passed in July 2010 by a majority of votes in the lower house and in the Senate, with Catholics in the government coalition and the opposition split for and against on a free vote of 'conscience' or conviction.

During a protracted and emotional debate, opponents of gay marriage proposed a civil-union law instead that would have barred gays from adopting or undergoing *in vitro* fertilization to have children, and enabled any civil servant to 'conscientiously object' to register gay couples. In the end, as the *Huntingdon Post* reported, 'parliamentary manoeuvres kept the Senate from voting on civil unions as the government bet all or nothing on the more politically difficult option of marriage'. Sen. Juan Pérez Alsina, usually a loyal supporter of the government, called marriage between a man and a woman 'essential for the preservation of the species'. But others compared the discrimination closeted gays faced to the oppression millions suffered under Argentina's dictatorships, and urged their fellow senators to show the world how much Argentina had matured. 'Society has grown up. We aren't the same as we were before,' Sen. Daniel Filmus said. 'From today onward, Argentina is a more just and democratic country,' said María Rachid, president of the Argentine Lesbian, Gay, Bisexual and Transgender Federation. The law 'not only recognizes the rights of our families, but also the possibility of having access to health care, to leave a pension, to leave our assets to the people with whom we have shared many years of life, including our children,' she said.

The law was passed during Cristina Fernández's first term as president. She had been elected in 2007 to succeed her husband

Néstor, who became her consort. The duopoly remained firmly at loggerheads with Bergoglio on a growing range of issues. When Fernández clashed with the farming sector after decreeing a sliding scale of new taxes on farm exports, Bergoglio blamed the government for needlessly provoking food shortages that badly hit the poor. As Mario Llambías, the leader of the farmers union, later recalled: 'In the middle of the dispute, Bergoglio spoke out about charity, the defence of justice, the need to fight corruption, and the search for the common good.' Bolstered by his words, farmers set up barricades, and middle- and working-class housewives in Buenos Aires demonstrated by banging pots and pans in exasperation at the rise in prices.

Bergoglio remained an ever-present thorn in the side of the Kirchner regime, questioning the legitimacy of its mandate to govern. Much as Fernández tried to rally her supporters claiming that she was the people's champion, it was the farmers, Bergoglio and his priests, disaffected Congressmen and opposition journalists who claimed to have the moral high ground – and the opinion polls, showing the government approval ratings in sharp decline, provided compelling evidence that the duopoly was not as popular as it claimed.

Then something quite unexpected happened, which for a while radically altered the political balance. On 27 October 2010, Néstor Kirchner died suddenly of a suspected heart attack, producing a remarkable real-life drama at the Casa Rosada. In a country with a tradition of venerating dead populist figures, however dubious their suitability for sainthood in their lifetime, Kirchner's funeral became a rallying point for the Peronist movement, with his wife Fernández staging a public display of personal mourning that drew sympathy from even those who had garnered opposition to her presidency. For hours, Fernández stood stoically by her husband's coffin as it lay in state, greeting a seemingly endless line of mourners with a kiss or an embrace, while regularly touching the casket. She was visibly a widow in pain but symbolically her composure remained presidential. She was dressed in black, wearing pearls (in gemmology they mean sorrow and tears). She was to remain dressed in black for many months, striking a dramatic pose of enduring grief.

Before announcing whether she might run again for president, she kept the country guessing. 'I've given everything there is to give,' she said, an echo of Evita's dying words. When in October 2011, she was re-elected with 54 per cent of the vote, the biggest victory margin ever for an Argentine president, she chose her own oath: 'To God, country, and Néstor,' she swore just as Evita had sworn enduring loyalty to Perón.

The day after Kirchner's death, Bergoglio led a requiem Mass in a packed cathedral, as just across the square, thousands more filed past his coffin in the Casa Rosada. 'This man carried in his heart, on his shoulders and in his conscience the anointment of his people,' Bergoglio declared. 'The people asked that he lead them. It would be a huge ingratitude if the people, be they in agreement with him or not, were to forget that he was anointed by the popular will. Everyone should now come together and pray for someone who assumed the responsibility of leadership.'

This loose English translation does not do true justice to the true meaning of this extraordinary statement by Bergoglio on such an occasion. The word anointment – *unción* in the original Spanish – had been used by Bergoglio in previous sermons. He would use it repeatedly in the future both before and after becoming pope to underline the spiritually transformative effect and impact of human solidarity and reconciliation. In the Catholic Church and also deep in the Hebrew tradition *unción*, anointment or unction of the gravely sick or dead has a transcendent aspect – a rite of passage that is believed to establish the 'faithful' in the 'spiritual' hierarchy.

But also striking is the word Bergoglio uses for leadership – *conducir* – the verb from the noun *conductor*. Although literally meaning driver or conductor, it is one of the best-known words of the Argentine popular political lexicon. It was the word immortalized by General Perón who used the word rather than *lider* (leader). This distinguished him from a tyrant or dictator and justified his own style of authoritarian populist leadership to his massed followers as someone whose central control, charisma and vision coordinated and guided people to a common goal, in the manner of an orchestra conductor.

One explanation of Bergoglio's speech is that it served as a reminder of the sympathy he felt for Peronism from the early days. Its founder embraced a political philosophy that, while rooted in populist Latin American notions of 'benign' personalized rule, echoed Catholic social teaching as laid out in 1891 by Pope Leo XIII's encyclical *De Rerum Novarum* ('The Rights and Duties of Capital and Labour'). It also pursued the third way, being as critical of the excesses of capitalism as it was of socialism. 'Even though Bergoglio and Kirchner saw each other as powerful adversaries, they shared points in common: their personal management of power and a tendency to take executive decisions to resolve situations,' wrote the Argentine historian and journalist Marcelo Larraquy.

However, the importance of Bergoglio's eulogy was also rooted in the way it underlined a spirit of reconciliation with the former adversary, and the assumption that all human beings are created by God and therefore redeemable in a Church made up of saints and sinners. Evidence that Bergoglio did not personally relish either confrontational politics (which had a tendency in Argentina to descend into personal slander) or disloyalty to the Vatican had surfaced earlier when he parted company with his outspoken chief media strategist, Fr Marco. This followed a series of widely reported comments made by Marco accusing Kirchner of being 'divisive and fuelling hatred' and a separate interview with *Newsweek* magazine when the priest took issue with Pope Benedict's critical remarks about Islam. We cannot of course know for certain whether Kirchner would have himself appreciated Bergoglio's conciliatory words on the former President's death, still less whether he had undergone some kind of last-minute conversion to the Catholic faith or whether, listening to his former adversary, he might have been turning in his grave.

The fact is that Kirchner's death and all the ritual that surrounded it for a while swung the balance of power firmly in his widow's favour. While Fernández, at fifty-nine years old, claimed to have retained her Catholic faith, she had no love for Bergoglio whom she still considered a political opponent. Only on one issue was she prepared to be influenced by her religious principles: her refusal to make decriminalization of the country's abortion laws government policy. According to a court ruling in Argentina in 2012, abortion remained a crime, except when carried out in order to prevent danger to the life or health of the mother, or when the pregnancy was the result of rape. But the high-court ruling was not always subsequently applied, with some conservative localities – like Salta, located almost a thousand miles from Buenos Aires – still requiring that rape victims seek court permission for an abortion, which in some cases was not granted.

'When it comes to a woman's body and her authority over her own body, what we have is a male-dominated, patriarchal majority in society and the Catholic Church,' said Mabel Gabarra, spokesman for the national campaign for free and legal abortion when progress toward further liberalization was halted. Though Argentina had its second woman president in modern history, and for a second consecutive term, who had shown herself progressive in other social policies such as legal same-sex marriage and transgender rights recognition, abortion was one battle that Fernández was not prepared to fight with Bergoglio.

There had also been a brief time, when Fernández had ruled with her husband, that a tentative olive branch was extended by

Bergoglio to Cristina and her sister-in-law, Alicia Kirchner, Argentina's Minister for Social Development. He had tried to coordinate with them State and Church funding for the *villas*. As a symbol of reconciliation Bergoglio gave Fernández a prayer card reproducing one of his favourite icons: Mary, Untier of Knots.

But such encounters became overshadowed by Bergoglio's increasingly outspoken denunciations of the corruption of state institutions such as when he galvanized popular discontent over the circumstances surrounding the worst train crash in Argentina's history on 22 February 2012. In the morning rush hour, a commuter train carrying mainly low-paid workers and unemployed crashed at the busy central station, known as Once, in Buenos Aires. Fifty-one passengers were killed and more than 600 people injured, the deadliest in a series of train accidents in Argentina during the reign of the Kirchners.

The train was carrying more than 800 passengers and travelling at an estimated sixteen miles per hour when it entered the station, slamming into the barrier of the platform, destroying the engine. The nation's Auditor General later claimed that years of failed safety tests and other problems had given the government more than enough reason to cancel the train operator's concession. Others pointed to high-level corruption including years-old allegations that a former transportation secretary had taken free vacations and other gifts from executives of the train company responsible, in exchange for favourable treatment. The company for its part blamed government price controls, saying that keeping fares to less than 25 cents a ride made it impossible to finance improvements.

Bergoglio implied that corruption was behind the crash and blamed unnamed officials for not complying with their duty of care towards the general public as he held a special Mass at the Metropolitan Cathedral in remembrance of the victims. 'Almost all the passengers of the train were commuting to make their living in an honest way. We must not get used to travel as if we were cattle.

Let us not get used to the fact that nothing is ever mourned in the City, that everything is fixed and paid for,' he stated. Fernández responded by declaring two days of national mourning – but this time there was none of the sympathy shown towards her when her husband had died.

By then there was an evident widening rift that went beyond appearances – the Archbishop who shunned ostentation in gesture and word, and the President who couldn't help appearing in public without a heavy layer of make-up. 'I put it on like I am painting a door,' Fernández told her authorized biographer, journalist Sandra Russo. A whole chapter was dedicated to her appearance, a subject that many Argentines and even high-level diplomats believed held the key to deciding who she really was. To her supporters, the dark eye shadow and mascara, the bright red lipstick, together with the decorative earrings, long dark hair, varnished nails, designer dresses and high heels showed that she had not allowed power to dilute the femininity and discreetly veiled coquetry that, according to the nuns that educated her, had characterized her since schooldays. In other words she remained human, defining her womanhood in a world where male power prevailed. As Fernández told one of her closest aides: 'I like to seduce. I don't want people to just obey me. I want to convince them.'

And yet Bergoglio, who had never ceased to be a Jesuit in his spirituality, was not in the business of seduction, but of genuine conversion, of wanting human beings to be stripped of their pretensions and discover the best of themselves.

In 2007, when her husband persuaded her to stand for election as president, Fernández oozed Argentine chic in her designer outfits, with her dark-auburn hair tumbling over her shoulders, as it had done in her student days. Her critics called her disrespectfully the 'mare' and 'Botox Evita'. They suspected her husband had passed her the baton simply to ensure the continuity of their dynasty or, worse still, that behind the mask was a populist despot in the making. Her rallies were massive and militant, with a sea of Argentine flags suggesting an essentially nationalist power-drive.

Her foot had rarely left the accelerator since. She initiated that first term by insisting she be called *Presidenta* (the female for president) while hanging on to her use of maiden and married name. Her husband Néstor as vice-president remained her principal political ally and adviser, confirming Argentina's highest office as an effective political duopoly or, as political analyst Pablo Mendelevich has termed it, a diarchy.

She generated controversial headlines almost from day one in office when an individual arrested coming into Buenos Aires from Caracas was found to be carrying a suitcase filled with large amounts of high-value dollar notes – allegedly secret funds for her campaign from her close ally Hugo Chávez. The incident provoked a major diplomatic spat with the US administration, whom Fernández accused of hatching a CIA conspiracy.

One of the first high-profile initiatives of her presidency had been to slap the export tax on the country's politically conservative farmers. Billed as part of a strategy for liberating the nation from its seemingly endless cycle and submission to the international financial system, the move provoked four months of strikes and blockades, and saucepan banging. Fernández, under pressure of events, was forced to reach a fragile truce with the farmers. She proved less compromising with her most vocal critics in the media who questioned her probity, her politics and her style. Fernández brought in new legislation to dilute the power of her most vocal critics in the powerful *Clarín* media group, in which Fr Marco and Sergio Rubin, one of the Bergoglio's authorized biographers, wrote on religious affairs. She slashed state advertising in *Clarín* and *La Nación*, two newspapers that criticized her government, as she lavished money on rival newspapers, radio and television stations that supported her.

In 2009, Fernández pursued her populist agenda by having her government take control of televising national football matches as part of its so-called 'Football for Everybody' (FPT) programme, wresting match broadcasting rights away from a private enterprise in which her *bête noire*, the Clarín Group, had a major stake – a move publicly endorsed by the country's controversial football legend, Diego Maradona.

Fernández at no point defended Bergoglio while he was Archbishop and Cardinal from those who alleged he had been complicit with the military during the Dirty War. On the contrary, lawyers and judges sympathetic to her government went on the offensive, forcing Bergoglio to publicly account for his record on the controversial issue. In November 2010, Bergoglio was cross-examined by human rights lawyers over allegations of complicity with the military regime made against him by the journalist Horacio Verbitsky, who had been himself a close political ally of Néstor Kirchner.

The cross-examination took place before a judge investigating human rights violations at the ESMA detention camp where the Jesuit priests Yorio and Jalics were held in 1976. Bergoglio asked for and was granted a special dispensation under Argentine law as a high-ranking official who was not charged of any crime. He did not have to appear in court at the public hearing but instead was allowed to give his evidence before magistrates and lawyers in the Archbishopric, behind closed doors

However, the content of the proceedings were subsequently leaked to *Clarín* and was aired extensively by pro-government media with lawyers acting for victims of human rights violations describing Bergoglio as 'reticent' and 'uncooperative'. The filmed version of the hearing, posted online, showed a very tired and seemingly uncomfortable Bergoglio rejecting any suggestion he had betrayed the Jesuit priests by not protecting them from arrest. He also told the hearing that he had been unaware that a property owned by the Buenos Aires archdiocese had been used as a secret detention camp by the military in 1979 to hide prisoners of the ESMA, which was being visited by a United Nations inspection team. This allegation was reported by Horacio Verbitsky in his book *The Silence*. Bergoglio's presence in the hearing was as a witness as he had not been charged with any criminal activity. His main accuser, Verbitsky, responded by publishing a copy of one of the documentary sources he had used to make his original allegation – a fax written to him by Bergoglio, prior to the hearing, providing the journalist with details as to where he could find the deeds of the property in question. The hearing added little to what was already in the public domain, and left public opinion on the issue divided between those who felt he had not done enough to protect victims of human rights violations and had collaborated with the military, and those (a majority) who believed he was beyond criticism.

Undeterred by Bergoglio's self-defence, the government continued with its campaign against opposition media, encouraging human rights activists to pursue *Clarín*'s owner Ernestina Noble and her two adopted children, after alleging that they had been illegally seized as babies from their natural families during the military regime. A judicial inquiry into the case collapsed after DNA tests failed to link Mrs Noble's adopted sons to the alleged 'disappeared' birth mothers. Fernández pointedly refused to offer any apology for the invasion of privacy and trauma caused.

Even more controversial were the Kirchner family's business dealings. These came under scrutiny with the release between 2008 and 2010 of the President's official declaration of assets. This showed an increase in the first family's wealth from $2.3 million in 2003 to $18 million in 2010, the most recent year for which assets had been declared. According to the declaration, most of their money came from property deals in the Santa Cruz province, and interests in apartments and hotels in Buenos Aires and El Calafate, the Patagonian tourist resort where Fernández had a holiday residence she used when not staying at the Casa Rosada or the presidential residence in Olivos. She and her husband denied any illegality and her opponents failed to get any judge to put them on trial – but such wealth contrasted with the growing poverty of Argentina's low-paid workers and unemployed slum dwellers. Details of Fernández's personal enrichment emerged amid fresh allegations of financial irregularities which besieged her vice-president, Amado Boudou.

By March 2013, Fernández's popularity ratings were once again in decline amid signs that the economy was beginning to falter. Political tension was also on the increase, threatening a divisive power struggle with *La Presidenta* trying to secure a succession in her interests. Her growing irritability suggested a harried figure less in control than in the early days of her presidency – and she was evidently ill-prepared for the shock of the leader of the opposition being elected pope.

Part Two

Among The Believers

Chapter Twelve
Power and the Shanty Town

Days after Jorge Bergoglio was elected pope, I boarded a local train in Buenos Aires's Retiro central station and followed the public transport journey he had made on several occasions as a bishop.

The station, with its imperial exterior and impressive steel interior (made in Liverpool before being assembled in Argentina) was designed by British architects and engineers in the early twentieth century. For many years it was considered to be one of the most important examples of structural engineering in South America. These days it retains something of its original magnificence but on the mid-afternoon train I boarded, such a memory quickly diminished and was replaced by a harsher modern-day reality of Third World Argentina.

Reverberating and creaking, the rusting Mitre Line train moved slowly out like an abandoned museum piece, the track lined on one side by makeshift constructions of brick and sheet steel, flat roofs linked by a chaotic network of cables, narrow unpaved streets, and improvised sewage systems. Just a few hundred yards away, on the other side of the tracks, just beyond the Casa Rosada, the cathedral and government buildings, downtown Buenos Aires boasts banking and foreign exchange centres, luxury apartment blocks, shopping arcades, polo fields and casinos.

But the train moved on, heading north, struggling on its loose couplings, carrying its own world within it. The carriages were filled with crack addicts and drunks, street vendors and cleaners, mostly young women, aged and silenced by poorly paid office and domestic work and long hours. Those of the passengers who had a job, a minority including garbage collectors, had been working all night and part of a day. They were now sleeping. Those who were awake were subjected to a regular roll call of cut-price offers, from biscuits and chocolate bars to paper handkerchiefs and holy pictures. A man, drunk and drugged, begged for some coins, then collapsed on the floor and went into a deeper sleep than all the others before a friend shook him up and teased him, asked him how his non-existent job was going. 'Are you working?' the addict shouted back without waiting for an answer and taking another swig from his bottle. 'Well, I'm not.'

A vendor passed offering chocolate biscuits filled with dulce de leche. 'Two packets for the price of one – just ten pesos. Take one as a present,' he traded. He was followed by a hunchback crawling on his knees. 'I can't walk because I can't afford the cost of an operation on my legs,' he said, begging. Behind him a young girl, looking not more than a young teenager with a ragged unwashed look, carried a baby. 'I have no money to feed my child,' she said, hands held out in supplication.

The track to my final destination was just over fifteen miles long but it was in such bad shape that the journey took well over an hour. Through the window, a government poster came into view, with the statement, 'We are improving our railways, feel part of this great work,' in large letters signed by the President herself, Cristina Fernández de Kirchner. This stretch of line was a great deal worse than when I first arrived in the city, in the early 1980s, and the capital's *villas* or poor neighbourhoods had grown despite a massive increase in state borrowing, foreign investment and public spending. My journey began with one big shanty town, and ended with another as the train finally reached José León Suárez, the nearest station to the Villa la Cárcova.

The neighbourhood was bordered on one side by the capital's ring road and a gigantic open garbage field on the other. While the first marked the limit of its projection towards the city centre, the latter was the lifeblood of those who collected garbage with their hands and tried to sell it off for recycling, not always successfully. The large field, divided by a putrid canal, set off toxic vapours in the afternoon sun, its rotting surface populated by birds of prey and children scavenging and competing for scraps in bare feet.

I had come at the invitation of a priest, José María Di Paola, popularly known as Padre Pepe, whom Archbishop Bergoglio once described as 'a man of God who does my soul and spiritual life a lot of good'. Padre Pepe was waiting for me by the station in his rundown Fiat Duya, a rosary and a cross jangling from his front mirror, the passenger seats covered in loose prayer sheets, and a dashboard with well-worn stickers of the gaucho saint Antonio Gil and Nuestra Señora de Caacupé, Virgin of Paraguay. With his scraggy long black hair, crumpled slacks and loose-fitting clerical collar, Padre Pepe looked like a mix of hippie tramp and a born-again Christian who had taken to the road. But he drove me into the shanty town with the self-assured air of a scout returning to his tribe, a missionary in touch with his flock.

Just turned fifty, Padre Pepe belonged to a generation of Argentine priests who owed their appointment to the present pope. During the 1970s, Bergoglio saw his role as head of the Jesuits as one of principally ensuring discipline and spirituality among young priests, dissuading them from venturing into areas that might draw them into the violent and confrontational politics that engulfed his country – but nonetheless instilling in them the Ignatian ideal of seeking new frontiers, among the poor. During the 1990s as a bishop first and then archbishop, Bergoglio saw to it that a new cadre of loyal soldiers of the Church, parish priests, belonging to no particular order, left the leafy upmarket neighbourhoods of the metropolis to spread the good news of Jesus Christ among the poor and dispossessed of the *villas* or shanty towns. After Bergoglio succeeded the deceased Antonio Quarracino as Archbishop of Buenos Aires in February 1998, he increased from eight to twenty-five the number of priests assigned to the slums of the capital, a network whose coordination he entrusted to Padre Pepe.

Padre Pepe stood out from his peers because of his mix of youthful energy and charisma, as well as the practical expression of the 'theology of the people' that had begun to be championed by Bergoglio since his replacement as head of the Argentine Jesuits and his subsequent move up the ladder of clerical office after the fall of the military. The so-called theology of the people was based on the belief that true Christianity – the expression of Jesus Christ through the act of selfless sacrifice on behalf of others – was to be found among the poor and marginalized sectors of society. In particular, it was to be found in the popular culture of devotion to the Virgin Mary and other religious icons which bound communities in an essential spirituality that surpassed material need.

At the heart of what Bergoglio embraced as the theology of the people – a third way between Marxism and unfettered liberalism and in line with Church social teaching – was a sanctified Peronism. However, Padre Pepe also drew inspiration, at a deeper spiritual level, from the example of the early missionaries in Paraguay and Argentina. They had created self-ruling and self-sufficient communities known as *reducciones* ('reductions') for native Indians in a way that for a while protected them from the social injustices of the Portuguese and Spanish empires. The reductions developed into deeply religious and creative civic societies of their own under the paternalistic guidance and instruction initially of Franciscan and later of Jesuit fathers, between the late sixteenth and late eighteenth centuries when the Jesuits were expelled by Carlos III of Spain and the Guaraní Indians were abandoned to a state of colonial subservice.

The losing battle the Jesuit missionaries fought to preserve their missionary enclaves in Paraguay and northern Argentina against the repressive colonial state and its slave traders was dramatically depicted in the film *The Mission* (1986), starring Jeremy Irons and Robert de Niro. The two actors played the roles of Jesuit fathers with contrasting attitudes towards how to deal with injustice – the first, played by Irons, believed in passive resistance and spirituality, the other in justified violent action – a dichotomy that would resurface among some Argentine priests before and during the military regime.

Years later, in 2012, an Argentine film *El Elefante Blanco* depicted contemporary life in one of the more notoriously violent *villas* known as La Ciudad Oculta or hidden city, telling the story of three fictitious friends: an Argentine priest, Fr Julián, a Belgian missionary, Fr Nicholás, and a local female social worker called Luciana. Together they work to try and resolve the problems of delinquency and gun crime which are rampant in the *villa* but gradually take divergent paths in the face of the obstacles they face: the complicity of the Catholic hierarchy with a corrupt state apparatus, police repression and the pervasive influence of rival organized drug trafficking gangs. While Fr Julián seeks dialogue with the authorities, and negotiates with the drug gangs so that neither side encroaches on each other's agreed territory, Fr Nicholás has an affair with Luciana and adopts an increasingly militant attitude, organizing anti-government demonstrations by the slum dwellers, and visiting the home of drugs dealers to intercede on behalf of the victims of their shootouts.

The leitmotif of the film, which gives it the title, is a gigantic abandoned tower block promised by successive governments as a new hospital but never built. It is a squat for rough sleepers, mainly drug addicts and drug dealers. The White Elephant is a symbol as much of government corruption and Argentina's endemic drug problem as of the Church's impotence in fighting both. The film has the bishop abandoning the shanty town to its fate, and ends with both priests shot by police after being caught up in a gunfight between them and a young drug addict they are trying to get to hospital in their car. Fr Julián is badly wounded and subsequently dies while Nicholás recovers and heads off to a monastery to try and rediscover a life of celibacy and contemplation before returning to the *villa*, chastened ideologically but with renewed spiritual energy to pursue a life among the poor.

Dealing with drug traffickers and drug addicts, and confronting corrupt authorities and occasional ecclesiastical bureaucracy, were part of existence in La Cárcova. Moreover Padre Pepe himself had formed an emotional attachment to a woman once, a relationship he openly discussed with his biographer Silvina Premat for her book *El Cura de La Villa*. However, while admitting that the film had brought the reality of Argentine slum life to a national and international film audience, Padre Pepe resisted the suggestion that Fr Julián was loosely based on him or any other of his colleagues, and accused the filmmakers of distorting life in the *villa*, adopting an unfairly negative and pessimistic view – of the slum dwellers and the Church. 'What the film *El Elefante Blanco* fails to reflect are the positive Christian values that many of the slum dwellers draw from their religious faith, their strong sense of human solidarity, of family, of caring for others – living the Gospel through their simplicity and instinctive creativity showing that poverty can be redemptive,' Padre Pepe told me as we shared a bowl of *mate* tea for the first time in his cramped office one chilly afternoon in late August (winter in Argentina).

Padre Pepe told his biographer that his love for a woman was not the reason he had a spiritual crisis, seven years into his priesthood, aged thirty-two, but the thought, prompted by the birth of a nephew, that if he went on being a priest, he would never have a wife and children. 'At times the thought went away and he felt he could find a different fulfilment remaining celibate – but then it would come back like a heavy weight that took away his peace,' writes Silvina Premat in her authorized portrait.

The year was 1994. Padre Pepe was working in another poor neighbourhood of the capital. His local bishop and immediate ecclesiastical authority was Jorge Bergoglio. Unlike the judgemental and politically corrupted bishop in *El Elefante Blanco*, Padre Pepe's real-life superior showed understanding for his priest's struggle and respected his honesty the day he owned up to his 'crisis' rather than keeping it repressed. Bergoglio turned down Padre Pepe's requests that he be granted a definitive licence to leave the priesthood (celibacy is a tradition rather than an article of faith in the Catholic Church) and instead told him to accept a temporary suspension and take time off to reconsider his future. 'Bergoglio saw that Pepe was an honest guy – who was truthful with himself and with others, that his doubt was a serious one and that he had to resolve it the best way possible, not under God's table but face to face with him, face to face with his bishop,' wrote Pepe's biographer.

Padre Pepe spent several months working as a human resources manager in a factory while having a relationship with the woman, a teacher, he had been attracted to when his 'crisis' first blew up. He also spent long hours listening to a monk who was an old friend and who told him he owed his faith to living in a community. At one point Pepe asked him for his definition of priestly celibacy. 'To love without possessing, to be loved without dependency,' his friend answered. Pepe discerned his true calling was to be back in the *villa*, as a priest. When Pepe asked Bergoglio's permission the Bishop embraced him, like a father, his prodigal son lost but found. 'I've come back, Monsignor,' said Fr Pepe. 'Come back? Surely not. You never left,' Bergoglio answered.

Days later it was 20 July – traditionally the Day of the Friend in Argentina. Padre Pepe and Bergoglio concelebrated a Mass together in the Jesuit church of San Ignacio, next to the order's Salvador school in Buenos Aires. To his initial surprise, the congregation was made up mainly of women ranging from their early twenties to their fifties. Only after the Mass was over did Bergoglio tell him that he had offered up the Mass at the request of a friend, a former prostitute he had converted to Catholicism. The other women were in their majority still in the profession.

There was much forgiveness to be asked for and mercy justifiably given in the world he had returned to, as a priest, Padre Pepe told me when I caught up with him twenty-eight years later. With his long black hair and beard and translucent eyes, the fifty year old had the restless air of a committed disciple that gave no hint of piety. His box-like 'office', near the chapel and community centre he had helped build, was stripped down to bare essentials: a small wooden table and chair and a small disordered filing cabinet. Along the wall was a simple cross, posters of Jesus Christ, St Francis of Assisi and the Virgin Mary, and a commemorative photograph of Fr Carlos Mugica, the radical priest who was shot dead by an assassin in 1974 after celebrating Mass in the shanty town where he worked.

Mugica's personality and politics still made him a controversial figure. On the fortieth anniversary of his death opinion remained divided as to the true identity of the gunman who killed him and whether it was the extreme-right Triple A (the most likely) or the Montoneros or some other left-wing terrorist group that was behind it. After his death, Mugica's body was claimed by his family, and taken away from the shanty town where he had sacrificed his life, to the city's grandiloquent cemetery for the rich and famous and buried in a grand marble pantheon where his Basque ancestors had been laid to privileged rest.

The memory of Mugica was suppressed by the military regime

that took power in 1976, only to be resurrected with the return of democratic rule. Mugica was given a new lease of life – or at least subjected to a sympathetic revisionism – when Archbishop Bergoglio and his *curas villeros* (the slum priests) embraced the theology of the people: theology not as a static abstract but as evolutionary, capable of responding to an ever-changing historical context with the timeless message of the Gospel at its heart. 'We feel part of the same timber as Padre Mugica . . . part of a certain continuity within the Church, because his essential ideas and that of other worker priests who preceded him endure. They chose to be in the *villa,* living alongside the poor which was in itself a transformative experience. The poor transmit certain values as a result of not aspiring to any power, and with that comes wisdom, clarity of thought,' Padre Pepe told me later as we shared a meal of pasta and wine with a small group of university graduates who worked in the shanty town as young volunteers.

While Mugica prioritized political action at a time of revolutionary Marxist-inspired fervour and reactionary right-wing repression, the populist era of the Kirchners required a different approach. Padre Pepe's focus was on the 'spiritually and socially redemptive possibility of popular culture' to which liberation theology gave less publicized content. Veneration of the Virgin of Caacupé put the slum dwellers in touch with those indigenous roots, which nineteenth-century Argentine generals had tried to eradicate but which the early Franciscan and Jesuit missionaries had sought to transform into a new multicultural land of paradise. The Santo Gaucho Gil, meanwhile, appealed to the historical populist nationalist narrative favoured by Peronism.

There were thus three strands of legend informing the iconography in the *villa.* The first, having to do with the Virgin of Caacupé, had an 'Indio José', an indigenous resident of one of the Franciscan *reducciones* or mission enclaves, having to hide from a rival tribe while wandering in the forest. José made a promise that if his life was saved he would carve a statue of the Virgin from the wood of the tree behind which he was hiding. The danger passed, and he fulfilled his promise, carving not just one but two identical Virgins. A sequel has the Franciscan mission being saved from a huge flood after the Indio José swam out and recovered a small case floating in the water. Inside was a statue of the Virgin.

The second icon, Santo Gaucho Gil, was a swashbuckling Errol-Flynn lookalike, with long flowing black hair and handlebar moustache, dressed in the scarf, baggy shirt and trousers of the Latin American cowboy. Antonio 'Gauchito' Gil is famed as a Latin American Robin Hood who lived in Argentina as an outlaw in the 1800s after refusing to fight against his fellow countrymen in a civil war. He is revered for sharing his spoils with the poor and protecting them to this day. Legend has it that just before a police sergeant slit Gil's throat, Gil told him he was killing an innocent man who after death could intercede on his behalf with God. His executioner should pray to him, Gil said, for his child's recovery from an illness. The sergeant did so and the child was cured, giving birth to the cult of Gauchito Gil.

Around 8 January every year, tens of thousands of Argentines travel long distances to the town of Mercedes, about 480 miles north of Buenos Aires, to pray at the roadside sanctuary of El Gauchito Gil. But posters and shrines to the Gauchito take pride of place in the shanty neighbourhoods of the metropolis all the year round. The saint is still not officially recognized by the Church. Nevertheless he is part of Argentina's populist historical narrative, and respected by Bergoglio's *cura villeros*, many of whom like Padre Pepe belong or are sympathetic to the Peronist movement, as a necessary force of social cohesion in a community largely made up of displaced and marginalized migrants.

The cult saint and the Virgin of Caacupé are celebrated with processions, prayers and drunken revelries where communities come together and let their hair down, occasionally yelping piercing cries of joy known in the indigenous Guaraní language as '*sapucay*'. Pilgrims offer Gauchito Gil everything from licence plates to wedding dresses to thank him for his miracles. He is revered by truckers and bus drivers who believe he protects travellers. Crimson banners on roads all through Argentina mark shrines to him, and the words 'Thanks, Gauchito Gil' are painted on many trucks. He is attributed with powers of identifying criminals and with a keen sense of what represents the common good. In each poor neighbourhood, oral history passes down tales of miracles being experienced by one family or another. Although lacking sufficient evidence to have him pronounced a saint, his emotional impact in many *villas* is bigger than any European saint or apostle passed down by universal tradition and official Church teaching.

Padre Pepe told me that devotion to these icons was a necessary refuge and support for those who would otherwise turn to violence, drugs or even self-mutilation as a way out of their desperation. He sees these folk-saints and Virgin myths as creative responses to the failure of State institutions. He saw his role as helping reaffirm people's faith while guiding it away from superstition and back to Jesus Christ. Or as another Argentine priest – Julián Zini, who has regularly visited Gil's sanctuary – put it: 'Because the Church did not evangelize enough by telling the faithful their intermediary with God is Jesus, people have sought out intermediaries closer to them and to their reality.'

Alongside these icons, and the huge annual pilgrimages to the sanctuary of the Virgin of Luján (declared in 1930 by Pope Pius XI Patroness of Argentina, Uruguay and Paraguay), the *villa* honours its third icon: Fr Carlos Mugica. Like El Gaucho Gil, he is not officially beatified as yet by Pope Francis but he was long ago blessed by Bergoglio as a Peronist folk-martyr who in his courageous witness to his faith anticipated the Jesuit's own conversion.

Mugica's remains have been transferred from his family mausoleum and now lie enclosed in a simple tomb in the chapel of the *villa* near Retiro station he helped build. The shrine includes the blackened bronze cross Mugica always insisted should never be polished as he didn't want to symbolize a church of ostentation. A small piece taken from the trousers Mugica was wearing when he was shot stands by the altar, encased in a simple glass frame.

'For Catholics, relics are like a part of a loved one. It is what's left of the loved one,' Padre Pepe said at the inauguration of the altarpiece on 9 October 2009. 'The fact that he is buried here means that he is present. It's a good thing because it shows our commitment to live by his example . . . Fr Carlos taught us to live the gospel of love, the gospel of Jesus. This tells us that we must not just think of our neighbour, but take care of him. Fr Carlos took care of the other. What he did will endure because it belongs to God, it's not an invention.'

Mugica's remains were transferred from his family mausoleum ten years earlier in October 1999 in a ceremony that involved not just the active participation of numerous priests and hundreds of *villeros*, but also Bergoglio, recently appointed Archbishop of Buenos Aires. The occasion was memorable, not just because it confirmed Mugica's iconic status, but because of the way it marked a future pope's reputation, rescuing it from the political and moral shadowlands he had occupied in his earlier days as a Jesuit. Bergoglio's insistence on that day that it should be one of Mugica's friends, Fr Botan, and not himself who should be the lead celebrant of the Mass was in itself a rare act of humility for an Archbishop of Buenos Aires. But Bergoglio did not remain silent. He used the occasion to make an unprecedented act of contrition for the past failings of the Argentine Church during the country's worst period of political violence and State-led repression. Turning from Mugica's remains to the large assembled crowd and media, Bergoglio said in a clear voice that would resonate well beyond the *villa*: 'Let us pray for Fr Carlos's assassins, and the ideologues that lay behind it, but also for the complicit silence of most of society and of the Church.'

Bergoglio's new cadre of priests may not have had rival political terror gangs or a repressive military regime to confront, but they faced a social and political reality that presented a huge challenge nonetheless. In the lead-up to Argentina's hosting of the World Cup in 1978, the military bulldozed large swathes of the *villas* and forcefully expelled their inhabitants, including those who had long lived near the River Plate stadium. With the return of democracy, vacant land in different parts of the city was again occupied by squatters and unlicensed building resumed. Now the *villas* were inhabited by unemployed Argentines escaping from the provinces or unable to afford the cost of dwellings offered by the State in the city because of spiralling inflation and indebtedness. During the 1990s the *villa* population was boosted by an influx of poor immigrants from other Latin American countries, attracted by the illusion of potential wealth to be made during a period of economic growth, however fragile its underpinning.

Some older priests who had survived the repression began to organize the slum dwellers into cooperatives, encouraging them to use their combined skills as construction labourers, electricians and plumbers to build with great care and planning: what the military had dismissed as *villa miserias* (misery slums) came to define themselves as simply *villas* – villages. But the sheer volume of squatters evading the law and taxation, combined with the ever-increasing homeless and jobless in desperate straits of survival, held back development. While the State failed to invest in adequate social services and infrastructure, the politicians interfered as much as they could, with the Peronist party particularly invasive. The system of so-called *punteros* or fixers, as local party officials were called, was endemically corrupt, with those supposed to be involved in looking after the interests of the community engaged in widespread graft and cronyism, in many cases linked to central government and state companies.

In 1998, during the Peronist government of Carlos Menem,

Padre Pepe was sent into Villa 21.24, one of the fastest growing and most notoriously violent slums in Barracas, the southeast neighbourhood of Buenos Aires. There, he found a community effectively abandoned by the State. The *villa* lacked security of employment, basic social services, schools and infrastructure. Lawlessness ranged from petty crime to increasing activity linked to the drugs trade run by local mafias, as well as by more powerful barons that straddled the continent.

Padre Pepe was under instructions from Bergoglio to set up his parish headquarters at the centre of the slum and to draw to his church, with the help of lay volunteers, those in need of social as well as spiritual support of one kind or another. Around a simply built whitewashed concrete chapel, lined with religious murals crafted by local slum dwellers, there developed a small complex of makeshift buildings and patios were people were fed, clothed and offered medical advice, with funds provided by Cáritas, the Catholic Church's charity. There was a small crèche for children, a dining room, spare beds for the elderly and a rehabilitation programme for those, in particular teenagers, who had developed a drug habit, smoking *paco*, 'the drug of extermination'. The programme included taking youths out of the slums to small activity camps in the countryside.

Soon after taking up his first major assignment, Padre Pepe arranged for a replica image of the Immaculate Virgin of Caacupé to be installed in the chapel and regularly paraded through the slum. She was a tiny unassuming Virgin, whose small size and characterless face was transformed in the popular imagination. Around her the slum dwellers, many of them Paraguayans, much darker skinned than she was depicted, would gather to pray and petition, an act of faith as well as a necessary gesture of communal solidarity. Such acts, Padre Pepe and Bergoglio hoped, would help guarantee a more peaceful and spiritual existence for *villeros*, otherwise susceptible to the power of criminals and a sense of hopelessness instigated by a corrupt State. But the programme, replicated by priests in other slum areas, proved mostly a palliative rather than a cure. In the absence of coordinated political action or indeed of a Church willing to get involved in forcing political change, the theology of the people was limited in its ability to engage with and indeed receive State assistance in any meaningful organized programme.

Despite the Church's best efforts to bring in a more benign regime, it was swimming against the current. *Paco*, a highly addictive and toxic drug, began to spread in a significant way through the slums of Buenos Aires after the country's devastating economic crisis in 2001. Made from the residue of coca leaves, *paco* was widely considered by Argentines to be the most dangerous drug on the market – more so than heroin or crack. It's a potpourri of cocaine waste, rat poison, kerosene and various industrial solvents. The effects from one hit last from five to ten minutes, but the initial intensity of the drug (often described as an 'orgasm') lasts for only a few seconds. Afterwards, the muscles tense and the body craves more, plunging the user into a deep state of depression and desperation.

Between 2001 and 2005 *paco* use in Argentina increased 200 per cent, with drug dealers selling a dose for one peso (the equivalent to 25 cents at the time), compared to ten pesos for cocaine. In the decade since Argentina's financial collapse in 2001, the country's economy recovered but *paco* continued to pose a serious social and health risk in large swathes of Buenos Aires occupied by slum dwellers.

During the early years of Padre Pepe's life in the slums, the instruction he and other priests received from their Archbishop Bergoglio was to try and minimize the risk to their own lives and those who sought their protection. This meant neither proselytizing in the areas controlled by drug gangs nor breaching the trust of those who came to church seeking help. As part of the stand-off, the priests tried to avoid being seen as open collaborators of the police. Instead, they focused some of their efforts in helping those who had no official residency papers get access to hospital treatment. It was a controversial strategy that was destined to fail as the drug culture became more pervasive in the slums, and the drug gangs increasingly violent.

Padre Pepe and other lesser-known priests in 2009 broke the fragile *entente cordiale* by issuing – with Bergoglio's blessing – a hard-hitting denunciation of the tragic impact illicit drugs were having on Argentine society, accusing drug gangs of ruining the lives of young people and whole families, and the State of being complicit because of its failure to intervene. 'Among us,' said the priests' statement, prominently signed by Padre Pepe, 'illicit drugs have been effectively decriminalized. You can possess and use drugs with barely anyone attempting to stop you. It is a matter of fact that neither the police nor any other representative of the State intervenes in the lives of these kids that have poison in their hands . . . These youths have had their minds and spirit ruined and have no possibility of living a civilized life.'

A month later, and after the statement was followed up with a high-profile media campaign featuring Padre Pepe, he received a message from one of the drug gangs that if he didn't silence himself and abandon the slum, he would be killed. The threat prompted Bergoglio to make a public statement in support of one of his most valued priests, in effect reconfirming himself as the Catholic Church's main field commander in the *villas* while also publicly holding the Kirchner/Fernández government responsible for what happened. Speaking in Buenos Aires cathedral in a widely publicized annual Mass for teachers, parents and schoolchildren, Bergoglio described illegal drugs as one of the main challenges facing the Church and society: 'Drugs are a nightmare, a very grave problem, an issue that should concern not just these priests but all of us. We have to protect our children because sometimes this nightmare world makes us forget the natural way we have of protecting our children.'

Hours earlier, Argentine President Kirchner's Minister of the Interior, Aníbal Fernández, had responded to media coverage of the threat to Padre Pepe by claiming that the Church and State were joined at the hip in a common battle against drugs: 'It's not just priests but officials who are threatened. It's an occupational hazard. The only difference is that we government officials don't go public on it.'

However, when Bergoglio spoke, he also pointed the finger at darker, more powerful conspiracies: 'The threats should not be belittled, because none of us know what might be their outcome. This intimidation comes from drug traffickers who are powerful merchants of a nightmare.' Bergoglio was not alone in suspecting that the Peronist government of Néstor Kirchner, elected in the aftermath of Argentina's economic collapse in 2001, was far from being one of the traffickers' opponents; many thought that the government was complicit, through a laissez-faire approach not unrelated to corruption, in allowing the illicit drugs trade to have grown as it had.

For a while Padre Pepe stayed on in the *villa*, with the support of the many people who looked to him as a true pastor. For a while he also counted on the backing of his own Archbishop Bergoglio who had experienced at first hand in the *villa* the Gospel being delivered in a spirit and language that could be understood by those most in need of it. Since becoming an archbishop, Bergoglio had become a regular visitor to the *villa*, travelling unaccompanied by public transport, and often turning up unannounced just before a Mass celebrated by one of his priests. He also paid personal visits to some of the poorest dwellings in the capital to listen to people's problems, pray with them and suggest whatever help was needed.

One of Padre Pepe's parishioners was a young unemployed woman called Miriam who had become addicted to *paco*. Fr Pepe had taken her into his community's care after she had miraculously survived being beaten up, gang raped and thrown into the local putrid canal. During her struggle to rehabilitate herself, Miriam met Bergoglio on one of his visits. 'I saw a father, I saw a light,' she later recalled. 'He said he wanted to help me train as a therapist so I could help other addicts and he managed to get me a scholarship to do a university course.'

On Maundy Thursday 2008, Bergoglio washed the feet of twelve former and recovering addicts in Padre Pepe's chapel, engaging in conversation with each one. Miriam was one of them; it was the first time in her life she had ever had a man humble himself before her with such respect and love.

Padre Pepe continued his work for another year. However, he came under pressure from Bergoglio who had become increasingly alarmed by the continuing death threats which be believed endangered the lives not just of the priest but many of his followers. Arrangements were made for Padre Pepe to take a low-profile sabbatical in a 'safe house' in a remote rural community in the northern province of Santiago del Estero.

After two years working in an educational and social assistance scheme for poorly paid rural workers, Padre Pepe returned to Buenos Aires when he was reassigned from Villa 21.24 to La Cárcova, a no less challenging parish where we met in 2013 and again in 2014. Time had not stopped still. With Bergoglio's support, other *cura villeros* had carried on with their mission of making the *villa* a place where humanity struggled but prevailed.

Chapter Thirteen
First Stop, Brazil

On Sunday, 28 July 2013, Pope Francis ended his six-day visit in Rio de Janeiro, celebrated by hugely enthusiastic crowds that had grown close to three million, a record attendance never seen before in this city famous the world over for its massive street parties.

I had anticipated his arrival by a few days, flying out from London to Brazil's major seaside city to test the mood as the faithful gathered to greet the newly elected pope – the first Latin American pontiff – on his first papal trip abroad. My flight out from Heathrow was delayed by several hours because a bird had been caught in the engine of the plane that was supposed to fly us across the Atlantic. Despite reassurances from British Airways that the engine was not severely damaged, I thought it best to pray and commend myself to God. Others of greater faith than me seemed more relaxed. For a while Heathrow's Terminal 5 seemed taken over by happy pilgrims, content with the nature of their journey, and thus with themselves. With its gigantic halls, packed with retail outlets, barely separated from the seating areas, the terminal was a temple to Mammon. Yet the pilgrims had brought their own modest provisions, for sharing, and sat on the floor. They had turned the departure lounge into a giant picnic area. The large majority were young Italian men and women, and a sampling of priests, among them missionaries, on their way to join thousands of others who had signed up to World Youth Day, to be celebrated by a pope few had experienced beyond the TV images of his appearances in Rome. Heathrow seemed as good a place as any to test what kind of Church was being stirred by the election of Jorge Bergoglio to the world's most important spiritual post, the supreme leader of 1.2 billion Catholics.

The leader of the largest and most enthusiastic group of Italians at Heathrow on the day was a tall, thin thirty-odd-year-old priest, Fr Alejandro Pala, carrying the weight of a bulging rucksack on his shoulders with the effortless air of a global hitchhiker. I asked him what motivated his vocation.

He replied, 'My parents were not particularly religious. After my first Communion I stopped going to Mass. I suffered heart problems, failing arteries. After an operation I started to think: Where is my life going? Will I ever play sport again, what will I do, what shall I study? I studied law, philosophy, but I felt empty. Then one day I was invited to a prayer meeting in the local parish. The priest welcomed me with a simple word: "Peace." He then said there were two paths to fulfilment: a happy marriage or a happy priesthood. He didn't say which one was for me. He just said, "Go away and think about it." I thought about it for four months. Then I was alone one night and suddenly the thought came to me: "What if I become a priest and devote my life to others?" It was an inner voice that seemed to ask me. And then a great sense of peace and liberation came over me. I was ordained by Pope Benedict and worked in a mission in Belo Horizonte.'

So what of Pope Francis?

'At first, many people were a bit perplexed. They didn't really know who he was. But more and more people have warmed to him, realizing he is a simple man, on the side of the poor. I hope he will deal with the Vatican bank,' Fr Alejandro replied.

A few yards away stood Elena Teschi, a vivacious twenty-four-year-old pharmaceutical student who seemed deeply attached to her mobile, when not looking up, taking in the surrounding scene and reflecting on it with a benign smile. This was her fourth World Youth meeting after those held by the previous pope in Cologne, Sydney and Madrid. Why did she keep going to these gatherings? I asked her.

'It is a way of taking a break from your daily life and finding the time and space to meet Jesus Christ who by dying on the Cross showed us love and mercy. Pilgrimage is a version of this. For the rest of the year it is difficult to find yourself. But this journey helps me get closer to God. It's a form of intense prayer. I find myself saying it quietly to myself, or out loud if there are others who I know who are on the same wavelength. I pray this: "I know you are the truth, I know I want to live like you. But it is difficult. I haven't the strength, I need guidance. Please *Papa Francisco*; help me in that process . . ."'

She continued, unprompted by further questions. It seemed a cathartic moment for her, and also an extended prayer. The sincerity of her words and the warmth of their expression seemed temporarily to blot out the commercialized frenzy of the airport terminal and draw us closer to sacred ground.

Elena shared her life – full of wounds of one kind or another – as if we were old friends. 'I've been in a difficult relationship with my parents as I've grown up, but I have learnt with others to love and be merciful. My faith is a personal thing. It wasn't passed on to me by my parents. I like being with other people, finding unconditional love. There was this woman who took the trouble to love me unconditionally and to get me to talk about my problems. She made me realize I had a lot of anger. Now I look forward to having a family, to being a mother, to being a wife. I am also learning to love my parents the way they are and to tell them what I feel like without being afraid. I feel I can say I love you although this is going on in your lives. It hurts me but I still love you. I'm not blaming you. I pray for Peace, and to be myself.'

So how did Pope Francis play into her life? I asked.

'I love Francis. He goes straight to the point. It is so helpful to hear him say things the way he says them. So straightforward. He is an example. He makes clear that God is loving. Behind this pope is Jorge Bergoglio – a humble priest and a caring pastor . . .'

Later, on the plane, I found myself sitting next to twenty-five-year-old Jean Paul from Myanmar, Burma, who was studying for the priesthood in Rome. He admitted to feeling uplifted by the enthusiasm of other students travelling with us, but also by the new pope. 'We can see the Church at its best in the spirit of these young people. They are prepared to sacrifice themselves for others. They see life as a community, and they see this pope as a true spiritual leader who speaks a language they can understand. Francis knows how to communicate in a simple way, and be close to the people. Benedict was a good man too but an intellectual. Francis wants to change the Church so as to have it firmly on the side of the poor. He wants there to be more reconciliation and less conflict.'

As we flew over the Atlantic, Jean Paul told me, in stuttering English, a little about himself, enough to remind me how challenged the celibate priesthood felt by the surrounding world. 'I was baptized when I was young, discovered faith through reading. As I got older my faith got stronger. As a human being I am vulnerable to temptation but after confession I feel recharged spiritually. I have been six years in the seminary. I've got eight years to go at least before I am ready to be a priest. I know we have to prepare ourselves well and that some priests are in crisis and need prayer – Will you pray for me?'

I said I would and then asked him if he thought there should be married priests.

'Married priests? This is a question I will have to look at when I study theology,' he replied. Then he thought a little more. 'But I don't think marriage is the solution. The solution comes from within – you have to contain your bodily desires. Find yourself in prayer. But it's difficult, very difficult, so pray for me. It's a long road.'

At the age of sixty-seven, it was a road that Fr José Álvarez, an Augustinian missionary, originally from Zamora, Spain, had been walking for some while. If celibacy was not at the top of his agenda it was because he was faced with more pressing problems, which left him little time to ponder about sexuality – his or anybody else's – living as he had been for years in one of Rio's worst *favelas* or slums. His parish was made up by three *favelas*, criss-crossing each other's boundaries and hugging the side of the small mountains that jut out around the city.

Hours before the Pope's arrival, Fr José's 'D-Day', he was struggling with a small group of volunteers to finish preparing for the arrival of over a hundred pilgrim students from Europe, who he had agreed to accommodate in a temporary dormitory he had set up in his Church. It was the safest part of an otherwise crime-ridden neighbourhood. 'For over thirty years this neighbourhood was abandoned by the State as it filled up with poor rural workers from the north and displaced unemployed from Rio itself. There was a big increase in the illegal drugs trade, with dealers selling every kind of drug from marijuana to crack.'

Back in 1983, on my first visit to Brazil, I visited neighbouring Vidigal, then the largest *favela*, as a young foreign correspondent based in South America. *Favelas* looked pretty, warm and beckoning, but then I had always seen them from a distance, I wrote at the time. At night from a plane, I had gazed down on them. They looked like candles flickering on water. In daytime, from the privileged view I had from my apartment building, the nearby *favela* on the ridge across the valley was rust coloured. Then in the dark it was filled with the soft light of lanterns. There was a distant dog bark and the sporadic cry of a child.

I took a taxi along the seafront filled with tourists and then walked into Vidigal. It was set out on a hill just behind the Sheraton Hotel. I was met by Fr Jesús, a Spanish Jesuit. He was waiting for me, reading his breviary by a rubbish tip. He took me to a building where there was a school and a chapel and invited me to join him for Mass. The chapel was built like a garage, but its walls were decorated with children's drawings and slogans evoking the Church's social conscience. There were no chairs, so people either stood or sat around the altar – a bare table on which was set a jug, a wooden cross and some loaves of bread. There was a lot of singing and when it came to the 'Our Father' everyone stood in a circle and held hands.

Fr Jesús told me he found a greater sense of community in Vidigal than in any neighbourhood in Rio. He knew that in other *favelas* that were growing around the city, there was already a sense not so much of community as ghetto. The residents quickly identified and disposed of outsiders. To be allowed in, you had to prove yourself a mugger or a murderer or both. The drug gangs would come in later. In Vidigal, by the grace of God, things were different then. The local community, helped by Fr Jesús, had organized its own electricity and internal water supply, its own schooling and health service. The money came mainly from the Church and the government.

The funds from the government might not have been so forthcoming had it not been for the visit that Pope John Paul II made in the early 1980s. He had been shown Vidigal as an exemplary 'City of Poor'. The military regime at the time, as subsequent elected governments would also do, blamed the poverty on the unscrupulous behaviour of the foreign banks, conveniently forgetting that it takes two sides to create a debt and the borrower is a corrupt State.

I remember that at the top of the hill in Vidigal there was a small chapel, marking the place where Pope John Paul II had celebrated Mass. Inside was a small glass box containing a large gold ring with the inscription, 'The ring was donated by Pope John Paul II on the occasion of his visit to Vidigal.' I asked Fr Jesús why he hadn't sold the ring and used the money for the *favela*. He told me that he had held a ballot on the subject of the ring and everyone in the *favela* had voted to keep it or give it to the city's museum. 'You see, it's not money people have here, it's social coexistence,' he told me.

Thirty years on, I struggled to see what had changed as Fr José took me on a walking tour of his three *favelas* – a large area of seemingly endless unpaved streets and narrow alleyways lined with haphazardly constructed one- and two-storey shacks, and garages, made up of metal sheeting, which doubled up as shops selling basic foods and drink. Fr José and his team of teachers and social workers ran a small primary school, a pharmacy and health centre, and evening classes for adults. He was particularly proud that he had managed to convince the Mayor's office to build a rudimentary football pitch. The kids loved football more than anything else. 'We are very committed to providing a trustworthy support to people here,' Fr José told me.

He was building a new chapel on the second floor of an abandoned building. It was next to a large hall run by the local Protestant Pentecostals, who Diarmaid MacCulloch in his *History of Christianity* describes as 'one of the most numerically successful' modern Christian movements. It was a reminder of the challenge the Catholic Church faces from the haemorrhaging of its support to less traditional evangelical movements that have spread across South America. Brazil, Mexico and Colombia account for over a quarter of the word's Catholic population, and the country has more Catholics than any other: 123 million. As the US Catholic priest and sociologist Andrew Chesnut wrote in the *Catholic Herald* on the eve of Pope Francis's arrival in Brazil, Catholicism had long ceased to be assured of its dominance in Latin America. In Brazil, as in most of the continent, the number of Catholics had been declining since the middle of the twentieth century, while the number of Pentecostals had been rising. As recently as the 1940s, 99 per cent of Brazilians were Catholic. Today that figure has plummeted to 63 per cent.

And yet, as Chesnut put it, it was 'within this context of precipitous decline that the cardinals chose a Latin American *confrere* as Pope . . . Having written off a major attempt to revitalise the Church in Europe and having realised the dynamism of the faith in Africa and Asia, Church leaders strategically opted to focus on the region that with 42 per cent of the world's Catholic population holds the key to future growth.'

According to Chesnut's published figures, since the 1950s tens of millions of mostly poor Latin Americans have converted to Pentecostal denominations such as the Assembly of God and the Brazil-based God is Love (*Deus é Amor*). The 'astronomical growth rate' from the 1940s saw the Protestant percentage of the Brazilian population increasing from 1 to 22 per cent, of which approximately three-quarters, Chestnut estimated, are Pentecostal.

Chesnut prophetically wrote a book *Competitive Spirits: Latin America's New Religious Economy* back in 2003 in which he noted that Pentecostalism appealed to millions who felt abandoned by and inadequately tended to by the Catholic Church. It is spirit-centred worship, complete with faith healing and exorcism, and emphasis on solutions to poverty-related afflictions such as drug abuse and family discord.

Fr José was under no illusion as to the challenges he faced in ensuring that his Church retained a meaningful presence in the *favelas*. When I asked him why, when so much had seemed to have changed in the world in the last thirty years, so little had happened in terms of real social progress, he pointed the finger not at the Church but at the State.

'Over the years it's become evident that many people are

implicated – politicians, policemen and drug traffickers . . . handing the *favelas* to the big drug gangs, those who move with great power and a lot of money. We have seen a cultural development which I call by one word – "death" – where some lives are valued more than others.'

A new government policy approved in the run-up to the World Cup of 2014 and the Olympics of 2016 involved special task forces of police and military storming *favelas*, carrying out sweeping arrests and establishing a permanent armed presence with security checkpoints controlling access to the neighbourhood. The so-called 'pacification' programme was supposed to create sufficient security for essential infrastructure development and the carrying out of basic public services like garbage collection. But the record was mixed. The provision of essential services remained far more primitive than in high-income residential and commercial parts of the city, while violence persisted, with the security forces yet to shed their reputation for repression and corruption.

Days before I visited him, one of Fr José's local Masses had to be abandoned by the congregation after they were caught in the crossfire of a shootout between police and armed criminals. Fr José told me that while police still tortured, assassinated and took bribes, one of the more enduring gangs use the term 'The Microwave' to describe the body of someone they have killed and whose ashes have been delivered to the nearest relative.

Towards the end of our day together, over a cup of coffee, Fr José pointed to the Sugar Loaf Mountain and its emblematic Christ overlooking the city. 'Look how beautiful Rio can look and Brazil has so much potential – a good climate, natural resources, people who can work well – and yet we still have more and bigger *favelas* than when you were last here.'

Despite it all, Fr José was full of hope. 'Pope Francis is winning the hearts of ordinary people. He speaks from the heart and reaches people's hearts. He is boosting the self-esteem of the underprivileged and those who feel marginalized. They see a pope who thinks of them, who remembers them. For Pope Francis it's not a question of taking political power, it's of preaching and acting out the Gospel message which Jesus did by being alongside the poor and the excluded. John Paul II got rid of all independent-thinking bishops and centralized Church authority and created a whole generation of priests who liked all the pomp and ceremony and were only interested in getting promoted up the clerical ladder, and this trend continued under Pope Benedict. My hope is that Pope Francis will bring the Church back to its people.'

From the moment he stepped onto Brazilian soil, Pope Francis showed the humility and human engagement that characterized his time as a bishop in Argentina and which had marked his first months in Rome. The greater the crowds of ordinary faithful – and the further the distance from the official ceremonies organized by government and hierarchy – the visibly happier and more relaxed he seemed to become. He showed himself at his best as a communicator with young people and the poor, displaying a deep sense of humanity in his visit to a hospital for young drug addicts and to one of the *favelas*. His meetings with lay officialdom left little room for complacency as the Popehad already taken the first steps to deal with alleged corruption in the Vatican's finances.

Later, as he moved around this sprawling city, Pope Francis blessed numerous babies while stepping down repeatedly from his Popemobile to bless invalids and draw himself more personally to pilgrims and their outstretched hands. If the week he was on Brazilian soil had the air of a campaign trail, then it was because Pope Francis was clear in his mission of evangelization, to win hearts and minds, to boost the faithful, speaking a language for our times and with a sense of Christianity's early roots as a Church of the people, full of hope in the future.

World Youth Day in Rio, with its gathering of young Catholics from around the world, proved a perfect platform to develop his ambition. Throughout the week he was there Pope Francis stressed the importance he attached to a grassroots renewal of the Catholic Church by appealing to his young followers to become key participants in a fresh and meaningful project of evangelization. 'We are building a Church and you must become protagonists of history,' he said at the final Mass on Rio's Copacabana Beach – or, as he told some youths who had travelled from his native Argentina, speaking in the slang of Buenos Aires, 'get out into the street and stir things up'.

Following an extended period of popular protests against the established political class, not just in Brazil but around the world, the Pope seemed in sympathy with those manning the barricades who demanded greater financial accountability of the State and the private sector.

It was evident that the conservative local hierarchy promoted by previous popes has over the last two decades become disconnected with the political calls for greater social justice. Pope Francis appealed directly to political leaders to tackle corruption and restore ethical government. Talking to local bishops and priests, he berated them for becoming too distant from their flock and urged them to focus on the pragmatic needs of their congregations.

Meanwhile, the populist nature of Pope Francis showed at the evening vigil on the Saturday of his visit, also on Copacabana Beach. A lifelong fan of San Lorenzo football club, Francis drew an analogy between a good team and a Church that did not betray its following, but drew it into a positive relationship with Jesus, and through him, with the world, making of it a more just, equitable and ethical place.

'Jesus asks us to play in his team but he offers us something greater than the World Cup – a life that is truly happy and fulfilled,' he said. In words aimed not just at young people, but all those who felt alienated by the institutional Church, he went on: 'We want to build a Church that is big enough to accommodate all humanity.' This was a universal pastor speaking, deeply conscious of the damage to the Church's reputation from sex-abuse scandals, financial corruption, and its perceived denigration of the love shared by people of the same sex.

In another speech, Pope Francis invited those listening to lend themselves to a rare moment of collective silence and contemplation, and to be open to and trust in the humanity of Christ, not to feel rejected, excluded or condemned. 'Do not look at the thorns and the stones but on the small grain of soil where seed can be sown . . . If you have erred, do not fear. Jesus understands.'

In his evident physicality with the crowds and his words, Francis projected a living witness to the beauty and dignity of life, and the fundamental unity of the human person.

A young Argentine priest told me in Rio, 'He has strengthened and won over many young people with his direct and unpatronizing way of addressing them. There is nothing sanctimonious about Francis. He is moving the Vatican from autocracy to accountability.'

Others went even further, including the Brazilian liberation theologian Leonardo Boff. He said that during Pope Francis's visit to Latin America, continent of struggle and yet of huge promise, this pope of immeasurable energy and inspiration had instilled a new dynamic into the Church's social doctrine and restored its option for the poor, which governments, voters, bishops and priests would be hard pressed to ignore. With Pope Francis, Boff said, a Church of the third millennium was being inaugurated, 'far from the palaces and in the midst of the people and popular culture'.

For those of us accompanying the Pope in Brazil, there were certainly many memorable moments. On the Friday night there was a rare hush among the multitudes – broken only by bursts of rabid applause – as Pope Francis spoke from the heart. Christ's Crucifixion was not defeat but a victory of good over evil, of hope over despair, the certainty of God's love for the sinner, and the prospect of redemption, he prayed. Whatever our personal suffering, we know we are not alone, for Jesus is with us, in communion, offering us love and happiness with his presence, he went on to say. Pope Francis spoke in a quiet and focused tone, which was not sombre but sought to engage the listener. The Cross was one shared with those who suffered the corruption and greed of politicians and the moral betrayals of bishops and priests, including those who sexually abused or pursued careers instead of true holiness in humility. This Cross too would help Latin America find a way to confront injustice and violence but also help the universal Church rediscover its humanity and sense of mission.

Such measured reflection in the midst of such a mass following of the faithful was evidence that Pope Francis, first and foremost, was a spiritual not a populist leader, and a humble one. And it showed that he respected the parameters set by his predecessor Benedict XVI, who in 2008 had criticized the tendency of some young Catholics and sectors of the media to view World Youth Day as a kind of gigantic rock festival. Benedict had stressed that the event should not be considered a 'variant of modern youth culture' but as the fruition of a 'long exterior and interior spiritual journey' by the young pilgrims involved.

On the last day of his visit, Pope Francis set aside his distrust of the media and granted a rare interview to Brazil's most popular station, Globo TV, before talking with the Vatican press corps on the plane back to Rome. He spelt out his determination to restore collegiality and accountability within the Church, pursue constructive dialogue with other faiths, and to confront with a new morality and social justice the 'idolatry of money' and what he termed 'the globalization of indifference' towards the poor.

In Brazil, Pope Francis showed the world audience his profoundly human side, reaching out and fuelling the enthusiasm of millions with his smile and direct eye contact. He showed himself – away from his native Argentina and Rome – a natural physical communicator, a populist priest and bishop of the people. The louder and more passionate the crowds, the more energetic his response; he was a pope at peace with his sense of mission amidst devoted Catholic youths he called 'disciples of the new evangelization' and the poor, to whom he had never felt closer.

There were rare moments when the occasion may not have quite appealed to more traditional Catholics, certainly in Europe. For example, the Stations of the Cross on the Friday were dominated by an eclectic modernist choreography, rock music, striking costumes, a giant neon-lit Cross behind the Pope's throne, and haunting voodoo-esque rattles marking the end of each station. Some scenes, like the appearance of a stripped and bloodied Jesus taking centre stage on a raised platform, were reminiscent of *Jesus Christ Superstar*, others of the London Olympics or of Rio's own carnival. The wooden cross garlanded in ribbons of Vatican colours, carried by youths in white garments and followed by a band from the Brazilian Navy and altar boys swinging incense only fuelled a sense of over-the-top theatrics. The organizers seemed to have one eye on winning over the Pentecostals, the other on the Olympics in 2016 – testing loyalties and reaction. But then they could have simply wanted to have another event with which young people could connect. This was, after all, World Youth Day. Even the less convinced older observers, like myself, thanked God for the moving testimonies by young pilgrims at each station, revealing their personal experiences of loss, pain and redemption. And in the end it was the Pope's words that restored a necessary note of spiritual sobriety amidst the invasive razzmatazz and near hysteria of the crowds.

The ceremony on Copacabana Beach was evangelical in its loud, simplistic assertion of faith, with a charismatic pope at its heart. It spoke to the converted and young people in particular – and would have touched hearts among evangelical Anglicans – but in a style that may have had a more limited appeal to the doubters, non-believers and peoples of other persuasions, not to mention traditional Eurocentric Catholics and high Anglicans.

In terms of ecumenical engagement, this papal trip fell short of Benedict's visit to the UK in 2010. In political terms it did not have the immediate impact of Pope John Paul II's visits to Poland, the UK and Argentina during the Falklands War, and Manila where governments were overthrown subsequent to the papal visit. And yet while breaking free of the negative, dogmatic and doctrinal pronouncements of his two predecessors, Pope Francis also showed humility as well as a connection with the disenfranchised and the poor. On balance this was a papal trip potentially as historic as Pope Paul VI's first pilgrimage abroad, not just because of the ground covered but also because of the nature of the Pope.

During a week that would endure in many memories, I followed the pilgrims for miles, through the inner streets, tunnels and coastline that weave their way across Rio – a city that nature invades, but where rampant consumerism and social inequality prevail. Around me were thousands of youths, from different parts of the world, although mainly Latin America, on their way to Copacabana to see Pope Francis. They had a spring in their step. It was a pilgrimage of a very committed kind. 'They've been taking cold showers and sleeping rough, but their happiness is undimmed. You can feel Jesus is present,' an Italian priest told me.

The long and wide beach and promenade of Copacabana had for years been a venue of choice for mass gatherings from the Rolling Stones to New Year's Eve, and of course part of the carnival. This World Youth Day seemed to have an element of all three in its youthful energy, celebration and mass euphoria verging on hysteria whenever Pope Francis came close. Only the hedonism was missing. Instead, there was of course much talk of Jesus and *alegría* (joy) dominated by chants proclaiming, 'Here we are, the youth of the Pope'. Rio seemed full of young boys and girls and priests and nuns who talked of their encounter with Jesus in mass gatherings like this. To engage with them in any detailed questioning of their beliefs was to encounter a solid wall of certainty on the sanctity of traditional marriage and family life, the authority of the Pope, the call to go out and evangelize. Not a grain of doubt before a pope that spoke to them directly, in transformative language easily understood, who stirred their enthusiasm to fever pitch.

'Your youth is showing that your faith is stronger than the cold and the rain,' Pope Francis told them on the beach where millions had gathered. It was raining and, for Rio, it was cold. The clouds hovered round the Christ Redeemer statue, clearing occasionally. 'You see, God is Brazilian, after all,' said João, a local waiter who celebrated the fact that his eighteen-year-old daughter had been inspired by Pope Francis to return to the Catholic faith.

Except for a few hundred local demonstrators protesting about the expense of the trip and the Vatican's stand against abortion and legalized gay marriage, the whole of Rio and much of Latin America was in awe of Pope Francis. 'Put Christ at the centre of your lives and in your hearts. Don't think that money is the solution. Don't get satiated with money. It just makes you weak. It's faith that gives you security and hope. Faith is revolutionary.

'Ask yourselves; are you ready to enter in this revolution of the faith?' he said in Rio.

In Latin America's southern cone, the Pope walked territory that was familiar to him, his directness of gesture and word striking a chord among the pilgrim young and the poor in Rio they would not easily forget. Francis took to the streets, deep into the depth of Rio's poor, in the *favela* of Manguinhos. He reached the shanty-town dwellers in an open car, stopping now and then to kiss and bless babies lifted to him by his security guards, then leaning towards the crowd, before stepping down among them, meeting them with his smile, his handshake, his warm blessing, the light breaking through the darkness and rain, in an enduring gesture of human solidarity. And then he stepped up to the makeshift stage, as to the mountain summit, and made them feel honoured, dignified, people of his world, and that of Jesus Christ, of the Beatitudes.

'In your generous welcome . . . you have shown a great sense of solidarity. And the word solidarity is not one that can be or should be silenced,' he told them. He called for greater social justice, and promised that the Church would be behind every initiative that promoted development and the dignity of ordinary men and women. 'A nation is built on these essential pillars: family, tolerance, education, housing, health, security . . . violence can only be overcome with a change in the human heart.' And turning to government and others in positions of authority, he urged them to recover a sense of the common good, while ending with a tribute to youth who, conscious of the corruption of some of their leaders, were calling for a better society. 'We need an enduring peace in our communities, one that brings genuine social justice. Do not lose hope!' he told the crowds. They cheered him loudly.

As a smiling Brazilian told me: 'The Pope has already performed a miracle. He has achieved what seemed impossible. He has managed to get ordinary Brazilians to fall in love with an Argentinian.'

A sense of spiritual transformation was palpable on the streets of Rio. And it seemed bound to be catching universally.

On the last day of Pope Francis's visit to Brazil, Argentine President Cristina Fernández turned up in Rio to stress her reconciliation with the person her late husband Néstor had considered his main political rival and opponent, and whose election as pope had taken her so by surprise. After a delayed reaction to the news which initially shocked her, Fernández had realized the risk, not least to the stability of her presidency, of not reconciling herself with the former Archbishop of Buenos Aires now that he was the spiritual leader of the worldwide Catholic Church.

Just as she had done at an earlier, largely protocol-induced meeting at which she met Pope Francis in Rome within days of his election, Fernández sought his blessing and pointedly distanced herself from Horacio Verbitsky, the journalist who more than anyone else had personified her and her late husband's governments' attempt to tarnish Bergoglio's reputation. The one-time political ally of the Kirchners was doggedly trying to recycle his stories about Bergoglio's alleged betrayals during the Dirty War. Fernández hoped instead to engage Pope Francis in an early diplomatic offensive to press Argentina's claim over the Falklands – but this proved illusory. She was reminded that while Bergoglio had been Archbishop of Buenos Aires, Francis was now Bishop of Rome with a responsibility that went far beyond narrow national interests. She settled for an exchange of sentimental gifts in which she gave the Pope a kit for preparing and drinking his beloved *mate*, the Argentine tea; he gave her a small pair of knitted shoes for her newly born grandson and holy pictures. For his part Francis began his papacy expressing his sincere hopes that his presence in the Vatican would help Argentines find peace and harmony within themselves – a spirit that had eluded them for most of their history.

In the months that followed the Brazil visit, Fernández obtained two more papal audiences – in March and September 2014 – to try and shore up her dwindling popularity as the Peronist party squabbled over who might eventually succeed her amidst deepening economic problems. Fernández was actively looking for other populist causes she hoped Argentines would rally round. The football World Cup that summer in Brazil provided her with an opportunity. Not only was Brazil the great continental rival, but it was a World Cup that Argentines, with a team led by the FC Barcelona star Lionel Messi, hoped to win. Moreover, with Pope Francis in the Vatican, Fernández fuelled the hope that Argentine football had God on its side, as in the days of the tempestuous but hugely talented Diego Maradona, voted the greatest footballer of the twentieth century.

Football, along with the Catholic Church and General Perón,

were major influences on Bergoglio as a young boy. 'Argentine Miracle: A Peronist on St Peter's Throne' was how the Argentine mass circulation newspaper *Clarín* had headlined his election. It was an exaggeration. But he was born into a Peronist constituency and, long before he heard the call of God, he had become a fan, like his father and most of his neighbourhood friends, of local football club San Lorenzo de Almagro at a legendary time in its history. In 1946, when Bergoglio was nine years old, San Lorenzo became Argentine champions.

In deference to his universal role, and no doubt the God of surprises and the unpredictable Holy Spirit, Pope Francis, while surely watching the TV in his modest living quarters in Rome, did not publicly endorse the Argentine national team as Fernández and many Argentines would have liked. The World Cup may have historically been a Catholic affair with Catholic countries winning fifteen of the nineteen tournaments prior to Germany's victory in the summer of 2014. But Brazil, the world's largest Catholic country, understandably resisted the idea that Argentine football had a monopoly on divine intervention. A popular World Cup T-shirt displayed the legend: 'You already have the Pope and Messi – Brazil World Champions 2014.'

The fact that when Argentina failed to win so did Brazil was taken as a blessing in disguise by those who still believed in an Argentine God. For Fernández and Argentine football there was further comfort to be had in September 2014 when the Pope enthusiastically received Diego Maradona and Argentine players who had signed up for a charity match for peace in Rome's Olympic stadium (Messi was absent through injury but would be later granted a papal audience of his own).

'It's given me a real kick to see an Argentine in such an important place as the Vatican, after we've had so many popes that only cared about politics but not about the kids who go hungry,' declared Maradona after handing Pope Francis a shirt with the Argentina colours and the Number 10 of his magical playing days. 'He has helped restore the Catholic faith I had when I was a kid.' While Maradona's conversion to piety and abstinence was widely thought unlikely, there was no doubting that the 'people's champion', born in a Buenos Aires slum, found himself more engaged by Pope Francis than by any of his predecessors.

It was all very different from the chemistry lacking from Maradona's previous papal encounter, with Pope John Paul II, from which the Argentine star had emerged unconvinced by the Polish pontiff's revolutionary credentials. As Maradona later recalled, marvelling at the Vatican's gold ceilings at the time, he had thought: 'Sell the ceiling, dude. Do something!'

Pope Francis was not about to sell off St Peter's, but he struck a humbler, more genuinely engaging figure than JP2, and was already leading by example in his commitment to greater social justice. Thus in September 2014, on her way to a meeting of the United Nations General Assembly in New York, President Fernández emerged from a lunch meeting with the Pope claiming that he backed the campaign by developing countries to stop so-called vulture funds undermining debt-restructuring deals like those at the centre of Argentina's US court battle. Argentina had slipped into default in July 2014 after losing a long legal battle with hedge funds that bought its debt at rock-bottom prices during Argentina's financial crisis, and then rejected the terms of debt restructurings in 2005 and 2010, pursuing the country through the courts to get full repayment.

Fernández and Pope Francis had discussed the debt burden, poverty and the 'exponential growth of wealth', the Argentine President told the media, adding that the Pope was concerned about 'the way hedge funds can oppress a sovereign nation'. Yet there was no public comment from the Pope or from his press office or in the Vatican's daily *L'Osservatore Romano*, which pointedly devoted more lines to a visit on the same day by Latvia's President

Andris Bērziņš, which was confirmed on Monday. Pope Francis had made his strong views about the injustice of global poverty and the 'new tyranny' of unfettered capitalism clear in his eighty-four-page document of 'apostolic exhortation', *Evangelii Gaudium*, in November 2013. He had said: 'Just as the commandment "Thou shalt not kill" sets a clear limit in order to safeguard the value of human life, today we also have to say "thou shalt not" to an economy of exclusion and inequality. Such an economy kills.'

Francis was cordial in his reception of the thirty-person official delegation that accompanied the Argentine President, bearing gifts. These included, in addition to a hand-carved statue of a Bergoglio favourite Marian icon, Our Lady of Knots, Argentine populist emblems like photographs of him as Archbishop on a visit to a shanty town with Padre Pepe, a portrait of the assassinated Peronist priest Fr Mugica, and a shirt signed by La Cámpora, the radical group of young party militants that organized pro-Kirchner rallies and occupied key government posts. The Pope was photographed smiling and seemingly at ease – but still pointedly refrained from making any partisan or nationalistic comment. He had enough experience of Argentine politics to be on his guard against being used as a tool for government propaganda. For her part, Fernández had shown a crass misunderstanding of what Pope Francis represented, and the role expected of him by Catholics and non-believers alike.

From the moment he stepped out for the first time onto the Vatican balcony and uttered his first words there was an evident paradox to Pope Francis being the centre of the world's attention. While he drew on his political, social and spiritual Latin American experience, his election as pope challenged him also to face up to his role of teacher, prophet and preacher, and, as a truly global spiritual figure, to transcend his own race and nationality.

Much as Fernández wanted Pope Francis's political endorsement, he showed himself in no hurry to convert to her personal political cause, even if he has remained a Peronist at heart. On the contrary, the defining characteristic of the first two years of the papacy was a humility in style and accountability and transparency in governance that was in striking contrast to the confrontational politics, bogus radicalism and sheer demagoguery that continued to be shown by the court of Kirchner/Fernández. Mrs Fernández remained obsessed with her make-up; Francis continued to wash feet.

That Fernández could not take Pope Francis's support for granted was signalled on 9 May 2014 by the most hard-hitting statement against the government from the Argentinian episcopal conference since the election of one of its own as pope in March 2013. In echoes of former Bergoglio pronouncements, the Argentine bishops decreed that something remained rotten in the state of Argentina. In a statement, which is unlikely to have been written without the Pope's approval, they declared that their country was 'sick with violence', and they compared public and private corruption to a cancer 'causing injustice and death'. This provoked President Fernández to activate her social networks and media friends to defend herself against what she called a 'deliberate attempt' to blame her administration for the insecurity alleged by the bishops.

The simmering Argentinian pot stopped short of overflowing into a full-scale crisis, at least on this occasion. Archbishop Victor Fernández (no relation), the rector of the Catholic University of Buenos Aires and a close ally of Pope Francis, responded to the President by stating in the pro-government newspaper *Página/12* that both President and opposition had been too selectively partisan in their interpretation of a text that was broadly in line with current papal 'global concerns'. This was followed by a meeting between President Fernández and three other leading bishops. Government aides spun this as a public display of renewed understanding with the Church of Pope Francis. Given the absence of an agreed joint statement, it appeared to be more of a damage-limitation exercise.

Meanwhile, in the midst of the row, there was no doubting whom a majority of Argentines supported. Opinion polls that May gave Pope Francis an extraordinary 90-plus per cent personal approval rating among his fellow countrymen – consistent since the early days of his papal election – with Fernández at only 25 per cent as head of government compared to 44.4 per cent only four months previously and over 50 per cent in the aftermath of her husband's death.

But Argentines themselves still couldn't agree on who was to blame for the kind of social injustice and political failure that the new papacy denounced. And but for the courageous voluntary and pastoral work done in the slums by teams led by priests like Padre Pepe, Argentina still gave the impression of struggling to find any sense of spiritual renewal or genuinely democratic political direction. Certainly Peronism in Argentina was proving more resilient than communism in Poland before the collapse of Soviet rule during the papacy of Pope John Paul II, and there was something of the Peronist that lingered in Pope Francis's conduct and worldview.

Chapter Fourteen
God's Banker

Following his election, Pope Francis accelerated the most significant reform ever of the controversial Vatican bank – officially known as the Institute for Religious Works (Istituto per le Opere di Religione, IOR), it had been the subject of periodical financial scandals and political conspiracies dating back decades. His predecessors had failed to overcome the resistance to change of deeply imbedded political interests linked to the Vatican's inner court and to rein in the excesses and mismanagement of the Catholic Church's accumulated wealth.

In the words of Jason Berry, the author of a detailed book on the subject of Vatican finances: 'For decades, IOR was a black hole of Vatican finances, an off-the-books asset that critics likened to an offshore bank, particularly after the Vatican paid a $250 million (£146 million) fine in 1985 to Italy for the IOR's role in the collapse of the Mob-controlled Banco Ambrosiano.'

Debate on how much a succession of popes knew about what exactly went on at the IOR – with its offices in the Apostolic Palace in Vatican City – had fuelled controversy over generations. Writing in 1981, one of the doyens of the Rome-based foreign correspondents, Peter Nichols, noted that a majority of cardinals were utterly in the dark about the secrets of a bank that handled not only the Vatican's own funds but those of national hierarchies, religious orders, clergy and an unknown quantity of privileged private clients on a major international scale. 'The fluctuations in the guesswork [about the true value of assets] are just too great to inspire a lot of confidence,' Nichols, the then London *Times* correspondent, wrote in his book *The Pope's Divisions*.

Thirty-three years later, the *Financial Times* reported after a detailed investigation of its own, that while the bank had been used in recent decades to channel cash, often secretly or with limited information to correspondent banks, to vulnerable Christian groups in Cuba and Egypt (and in communist days to the Polish trade movement), it had also been open to abuse by tax cheats and organized crime. But the circumstances surrounding the bank changed in 2008 when the euro crisis led to pressure from the Organisation for Economic Co-Operation and Development, Europe's Stability Board and the Financial Action Task Force for a crackdown on states that failed to comply with tougher international regulations – and that included the Vatican. In the final years of Benedict XVI's papacy, with the Italian media regularly running stories about police probes into alleged financial scandals, the IOR came under increasing pressure from Italy's then central bank governor Mario Draghi (a future president of the European Central Bank) to halt servicing privileged clients suspected of money laundering.

In 2009, an increasingly frail Pope Benedict tried to signal he was taking control of the situation by having appointed someone he personally trusted, an Italian banker and a university professor in financial ethics, Ettore Gotti Tedeschi, to take over the presidency of the IOR. Tedeschi was head of Banco Santander in Italy and a member of the conservative Catholic lay organization Opus Dei, which was influential in the Vatican. However, Tedeschi was forced to resign in May 2012 after a no-confidence vote from his board and for 'failing to carry out various duties of primary importance', according to a statement by the Vatican spokesman Fr Lombardi. It later emerged that bank officials took key decisions without always informing the Pope and that Benedict XVI discovered his friend Tedeschi's fate only after he had been ordered out.

The fact that Tedeschi was a member of Opus Dei and close to Benedict in the end proved inadequate protection against the Vatican's internal intrigue. Tedeschi was placed under investigation for allegedly omitting data in wire transfers from an Italian account after prosecutors seized 23 million euros from a Rome bank account registered to the IOR amid suspicion of violations of money-laundering rules. Further allegations published in the Italian media but never substantiated claimed that Italian police had raided Tedeschi's home and found dossiers containing incriminating information on *faccendieri* (frontmen for the Mafia) politicians, priests, bishops and shady accounts.

Tedeschi denied any impropriety, with friends suggesting that his attempts at forcing greater accountability and transparency within the IOR had faced rearguard resistance from a group of cardinals and other unidentified political lobbies. The same friends suggested that Tedeschi feared for his life – not unreasonably given the Vatican's cloak-and-dagger history. Thirty years previously Robert Calvi, the former chairman of the Italian Banco Ambrosiano in which the IOR was a major shareholder, was found hanging from Blackfriars Bridge in London.

In the run-up to Tedeschi's resignation, the IOR certainly gave the impression of being under siege from some of its major clients, with its management embroiled in conspiratorial personal battles involving senior figures inside the Vatican, and a pope that was fast losing the will to stay in office, let alone impose his leadership. In March 2012, JP Morgan closed the bank account it held for the Vatican because the IOR was providing insufficient information about funds that it was asking the US bank to move around the world. As the manager of a large European bank later told the

Financial Times: 'We would say, "We need to answer the regulator on this matter." They would say, "We answer to God."' But God was unable or more likely unwilling to stem the mounting pressure for reform. Moneyval, the Council of Europe's financial investigation arm, reported in July 2012 that the Vatican's financial regulator lacked any effective clout and that the IOR was non-compliant on six out of sixteen core standards.

In January 2013, a sense of crisis at the IOR surfaced during the peak New Year holiday period when ATM cash machines inside Vatican City were temporarily disabled under orders from the Bank of Italy. Even long-term clients such as religious orders found it difficult to access their accounts despite there being no suggestion of any involvement in criminal activity. In the final days of his papacy, Benedict made two key appointments he hoped would restore the bank's credibility. In September 2012 he appointed the youthful and energetic forty-one-year-old Swiss lawyer, René Bruelhart, as the head of the Vatican's financial regulator (the Financial Information Authority) set up in 2010. Widely respected by senior western intelligence officials for his work in tracing Saddam Hussein's overseas financial assets, Bruelhart had also built a reputation for diligent forensics when helping to uncover the Siemens contract scandal of 2006, which involved bribery of government officials. The second appointment was that of Ernst von Freyberg as the new Vatican bank chief on 15 February 2013, just days after Benedict had announced his intention to resign, filling a post left vacant since Tedeschi's departure. Von Freyberg was an aristocratic German lawyer-financier, founder of a Frankfurt-based financial advisory company called DC Advisory Partners, and chairman of a major German engineering firm. He was also a member of the well-funded and highly influential network of the great and good – the Catholic order of the Knights of Malta – as well as a regular pilgrim to Lourdes.

According to Giovanni Maria Vian, editor of *L'Osservatore Romano*, the Vatican's semi-official mouthpiece, Pope Benedict decided to retire after a trip to Mexico and Cuba in May 2012 although it remains unclear as to how far an 'inner circle' of cardinals and confidants were made aware of his departure plans before the public announcement. That Benedict confirmed the new appointments already knowing that he was not going to be pope much longer suggests that he had one eye on his legacy, cleaning up the controversial, unfinished business that had overshadowed his papacy. He felt he owed it to his successor to hand over a steadier ship rather than one buffeted and seemingly at the mercy of a perfect storm.

'Pope Benedict was a teaching pope, a theologian and intellectual. His idea of hell would be to be sent on a one-week management training seminar,' one Vatican insider told the BBC's Mark Dowd. 'His misfortune was to accede to the papacy at a time that there was a power vacuum, in which a number of middle-ranking members of the Roman Curia, the Church's civil service, had turned into "little Borgias" as another clerical official put it,' reported Dowd. Pope Francis would himself refer to the Curia as the 'leprosy of the papacy', filled with clerics who were both narcissistic and self-referential. Over a period of time dating back to the final years of Pope John Paul II, the heart of the HQ of the Roman Church had become dominated by in-fighting cliques. This was what the man responsible for Vatileaks, the Pope's butler Paolo Gabriele, said he wanted to expose by photocopying and leaking documents, part of a series of 'exposures' given wide coverage in the media.

The latest scandal surrounding Vatican finances first came to light in January 2012 when Italian journalist Gianluigi Nuzzi published letters from Carlo Maria Viganò, formerly the second-ranked Vatican administrator to the Pope, which had been given to him by Gabriele. In the letters Viganò begged not to be transferred as nuncio to Washington, DC after exposing alleged corruption that cost the Holy See millions in higher contract prices. Over the following months the scandal widened as documents were leaked to Italian journalists, uncovering power struggles inside the Vatican over its efforts to show greater financial transparency and comply with international norms to fight money laundering. The scandal escalated in May 2012 when Nuzzi published a book entitled *His Holiness: The Secret Papers of Benedict XVI* consisting of confidential letters and memos between Pope Benedict and his personal secretary. The book portrays the Vatican as a hotbed of jealousy, intrigue and underhanded factional fighting. It also revealed details about the Pope's personal finances, and included tales of bribes made to procure an audience with him.

Some veteran Vatican observers suggested that the leaking of the documents was clearly intended to embarrass and force out the man at the centre of the papal civil service, Cardinal Tarcisio Bertone, Benedict's powerful Secretary of State, or 'Prime Minister' as he was seen by some bishops, clergy and diplomats. Bertone had become unpopular among several bishops who questioned his competence as an administrator. He resigned in September 2013, six months into the Francis papacy after no one in the Vatican had spoken out in his defence; he claimed that he had become the whipping boy for the deep administrative malaise that had set in during Benedict's papacy, which was criticized for its disfunctionality and Eurocentrism. He quit after commenting that the leaking of confidential documents seemed 'carefully aimed, and sometimes also ferocious, destructive and organized', and lashing out at an unnamed 'mix of crows and vipers' within the Italian media and the Church. 'It would seem that the Secretary of State can decide and control everything, but it is not so. There were problems we could not properly face because they were as sealed in the management of certain people who did not network with the Secretary of State,' Bertone said.

Whatever the conspiracies that may have been behind Bertone's resignation – and somewhat ambiguous statement – it was clear that his days in the Vatican were numbered once Pope Francis had been elected. The theme of collegiality was one much emphasized during the Second Vatican Council but its practice had fallen by the wayside during the papacy of John Paul II. Only during the years of Benedict XVI leading up to his succession was the issue revived to the point of being seriously discussed in the meetings of cardinals that preceded the 2013 conclave. By then Vatileaks had exposed the corruption, careerism and inefficiency in the Curia, to which many people felt Bertone had contributed.

The subsequent announcement within a month of the papal election that Pope Francis was setting up a group of eight senior bishops to 'advise him in the government of the Universal Church' was much more than just a knee-jerk reaction focused on a shake-up of the Curia. Rather, it was the start of a process of much wider examination of issues affecting matters of Church teaching as well as organization. The group was in effect an advisory council tasked with helping the Pope decide on key issues that came across his desk. The hugely experienced Vatican reporter John Allen summarized the eight cardinals (George Pell of Sydney, Óscar Maradiaga of Honduras, Francisco Ossa from Chile, Patrick O'Malley from the US, Oswald Gracias from Bombay, Laurent Pasinya from Kinshasa, Reinhardt Marx from Germany and Giuseppe Bertello, a career papal diplomat) as 'strong personalities rather than "yes" men inclined simply to tell the Pope what he wanted to hear'.

True, there was not an identifiable theological or political radical among them. Indeed, all of them owed their career paths to the previous two popes, and like Pope Francis had no record of doctrinal challenge to traditional Catholic teaching. And yet between them the cardinals represented a significant transcontinental geographical span, and each had at some point been critical of the way the Catholic Church was managed. Pell had criticized the disfunctionality that characterized the Benedict years; Maradiaga had crossed swords with powerful Vatican figures like Cardinal Angelo Sodano before becoming Bergoglio's unofficial campaign manager at the conclave; Gracias and Pasinya had argued for local churches and regional conferences to have more devolved powers; O'Malley, a Franciscan, had impressive credentials in spearheading 'clean-up and heal' missions in several US dioceses, including his own one of Boston, that had been engulfed in sex abuse; Marx was a strong proponent of the Church's social teaching. And then there was Bertello: seemingly untainted by Vatileaks, he had a civil servant's under-standing of the complex inner machinery that Pope Francis now had to deal with on a daily basis, having overseen the administrative and technical services on his appointment as 'governor' of Vatican City State in 2001. 'Francis has turned to prelates likely to give him real advice, not just a rubber stamp,' Allen concluded.

Another significant appointment within months of the papal election was that of fifty-eight-year-old Archbishop Pietro Parolin, a widely respected diplomat, to the key role of Secretary of State. The role was restructured so he could focus on international diplomacy, his main strength. A graduate of the elite finishing school for papal diplomats, the Pontifica Accademia Ecclesiastica, and of the Jesuit Gregorian University where he studied canon law, Parolin had a reputation as a soft-spoken, engaging priest with a good track record of competent diplomatic service in posts in Africa and Latin America. He also had several years of experience of learning from those more senior than himself, working inside the Vatican, under Pope John Paul II and Benedict XVI. Parolin's promotion by Pope Francis signalled that the Vatican, the world's oldest diplomatic entity, was poised once again to play an important role in peace-making, the promotion of human rights and advocacy of the poor. This was particularly relevant to Latin America, where following the death of Venezuelan President Hugo Chávez on 5 March 2013 – just days before the election of Pope Francis – populist civilian governments in Venezuela, Argentina, Bolivia, Ecuador and Cuba, as well as Venezuela itself, were left politically less secure and with little option than to defuse antagonisms towards the Catholic Church.

Meanwhile at the Vatican bank, when von Freyberg first took up his appointment, he diplomatically stated publicly that the IOR was a 'well managed and clean financial institution' and merely suffered from a bad reputation linked to old scandals. But the narrative was soon to shift. He subsequently admitted that more drastic measures were needed to clean up the bank's bad image and provide greater transparency. He said this after sacking the IOR's head of daily operations, Paulo Cipriani, and his deputy, Massimo Tulli.

And yet days before Pope Francis's visit to Brazil (his first foreign trip since his election and one designed to reassert Catholic influence universally) the Vatican was embroiled in yet another alleged scandal on its own doorstep. A report in *L'Espresso* magazine alleged Mgr Battista Ricca, an Italian priest and career Vatican diplomat, had led a secret and troubled gay life. Ricca was not only director of the Domus Sanctae Marthae, where Francis had chosen to live (indeed, Francis often ate with Ricca), but on 15 June 2013, the Pope, seemingly without consulting von Freyberg, named Ricca to be his clerical representative at the Vatican bank, and to act as liaison between the lay management and the commission of cardinals advising the Pope.

The allegations traced Ricca's career back to his days when he worked in the papal nunciature in Montevideo, Uruguay, in 2000 and 2001 after serving on diplomatic missions in Congo, Algeria, Colombia and finally Switzerland. While in Berne, Ricca befriended a captain of the Swiss Army, Patrick Haari. The two arrived in Uruguay together, and Ricca asked that his friend be given a role and a residence in the nunciature. The nuncio rejected the request. But a few months later the nuncio retired and Ricca, having become the chargé d'affaires '*ad interim*' until the appointment of the new nuncio, assigned Haari a residence in the nunciature, with a regular position and salary. When the new nuncio, Janusz Bolonek of Poland, arrived in Montevideo at the beginning of 2000, he disapproved of the 'ménage' and informed the Vatican authorities about it, insisting repeatedly to Haari that he should leave. But no action was taken.

Sandro Magister, the author of the *L'Espresso* report, stated that while in Montevideo Ricca has once been beaten up in a meeting place frequented by homosexuals, and on another occasion been found trapped in the elevator of the nunciature with a gay rent boy known to the police. Haari was eventually dismissed and Ricca transferred to a lower profile nunciature in Trinidad and Tobago before being recalled to the Vatican. Back in Rome, Ricca discreetly resumed his career in the Curia, eventually joining the Secretariat of State with responsibility for all financial expenditure in all the nunciatures in the world. While in Uruguay and in Rome, Ricca's homosexuality and past escapades were known to dozens of bishops, priests, nuns and lay persons, but his personal file had been effectively covered up for years. What made the report worthy of serious consideration was not only Ricca's closeness to Pope Francis but the fact it was written by Magister, no fly-by-night hack but a veteran reporter on Vatican affairs known to have good sources within the Curia.

Before flying to Brazil, Pope Francis authorized Father Lombardi, his press officer, to deny the allegations, saying that Magister's report was 'not trustworthy,' and he did not ask for Ricca's immediate resignation. Soon a counter-narrative began to circulate among other Vatican insiders suggesting that the Ricca file had been leaked to Magister by members of the Curia as a warning to Pope Francis to tread carefully in shaking up the establishment as there were no small number of similar skeletons in the cupboard that might tumble out as a result. Once his high-profile first foreign trip was over and he was on the plane back to Rome, Pope Francis told the Vatican press corps accompanying him that a preliminary investigation had been conducted regarding charges of immoral conduct against Ricca and the investigation 'found nothing'.

Pope Francis said: 'I did what canon law requires, which is to conduct a preliminary investigation. We didn't find anything to confirm the things he was accused of, there was nothing . . . I'd like to add that many times we seem to seek out the sins of somebody's youth and publish them. We're not talking about crimes, which are something else. The abuse of minors, for instance, is a crime. But one can sin and then convert, and the Lord both forgives and forgets. We don't have the right to refuse to forget . . . it's dangerous. The theology of sin is important. St Peter committed one of the greatest sins, denying Christ, and yet they made him pope. Think about that.'

The Ricca story barely featured when the Pope was in Brazil and subsequently retreated altogether from the main news coverage, in the absence of any evidence of wrongdoing. It had, however, left lingering questions about Pope Francis's judgement, not only in forging a friendship with someone whose private life made him vulnerable to being embroiled in controversy. He had also appointed him as his apparent 'eyes and ears' at the Vatican bank at a critical juncture in its history – with a papal pledge to assert a new period of transparency and accountability. When did Francis himself first know about the facts of the Uruguay period, and why did he seemingly believe that they were not serious enough to be used not just to discredit Ricca but also pressurize his own papacy? The answers proved elusive while researching this book.

The controversy which involved allegations of Ricca's homosexuality proved short-lived when Pope Francis refused to be pressured into sacking him. Ricca's main job and one that took up much of his time was running four Vatican residences, among them the Domus Sanctae Marthae where Pope Francis had chosen to live. His role at the IOR was, according to a well-placed priest familiar with the Vatican's inner workings, 'largely an honorary appointment with very little actual responsibility'. The source (not part of any lobby but a genuinely spiritual man of unquestioning loyalty to the Pope) was adamant that Ricca had been a victim of the kind of speculative conspiracy that sectors of the Italian media had turned into their tradecraft. As the source, a member of the Vatican Curia, told me: 'Of course once you start throwing dirt at somebody, it sticks. But that is hardly just, and I have no reason to believe that what Magister wrote was fair. After all, people are to be considered innocent until proven guilty, a principal that we seem to be losing sight of increasingly. He hasn't been proven guilty of anything and yet everyone assumes that he is a very shady character indeed, and should not be trusted with responsible roles when it seems to me that in fact he is a perfectly okay member of the diplomatic service who has been entrusted with a largely honorary role, which is not going to take up much of his time.'

Ricca was clearly no Archbishop Paul Marcinkus, the American president of the IOR in 1971–89 who found himself at the centre of the biggest scandal affecting the bank – the collapse of Banco Ambrosiano. Whatever Ricca's sexual proclivities, they did not impact on the reform process that Pope Francis inherited and was determined to deliver on his watch.

From the outset of his papacy Pope Francis set the tone on financial correctness, speaking out against the idolatry of money, all-encompassing corruption and tax evasion that has reached global dimensions: 'The worship of the ancient golden calf has returned in a new and ruthless guise in the idolatry of money and the dictatorship of an impersonal economy lacking a truly human purpose.'

Behind the scenes he put the weight of his authority and popularity behind clear moves to have the Vatican practise what it preached, ensuring that the way it ran its finances and those of others became emblematic of a new solidarity with the worldwide faithful – ethically sound as well as efficient.

As an experienced Western government diplomat assigned to the Holy See told me: 'Benedict put the reform of Vatican finances on the right track by deciding, under pressure, to open up the bank to financial scrutiny. Once the accounts were opened up and regular inspections were underway the process became irreversible. It was courageous of Benedict but it was Francis who followed things through, taking the reform several steps further on. The commission Pope Francis appointed took its work very seriously, and embarked on proper investigations.'

On 26 June 2013 Pope Francis chose five Vatican insiders to be part of his newly set up commission of inquiry into the conduct of the IOR. The president of the group was Italian Cardinal Raffaele Farina, seventy-nine, head of the Vatican Library. Other appointees were Spanish Bishop Juan Ignacio Arrieta, a sixty-two-year-old Opus Dei canon lawyer who was secretary at the Pontifical Council for Legislative Texts; French Cardinal Jean-Louis Tauran, seventy, one of the Holy See's best diplomats and its top official for interreligious dialogue; Mary Glendon, seventy-four, the American lawyer who headed the Pontifical Academy for Social Sciences and was a former US ambassador to the Holy See; and Mgr Peter Wells, fifty, the American who served as 'assessore' or No. 3 in the Secretariat of State. 'Anyone hoping that the commission of inquiry might be composed of people with outside objectivity and no inside personal interest would be very disappointed with this group. On the other hand, those likely to be most threatened by such a commission and the Pope's reforms might feel some reassurance by the names on this list,' wrote the Tablet's Robert Mickens cautiously.

Pope Benedict XVI had sought external oversight on the Vatican finances. During his papacy, Lord Camoys, head of one of England's most prominent Catholic families and a leading British investment banker, and Peter Sutherland, Ireland's former Attorney General and non-executive chairman of Goldman Sachs, were both recruited as unpaid consultants. These were largely honorary roles with no executive powers, requiring only occasional visits to Rome to meet members of the IOR board and Administration for the Patrimony of the Apostolic See (APSA). The latter had historically handled the income side of the Vatican's official budget, namely its substantial real estate and stock-market holdings. But Pope Francis signalled that whatever he had inherited from his predecessor, he needed to consult further about what more needed to be done, and the nature of advice and the way it was acted on had to be his own decision. Such governance reflected that something of the Jesuit provincial had re-emerged, but he had learnt to act differently than in the past when he was accused of being too authoritarian and not listening enough.

The challenges that remained were underlined just two days after the announcement of the new commission, when Mgr Nunzio Scarano, a Vatican official who has at least two accounts at the IOR, was arrested along with two accomplices after being suspected of trying to smuggle 20 million euros (£17 million) from Switzerland into Italy. The arrest of Mgr Scarano, a former banker and a chief accountant at APSA, was said to have especially perturbed the Pope, who has often warned clerics (and others) to be wary of 'money worshipping'. In fact, the Vatican had already suspended the cleric – social networks nicknamed him Monsignor Cinquecento in reference to the 500-euro bills he was alleged to habitually carry around with him – several weeks earlier after it learnt he was also under investigation over financial dealings in his native Salerno, a port city just south of Naples.

And yet there appeared to be a fresh wind blowing from the new pope's directives. That July 2013, Peter Sutherland, the chairman of Goldman Sachs, flew into Rome having retained his consultancy role under Francis. He continued to keep his distance from involvement in the day-to-day management of the Vatican's financial affairs, believing that such a task did not fall within his terms of engagement. Nevertheless he was impressed by Pope Francis's reforming spirit and was prepared to help him as far as he could. His visit proved to be somewhat different in character to those he had made to Rome during the Benedict era. Having played a bit part previously, Sutherland briefly took centre stage – if still outside the public eye. This time he found himself visiting not the Apostolic Palace but the Domus Sanctae Marthae where he found Pope Francis having his daily self-service breakfast in the dining room like any other priest or bishop. He was then asked to address a closed-door meeting of the Council of Cardinals, the pontiff's most senior advisers, with a very clear message: the need for transparency.

That the assembled audience were receptive to what Sutherland had to say was not that surprising. Pope Francis had been elected with the expectation that the Church would put its own house in order. The arrest of Mgr Scarano had focused minds. In the months that followed the Swiss Bruelhart and the German von Freyberg tried to complement each other, as a kind of CEO and chairman respectively with a crisis management team reviewing all accounts and tracking money transfers. Von Freyberg told the *Financial Times* that he considered it his task to 'get IOR super compliant and a respected member of the financial system, and out of the newspapers'. And yet von Freyberg's term in office at the IOR did not go unquestioned. His decision to bring in Promontory Financial, a global risk-control group, to help in the screening of an estimated 18,900 accounts at a cost initially and somewhat vaguely described as 'well above seven digits' raised questions as to whether this might not prove an excessive expense, which sat awkwardly alongside a pope that made humility a central aspect of his Church's mission.

Nevertheless, Pope Francis believed that bringing in outsiders to the Vatican bureaucracy like himself was a necessary part of his reform process. Not only did he raise no objection to Promontory Financial but also approved the appointment of Juan Zarate, the former US government terrorism adviser, to the Vatican's internal financial watchdog in June 2014. Zarate formed part of a continuing policy of having appointed high-profile external non-Italian advisers to the bank as a political counterweight to the more deeply entrenched vested interests of the Curia. A month later, von Freyberg quit his appointment after seventeen months in the job. While overseeing the closure of numerous questionable accounts, not strictly tied to the Church, he had also completed a business plan for the restructuring of the IOR as part of an ongoing process of modernization of Vatican finances. This was in parallel to changes in the Curia, with George Pell, the Australian cardinal, heading up the new Secretariat of the Economy.

As part of the declared policy of increased transparency and accountability, von Freyberg issued a long and detailed farewell statement along with figures that underlined the controversial nature of the bank's reform, and as Sandro Magister put it, 'threw up not a few curiosities'. This was only the second successive year in the bank's history that its accounts had been published. In October 2013, under pressure from Pope Francis, the IOR issued its first annual report which showed that the bank had 19,000 clients from around the world, 33,000 accounts and 5 billion euros in assets. It showed that few loans were made, but the bank held deposits, transferred money and made investments. Half the bank's clients were religious orders, another 15 per cent Vatican institutions, 13 per cent cardinals, bishops and clergy, and 9 per cent Catholic dioceses around the world. The rest of the clients were made up of those who had or should have had some 'affiliation to the Catholic Church', the report stated somewhat ambiguously. The bank was also awash in donations and cash from Sunday collections and charitable giving – about a third of its business. Alongside these accountable flows of money were an unpublicized number of dubious transactions involving accounts which had been set up with the aim of protecting the identity of the ultimate beneficiary, and by clients lying about their status. These accounts were suspected of having been set up for money laundering and tax evasion.

The figures released just under a year later showed that the restructuring of the IOR in order to weed out suspicious activity had resulted in the bank's net profits falling from £69 million (€86.6 million) in 2012 to just £2.3 million (€2.9 million) in 2013. As part of the clean-up, the accounts of more than 2,000 individual and institutional clients were blocked and a further 3,000 'customer relationships' curtailed. Those who had ceased to do business with the bank in recent years included some correspondent banks who had thought it prudent to do so rather than risk having their reputation tarnished as prosecutors and regulators homed in on the Vatican. The huge drop in net profits was due to write-downs on millions of pounds' worth of bad investments in externally managed funds, made before the reform process began in 2013. It also included €8.3 million in fees paid to Promontory Financial, with the company's employees accounting for 25 per cent of the staff of the Vatican bank.

At a Vatican news conference, von Freyberg told reporters that it made sense for him to leave as the IOR entered a new phase: 'At the beginning of my mandate, I repeatedly said that I would proceed with zero tolerance for any suspicious activity. It is fair to say that over the past months this often painful but very necessary process has opened the door to a new, unburdened future of the IOR – as a financial service provider that is fully and solely dedicated to serving the mission of the Catholic Church.'

Now that accounts had been closed and dubious investments off-loaded, a second phase of reform was set to begin, involving the slimming down of the bank's remit and the replacement of von Freyberg by a full-time president with experience in asset management. Von Freyberg was replaced by Jean-Baptiste de Franssu, the French chairman of INCIPIT, a mergers and acquisitions consulting firm. Von Freyberg's business plan envisaged ensuring that the IOR's exclusive role be eventually that of 'savings and loans for religious congregations', which made up the majority of its account holders, channelling all asset management activities, which had been run by several institutions, to one entity. In a show of unity, von Freyberg, de Franssu and Cardinal George Pell all emphasized the need to continue to consolidate financial operations in a process marked by transparency, coordination, professionalism, ethical values and compliance with international regulations.

Cardinal Pell, in February 2014, had been appointed by Pope Francis to the newly created role of Prefect of the Secretariat for the Economy. The Vatican also announced a new Council for the Economy comprising eight cardinals or bishops representing different parts of the world, and seven lay experts of different nationalities with strong professional financial experience. The developments were part of a restructuring of the Holy See's economic affairs, which were also the subject of the discussions of the group of eight (C8) cardinals picked by Francis to oversee reform of the Curia. Cardinal Pell was part of the C8. The changes were aimed at enabling more formal involvement of senior and experienced experts in financial administration, planning and reporting, and ensuring better use of resources and improving the support available for various programmes, particularly works with the poor and marginalized – even at the risk of creating new and more diverse layers of bureaucracy.

While only time would tell whether the new structures would improve not just the inner working of the Vatican but also its relationship with the wider world, the reforms on paper at least transformed the controversial hardliner Pell into the Vatican's equivalent of a Chancellor of the Exchequer. He would have authority over all economic and administrative activities within the Holy See and the Vatican City State, and prepare the papacy's annual budget. The Secretariat of the Economy's responsibilities included management and oversight of APSA, which returned to focusing on what it was founded to do: manage the portfolio of Vatican real-estate holdings and the financial settlement paid by the Italian government in 1929 with the signing of the Lateran Pacts, in which Italy and the Vatican recognized each other's sovereignty and boundaries.

In his first statement following his new appointment, Cardinal Pell predicted that the financial reforms of the Francis papacy would help make better use of the Vatican bank's resources to help the poor and disadvantaged. Pell had been openly critical of the exclusiveness of the Italian-dominated Curia during Benedict's papacy, and in his own country had built a reputation as an efficient manager of aid funds with a good financial brain.

Pell was conservative on matters of Church teaching. In 2007 he had become embroiled in a row with New South Wales politicians over a Bill that would allow stem-cell research in the state. At the time he threatened to refuse Communion to MPs who voted in support of the Bill. In November 2012 Pell drew further criticism from Catholics and non-Catholics after accusing the media of exaggerating the Church's involvement in child abuse. 'What is important for the press and the public to realize is that because there is a persistent press campaign against the Catholic Church's adequacies and inadequacies in this area, that does not necessarily represent the percentage of the problem that we offer,' he said. 'In other words, that because there is a press campaign focused largely on us, it does not mean that we are largely the principal culprits. We are not interested in denying the extent of misdoing in the Catholic Church. We object to [the extent of misdoing] being exaggerated, we object to being described as the only cab on the rank.' In August 2014 he draw outrage from child sexual abuse victims and their advocates after telling a royal commission into institutional responses to child sex abuse, that the Catholic Church was no more responsible for child abuse carried out by Church figures than a trucking company would be if they employed a driver who molested women.

The promotion of Cardinal Pell to a key advisory role within the Vatican sent out particularly mixed signals for those trying to look into the longer term future of the papacy.

Chapter Fifteen
The Long Shadow of Abuse

It was early August 2014, high summer in Spain, when a young university lecturer from Granada who went by the name of 'Daniel' and claimed to be a member of Opus Dei, received an unexpected call from an unknown number on his mobile phone. The caller initially identified himself in Spanish as Fr Jorge. When Daniel said he did not know any priest of that name, the caller said, 'I am *El Papa Francisco*.'

'Daniel' was the alias of a protected witness who was increasingly traumatized by the unresolved nature of his memory and the thoughts of others who might be suffering a similar fate. Days earlier, according to a report first aired publicly on the well-informed Catholic Spanish news service *Religion Digital* he had written a five-page letter to Pope Francis. In it, Daniel detailed the repeated sexual abuse he alleged he had suffered at the hands of priests in his childhood and adolescence.

On the phone, according to the report, Pope Francis expressed the profound impact the letter, which he had read several times, had on him and asked for forgiveness on behalf of the Church before assuring him that justice would be done.

'I received the letter,' Pope Francis later confirmed when asked about the Daniel case by Spanish journalists as he returned from a visit to the European Parliament in Strasbourg in November 2014. 'I read it, rang its author and said: "Tomorrow go and see the bishop." I told him that I had written to the bishop to get going and investigate.'

By then the Daniel case was being widely reported in the Spanish media, including the arrest by Spanish police of four suspects, three of them priests, after an unknown number of clergy had been suspended from their duties by the Archbishop of Granada. The day before the arrests the Archbishop of Granada and other clerics took the unusual step of prostrating themselves in the cathedral during Sunday Mass, 'asking forgiveness for the sins of the Church, for all of the scandals that have, or might have, occurred among us'. Such an act of penitence traditionally took place once a year, on Good Friday, but Archbishop Francisco Martínez had chosen to do this because of the seriousness of the allegations.

In its preliminary stages, the Daniel case raised familiar questions about how much the local Church hierarchy might have known about the activities of priests in a particular diocese, and whether the way the local Archbishop had acted was within the legal parameters of secular and canonical law. But the case also broke unexpected ground in Spain, a country where despite media exposure of a small number of earlier alleged sexual abuse cases, the still powerful Catholic Church had remained relatively protected from secular scrutiny. This was despite losing its previously virtually unassailable position of authority during the dictatorship of General Franco. Above all, Pope Francis's extraordinary personal intervention, while abiding by the 'zero tolerance' approach to sexual abuse cases promised by his predecessor Pope Benedict XVI, signalled a new way of dealing with the issue in gesture, and action.

Four months earlier, in an 11 April 2014 speech delivered to the International Catholic Child Bureau, Pope Francis had also asked for forgiveness on behalf of priests who abused children, but in general terms and without identifying his defence of any one victim. The Pope's unscripted comments were hailed at the time as his 'strongest statement yet' on the sex abuse crisis. Pope Francis said he was aware of the 'personal and moral damage . . . carried out by men of the Church', and insisted the Church must be 'very firm' in fighting sex abuse. 'We do not want to take one step backward in dealing with this problem,' said Pope Francis, 'because you cannot take chances with children.'

In July 2014 Pope Francis arranged a publicized meeting in Rome with six victims of clerical sex abuse from three European countries. He begged forgiveness for the 'sacrilegious' crimes committed by the 'sons and daughters of the Church who betrayed their mission, who abused innocent persons'. The Pope told the six – two from Britain, two from Germany and two from Ireland – that the Church would 'weep' for its 'grave sin' and must make amends for the suffering it had caused. In pledging that bishops who fail to report or cover up abuse would be held accountable, Pope Francis appeared to be upping the stakes still further on the subject. 'I ask for the grace to weep, the grace for the Church to weep and make reparation for her sons and daughters who betrayed their mission,' he said.

During a Mass for the group of survivors at the Domus Sanctae Marthae, the guesthouse Francis has made his residence, he denounced the abuse of minors as 'worse than despicable'. He said: 'It is like a sacrilegious cult, because these boys and girls had been entrusted to the priestly charism in order to be brought to God.' In his informal homily, prepared without notes, Pope Francis referred to the moment when Peter weeps after denying Christ. Francis asked for forgiveness and told the survivors that abuse by clergy had been too long hidden and 'camouflaged with a complicity that cannot be explained'. He lamented that child sex abuse leaves 'lifelong scars' and acknowledged that victims have been driven to addiction and even suicide by their experiences.

Among those who were with the Pope that day was Englishman Peter Saunders. When he was a young child he was abused by two priests. As an adult he set up the charity the National Association for People Abused in Childhood. Reflecting on the Pope as a person and what he had said, Saunders later commented that only time would tell how the promises to hold all accountable would pan out, although he believed Pope Francis to be sincere. The meetings followed two damning reports of the Church's past record by the UN in early 2014. The UN Committee on the Rights of the Child said the Church had 'systematically' adopted policies that allowed priests to rape and molest tens of thousands of children over decades. The UN Committee Against Torture found that the Vatican 'resisted mandatory reporting' of child abuse and instead transferred offenders to other dioceses, allowing more abuse to take place.

It took Pope Francis nine months in post before he announced his plans to establish a special commission to advise him on the issue and to draw up reforms of Church processes in dealing with those involved. The initial eight-person commission was formally set up in March 2014, on the first anniversary of the papacy. The most prominent appointee was Cardinal Seán Patrick O'Malley, a Capuchin Franciscan who became Archbishop of Boston in 2003 after Cardinal Bernard Law's resignation. With a mixture of humility, transparency and directness, O'Malley earned a reputation for helping restore some of the Catholic Church's integrity in a city historically proud of its Catholic roots and influence. He helped settle the claims of hundreds of victims, established a policy requiring that perpetrators be turned over to civil authorities, and published the names of guilty priests. O'Malley was widely praised by both Church leaders and victims.

The papal commission in its early history also included prominent lay British and European psychologists and psychiatrists, and Marie Collins, who was sexually abused by a cleric in the 1960s and is a leading campaigner on the issue in Ireland. Another victim, Peter Saunders, would be invited to join later. From the outset the commission featured two priests, the Jesuits German Fr Hans Zollner and the Argentine Humberto Miguel Yáñez, who respectively taught psychiatry and moral theology at the Jesuit-run Gregorian University in Rome.

Zollner, vice-rector and the latest head of the Institute of Psychology at the prestigious Gregorian, had particularly impressive credentials in terms of his understanding both of how the Vatican worked and the dynamics of abuse, as was pointed out by John Allen in the *National Catholic Reporter*. Zollner co-authored *The Church and Paedophilia – An Open Wound: A Psychological and Pastoral Approach* in 2010, and two years later chaired a major international summit on the sex abuse crisis held at the Gregorian, at which Yáñez was among the speakers.

Yáñez had entered the order when Bergoglio was provincial and was later taught by him at the Colegio Máximo at San Miguel near Buenos Aires. He came to look up to Bergoglio as a spiritual father who, while giving him a certain freedom to think for himself, also instilled in him the need for coherence in his life and apostolic and ministerial commitment. While some other Jesuits of his generation had distanced themselves from Bergoglio during those years, considering him too disciplinarian and theologically conservative, Yáñez was not one of them. Instead, he recalled his days as a Jesuit scholastic with great satisfaction. Like Bergoglio he became a follower of liberation theology with a focus on non-Marxist popular religiosity, which he believed was more suited to Argentina's political and social reality.

During the early years of the Kirchner/Fernández government he was head of the Argentine Jesuit think-tank CIAS, from which he organized a series of conferences on democracy. Many of the CIAS discussions reflected Bergoglio's criticism of Argentina's failed politics and corruption in 2002–12. Yáñez was thus a true Bergoglio loyalist, as well as a friend who could be trusted to be Pope Francis's eyes and ears within the commission, even though the charismatic Cardinal O'Malley was the effective head.

Within a month of his election, Pope Francis had acquired a reputation for introducing himself simply as 'Fr Jorge' in personal phone calls to new and former associates. He famously even phoned his old newsagent in Buenos Aires in order to apologize for having to cancel his subscription. Other recipients of calls included personal male and female friends who needed comforting or whom he trusted for advice, as well as those to whom he wished to convey a sense of deep contrition, such as 'Daniel'.

Given the commission's expertise and commitment to dealing with the issue of abuse, the widespread expectation was that it would move the Church from its previously piecemeal approach to more coordinated and concerted action. If the Francis papacy was perceived by some sectors of the secular world to move initially with leaden steps on the issue, this was not how it was viewed within the Vatican itself and those who had had dealings with the issue under Benedict XVI. As Fr Zollner commented in an interview with the *National Catholic Reporter* soon after the papal resignation, Benedict XVI deserved credit for taking the important first steps, but evidently there was much more still to be done.

As John Allen has pointed out, one of the reasons many Catholics as well as non-Catholics found it difficult to portray Benedict as a reformer, not least in the United States, was the perception that bishops had not been held accountable for the protection of children in their dioceses. One of the challenges facing his successor was how to coordinate the correct adherence to civil and canon law, and ensure good practice across the Church when bishops and priests operated in different secular jurisdictions and cultures.

Thus, months after the new papal commission on sex abuse was set up, Cardinal O'Malley publicly criticized inconsistencies in response to the failure of bishops to take responsibility for the protection of children in their diocese. He pressed for urgent action to be taken by the Vatican, for example in the case of Bishop Robert Finn of Kansas City-St Joseph in Missouri. Finn waited six months before notifying police about the Revd Shawn Rattigan, whose computer contained hundreds of lewd photos of young girls taken in and around churches where he worked. Rattigan was sentenced to fifty years in prison after pleading guilty to child pornography charges. Finn pleaded guilty to a misdemeanour charge of failure to report suspected abuse and was sentenced to two years' probation in 2012. Finn was the highest-ranking Church official in the US to be convicted of failing to take action in response to abuse allegations – but the Vatican moved slowly against him.

By contrast, in Africa, a key continent for Catholic missionary work, Pope Francis faced challenges of a different nature as Hans Zollner told John Allen: 'This is not the Anglo-Saxon legal system and puritanical moral system. In many African countries, for example, it's normal to marry a girl at 14, 15 and 16, and to have children at that age. In Angola, there are initiation rites for boys at the age of 13 to 16. They stay in "boy camps" for one to two years, where they're introduced to sexuality, including what by our standards would include abuse. We have to understand a bit more what sexuality means for the peoples of Africa, and how they understand sexual interaction with minors. The civil law may be completely different from the practice. If the culture, or the tribe, or the family says that you marry at 16, then it doesn't matter what the law says. Actually, that's often true in India with the caste system.'

India, it is worth noting, according to the *National Catholic Reporter*, is where the Catholic Church is growing at a rate ahead of overall population growth, so it is estimated that by 2050 there could be almost thirty million Catholics, well ahead of the Catholic population of Germany, for example, and close to Poland.

Pope Francis's sermons after his election made it evident that while he believed it was high time for the institutional Church to break out of its self-protective, excessively clerical silo mentality, he was still a Jesuit who believed in carefully examining the facts in front of him before rushing into judgement – and the paperwork that piled up in his in-tray on a variety of subjects was immense. As it turned out, within weeks of the papacy, Francis was showing himself not only categorical in his acceptance of the Church's need to assume greater responsibility over the issue, but making sure that his words translated into action. He broke down the barriers that had hitherto protected the perpetrators of abuse, and ensured that cases were addressed without delay and acted on with just and necessary rigour.

On 5 November 2014, Pope Francis published a short document signalling his willingness to take a stronger hand in removing some bishops from office. The one-page edict dealt primarily with the age of a bishop's retirement, suggesting that bishops should not be reluctant to step aside earlier than the mandatory age of seventy-five for the good of the Church. But in one key sentence he added: 'In some particular circumstances, the competent Authority [the Pope] may consider it necessary to ask a bishop to present the resignation of his pastoral office, after letting him know the motives for such a request and after listening attentively to his justifications, in fraternal dialogue.'

The power of a pope to sack a bishop had always been presumed among Catholics and was used by Benedict XVI, but here it was spelt out as if it was felt necessary not just in public relations terms, but in terms of the Pope's own authority, clearing up any ambiguity about his power to act, and the need for bishops to be accountable. The canonical document – a widely commented upon *aide memoire* – came months after Pope Francis had 'accepted the resignation' of the German Bishop Franz-Peter Tebartz-van Elst, who had reportedly spent some 31 million euros ($43 million) on a new residence and complex in his Limburg diocese in western Germany while at the same time reducing salaries for staff in the name of financial austerity.

Pope Francis later removed a Paraguayan bishop, Mgr Rogelio Livieres Plano of Ciudad del Este who has been accused of protecting a priest suspected of sexually abusing young parishioners. Meanwhile, closer to home Pope Francis's 'zero tolerance' on sexual abuse was underlined by the action taken against the apostolic nuncio to the Dominican Republic, Jósef Wesołowski, after he was alleged to have paid for sex with minors in accusations that arose in late 2013. He had already resigned from his position of nuncio on 21 August 2013, but he was placed under house arrest in the Vatican (he was too ill to be imprisoned) where he remained at the end of 2014, awaiting trial.. The Vatican ruled that Wesołowski would be 'laicized', a canonical penalty that bans the person involved from celebrating the sacraments, while making it clear that it would fully cooperate with the criminal prosecution. Although there was no extradition treaty between the Vatican and the Dominican Republic, officials expressed their willingness to hand over Wesołowski to its civil authorities, further clarifying that as the nuncio had been removed from his post, he no longer had diplomatic immunity.

As the Jesuit commentator and author Thomas Reese has written in the *National Catholic Reporter*, when it comes to its record of dealing with sex abuse, 'the Church deserves to be raked over the coals'. As Reese pointed out, the Church made various critical mistakes in its response to abusive priests and dealing with the victims, all of which proved to be disastrous. Since the early 1990s the Catholic Church had paid at least $2 billion in the United States alone to settle abuse claims.

However, in Spain and many Latin American countries such as Argentina, where the Church historically has exercised considerable power and influence over the secular authorities, the potential scope of abuse crime surfaced belatedly with no record of victims receiving restitution in public settlements.

Pope Francis's own past record on the issue while he was a

bishop in Argentina never became as much of a subject of public controversy as his alleged shortcomings on the human rights front as a Jesuit priest during Argentina's military dictatorship. Yet his past record in handling allegations of sex abuse, it has belatedly emerged, was one that in European countries would have provoked criticism – and in the United States did. According to well-placed clerical sources in Argentina, interviewed for this book, Bergoglio as archbishop disagreed with psychiatrists who argued that priests required regular mandatory counselling both during and after leaving the seminary. It is also claimed that there were occasions when he brushed aside concerns about the sexual misconduct of some of his priests.

'Bergoglio when he was archbishop did not reject psychology outright, and allowed psychological tests of those training for the priesthood in seminaries for which he had oversight as a bishop. He also advised several ordained priests to submit themselves to therapy,' recalled Fr Gustavo Irrazábal. He was a professor in moral theology and trained lawyer who taught at a main seminary in Villa Devoto, Buenos Aires, in 2000–2006 when Bergoglio, who had himself trained at the seminary, was his archbishop. 'However, when I was in charge at the seminary I suggested to Bergoglio that psychological assistance should not be limited to those identified as needing therapy but permanently to all priests including those who did not seem to present any psychological disorders when they were ordained. He opposed that.'

While studying for his doctorate at the Gregorian University in Rome, Irrazábal had become influenced by the theories of Luigi Rulla, an Italian Jesuit and psychiatrist, based on empirical tests and interviews with US religious and seminarians during the 1960s. The result of the investigation, complemented by philosophical and theological approaches to the subject, was published as *Anthropology of Christian Vocation* in the early 1970s. With a focus on the risks from repressed sexual or aggressive impulses arising largely from buried or unintegrated childhood experience, Rulla argued that even when a person orientates himself fully towards the values and ideals of a religious life, the nature of his relationships and secret practice may be determined by unconscious needs and attitudes in conflict with these values.

Rulla's theories have remained controversial, and are questioned on empirical and theological grounds by anti-Freudian secular therapists and clergy who have taught in seminaries. However, Bergoglio, who was at odds with fellow Jesuit Rulla and his disciples, also had his critics, not least among his own priests in Argentina. Some argued that he placed too much focus on spiritual discernment, prayer and religious ritual, and the devil – to which he made frequent references in his homilies before he became pope – while only belatedly grasping the human dimension to vocational crisis.

'The problem I believed we faced was the fact that many seminarians while not presenting disorders while in the seminary, did so after becoming priests, showing themselves ill-suited to their vocation, and therefore conflictive and unhappy,' said Irrazábal.

A few months into the Francisco papacy, I interviewed Fr Nacho Puente Olivera, a Buenos Aires priest. Older members of his family had been friends with Bergoglio since he was a child but he had grown disillusioned with the institutional Church, a fact he blamed on its complicity with the military regime he held responsible for the disappearance of close relatives. I later learnt that Olivera had subsequently left the priesthood to marry and dedicate himself to social work soon after our encounter.

While still a priest Olivera told me that, three days before Pope Benedict announced his resignation, he had a meeting with Bergoglio in the Argentine capital, during which he expressed, not for the first time, his concern about the sexual misconduct he had witnessed among other clerics. As he recalled, 'I expressed my concern about a priest we both knew and who I believe was going through some kind of personal breakdown. I had glimpsed him masturbating in the priests' house we shared through the open door to his study. Bergoglio said he would move me to another more important parish but leave the other priest where he was. I struggled to understand. I was speechless. Afterwards all that came to mind was the suspicion that I was being promoted as a way of silencing me.'

Fr Nacho said, 'When I challenged Bergoglio about certain cases I knew about, his reply was that we had to show forgiveness and support. To which my response was I agreed that there were numerous priests that needed help in coming to terms with their sexuality but we shouldn't wait till it became a public scandal before reacting and taking action. We had to deal with problems affecting the psychological breakdown of a person, bring therapy in much sooner, contain the situation before it risked getting out of control.'

There were other cases Nacho told me about – priests who had themselves been abused as teenagers by other priests – but nothing was done because the institutions involved had strong links with key figures in the Vatican where some members of the Curia turned a blind eye. The abusers were in effect protected although there is no suggestion that Bergoglio was complicit, still less actively involved in the cover-up.

Fr Nacho continued, 'Bergoglio when he was a bishop and Benedict was pope felt there was nothing he could do in Rome. He didn't seem able to confront Rome over the issue. But my feeling was that sooner or later he would have to take responsibility. I used to say to Bergoglio, "I don't think you realize that this is only the tip of a wider crisis the priesthood is going through under the pressures of modern society; a bishop I know who is an alcoholic; the priests I know who are suffering from acute depression, others who are repressing the fact they are homosexual and they all fear being discovered. Abuse makes everyone involved feel dirty."'

In September 2013, halfway through Francis's first year as pope, one of only a few publicized criminal cases lodged against an Argentine priest surfaced when Fr Julio Grassi was jailed, four years after being convicted of sexually abusing a pre-pubescent boy in his care at a home for children and abandoned youths. Three courts in Argentina had already confirmed his 2009 conviction before the Supreme Court of Buenos Aires province ratified the fifteen-year prison sentence The charitable foundation, for which the young, dynamic, media-savvy Grassi raised funds by tapping the wealthy, had won praise from the country's politicians and the Church, including Bergoglio. It was called the Felices los Niños, the 'Happy Children' foundation.

An investigation carried out by the *Washington Post* and published on 18 March 2013, five days after Bergoglio was elected pope, found that in the years after his conviction, Bergoglio as Archbishop of Buenos Aires declined to meet with the victim of the priest's crimes or the victims of other predations by clergy under his leadership. He did not offer personal apologies or financial restitution, even in cases in which the crimes were denounced by other members of the Church and the offending priests were sent to jail. 'He has been totally silent,' Ernesto Moreau, a member of Argentina's UN-affiliated Permanent Assembly for Human Rights told the *Post*'s Nick Miroff. Victims asked to meet with Bergoglio but were turned down, Moreau claimed. 'In that regard, Bergoglio was no different from most of the other bishops in Argentina, or the Vatican itself.'

Again, there is no evidence that Bergoglio played a role in covering up abuse cases. Several prominent rights groups in Argentina say the Archbishop went out of his way in recent years to stand with secular organizations against crimes such as sex trafficking and child prostitution. They say that Bergoglio's resolve strengthened as new cases of molestation emerged in the archdiocese and that he eventually instructed bishops to immediately report all abuse allegations to police. In September 2012, after an Argentine priest from a rural area was convicted of abusing dozens of boys between 1984 and 1992, Archbishop Bergoglio's office released a statement saying the case had 'reaffirmed our profound shame and the immense pain that result from the grave mistakes committed by someone who should be setting the moral example'.

However, the case of Father Grassi proved particularly troublesome to children's advocates in Argentina because Bergoglio was widely viewed as close to the young priest, who told reporters before his conviction that he spoke with Bergoglio often and that the Archbishop 'never let go of my hand'. Grassi was not expelled from the priesthood after the initial guilty verdict. Instead, Church officials, led by Bergoglio, commissioned a lengthy private investigation by a leading Argentine lawyer which concluded that the case against him had been based on false evidence, supporting Bergoglio's view that Grassi was innocent. The report was submitted as part of the priest's legal appeal, which initially helped Grassi avoid jail time, staying under loose house arrest instead.

One of Argentina's best-known advocates for child-abuse victims, Sister Martha Pelloni, said she was called in several times to consult with psychologists who treated Grassi's alleged victims. She said the meetings left her with no doubt that the priest was guilty, despite the Church-commissioned report attempting to exonerate him. He was eventually convicted on the charges made by one of the boys. 'A lot of Catholics have wanted to protect and defend him,' she said. 'But the abuses were real.' A lawyer for the prosecution, Juan Pablo Gallego, described Grassi as 'a convicted paedophile, who was out of control'.

Bergoglio appears to have changed his mind about Grassi after being presented with further incriminating evidence about the priest in a personal meeting he granted Eduardo Valdés, a lawyer acting for one of the young abuse victims. Valdés was a well-known figure in the Peronist movement who had served as deputy to the

Foreign Minister Rafael Bielsa in the first Kirchner government. While Bergoglio regarded Néstor Kirchner as an anti-clerical demagogue, he trusted Valdés, a committed Catholic who did not slavishly follow the President's command on every issue. Valdés quit the foreign ministry in 2004 and returned to private practice after becoming involved in a diplomatic row with Cuba over the extradition of an Argentine national – a move Kirchner felt got in the way of his friendship with the Castro brothers.

Valdés's case was that of 'Gabriel', the first abuse victim to testify against Grassi. 'When I went and saw Bergoglio [after Grassi's conviction],' Valdés told me, 'he said, "To God what is God's, and to Caesar what is Caesar's" before adding, "From now on I hope you can refer to Grassi, not Fr Grassi – because the Church has nothing to do with this."' (In October 2014 Valdés was appointed Argentina's ambassador to the Holy See, having played a key role in building a cordial relationship between President Fernández and Pope Francis.)

Fr Grassi still insisted he was innocent. 'In my life, all I have done was to help the children in need,' he told the criminal court in the city of Morón. 'The prosecutors have lied and set up a case against me . . . I am in peace, I believe in God,' Father Grassi said after being jailed.

In another notorious Argentine abuse case, a priest in the Archdiocese of Buenos Aires was assigned to work with children even when church leaders knew of allegations against him. After local parishioners accused Father Mario Napoleon Sasso of molesting children in a poor, rural province of eastern Argentina in the early 1990s, he was sent to a private rehabilitation centre for wayward clergy, La Domus Mariae (the House of Mary), north of Buenos Aires. He lived for two years at the centre and was then reassigned to work in a soup kitchen for poor children in a town outside the capital. There, he went on to sexually abuse girls as young as three.

Ernesto Moreau, who was the attorney for the victims' families, told the *Washington Post* that in 2003 he accompanied two nuns and a priest who had denounced Sasso, along with the victims' families, to a meeting with the Vatican emissary in Buenos Aires. He said the families were told to be 'patient' and were offered gifts of rosaries 'blessed by the Pope'. 'They just wanted to cover it up,' Moreau said. Three years later, as the evidence against Sasso mounted, the families asked to see Bergoglio, Moreau said, but they never received a response. Sasso was convicted in 2007 and sentenced to seventeen years in prison. He has since been released on parole.

In the same *Washington Post* article pubished on 8 March 2013, Sister Pelloni, however, praised Bergoglio for taking an increasingly firm stance against predatory clergy during the years leading up to his papacy. Argentine law makes it a crime to fail to report allegations of abuse against children. 'Now if you go to a bishop with a claim, they'll say, "Report to the police",' she told the newspaper. 'Bergoglio must have ordered that.' Yet past victims of sexual abuse might have been spared if their cases, too, had received such decisive action, Bergoglio critics contend.

In a rare published comment in 2012, prior to becoming pope, Bergoglio said: 'The idea that paedophilia is a consequence of celibacy is ruled out. More than seventy per cent of cases of paedophilia occur in the family and neighbourhood: grandparents, uncles, stepfathers, neighbours. The problem is not linked to celibacy. If a priest is a paedophile, he is so before he is a priest. Now, when that happens, we must never turn a blind eye. You cannot be in a position of power and destroy the life of another person. In the diocese it never happened to me, but a bishop once called me to ask me by phone what to do in a situation like that and I told him to take away the priests' licences, not to allow them to exercise the priesthood any more, and to begin a canonical trial in that diocese's court. I think that's the attitude to have. I do not believe in taking positions that uphold a certain corporative spirit in order to avoid damaging the image of the institution. That solution was proposed once in the United States: they proposed switching the priests to a different parish. It is a stupid idea; that way, the priest just takes the problem with him wherever he goes. The corporate reaction leads to such a result, so I do not agree with those solutions. Recently, there were cases uncovered in Ireland from about twenty years ago, and the present Pope [Benedict XVI] clearly said: "Zero tolerance for that crime." I admire the courage and uprightness of Pope Benedict on the subject.'

From the moment he was elected pope with the remit of pulling the universal Church out of its perceived institutional and moral malaise, Francis knew he had to assume much greater responsibility for dealing with the sexual problems of the worldwide clergy than he had ever had to face as Archbishop of Buenos Aires. And in Rome he was evidently more prepared to listen to expert advice on sexual abuse than he had been in Argentina. And yet he had to struggle against his own Jesuitical instinct to reach his own verdict without having it prejudged by others. He also thought it best to forgive rather than condemn. Such an attitude sprang from his experience of having his own reputation tarnished by his detractors over his role as the head of the Jesuits in the Dirty War. But if he was to re-establish the Church's credibility, there could be no room for equivocation. As pope, he had to be the first to say that no sexual abuse could be tolerated, wherever it occurred in the Catholic Church – and he did.

And while Francis clearly expressed his *mea culpa* over the Church's historical record on the issue, dealing effectively with the problem of sexual abuse within the institution remains one of the key challenges of his papacy.

The American Jesuit commentator Thomas Reese, in an article published in the *National Catholic Reporter* on 7 February 2014, analysed where the Catholic Church went wrong:

In terms of the alleged abuse itself, the initial response was one of denial, the second was to deal with abuse as a sexual sin – demand repentance and the promise of reform, while the third was to deal with abuse as a psychological problem that could be cured. Priests were sent to counselling and therapy. Incompetent psychologists assured bishops they could fix the priests. They argued that it was essential, if the therapy process was going to work, that priests have the chance of returning to ministry. They tried to imitate the successful model of dealing with alcoholic priests.

While a 10 per cent recidivism rate might be considered extraordinarily successful in the criminal justice system, it was not good enough if it placed children at risk. Zero tolerance was the only solution.

As for the response from the victims, legal action not only proved costly for all concerned but alienating, which undermined engagement and the possibility of reconciliation as well as restitution. Battle lines were also drawn within the media and within the Church itself, turning the issue into something that divided Catholics. Fr Reese wrote:

The bishops saw the 'secular, liberal media', which opposed them on abortion, gay marriage and contraception, as trying to destroy the church. They saw prosecutors and politicians trying to interfere in the running of the church. They saw victims' lawyers as filling their pockets with big payments. They saw liberal Catholics pushing an agenda of married priests, women priests and democratic reform in the church. Seeing the crisis as a power struggle made it almost impossible for the church to do the sensible thing: Have a bishop admit his mistakes, take full responsibility and resign.

Reese, a recognized expert, welcomed Pope Francis's decision to have an international commission study the sexual abuse crisis and come up with a list of best practices so that the Church could learn from the US Church and not make the same mistakes. And yet, as he pointed out, in the early days the Europeans thought sexual abuse was an American problem – until it hit Ireland, England, Scotland and German-speaking countries. 'Today, I fear Latin American and African bishops think this is a "First World problem",' wrote Fr Reese.

In fairness to the UK, the bishops of England and Wales were well ahead of their US and European counterparts in recognizing the problem. Following an inquiry led by the judge Lord Nolan, a legal expert on standards in public life, stricter guidelines relating to child protection were introduced in 2001. Since then, English Catholic leaders have maintained the Church has 'gold standard safeguarding' with much improved systems in place for reporting allegations to statutory authorities and for dealing with those involved. In more recent years, fewer cases of sexual abuse have arisen even if the system has been shown not to be foolproof.

'Anyone wanting to become a Roman Catholic priest must be someone with a very thick skin and an unflinching faith,' reported the BBC's Duncan Kennedy in May 2010 in a dispatch from Rome.

At the time, Catholic priests were at the centre of the latest wave of child abuse scandals. Church authorities in Europe and North and South America were alleged to have failed to deal properly with those in their charge, moving them to new parishes where more children were put at risk. Pope Benedict XVI himself stood accused of being part of a culture of secrecy, and of not taking strong enough steps against paedophiles when he had that responsibility under Pope Paul II as the Cardinal Prefect of the Doctrinal Congregation in Rome. En route to Portugal in 2010, Pope Benedict XVI said the clerical child abuse scandal showed that: 'Today we see in a truly terrifying way that the greatest persecution of the Church does not come from outside enemies, but is born of sin within the Church.'

More than three years later, I travelled to Rome to test the mood of aspiring priests and their teachers following the election of Pope Francis. I booked myself a room in the Pontifical Beda College, a seminary specializing in people with late vocations but also catering for younger students from around the world. Beda lies a couple of blocks away from the magnificent Basilica of St Paul Outside the Walls, which houses the alleged remains of St Paul, generally considered one of the most important figures of the first century of Christianity.

My host was Mgr Roderick Strange, the seminary's rector, a highly intelligent and engaging priest I had befriended in my early days as a Catholic journalist. Rod was an authority on Cardinal Newman, the convert from Anglicanism who helped shape the reforming spirit in the Catholic Church. I was drawn to Rod by the huge admiration for Newman I had inherited from my great-uncle James – an Anglican and one of Newman's first publishers. Rod admitted once that one of his favourite Newman quotes was 'The best preparation for loving the world at large, and loving it duly and wisely, is to cultivate an intimate friendship and affection towards those who are immediately about us.'

When Rod was asked in an interview whether Newman's views on friendship informed his own faith, he responded: 'Newman combined qualities that can sometimes be in tension in others. So, for example, he was a champion of dogma, but also a keen advocate of theology. He was also said to be "never less alone than when alone", a man who prized solitude, while he was at the same time blessed with a gift for friendship . . . he recognized that if we are to fulfil the great commandment to love God and our neighbour, we will not do that by a vague, broad, general philanthropy. We have to love particular people. Through these particular loves we make the great commandment a reality in our lives.'

Discussing priestly training, Rod talked about the need for the priesthood to develop on a firm foundation, and the importance of finding the 'right balance of heart and mind, reason and feeling, body and soul so as to be humanly integrated, being our true selves'. He added that priesthood was 'about more than just prayer, flair and care'. As he put it in an interview with the BBC: 'Of course, we want someone who can pray, someone who shows intellectual flair and who has a sense of pastoral care, but also someone who has a grounded, solid, integrated, mature personality.'

Beda was founded in 1852 although the building currently housing the seminary was inaugurated by Pope John XXIII in 1960, the year that ushered in a decade of profound upheaval within the Church. When I visited in October 2013, the atmosphere was one of a senior common room at a well-heeled Oxford or Cambridge college. Open-neck shirts are the signature dress style of the seminarians, with only Mgr Strange wearing a dog collar – a token gesture towards convention that belies his liberal theology.

Among the late-vocation students I met was Ron, aged fifty-three. He distinguished himself from all the others by wearing a well-tailored suit, cravat and, on his walks beyond the seminary, a broad-brimmed hat. He was born into a Catholic family in 1960, delivered by a half-blind midwife in the front room of his cramped terraced Dublin home near the Quays. He was educated by the Christian Brothers before training as a psychiatric nurse, a profession he followed in various London hospitals over the years. In 1986 he worked in a ward for infectious sexual diseases, when Aids was spreading with as yet no anti-HIV medication available.

'One day,' he told me, 'I was having a cigarette after seeing three clients who were all racked with guilt because of the sexual infidelity they had committed: a businessman in his thirties, married with two children, who after a business trip was pretty upset about what he was going to tell his wife. Then there was a twenty-eight-year-old woman who had had an abortion in her teens and had been married for about two years and couldn't have sex and discussed the possibility of guilt and shame and post-traumatic stress. And there was another guy who was diagnosed in the clinic at the time with gonorrhoea and he was really angry and he was threatening all sorts of violence against his girlfriend. So I was outside the clinic having a cigarette and looking at the planes going by and I thought those three clients I've seen this morning are far better off going to a priest, and it was a thought that I had myself. It wasn't a schizophrenic hallucination popping into my mind. It surprised me because I asked myself – where did that come from? Well, what I was thinking of was the sacrament of reconciliation: so they go to a priest, they confess their sins, they get absolution, and feel a hell of a lot better and probably more cognizant to cope with their extreme anger, cope with their guilt, cope with their infidelity, and make a clean breast with their wife and their partner. And then it led from there to what happens to me. Where did those thoughts that I had about priesthood go and why did they evaporate for at least two decades of my life?'

Ron said in his youth he had been bisexual, moving from a woman to a man, developing into being gay. I asked him if he had an issue with celibacy.

'No, no, I haven't had a relationship going on two decades,' he answered. He and other seminarians had gone through some psychological tests and something called the Minnesota Multiphasing Personality Inventory (MMPI). 'Rather than filling in forms as I was used to from the late 1970s, it was a computer programme with questions like: When did you first start masturbating? What kind of sexual fantasies do you have? Do you look at pornography? When was the last time you looked at pornography? When was the last time you entertained any thoughts about children? Have you entertained children? Have you ever taken them out?'

Ron passed the test. Otherwise he would not have been at Beda. But different seminaries had different standards.

'I have heard of priests doing their seminarian training without doing the psychometric testing as a pre-screening exercise, being quite resistant to the idea, thinking it's a load of navel gazing,' Ron said. And he sympathized with those priests who had to get criminal record (CR) clearance every time they move to a new job involving children or young adults. 'Three CR clearances to do your job as a priest seems to me a bit excessive.' The system had become unfair and discriminatory; the priesthood had become over-regulated in the age of Pope Francis – or so he claimed.

I next visited the neoclassical palazzo in Rome's Piazza della Pilotta, which today houses the Gregorian, the university originally founded by St Ignatius. Regarded as the global theological nerve centre of the Catholic Church and of the Jesuits, it boasts more cardinals and popes among its alumni than any other single educational establishment in the world. There, in the age of Francis, I met Fr Jacquineau Azetsop, a young Jesuit priest from Cameroon. He shared these questions as we sat drinking coffee in the spacious modern common room used by the order: 'Where are we as a Church? What are we looking for? What is the meaning of priesthood for today? What are the challenges of the priesthood today? And are these challenges specific to the priesthood? Or are they challenges that the entire society is confronted with?'

And this is what Jacquineau understood: 'At the level of the individual, one of the anthropological foundations of celibacy, of chastity is this: I free myself to be entirely available to people, to the Church, to society, and this is something that is countercultural. I have been living in the US for four years and even there I find that chastity is countercultural. Society does not appreciate celibacy while having a sexual relationship with somebody seems to be valued by society. This is in every culture. Even the Buddhist monks in Tibet have to make an effort to transcend what seems to be an important social value in order to lead their monastic life.

'The second point is at the level of society, I have heard people say. "You want to be a priest? Ah, that's bullshit, no one wants to do that anymore," they say. And for sure, I have the impression that a vocations crisis will come to us soon also in Africa because we have more people who want to be Christian but no way do they want to be priests. They want to get married, they want to have children. And yet religious life began with *fuga mundis*, running away from the world, running away from society, to be faithful to Jesus. You will see that many of the seminaries are built on the outskirts of cities so people can be away from society, they can study well and pray. Well, does that work? That's the question. I don't say yes or no.'

Depending on your meaning of 'religious life', the first apostles didn't run away from society, I could have said. Jacquineau was in a stream of consciousness so I thought it best not to interrupt.

He continued: 'But you go into some convents and people go out once a month. By contrast I remember when we were Jesuit novices we used to go out twice a week. Our novice director used to say: "You are being trained for the world, for people, you have to know them, you have to learn your way around, you have to know the challenges you have chosen by being with people from the start, not tomorrow, but from now, from the start." My point is that it's important that priestly formation allows people to be who they truly are and to express themselves as who they are within the framework of what they have chosen. St Ignatius never wanted us to be monks. He wanted people with a mission, to serve people outside. So there is a great sense of freedom in the Society of Jesus. But I would say that freedom is a chance and a risk. It is up to the person to use it well.'

I left the Gregorian feeling that, in the age of Francis, I had shared a coffee with someone who thought he could make a good African pope one day.

★

Weeks earlier, after Benedict's resignation and just prior to Francis's election, Cardinal Keith O'Brien, the leader of the Scottish Catholic Church, resigned amid allegations, subsequently shown to be true, that he had been involved in inappropriate sexual behaviour with young priests.

I later visited Scotland. I met with parishioners and priests familiar with the case, leaving me in no doubt that O'Brien had led a double life. In public he cut the figure of a charismatic spiritual leader, who courted publicity and was accessible to campaigners requiring the imprimatur of a senior bishop on any issue that the Vatican remained ambiguous or indecisive on. An example was his personal support for the campaign for the beatification of Archbishop Romero. He was publicly protective of the social and employment rights of Scottish Catholics who still faced discrimination from Protestant-dominated national and local government authorities. He was courted by pro-independence Scots. He was also outspoken in defending Catholic teaching in terms that attracted widespread censure from non-Catholics and turned him into a controversial political as well as religious figure. He notoriously called gay marriage a 'grotesque subversion' and 'madness'. When the accusations of sexual misconduct were shown to be true, he was exposed as a hypocrite.

For the papacy of Benedict XVI, already under pressure, it was a public relations disaster, undermining once again its authority on sexual teaching. While in Scotland, I found local Catholics in shock, some of them angry, but most of them disorientated as they grappled with the challenges of retaining their faith after a traumatic betrayal by one of the Church's once hugely admired princes.

Ted Coyle, an elderly Scottish Jesuit brother, told me of the personal admiration he had developed towards O'Brien over the years, without ever suspecting there was another man behind the mask. Ted talked of his childhood memories of Glasgow, when he and other working-class Catholics had suffered the abuse of the Orange Order and other Protestant sects. '"*Fenian bastards*," they would call us, and many of us had Irish ancestry. It was a history of discrimination O'Brien was conscious of and built his reputation battling against,' Ted recalled.

He still kept two letters O'Brien had written to him before the scandal surfaced in the media – one in which O'Brien had agreed to celebrate Ted's sixty-five years with the Jesuits; the other in which he asked to be joined in prayers of thanksgiving for his own twenty-five years as bishop. 'I wish the priests he behaved inappropriately with had come forward much sooner. It would have saved everyone a lot of trouble,' Ted told me.

Ted was just one of many Scottish Catholics to whom I talked who said they had never been given cause to suspect that O'Brien was anything other than his public persona. 'O'Brien enjoyed the trappings of leadership and the aura of his post but we never saw any suggestion of sexual misbehaviour,' said Des, a local teacher whose school had often been visited by O'Brien. A Scottish priest, talking to me on the condition of anonymity, told me about how his own tortured life (he was a recovering alcoholic who had fallen in love with a woman) contrasted with O'Brien's secret abusive conduct with a small cabal of vulnerable priests. 'Jim' (not his real name) said that celibacy was not the issue that defined priesthood: it was love. 'You cannot do celibacy without love,' he told me.

'Jim', shattered as he was by the O'Brien saga, now believed in Pope Francis. 'He is humble, like John XXIII who evoked the Jesus of the Gospels.' He had taken heart from Francis's criticism, delivered just days earlier, of clericalism, of Vatican 'courtiers' and the institutional Church's historical entanglement with worldliness.

'The [Vatican] court is the leprosy of the papacy,' Francis said. 'Heads of the Church have often been narcissists, flattered and thrilled by their courtiers,' he added. Acknowledging that courtiers 'sometimes' still exist, Pope Francis said the real problem with the

Roman Curia was that it was too 'Vatican-centric' and concerned with its own 'temporal interests' to the point that it 'neglected' the rest of the world. 'I'll do everything I can to change it,' he declared. He pointed out that the Holy See was not the Church, but was at the service of the Church.

The Pope's comments were made in an interview with Eugenio Scalfari, an agnostic left-wing intellectual and the founder of *La Repubblica*, a newspaper not known for its deference towards the Vatican in the past. The comments were published in October 2013 as Pope Francis held his first meeting with his Council of Cardinals, the group he had formed within a month of his election to advise him on universal Church governance and the reform of the Roman Curia. The Pope described the eight as 'wise people' who shared his feelings. 'This is the beginning of a Church with an organization that is not just top down, but also horizontal . . . a long and difficult road,' he said.

Weeks later I was in nominally Catholic Spain, in Sitges, a seaside town south of Barcelona. Famous as an original Roman settlement and the home of some of the artists of the modernist movement, the town had a large international gay community. Discreet homosexuality had survived as a small enclave in the days of Franco but gay rights mushroomed in democratic Catalonia. Sitges prides itself in staging the longest Gay Pride festival in the world. But Sitges is both multicultural and multisexual. Historically the influential and long-standing gay community – Sitges has a gay mayor – was no match for the San Bartolomé y Santa Tecla, the town's main church, named after the early Christian Spanish martyrs, which has survived sieges and civil wars across centuries and remains the town's towering emblem.

The end of October is a blessed time in the town's seasonal calendar. The summer tourists have long gone. The weather is mild and sunny, with light winds caressing the shoreline. The church stands on its hilltop perch, the highest landmark, rain or shine. During the years I regularly holidayed in Sitges, attending Mass on Sundays, I got used to the booming amplified voice of the parish priest, Father Josep, as he enthusiastically led his congregation in song and prayer. His sermons delivered the modern relevance of the Gospel without dogma, focusing on the humanity of Jesus and his disciples.

We met near the confessional, beyond the silverware of the sacristy which had been recovered after the Civil War (the anarchists in 1936 had looted the church and the adjacent chaplaincy and thrown a cross and statues of the saints onto the nearby beach). Fr Josep was squatting on one of a pair of two small stools. I sat on the other one facing him. We were on a level. I asked him to tell me how he saw his mission.

'I like to think of my parish as an open window to the world. Jesus, as you know, didn't have much time for the Pharisees and the high priests, but he cared and always had a word of encouragement for those in need. I think right now, when the world, our society, is in such a crisis, Jesus is more necessary than ever, and Pope Francis is helping us to have faith, to hope. He reminds me of John XXIII, a good person, a warm person. John XXIII's papacy only lasted five years, but he worked hard to change things.'

I asked Fr Josep if there had been an increase in church attendance since Pope Francis's election. It seemed to me there had been. 'I'm not one for numbers. I don't count them in or out. But what I do know is that people are being more positive about the Catholic Church. I think Pope Francis is winning hearts and minds . . .'

Sitges's most popular gay area was called 'Sin Street', not as a judgement but a fact. It was where sexuality had for years been most openly flaunted as well as tolerated. The Gay Pride parade passed by Josep's church. I asked him how his pastoral mission managed in a community that showed a tendency to narcissism and hedonism.

'What you are asking me is what do I think about gays? Well, I'll tell you. We have a large gay community and many gays come to my Mass. Sometimes they take Communion, and sometimes they ask me to hear their confession. I try to finds words, not of condemnation, but, quite the contrary, of understanding. I tell them, "Look, I understand your situation, I understand your life," so that they know that they can be good followers of Jesus and his Gospels.'

But what if a gay couple was married and they wanted to receive Communion – what then?

'It's not for me to judge,' Fr Josep answered. 'The bread of the Eucharist, the bread which Jesus has given us, is the bread of the poor. We each have our conscience, and each does what he can and what he wants . . .'

So no condemnation? I asked.

Fr Josep paused, then smiled before saying: 'No, no, no . . . The Lord didn't come to condemn the world, but to save it . . .'

The publicity poster celebrating the annual reunion of overweight bearded gays from around the world showed a bear alongside the Church of San Bartolomé y Santa Tecla. I remarked that what made Sitges so popular was the way it seemed to effortlessly accommodate the secular and the religious.

Fr Josep agreed. 'Yes, this is what Sitges is about. It has its carnival and its religious service. Gay Pride Week and Holy Week. One doesn't take away from the other. People coexist, they tolerate each other and – don't forget – the gay community helps the local economy: the small shops, the hotels, the bars, and that helps everyone. The key to life is to be able to live and let live, to not get angry, or criticize, but be open. Talking, people understand each other. And that's it.'

Given the sensitivity of the subject of sexuality and sexual abuse, this was one of the more challenging explorations I embarked upon in writing this book. My research had been drawn from several years of record and experience, from the discovery of child abuse at my own Jesuit school and elsewhere in England, to reports of a plethora of cases in the US. In Rome, I had talked to those training to be priests, and their trainers, retraced the steps of a hypocritical and disgraced cardinal in Scotland, before ending up with a priest and a congregation that looked to Pope Francis for a Church teaching focused on love rather than sin. It said something about the enduring male domination of the Catholic Church that women had barely been mentioned.

Chapter Sixteen
Women and Synods

When in 1943, Jorge Bergoglio, aged seventeen, first felt the call to the priesthood on a visit to his neighbourhood church in Buenos Aires, the response from the closest women to him at the time was mixed. His mother reacted badly. She thought the 'call' was nothing more than a figment of the imagination, the impulsive decision of an immature schoolboy. A part of her may have also been concerned that her dream of seeing her son married with children might evaporate.

'My mother experienced it as a plundering,' Bergoglio later recalled. She later refused to accompany Bergoglio when he entered the seminary. 'Don't get me wrong: she was a religious woman and a practising Catholic,' he told his official biographers Sergio Rubin and Francesca Ambrogetti. 'She just thought that everything had happened too fast, that it was a decision that required a lot of thinking about.'

As often happens, the adolescent youth sought understanding and a soulmate in a grandparent, and – being from an Italian family – the matriarchal *La Nona*. His grandmother's reaction could not have been more different. 'Well, if God has called you, blessed be,' she counselled, before adding, 'Please never forget that the doors to this house are always open, and no one will reproach you for anything if you decide to come back.' Her supportive attitude seemed to the young Bergoglio like a vital lesson on how to treat people who are going through a period of transition in their lives.

It is not hard to see how Bergoglio's *Nona* would have underpinned his devotion, as a cradle Catholic, to the Virgin Mary, not just as mother of Christ but as a powerful intercessor, one blessed with a unique understanding of God's humanity. His homilies and writings as priest, bishop and latterly pope put the Virgin Mary at the heart of his spirituality and his sense of what is true holiness. One of his often thumbed Gospel references has Mary running to see her cousin Elizabeth – who had thought herself barren but is pregnant with the future John the Baptist. 'The Virgin is always like that, our Mother, always running to our aid when we need her,' Pope Francis reflected in May 2013 during one of his regular homilies in Sanctae Marthae.

If Pope Francis's ideal of woman is viewed through the prism of his Marian devotion, one cannot separate Bergoglio from Argentina – provider of the political and social context in which he spent the bulk of his adult life – and its related myths involving womanhood. Of these the figure of Perón's second wife Evita, the national legend, looms large in the collective Argentine psychology. She was a second-rate actress who seduced an officer with a huge political ambition and ended up as First Lady of Argentina from 1946 until her death in 1952.

Her almost rags-to-riches story came to be easily mythologized by the aspiring young immigrant nation Bergoglio was born into. Once in power, Evita wore Paris couture, expensive jewellery and luxurious furs. She set an example to those who lived the Argentine dream – that in a country so rich with resources, there should be no poverty – even if the reality had long been that you only got rich living off your wits and at the expense of others. Standing faithfully alongside her husband, she gave the vote to women and rallied the workers and the marginalized poor while she raged against the unjust oligarchy. This appealed to the emerging middle classes of Italian descent that longed for the displacement of old oligarchies of Spanish descent and resented the commercial power the British had come to exercise on their country.

Her foundation financed hospitals, schools, orphanages, football pitches and old people's homes, distributing food, medicine and money – and each act bolstered support for her husband. She said her followers expected her to look good, much as devout Catholics dress up their Virgin statues. The mythology came to transfigure her into a saint; her agonizing death from cancer seemed martyrdom; the embalming of her body a necessary insurance against her corruptibility.

Her bestselling autobiography, *La Razón de Mi Vida* (*My Mission in Life*), which would have formed part of Bergoglio's library, blends subservience to her husband with a far from clear view of the place of women in society. Genuinely feminist perceptions ('the world today suffers from a great absence: that of women . . . we are absent from all the great centres constituting power in the world') are mixed with a sentimental reassertion of women's traditional role ('The number of young women who look down upon the occupation of home-making increases every day. And yet that is what we are born for').

Her early death in 1952 meant that the reputation she had built up was not too damaged by the increasing attacks of Peronism on the working class. In death she was transformed into a Saint of the Poor, easily managed in a predominantly Catholic country. In reality she was a corrupt and power-mad manipulator of the masses, helping bring about, in Juan Perón's own words, 'a fascism that is careful to avoid all the errors of Mussolini'.

Evita created a women's branch of the Peronist movement but ran it with an iron rod, and propagated an uncritical mass of support for Perón. Her book, published two years after Simone de Beauvoir's *The Second Sex*, eludes any discussion of female sexuality, still less liberation. And yet Evita came to symbolize, for many Argentine males, the ideal woman, and for working-class and lower-middle-class Peronist Catholics like the Bergoglio family, a Virgin Mary-style icon, an integral part of a popular religious culture.

Peronism, along with Catholicism, set the parameters of Bergoglio's attitude towards women. As already mentioned, a baroque painting of the Virgin bearing the title *Mary, Untier of Knots* had a great impact on the future Pope. He was at that time in 'turmoil', having had to temporarily leave Argentina for Germany, purportedly to do some academic research but effectively because some of his fellow Jesuits wanted to see the back of him.

Later, when he took up residence in a Jesuit seminary in the northern Argentina city of Córdoba, Bergoglio won the trust of local prostitutes who would come and unburden their consciences, while denouncing the exploitation and cruelty to which they were subjected by their pimps and clients. If they kept returning to have their 'confessions' heard, it was because they considered him non-judgemental. As for Bergoglio, he saw in the women vulnerable hearts struggling, like he was, in adverse circumstances – friends in distress.

As a bishop in Buenos Aires, Bergoglio took a public stand against human trafficking of all kinds, using well publicized open-air Masses in squares, railway stations and other public spaces to denounce the extent to which Argentine society tolerated the abuse of immigrant child labour, and the interconnected organized criminality which controlled prostitution together with the illegal drugs trade and gambling. During these years Bergoglio came to be seen as a true pastor and political ally by the NGOs and charities. This was in contrast to the political class's abandonment of a range of issues, from the threatened rights of indigenous communities to the victims of domestic violence.

One of his more controversial alliances was with La Alameda, which began in 2001 as a small community group running soup kitchens for displaced Bolivian and Paraguayan immigrants most deeply affected by the financial crisis. The group then grew under the leadership of a school teacher, Gustavo Vera, into a charity dedicated to exposing the human rights abuses committed against garment workers in clandestine 'factories' and women forced to take up prostitution by criminal gangs. The organization also came to incorporate the campaign for better working conditions of the city's (waste collects), many of whom lived in the shanty towns. Their leader was Juan Grabois, whose father Roberto had been a member of Guardia de Hierro, the right-wing Catholic faction within the Peronist movement with which Bergoglio had developed close links in the early 1970s.

In 2008 Vera, with Juan Grabois's support, contacted Bergoglio and told the Archbishop that they needed his political as well as moral support because La Alameda volunteers were being threatened by corrupt policemen and pimps, who seemingly were able to operate without any fear of government intervention. In the following weeks Bergoglio began to make some well-publicized visits to meetings organized by La Alameda, travelling by public transport, and regularly celebrating Mass in makeshift venues at which there was a large turnout of waste pickers, textile workers and prostitutes.

While his promotion to the diocese of Buenos Aires added considerably to his public duties, and challenged his attempts to keep his private life out of the media limelight, Bergoglio still made time for personal engagements and friendships even if these risked damaging his reputation among conservative Catholics. He maintained this human trait for personal relationship on being elected Pope.

In the close personal friendships he developed with women, perhaps that with Clelia Luro was one of the most remarkable given the extent to which her life seemed to challenge Church teaching. In 1966 Clelia, then a thirty-nine-year-old separated from her husband and a mother to six children, fell in love with Jerónimo Podestá, the Bishop of Avellaneda.

Podestá, five years older than Clelia, was a Peronist who believed that the CIA had fuelled divisions between the Church and General Perón before his first government fell. He was one of the politically radical Argentines among a generation of Latin American priests and bishops deeply influenced by the Second Vatican Council. As Bishop of Avellaneda (an industrial suburb of Buenos Aires) between 1962 and 1967, Podestá encouraged his priests to work in factories and slums but his radicalism brought him into conflict with the papal nuncio and other bishops who eventually stripped him of his appointment.

In 1972 he was stripped of his authority to celebrate Mass, hear confession and ordain priests. He then married Clelia who had worked for him as his personal secretary when he was a bishop. By then, hardline military officers, plotting a coup, considered him a political subversive and he had received death threats from the right-ring Peronist death squad, Triple A. He and Clelia went into exile, spending the next ten years in Paris, Rome, Mexico and Peru. In April 1982, caught up in the nationalist fervour that gripped a majority of Argentines following the military occupation of the Falklands Islands, Podestá donated a chalice he had used to celebrate his first Mass as priest to the junta's Patriotic Fund in support of the war effort.

The fund was launched with a marathon twenty-four-hour benefit performance broadcast live nationally on 9 May 1982. Anchored by an Evita-lookalike called Lidia 'Pinky' Satragno and Jorge Fontana, the *24 Hours of the Malvinas* had a long procession of personalities including musicians, politicians, bishops and journalists donating something to the Patriotic Fund. Gifts ranged from the accordion of the country's most famous tango composer to medals brought by politicians. The widow of Captain Giachino, Argentina's first hero of the Falklands – killed while attacking the

Governor's house in Port Stanley – handed over his knife and badge. Emotion spilled out into the streets, stirred up by Pinky and Fontana, most of the radio channels in the country and priests at their Sunday Masses.

The Malvinas War caused Podestá briefly to abandon his uncompromising opposition to military rule. However, throughout the 1970s, 1980s and 1990s Clelia and Podestá remained active in radical Catholic social action groups. Podestá was president of a group called the Latin American Federation of Married Priests, which faced opposition not just from members of the Argentine hierarchy, including the Archbishop of Buenos Aires Quarracino, but also from some celibate priests who felt betrayed by Podestá's marriage. They felt it distracted Podestá from his commitment to the poor and social justice. For her part Clelia became a radical feminist, campaigning for women priests while developing support groups for women, like her, who were held morally accountable and condemned by the ecclesiastical authorities for having contributed to priests breaking their celibate vows.

In 2000, two years after Bergoglio succeed Quarracino as Archbishop of Buenos Aires, Podestá was diagnosed with terminal cancer. As Clelia recalled: 'A month before he died Jerónimo told me, "I'm going to give the Archbishop a ring." I said to him: "What on earth are you going to do that for? Remember, Quarracino wouldn't even receive you." And he answered: "But Bergoglio is not Quarracino. He is a Jesuit, he is intelligent and he is going to listen to me."'

A few days later Podestá was hospitalized for the last time. No one from the Church approached Clelia to offer support – no one, that is, except Bergoglio. He rang Clelia as soon as he heard the news, broke away from an official meeting and made his way as quickly as he could to the hospital. When he arrived Podestá seemed to be in a coma. 'I've brought you something to pick you up,' Bergoglio said, holding Podestá's hand. It seemed to tighten.

Then Bergoglio anointed Podestá's forehead with pure plant oil and prayed words of comfort, peace and courage to Podestá, forgiving him his sins. Clelia was left in no doubt that she was in the presence of the Holy Spirit. It brought with it confidence in a benign God, and forged an enduring friendship with Bergoglio.

'From that moment I felt an enormous sense of gratitude towards him, and love,' recalled Clelia in an interview conducted soon after Bergoglio was elected as pope. 'Above all else he is a man of small gestures, ones that make you have faith – Bergoglio is a man of good gestures and also of kind words but he shows what he is by his actions.'

For the next twelve years, Bergoglio and Clelia's meetings were periodical if irregular. But a close friendship was maintained by the personal phone call Clelia received every Sunday from Bergoglio, sparking off a conversation often lasting nearly an hour. Clelia saw Bergoglio the day before he left for Rome for the conclave in March 2013. 'I told him, "That's it, you won't come back this time." He said, jokingly, "Now don't be a naughty witch." I said, "No, I am sure, I don't why but I just feel that this time you really are going to stay there. Last time you refused to be pope. But this time you won't be able to refuse." And he said, "Yes, I know, Clelia." Days later when I started to see the black smoke, I said to myself, "They can't make their minds up quite yet, but Bergoglio is going to come through and win." And so it happened.'

Eight months into the new papacy, Clelia died. In one of her last communications with her old friend, she sent Pope Francis a signed copy of a book of memoirs she had written with Podestá about their forty years of married life together, bound by love and the moral, social and political conviction that celibacy in the Catholic Church should be optional. In her covering note, she said she hoped he would share her experience with his Council of Advisors.

★

It was a month later that I caught up in London with another good friend of Clelia who shared a common experience, having been married to a former priest, lived in Latin America and met Bergoglio. She was Margaret Hebblethwaite, a Catholic journalist and widow of the former Jesuit priest, Peter Hebblethwaite.

Margaret and I had worked together when she was assistant editor of the *Tablet* in the early 1990s. In 2000, six years after Peter died, she gave up her job to go and live in Santa María de Fe, Paraguay, as a sort of freelance missionary. She would later recall that she had fallen in love with the small town, which had originally been a Jesuit mission (or reduction) for the Guaraní Indians. She waited four years for her youngest child to grow before settling there, inspired by liberation theology, with the aim of immersing herself in the poor. She set up an education charity and other community projects.

The first December after Pope Francis's election, we met for lunch in a Lebanese restaurant off the Edgware Road during her annual Christmas visit to her children. As we shared a *mezza*, she recalled her first meeting with Clelia and Podestá at a conference for married Catholic priests and their families in Brasilia, Brazil's administrative capital, in the mid-1990s: 'Podestá was the one married bishop to turn up. He was one of the speakers, Clelia went around with a huge cross round her neck, as if she was a bishop. She was strong and dynamic, a great militant feminist.'

Three years later Margaret travelled to Buenos Aires as part of research on potential candidates for a future papacy and was introduced by Clelia to Bergoglio after he had celebrated Mass. She was to see him on two further occasions before he became pope.

'He came across as someone who was interested in you, and he was interested in working with the poor. He showed warmth towards Clelia, towards me. I am an enormous fan of Pope Francis. If I were to register a very slight sense of disappointment it would be that he hasn't done enough about the women issue. He has done some fantastic things about honesty, poverty, attitudes towards different pastoral circumstances, divorcees, homosexuality. He has done something on women but not much. He's said that they ought to occupy more important positions, and he washed the feet of two Muslim girls in the prison on Maundy Thursday, and that meant a lot to me because in the Paraguay town where I live there was a very traditional parish priest who insisted on having twelve men for his washing of the feet, and I remember telling a friend of mine: "Twelve men, it makes one feel so excluded." The following year they added a woman as a token gesture but kept the twelve men as if the twelve were the only real disciples of Christ. So I was really pleased that Pope Francis, in defiance of these stupid rules, just went and washed the women's feet. But it's not enough.

'And the thing that really makes the Catholic Church lack credibility more than anything else is the women issue and exclusion from the priesthood that goes along with it because it is out of sync with society and history. I mean this thing about only men having positions of authority comes out of culture and the Church has locked itself into that culture and committed the sin of blasphemy against the Holy Spirit by saying this is the will of God, that only men can be priests. I have never had the counterargument expressed so succinctly as by a United Reform Church minister who did a retreat with me once: she said, "If women cannot represent Christ, then how can Christ represent women?"'

As we continued sharing our meal, I reflected at one point that her husband was just one of several intelligent and inspirational individuals she and I had known who had left the priesthood and got married. I asked Margaret whether she thought these priests had left because the priests couldn't handle orders from the Vatican or simply because as men they had fallen in love with women.

Margaret told me: 'In the old days, before the Second Vatican Council, the idea was, okay you are all baptized Catholics, most of you don't take it terribly seriously but if you are really committed and want to give yourself 100 per cent you become a priest or a nun, and people did. Then when people raised the possibility of a 100 per cent vocation through marriage the whole thing came apart. All these people left because their theology had changed and their theology no longer supported their life choice. It was no longer necessary.'

I thought she had avoided answering the question so I put it again, more bluntly: At the end of the day do these people leave the priesthood because they fall in love with a woman, and thus the woman has beaten God?

'No,' Margaret answered, 'it's not a battle between a woman and God. It's just that after the Second Vatican Council, for some priests, falling in love with a woman became part of loving God.'

But I imagine the man struggles with 'Am I a priest, am I not a priest?' I asked.

And she answered: 'Yes, it's part of the road.'

It was at Beda College, the male seminary in Rome, that I met Sister Gertrude, a visiting nun on a short study holiday from her native United States. My first sighting of her was of a diminutive, youthful-looking woman, with cropped hair and taut muscles, in trainers and tracksuit. She was about to go for a long distance run, along the legendary Via Ostiense, well beyond the nearby basilica which Catholics believe houses the remains of the martyred St Paul. I was to discover that running and God were Gertrude's two enduring passions. She talked about both with a breathless energy. She seemed wired both physically and spiritually; her one-time profession (now hobby) and her faith forged on the same coin.

Gertrude was a member of the Benedictine sisters of Mount Angel Oregon – an order she had joined at the age of thirty-three. Her life prior to that – from early schooling through to university – had been almost just one athletic challenge after another. Her first big break came in 1993 when she met her coach. 'He was someone who had done Ironman and done triathlon, he was an experienced coach. Anyway, he started coaching me and I just shot off to an entirely different plain. I started winning races everywhere round the States and I qualified for the Ironman gold triathlon championships in Coney, Hawaii. I was going to finish in the top ten when I ended up in the medical tent, throwing up with severe hyponatraemia. Well, of course I recovered. The next spring I qualified again and then I realized: I have to focus on shorter distances, which is really my speciality. So I started zoning in on that and continued to do well and then it got to 1997 when I thought there has to be something else to life than this. I mean I'd made a lot of money for a single person, I am winning these races and my big deal is, some Monday morning, to see my name in the papers.'

Gertrude joined the US Peace Corps.

'I lived pretty much in the bush, rode a bike around, supposed to help people with this post-apartheid educational system and most people were not really interested. I was in South Africa for just under two years and then I returned to the US and didn't know what I wanted to do. I sure didn't want to do what I was doing before. I tried but it lasted a couple of weeks and I just was not into it. So I bought a car and started driving across the United States, with my tent and my bike. I didn't really know where I was going necessarily, so I just camped and met people and kept trying to find some place to be and somehow – well, Divine Providence – I kept heading west, for some reason, and eventually I ended up in Oregon.

'I found out that there was a "seminary" – I didn't know what that meant – in Mount Angel Oregon and they had graduate programmes for anyone who was interested in studying theology. I didn't really know what that meant either although I did have a feeling I wanted to do something for the church and I didn't know what that meant either. I'd always gone to Church. I had experimented at one point in my life to not go and I didn't really like it. But I kept on going to Church and I was very faithful and everywhere I travelled I was also sure to find a parish. So I always went. I sometimes got involved as a lector but I never let anything interfere with my racing. So I knew at that time in 1999 that I wanted to do something.

'So I called the seminary and the Dean answered and he asked: "What are you doing?" And I said: "Well, I am not really doing anything." He said: "Why not come up and see what this place is like?" So I drove up to this place, and I pulled into this little town and thought, well this a cool place and I spent the night there and the next day I got up and was sitting at the breakfast table and I said: "I know you people don't know me at all, but I wondered if you could give me some direction as I really don't know what to do with my life." The wife of the Dean was a medical doctor and had just finished her theology degree at the seminary. She said: "Why not start this programme of theology?"'

Up the road lived the Benedictine Sisters.

'So I started to learn about the Benedictine life and I thought this is what I have been looking for. That was in August 1999, and that following February I started all these psychological tests to join the place – the oral interview had a psychologist asking me if I'd ever had a lesbian relationship; they tried to see if I came from a dysfunctional family or not, to check out whether I was lying about my past.'

After her initial 'screening', Gertrude entered the order as a 'postulant', then became a 'novice', before eventually taking her vow of 'perpetual monastic profession' with which she renounces personal possession of material goods. Chapter 58 of the Holy Rule of St Benedict invites 'stability, fidelity to the monastic way of life, and obedience'.

So did this amount to chastity, poverty and obedience, I asked?

'We don't really use the word poverty, because we have what's called the common life, meaning everything is held in common. So if, for example, I was to get a gift, according to St Benedict I would take that to the Prior and she decides whether or not I can have it or whether someone else deserves it more than I. It's really a life of common ownership and simplicity. Okay, of course I do have things which I would use and no one else would because I need them for my work, but in a sense everything I have is everybody's stuff.' Even her running shoes.

Whatever words she used for it, it struck me as an extraordinary commitment, one that set Gertrude apart from a majority of women in society. Didn't she think it a difficult path – had she never wanted to have a relationship with someone? I asked as we sat there sharing coffee one autumn afternoon in the Roman seminary, mainly otherwise occupied by men.

Gertrude laughed. 'I had plenty of relationships in my life before I became a nun. I also used to get drunk a lot. I guess I am lucky to be alive. I always thought I would be married, have a huge family and do my stuff, but that wasn't God's plan, and I was shocked because all of a sudden I found myself living with this group of women, all significantly older than me and I kind of liked it. I liked the peace of the monastery, the stability, the regularity of the life as it's lived: Benedictine spirituality is based on a relationship with the Word. Our prayer life consists of, in common, five times, sharing the practice of Lexio Divina [Sacred Divine Reading].'

I asked Gertrude if, when she wasn't running, she found the Lexio quite therapeutic.

She answered: 'It suits me very well. I'm fine with the rosary but I never pray it. I mean, St Benedict lived from the years 480 to 547 and there was no rosary. That came with the Mendicants. I mean, if you read his Rule on the Daily Manual Labour, you will read Manual Work, the Celebration of Divine Office and Lexio Divina . . .'

So did she think women had fewer problems with celibacy than men?

'I am a very healthy forty-nine-year-old heterosexual woman

but it's not my call to be married and I find that a life of celibacy is one in which I can be friends with and love a lot of people. That is what really the life is about. I mean, everyone should be able to be chaste and celibate, in terms of honouring one's body, having boundaries. I mean, if you are married, you have to have boundaries, with others. But if I was married I would never have the opportunity to stay in different monasteries, and go and study and stay in seminaries. I would have children and a husband to look after, they would be my first priority. I keep very fit still. I am running about forty to fifty miles a week, running the half-marathon on Sunday here in Rome, and I'm glad I have had that in my life, because so many people can't even get started with their exercises. Celibacy? You know, I'd like somebody to listen to me, and be loved, but that doesn't necessarily mean sexual intercourse. It doesn't at all. A chaste celibate life is just so much more than sexual intercourse.'

I asked Gertrude whether men found celibacy more difficult than women. Was it her experience of monastic men, or priests, that they were in touch with their own sexuality?

She answered: 'That I can answer straightaway. No, I don't think people in general are in touch with their sexuality . . . But let me go off on a tangent. There is something I don't comprehend about religious life in the Church. People have this expectation generally speaking that if you are a nun or a sister you should be wearing a veil and have a habit on whereas the men seem freer to wear what they like. There are some who think that if you are not wearing a veil you are not a sister. I have a monastic habit and I wear it when I like to wear it and I like it a lot.'

What made her like it? I asked.

'I feel I am part of something which is bigger than myself.'

I told Gertrude that part of the problem I found in Rome was seeing too many priests dressed from head to foot in clerical gear and looking rather precious and self important. Were some of them repressed homosexuals, as several interviewees had suggested to me?

Gertrude said: 'I think people are kidding themselves if they think they are not accepting gay men as priests. That's crazy. If you take a group of 200 guys you can't say they are all heterosexual. I don't have any trouble with homosexuals. I know homosexual people who lead more chaste lives than heterosexuals. As long as a person leads a chaste, celibate life, what does it matter? It all boils down to human formation, and the environment . . .'

Earlier that day, Gertrude had been to St Peter's Square for the weekly papal audience with the public. So what did she think of Pope Francis?

'Ever since John XXIII I've been thinking I wish I had a pope I could connect with . . . then Francis is elected and my first thought is "That's my pope!" I love this guy, he is my type of man. He is a kind of guy that you just want to go up and hug and he would not mind, and he would just talk to you. I feel I can relate to him as a human being. I see him with the people and see how he touches people. He is a human being who believes in practical things, instead of reciting a bunch of rules. He is the kind of guy you can sit down and have a beer with. I am appalled that there are people who criticize him when all he is doing is preaching the Gospel, respecting each individual – his or her humanity . . . I mean they criticize me when I run and I run ten kilometres a day. Why would I stop? It's a gift I've been given.'

Gertrude – the running nun – seemed in a hurry, like Pope Francis. Not all nuns were as happy with the papacy as she was. Those more radical than she is believed Pope Francis to be as anti-feminist as his predecessor. This perception had grown after Cardinal Gerhard Ludwig Müller, the Vatican orthodoxy watchdog, had reprimanded officers of the Leadership Conference of Women Religious (LCWR), the largest umbrella group for US religious women. Müller backed US bishops who criticized the group for their support for Sister Elizabeth Johnson, a theologian and author of *Quest for the Living God*, on the grounds that her book contained 'misrepresentations' and doctrinal errors. The LCWR has been accused of supporting radical feminist issues, including the ordination of women priests, in conflict with current Catholic doctrine.

Gertrude was quite unlike any nun I had ever met – but then that probably says as much about enduring male perceptions as about my own traditional Spanish Catholic background. My Spanish ancestry includes a great-aunt – Madre Maravillas de Jesús – the daughter of an aristocrat who became a mystic Carmelite nun. She survived persecution during the Spanish Civil War, hiding in a Madrid flat, then fleeing to Lourdes, before returning to 'liberated' Salamanca and spending over thirty years praying behind grilled windows, when not founding convents and distributing charity to the poor. One of my Spanish cousins, Gregorio, wrote than when she died, aged eighty-three, the year before Franco in 1974, surrounded by her sisters, her final breath 'expelled a profound and inexplicable scent of nard flower'. Madre Maravillas was beatified by Pope John Paul II in May 1998 after two miraculous cures were claimed on her behalf in Spain and Argentina respectively.

In July 2014, the Church of England's General Synod – as distinct from the Catholic Bishops Synod – voted to allow women to become bishops for the first time in history. The General Synod is the deliberative and legislative body of the Church of England. Its assemblies are a mixture of legalistic formality and self-conscious transparency and accountability, with a touch of piety thrown in – a kind of Catholic episcopal conference, political party conference and anarchic retreat rolled into one. Over the years, the General Synod has had a tendency to fall about itself in passionate argument and theological anxiety, reflecting the different currents that have developed since the Reformation within the worldwide Anglican communion, over which the Church of England is supposed to preside as the Mother Church, but struggled to do so, lacking the Vatican's tradition of authority and centralized control.

And yet on the occasion of their annual summer gathering at the university in the ancient city of York (founded by the Romans in AD 71), the tricameral Synod came together in a rare show of unity with the required two-thirds majority in favour of women bishops. The crucial vote in the House of Laity went 152 in favour, 45 against, and there were 5 abstentions. In the House of Bishops, 37 were in favour, 2 against, and there was 1 abstention. The House of Clergy voted 162 in favour, 25 against and there were 4 abstentions.

'It is hard to exaggerate the significance of today's decision at the York Synod,' reported Robert Pigott, the BBC's religious affairs correspondent, in his live coverage. Before he announced the vote, Archbishop of York John Sentamu asked for the result to be met 'with restraint and sensitivity'. But there was a flurry of cheers, and heart-felt applause. Later, groups of women delegates toasted with champagne.

The vote broke with a tradition of exclusively male bishops inherited from the first Christians almost 2,000 years ago. Pigott commented, 'Some Anglicans see it as a "cosmic shift" – arguing that the Church's theology has been changed by its acceptance that men and women are equally eligible to lead and teach Christianity . . . With the decision, the Church is acknowledging the importance secular society places on equality, signalling that it wants to end its isolation from the lives of the people it serves.'

Women bishops were already in office in a number of Anglican 'provinces' outside the United Kingdom including the USA, Canada, South Africa, Australia and New Zealand. And yet Anglicans in the southern half of the globe, who are now the majority, were largely opposed to female bishops. July's vote came more than twenty years after women were first allowed to become priests in the Church of England. More than one in five priests in the Church was now female. The result in July overturned centuries of tradition in the Church of England that has been deeply divided over the issue. In recent years, members of the Church of England, including clergy, had joined the Catholic Church because they disapproved of women priests.

No one was doubting the potential problems that still lay ahead in gaining wider acceptance within Christianity. The approval of women bishops threatened a negative impact in terms not just of the unity of Anglicanism but crucially the relations between the Church of England and the Catholic Church. Justin Welby, the former oil executive who became the Archbishop of Canterbury in 2013, was the senior bishop and principal leader of the Church of England, and the symbolic head of the worldwide Anglican communion. He had a responsibility not just for keeping his own house in order but also in building ecumenical bridges with Rome – a task in which he had striven to find common ground with Pope Francis. His comments on the vote were those of a diplomat putting the best possible interpretation on a possible crisis and trying to contain the negative fallout. Welby's immediate statement was this: 'Today marks the start of a great adventure of seeking mutual flourishing while still, in some cases, disagreeing. The challenge for us will be for the Church to model good disagreement and to continue to demonstrate love for those who disagree on theological grounds.'

And yet those who had voted against remained far from pacified, claiming, like lay member Susie Leafe, director of the conservative evangelical group Reform, that the Synod had disappointed a quarter of the membership of the Church of England who believed women bishops were at odds with their theological convictions.

In his response to the dissenters, Welby pointed out that the resolution approved by the Synod contained concessions for those parishes that continued to object to the appointment of a woman bishop – giving them the right to ask for a male alternative and to take disputes to an independent arbitrator. And he followed this up by writing to Catholic bishops to reassure them that the Church of England was continuing its 'quest' for unity. He acknowledged that while some Anglican Churches would welcome the result of the vote, 'we are also aware that our other ecumenical partners may find this a further difficulty on the journey towards full communion' and that dialogue now faced 'new challenges'.

Addressing the issue of what impact the vote might have on the Catholic Church, the veteran British religious affairs journalist Ruth Gledhill recalled a pivotal moment at the 2008 Lambeth Conference gathering of bishops from throughout the world. They were addressed by Cardinal Walter Kasper, the then president of the Pontifical Council for Promoting Christian Unity. He was globetrotting the ecumenical conference circuit and was regarded by those present as a pro-Anglican Catholic bishop. With women bishops by that time well advanced on the Church of England agenda, they were anticipating friendly words from Rome. Instead Kasper reaffirmed the Catholic Church's traditional teachings on the issue of women and hinted at what would become the *ordinariate*. (In November 2009 the apostolic constitution *Anglicanorum Coetibus* established *ordinariates* to enable 'groups of Anglicans' to join the Catholic Church while preserving elements of their liturgical and spiritual patrimony.)

In his address to the conference, Kasper cited correspondence between Pope Paul VI and Pope John Paul II with successive Archbishops of Canterbury. John Paul II stated: 'I declare that the Church has no authority whatsoever to confer priestly ordination on women and that this judgement is to be definitively held by all the Church's faithful.' This was not what the Anglicans wanted to hear. But there was more. For Kasper, the decision to ordain women implied a turning away from the common position of all Churches of the first millennium. He was clear about the implications: 'While our dialogue has led to significant agreement on the understanding of ministry, the ordination of women to the episcopate effectively and definitively blocks a possible recognition of Anglican orders by the Catholic Church.'

Fast-forward to the aftermath of the vote in the summer of 2014: it was clear that senior Catholic bishops in Britain were not exactly celebrating the vote of the York Synod even if most of them, not least Pope Francis himself, would have agreed with Welby's statement that with 'so much troubling our world today', common witness to the Gospel was of greater importance than ever.

Archbishop Bernard Longley, the Catholic chairman of the Anglican–Roman Catholic International Commission (ARCIC), said that the decision 'sadly places a further obstacle' on the path to unity, but added that the bishops were still committed to ecumenical dialogue. Longley described as 'ecumenically fruitful' one of the House of Bishops's declarations following the Synod vote, which stated that those who could not accept women's ordination 'continue to be within the spectrum of teaching and tradition of the Anglican Communion' and that they should be able to 'flourish' in the Church of England. In Rome, Archbishop Longley's co-chairman of ARCIC, Church of England Archbishop Sir David Moxon, who was also the Archbishop of Canterbury's representative to the Holy See, said: 'The Roman Catholic responses so far have been gracious, honest and constructive.'

As for other reactions, the letters pages of the liberal British international Catholic weekly, the *Tablet*, provided as always an excellent platform for diverse if sensible opinion on which it was worth reflecting. One of the letters was from a respected ecological theologian, Dr Edward Echlin, Honorary Research Fellow, University College of Trinity & All Saints, Leeds, and author of *Earth Spirituality*. Echlin wrote:

We need not fear that women bishops will damage relations with Rome. The two Churches have made enormous progress towards reconciliation and unity since *Apostolicae Curae* in 1896, and even since Vatican II. Our shared commitment to God in Jesus and the Spirit and in our mission and ministry, including environmental healing, will continue. Our ecumenism is less about structures and genders than a spirituality in service of the world.

In another letter to the *Tablet*, Pippa Bonner, for twenty years a member of the Catholic Women's Ordination group, celebrated the fact that the vote for women bishops had finally been passed in the Church of England. Bonner wrote:

> I would ask Catholics to pray and reflect on the role of women and what we can offer in our Church too . . . We want to stay within our Church and see women being able to test out a vocation to priesthood. We have a shortage of male priests and maybe now is the time to consider women as deacons and priests in a renewed church.

But while feminist Catholics believed that the Synod has done their Church a favour by adding fresh impetus to the campaign in favour of the ordination of women, Catholic clergy remained cautious. Thus an expert in ecumenical relations Mgr Mark Langham, the Catholic chaplain of Cambridge University, described the situation post-York as 'a critical moment for ecumenical dialogue'. He argued that Anglicans did not really understand how difficult the ordination of women in their Church was for Catholics, noting that the Vatican's main advisory board on doctrinal matters, the Congregation for the Doctrine of the Faith, had asserted this was a doctrinal issue, intrinsic to the theology of priesthood. He wrote:

> Thus, it is true to say that hope of union has receded. There

is no mid-point now between having women bishops and not having them. From speaking of unity, realistically dialogue now considers how two traditions, one of which ordains women bishops and one which does not, co-exist. The rug has been pulled from under those who longed for unity within the foreseeable future.

Mgr Langham added that ecumenists nevertheless had reasons to remain optimistic.

They have come too far, and weathered too many disappointments, not to continue to have faith in the movement. Ecumenism, they point out, is not a human construct, but a divine imperative. Wonders have happened; the Holy Spirit is not discouraged. At a time when, institutionally, we seem far away apart, faith in God's will for unity has to be stronger than ever.

The ecumenical sentiment was shared by Pope Francis who, when he was Archbishop of Buenos Aires, forged a personal friendship with Gregory Venables, the British-born Anglican bishop of Southern Argentina, and had since strengthened ties with Welby, the Archbishop of Canterbury. In fact, there were striking similarities of circumstances between Welby, the old boy from Eton turned oil executive turned evangelical Protestant, and Jorge Bergoglio, the Jesuit turned Pope who venerated popular icons of the Virgin Mary.

The fact that Welby was enthroned two days after Francis was inaugurated was a coincidence. But there were important parallels, as the British Catholic commentator Damian Thompson pointed out in an article for the *Spectator* magazine.

Both men were plucked from senior but not prominent positions in their churches with a mandate to simplify structures of government that had suffocated their intellectual predecessors, who also resembled each other in slightly unfortunate ways. Rowan Williams [Welby's predecessor] and Benedict XVI seemed overwhelmed by the weight of office; both took the puzzling decision to retreat into their studies at a time of crisis in order to write books – Dr Williams on metaphor and iconography in Dostoevsky, Benedict on the life of Jesus. When they retired, early and of their own volition, their in-trays were stacked higher than they had been when they took office. Their fans were disappointed and the men charged with replacing them thought: we're not going to let that happen again.

And yet Francis and Welby parted ways on the issue of women in the Church. 'The Church acknowledges the indispensable contribution which women make to society through the sensitivity, intuition and other distinctive skill sets which they, more than men, tend to possess,' wrote Francis in *Evangelii Gaudium*. 'Women in the Church must be valued not "clericalized".' Francis's negative sentiments about feminism have persisted, fuelling criticism. Women Catholic writers such as the prize-winning columnist Jamie Manson, writing on 13 May 2014 in the *National Catholic Reporter*, argued that Pope Francis distorted the struggle for women's equality in his interview with Jesuit Fr Antonio Spadaro, when he said, 'I am wary of a solution that can be reduced to a kind of "female *machismo*", because a woman has a different make-up than a man. But what I hear about the role of women is often inspired by an ideology of *machismo*.'

Pope Francis said in an interview with *La Stampa* that he believed in feminine genius, but not in women priests. To say, as the *Tablet*'s Abigail Frymann did, that this was a disappointment for Catholic women and men for whom the patriarchal priesthood was not a matter of faith was an understatement.

She was not alone in finding that when Pope Francis spoke

about women he sounded condescending or patriarchal, as perhaps befitting a near-octogenarian, celibate Argentine churchman of Italian stock – however well-intentioned and however much he had shown himself to be in touch with his feminine side in his personal friendships with individual women. In the first two years in his papacy, Francis spoke on several occasions of the need to develop a 'deeper theology of women', and of his determination to promote women to senior positions in Rome. A 'veritable quote machine' was how David Gibson, a reporter for the widely followed secular US-based *Religion News Service*, described Pope Francis in a report posted in November 2014. But Gibson, an otherwise generally enthusiastic supporter of Francis, noted that what the Pope sometimes said went down badly with women seeking genuine equality within the Church. They believed that genuine reforming action in this area was way down the list of priorities.

'I am at a loss to see how this could be other than insulting to women who'd already given up their families of their own to serve God,' the *Washington Post*'s Melinda Henneberger wrote after an address Pope Francis gave on 8 May 2013 to nuns from around the world gathered in Rome: 'Please, let it be fruitful chastity, a chastity that generates sons and daughters in the church. The consecrated mother is a mother, must be a mother and not an old maid (or "spinster") . . . Forgive me speaking this way, but the motherhood of consecrated life, its fertility, is important.'

In the early years of his papacy, Francis had so far failed to break the mould regarding the role of women, even if his intentions were good. In the eyes of his critics, when Francis talked about women, it wasn't just that he wasn't being progressive: he simply didn't have the language with which to address them and that was only likely to change if more women were given genuine positions of influence within the Vatican. But there were other similarly controversial issues in his in-tray that touched on women's place in society, and that of men.

★

Ahead of the Catholic Synod of Bishops on the Family in October 2014, several cardinals came out against proposed changes to Church practice that would allow divorced and civilly remarried Catholics to receive Communion. They included the Australian George Pell, entrusted by Pope Francis as the new Prefect of the Economy, and the German Gerhard Müller, who was head of the Vatican's Congregation for the Doctrine of the Faith.

'Doctrine and pastoral practice cannot be contradictory,' wrote Cardinal Pell. 'One cannot maintain the indissolubility of marriage by allowing the "remarried" to receive Communion.' The cardinal called for a clear restatement of traditional teaching to avoid any expectation of change that could trigger widespread protests when it was disappointed, as had followed Pope Paul VI's affirmation of Catholic teaching against contraception in 1968. 'The sooner the wounded, the lukewarm, and the outsiders realize that substantial doctrinal and pastoral changes are impossible, the more the hostile disappointment (which must follow the reassertion of doctrine) will be anticipated and dissipated,' added the cardinal. His comments came in the foreword to a book-length response to a proposal made in February 2014 by Cardinal Walter Kasper, the German theologian whom Pope Francis had confirmed as president emeritus of the Pontifical Council for Promoting Christian Unity, that the Church could find a 'toleration' of civil marriages following divorce, in some circumstances.

At the start of his pontificate Pope Francis praised Kasper's book *Mercy: The Essence of the Gospel and the Key to Christian Life*, in which he argues that the concept of mercy had been badly ignored by theologians and needed to be rediscovered by the Church and by society at large. Francis himself raised expectations that the Catholic Church might make it easier for divorced and remarried members to receive Communion when he told reporters accompanying him on his plane back from Rio de Janeiro in July 2013 that the Synod of Bishops would explore a 'somewhat deeper pastoral care of marriage'.

Pope Francis added at the time that Church law governing marriage annulments also 'has to be reviewed, because ecclesiastical tribunals are not sufficient for this'. Such problems, he said, exemplified a general need for forgiveness in the Church today. 'The Church is a mother, and she must travel this path of mercy, and find a form of mercy for all,' the Pope said.

But writing in the Vatican's official newspaper in October 2013, the German Cardinal Müller reaffirmed Church teaching barring such divorced Catholics from the sacrament of Communion without an annulment of their first, sacramental marriage. While he acknowledged that a 'case for the admission of remarried divorcees to the sacraments is argued in terms of mercy', he said such an argument 'misses the mark' in regard to the sacraments, since the 'entire sacramental economy is a work of divine mercy and it cannot simply be swept aside by an appeal to the same'.

The following February Pope Francis asked Kasper to address a gathering of cardinals on the subject. Kasper gave a speech which underlined his sympathy for the pressures faced by married couples in a modern society and the complex motives that might lead to divorce. 'I did not say you can admit all [divorced and remarried] to Communion,' Kasper told the *Tablet*'s Christopher Lamb. 'There are different situations: there are those who abandon a marriage and those who are the innocent party. I am not abandoning the indissolubility of marriage – we cannot do that! But a Christian can fail.' In other words the modern Church had to move away from the judgemental and make a pragmatic shift to put pastoral practice before doctrinal rigidity.

That both Müller and Kasper were allowed to speak out suggested that they had been entrusted by Pope Francis to be part of a process of dialogue and engagement very typical of the Jesuit way of finding resolution in conscience and faith. Pope Francis had himself talked eloquently, in his interview with fellow Jesuit Antonio Spadaro, of his wish that those who felt excluded by the Church should be made to feel loved and reconciled. Divorce might not have been the kind of global headline-grabbing issue that abortion or sex abuse or war had proven to be, but estranged Catholic married partners around the world were affected by the Church's traditional ban on Communion. This left them feeling in many cases unfairly excluded from the heart of their faith, adding to the pain on those already feeling wounded and struggling.

In September 2014 Pope Francis conducted the wedding of twenty couples in Rome, some of whom had been cohabiting – a state which used to be called 'living in sin' – others of whom had been married before. Both kinds had children who were made welcome at the ceremony. The gesture appeared to be a clear signal that Pope Francis was prepared to address the issue of marriage as something worth valuing, but within a broader context of understanding the challenges faced by those involved.

Weeks later there was disappointment for those expecting a major shift in Catholic teaching on divorcees and gays at the Catholic Synod of Bishops on the Family held in Rome, the first such major conference of the new papacy. Compared to the rough, somewhat chaotic cut-and-thrust of debate involving women and lay participants at the Church of England's Synod, the Roman Catholic version presented itself as a strictly ecclesiastical and orderly affair. While the Anglicans tended to debate openly and emotionally over a range of issues, the Catholic 'princes of the Church' exercised restraint when discussing a text prepared well in advance by a Vatican office. In 2010, on the rare occasion a handful of observers – all from the officially vetted Vatican radio – were allowed a peep into a Catholic Synod, the observers found the experience both fascinating and also deeply frustrating. Thus, while they witnessed an angry confrontation between two bishops on the Church in the Middle East, they were not allowed to report what they had seen and heard.

The Catholic Synod in October 2014 not only had the Vatican preparing an early text based on answers to a questionnaire circulated across the Catholic lay and clerical world, but allowing an unprecedented level of transparency. Pope Francis insisted that the voting tallies be published for each of the initial draft paragraphs and that the text be published in full. Thus the media was aware from early on in the proceedings that a ground-breaking 'mid-term' draft document called for the Church to recognize 'seeds of the Word' present in cohabiting couples, those in civil marriages and the divorced and remarried. It also stated that the sexual orientation of gays should be valued as they have 'gifts and qualities to offer parishes'. These draft paragraphs, which allowed Communion for the divorced and remarried in certain circumstances, got substantial backing from the Catholic Synod but fell short of the required two-thirds majority.

The New Ways Ministry, a US Catholic gay rights group, said it was 'very disappointing' that the Synod's final report had not retained 'the gracious welcome to lesbian and gay people that the draft of the report included'. Another gay and lesbian group, Dignity USA, said: 'Unfortunately, today, doctrine won out over pastoral need. It is disappointing that those who recognized the need for a more inclusive Church were defeated.' Reports in the secular media, including the BBC, suggested that the vote had been a rebuff for Pope Francis, underlining the entrenched positions of traditionalists within the Church.

Certainly, the Catholic Synod revealed that elements within the institution were out of touch with the loving message of the Gospels, and depressingly lagging behind the progress of civil society. There were bishops, for example, who suggested that couples in a second marriage after divorce might be allowed to receive Holy Communion but only after submitting themselves to a 'very long and demanding penitential way.' As the *Tablet* argued, this sounded as if the Church was being urged to impose further suffering on those who had already suffered much. Meanwhile, the inclusiveness of many bishops voting fell short of the testimony given at the Synod of a gay man who was welcomed home with his partner by his loving Catholic family, which embraced him warmly because 'He is our son.' And all this was discussed and voted on by the exclusively all-male conference of (allegedly) celibate bishops.

It was all very well religious commentators loyally aping the comments of some bishops that the 2,000-plus institutions of the Church tended to think in centuries, when contemporary twenty-four-hour news cycles demanded changed headlines in a matter of hours. A modern papacy had to speak a language that was relevant as well as truthful if it was to retain its spiritual authority. According to some of those present, Pope Francis, far from being rebuffed, had set the Church on a more positive path, if not at the hectic pace that a society seeking instant gratification demanded. As Vincent Nichols, Archbishop of Westminster and one of a new generation of cardinals appointed by Pope Francis, put it: 'You may have heard or read that this Synod has been about changing the teaching of the Church on marriage, family life or sexual morality. This is not true. It was about the pastoral care that we try to offer each other, the "motherly love of the Church", especially when facing difficult moments and experiences in family life.'

In a letter read out to English Catholics on 26 October 2014, the Sunday after the end of the Rome meeting, Nichols pointed out there had been no suggestion at the Synod that the Catholic Church might somehow give approval to the notion of 'same-sex marriage' or that its teaching on sexual morality was to change. However, the emphasis was less on sin and proscription than on compassion and inclusiveness. Thus 'every person was endowed with unique dignity, both as an individual and as a Christian, so that Church teaching had to be translated into loving care'.

Nichols continued: 'You may have heard that the Synod represented a "defeat for Pope Francis" or that he was disappointed at its outcome. This is not true. At the end of our meeting Pope Francis spoke at length about his joy and satisfaction at its work. He told us to look deeply into our hearts to see how God had touched us during the Synod, and to see how we may have been tempted away from the promptings of the Holy Spirit. The Synod, he insisted, has been a spiritual journey, not a debating chamber. In fact, the very word "synod" means making a walk or a journey together. That's what we did.'

According to Nichols the Synod's canvas had been far broader and more embracing than that suggested in the shorthand of the secular media – the journey, an exploration 'of all the problems facing the family today', from the effects of war, immigration, domestic violence, polygamy, inter-religious marriages, to cohabitation, the breakdown of marriage, divorce and the situation of those who have ended a valid marriage and entered another union or marriage. While 'the vastness of the picture and the suffering it represented was, at times, overwhelming', the Synod also looked 'at the great joy of family life and the importance of marriage at its heart'. As Nichols put it: 'We listened to husbands and wives speaking of the difficulties they had overcome, the struggles they face and the deep joy they experience in their mature marriages and family lives. They were moving moments. A lovely description of the family was offered: the family as "a sanctuary of holiness" with emphasis always on the sharing of prayer at the heart of family life.'

From a purely secular point of view, there was nothing much here of comfort for gays who wanted to marry their partners out of love and respect, or for those who through no fault of their own had seen their first marriage end in ruins and perhaps found true love the second or even the third time round. They could not understand why they should be denied access to the body and blood of Christ at the heart of their faith. It was also far from clear how many young people would really relate to the sanctimonious utterances that some bishops had us believe was a new language.

And yet in his final address to the Synod, Pope Francis spoke with authority as well as understanding, urging the bishops to accept that theirs was a work-in-progress, and not to yield to 'temptations'. The latter included a 'temptation to hostile inflexibility, that is, wanting to close oneself within the written word (the letter), and not allowing oneself to be surprised by God, by the God of surprises (the spirit)'. But he warned too of those who were tempted 'to come down from the cross to please the people and not stay there, in order to fulfil the will of the Father'. This was a pope treading a theological middle ground, and yet in his refusal to stand still or to put up the shutters, he was not fitting into the progressive-conservative blueprint.

He closed the Synod by beatifying Paul VI – the Pope who in his lifetime never gave the Catholic Synod the powers that Vatican II mandated but who nevertheless Francis thought worth quoting as setting up the possibility of future change 'by carefully surveying the signs of the times, making every effort to adapt ways and methods . . . to the growing needs of our time and the changing conditions of society'.

Some Catholics felt such hopes of change had been squandered by subsequent conservative papacies, while others lamented that Vatican II had itself left the Church divided. Pope Francis seemed conscious that he needed to take the whole institutional Church with him and that perhaps the early drafts of the Synod paper was, as the *Tablet*'s Christopher Lamb suggested, for the bishops, 'too radical, too soon'.

And yet there was an important sense in which the Synod was showing the fruits of having Pope Francis as its head. It seemed to draw on his experience of the Latin American bishops conference (CELAM) in Aparecida in 2007, which he played a key part in managing. As he described the conference at the time: 'The work progressed from the bottom upwards, not the other way round . . . based on open dialogue, with every bishop given the opportunity to openly speak his mind.'

'Our guideline was to include everything that came from the foundation, from the People of God,' the then Cardinal Bergoglio said, 'we didn't strive for synthesis; we strove for harmony' – and that had meant resisting the more radical positions by liberation theologians, as well as the reaction of recalcitrant conservatives.

Only time will tell whether CELAM, the uniquely strong continental body made up of Latin American bishops, will furnish a model for the realization of one of the key goals of Vatican II. As defined by two Vatican experts, Stefan von Kempis and Philip F. Lawler, in their book *A Call to Serve*, this goal was the 'establishment of an active and influential worldwide Synod of Bishops'. But in October 2014, there were signs of a more open culture of discussion and debate among the leaders of the Catholic Church than had been seen for many years – a process with which Pope Francis was clearly happy, not as an end in itself but part of that Jesuital exercise in discernment out of which he believed there would be a positive outcome, sooner or later – delivered, like his own election, by a God of Surprises.

Chapter Seventeen
A Pope for All Seasons

From the outset Pope Francis's papacy was marked by gesture and charged with symbolism. 'Gestures and acts in themselves can have consequences that are not foreseen or planned for,' I remember being told by the Catholic writer Vicky Costick as Pope Francis's second year neared its end. 'The challenge of true reform is whether he can promote an "adult church" . . . priests well-formed not "addicted to paedophilia", children respected, women promoted.'

Pope Francis did not travel across the world on his first apostolic visit beyond Rome but the location he picked, Lampedusa, was at the sharp end of the global north-south divide of wealth and poverty. It allowed him to reawaken consciences over a global scandal and denounce an injustice that cut across national boundaries – Europe's sea of death for migrants as a result of war and escalating inequality. Lampedusa, the small Sicilian island about eighty miles (120 kilometres) from Tunisia, was one of the nearest gateways to Europe for Africans fleeing conflict and poverty. Tens of thousands of migrants had made the dangerous crossing in recent years, usually packed into rickety wooden boats exposed to the elements. Some perished before making the shore. Those who survived faced further repression and exploitation. 'Pope Francis, only you can save us,' read a banner on one of the boats. 'You're one of us,' said a sign hanging from an apartment near the port. Some residents threw flowers into the water and chanted '*Viva il Papa*' as his vessel docked.

Pope Francis rode in an open-topped car – rather than the Popemobile often used by predecessors – to the site for the Mass, near a 'boat cemetery' where the hulks of shipwrecked migrant boats lay in the sun. He used a wooden chalice carved from one of the boats. His altar was a small, painted boat. The Pope called for a 'reawakening of consciences' to counter the 'indifference' shown to migrants. 'We have lost a sense of brotherly responsibility,' he said, and 'have forgotten how to cry' for migrants lost at sea. He denounced the traffickers who exploited migrants and took great risks with their lives.

Francis's empathy for their plight, underlining his drive to put the poor and dispossessed at the heart of the Church's mission, echoed his own family history. He owed his existence to the fact that his Italian immigrant grandparents missed the boat they had first booked to take them to the new life in Argentina. The boat had subsequently been shipwrecked and sunk with many of its passengers perishing.

Later as a bishop he defended the rights of exploited immigrant labour and their impoverished families in the shanty neighbourhoods of Buenos Aires. As a pope he had taken a new name in tribute to Francis of Assisi, the twelfth-century saint whose basic concerns had to do with *paupertas* (poverty), *umilitas* (humility), and *simplicitas* (simplicity). As Catholic theologian Hans Küng remarked, if no previous pope had dared to take the name of Francis, it was probably because the expectation seemed to be too high.

As the first Latin American pope, theologically and politically forged in his native Argentina, while owing the core of his spirituality to his training as a Jesuit priest, Pope Francis had a secular and spiritual perspective quite unlike that of his predecessors – in particular the two most recent, Benedict XVI and John Paul II, both Europeans who experienced the Second World War, and whose attitudes were shaped by the cold war. Catholic social teaching dating back to the late nineteenth century was as critical of the excesses of capitalism as it was of socialism. But in practice the Vatican had over the years become more tolerant of capitalism, while casting a wary eye on the more radical expressions of socialism. One reason was the perception that Marxism was inherently atheistic, and by definition confrontational. Another was the dominance of Italians within the hierarchy who credited Christian Democracy with having created Italy's capitalist post-war 'economic miracle'.

By contrast Pope Francis tended to see capitalism in terms of its effects on the Third World and what he had experienced in Argentina was not liberal, but corrupt and crony-ridden. Thus did he write in his first Apostolic Exhortation, *Evangelii Gaudium* ('The Joy of the Gospel'): 'Today everything comes under the laws of competition and the survival of the fittest, where the powerful feed upon the powerless.' He also wrote:

> While the earnings of a minority are growing exponentially, so too is the gap separating the majority from the prosperity enjoyed by the happy few. This imbalance is the result of ideologies which defend the absolute autonomy of the marketplace and financial speculation. Consequently, they reject the right of states, charged with vigilance for the common good, to exercise any form of control.

Such comments did not go down well with some rich German Catholics who accused Pope Francis of failing to understand the welfare benefits of a well-ordered market economy in a functioning democratic and accountable northern European setting. In the US the Pope was confronted with long-entrenched arguments in favour of free markets and unregulated private investment, and the limits that should be put on government intervention. Critics ranged from talkshow host Rush Limbaugh – who denounced the Pope's economic views as 'pure Marxism' – to conservative priests and judges. For his part Pope Francis told the Italian *La Stampa* newspaper that 'Marxist ideology is wrong. But I have met many Marxists in my life who are good people, so I don't feel offended.'

If Argentine politics and history were what had moulded Pope Francis's attitudes and style – not least a sense that pure Peronism provided a third way between communism and capitalism – his views on the political economy and his populist techniques had the potential to reach out and engage with protest movements across continents that no longer believed in the established order, and saw a need for change. In the UK, Catholic Scots with Irish roots, part of a wider movement, pressed for independence; in Catalonia, local priests and some bishops supported a campaign for a referendum on independence as a just cause despite its being declared illegal by the Supreme Court and blocked by the Spanish government in Madrid. Others involved in militant grassroots politics across Europe found in Pope Francis someone they could identify as having broken, to some extent, with his institutional 'caste'. Those who had given up hope on long-established socio-economic and political systems to narrow the gap between the very rich and the many poor, end wars and save the planet from climate warming found a similar language of denunciation emanating from the papacy. And yet Pope Francis and the new emerging radical politics of the left were at odds on subjects that touched on traditional Church teaching.

As Juan Carlos Monedero, one of the founders of Podemos, a new radical party in Spain, told me in December 2014: 'We have very good relations with socially committed Catholics and we see Pope Francis as having a greater commitment to confronting social injustice than either Benedict XVI or John Paul II. He is pushing ahead in areas his predecessors never dared to tread. And yet we don't share his traditional Catholic views on gay marriages, women and abortion.'

Meeting with 4,000 Catholic doctors a month earlier, Pope Francis reiterated his often stated view that abortion and euthanasia were sinful, and stressed that each human life, no matter the condition, was sacred. Pope Francis recalled that many times in his years as a priest he heard people object to the Church's position on life issues, specifically asking why the Church is against abortion. He said now, as he said then, that the Church was not against abortion because it was simply a religious or philosophical issue, but also because abortion 'is a scientific problem, because there is a human life and it's not lawful to take a human life to solve a problem'.

And yet this was a papacy that could not and did not stand still on a whole range of issues. Uprisings elsewhere in the world posed a direct threat to Christianity, forcing the Vatican to recalibrate its diplomatic chess game. As argued by Massimo Franco, columnist of the Italian *Corriere della Sera*, on the first anniversary of the new papacy, Pope Francis was the first 'global pope' of the modern era, less allied to the US than Pope John Paul II had been, and less Eurocentric than Benedict XVI. While his two predecessors were both Europeans shaped by the cold war, the new Pope's foreign policy meant promoting and accepting pluralism and a reinvigorated balance of powers. As Franco, author of *The Vatican According to Francis*, wrote in a paper delivered to the Royal Institute of International Affairs in London: 'The Pope developed this vision during his years as archbishop of Buenos Aires, a global, Latin American megacity where interfaith relations and inequalities are the rule.' Diplomats listening to Francis's first annual 'state of the world' address in January 2014 noted with interest, even astonishment, that Europe was barely mentioned. A more nuanced perspective suggested a convergence of interests between the US and Pope Francis in Latin America, the area of the world in which he stood to have the biggest impact politically, at least in the short term.

In his early months in office, Pope Francis appeared to be in a hurry to break out of his office and engage with the crisis-ridden world while seemingly increasingly disturbed by its capacity for violence. In September 2014, Pope Francis spoke of a whole series of simultaneous conflicts around the world being effectively a 'Third World War' for which he blamed the arms trade and the 'plotters of terrorism', who were sowing death and destruction. 'Humanity needs to weep and this is the time to weep,' Francis said as he prayed before Italy's largest war memorial in Redipuglia, where more than 100,000 soldiers who died in the First World War are buried.

In the first autumn of his papacy, Pope Francis intervened to join those concerned about the spiral towards a war in Syria by speaking out against a military strike – evidence, according to Massimo Franco, of a de facto alliance between him and Russia's Vladimir Putin. Twelve months on, the USA was bombing ISIS in Syria, and Russia's relations with the West had deteriorated to their lowest level since the cold war over the Ukraine crisis. This put under pressure the Vatican's new role as a soft power that was no longer the religious corollary of NATO, content with the US as global policeman. Pope Francis consequently appointed English Archbishop Paul Gallagher, an experienced, multilingual and highly respected diplomat, as Secretary for Relations with States, with the aim of bringing fresh impetus to the conduct of foreign policy.

Within the Vatican, Pope Francis drew on his years of political manoeuvring and administrative experience, carefully consulting on reform before taking any premature step that might end up backfiring. On his election, he inherited a highly centralized organization whose silo mentality had allowed scandals to proliferate under his predecessor. Pope Francis looked back on his time as a Jesuit provincial as a learning curve from which he drew important lessons. As a Jesuit provincial his authoritarianism had divided his order. By contrast when he became archbishop he would have meetings with his six auxiliary bishops every two weeks and several times a year with the council of priests. 'They asked questions and we opened the floor for discussion. This greatly helped me to make the best decisions,' he recalled.

The theme of collegiality was one much emphasized during the Second Vatican Council but its practice had fallen by the wayside during the papacy of John Paul II, after he raised false expectations with his 1995 encyclical *Ut Unum Sint*. Despite the encyclical's call on Christian leaders to help the Pope find a new 'way of exercising [papal] primacy', no reform was put in motion. Only during the years of Benedict XVI was the issue revived to the point of being seriously discussed in the meetings of cardinals that preceded the 2013 conclave. By then Vatileaks had exposed the corruption, careerism and inefficiency in the Curia, the Church's central bureaucracy. Nevertheless the maintenance in their posts of some well-known faces of the Benedict era reflected Francis's respect for his predecessor, and a conciliatory spirit. His reform needed to be carefully considered, and not done in a way that might appear vindictive.

His papacy set off as it intended to continue, along the Ignatian path of spiritual discernment, with only one dogmatic certainty – that God is in all things. 'We must walk united with our differences: there is no other way to become one. This is the way of Jesus,' he told the Jesuit Antonio Spadaro.

The quest for unity within the Church, respecting its diversity as a potentially integral part of its universality, was one of the reasons Pope Francis happily endorsed the canonization of John XXIII and John Paul II in April 2014, whose papacies were markedly different in style and content, and yet created a strong following beyond the purely religious field. The issue of sainthood had threatened to provoke controversy six months earlier with the beatification of

500 Spanish Civil War 'martyrs'. In a ceremony in the ancient Roman imperial city of Tarragona, thousands of relatives and followers of Spanish bishops, clergy, seminarians and nuns who were executed during the Civil War saw them brought a step closer to sainthood, after being declared martyrs.

During the last years of the General Franco dictatorship in the late 1960s and early 1970s, some progressive Church figures had focused on reconciliation between the two sides of the Spanish Civil War. More recently the beatification had benefited from a strong lobby composed of conservative members of the Spanish hierarchy, such as the outspoken Archbishop of Madrid Cardinal Antonio Rouco Varela, supporters of the centre-right Popular party, and surviving remnants of the Franco era who had always denounced the violent anti-clericalism or 'Red Terror' of the extreme left and anarchists. The choice of Tarragona for a major concelebrated Mass had a strong symbolic charge. For it was here, in the time of the Romans, that Iberian early Christians were put to death. It was here too that during the Spanish Civil War, over 150 clerics were executed, a higher concentration than any other town.

But the beatification had its opponents, including those who felt it responded to the political agenda of the right, it glorified members of the Church who had sided with the Spanish military uprising in 1936 and ignored those who, in conscience, had felt their Christian calling required them to fight against the neo-fascist Franco and the privileged classes that supported him and his generals.

When a similar ceremony of beatification of a group of Spanish Civil War 'martyrs' took place in Rome, Pope John Paul II presided. Subsequently Benedict XVI decided that beatifications should be done locally and would not normally be done by the Pope (the beatification of Cardinal Newman in England in 2010, which Benedict did preside over, was unusual). On this later occasion, at

Tarragona on 12 October 2013, Pope Francis stayed away, sending instead Cardinal Angelo Amato, prefect of the Congregation for Saints' Causes. Amato, who would become a key member of Pope Benedict's inner circle inherited by Pope Francis, gave a speech seemingly well tuned in to the sensitivities of his immediate congregation, describing Spain as 'a land blessed by the blood of martyrs', given that more than 1,000 Spaniards had been beatified in the last ten years. Contrary to what some sectors of the Spanish media had predicted, there were however no outpourings of right-wing national Catholic sentiment reminiscent of Franco's days; at the ceremony one militant who tried to unfurl a Spanish flag was quickly surrounded by the relatives of those being beatified and told this was not a place for political symbols.

Instead, on a beautiful sunny Mediterranean day, the atmosphere was both reverential and festive, part popular pilgrimage, part World Youth Day, with old and young sharing communal picnics, singing and praying in groups as they waited for the hierarchy and politicians to turn up. What attracted the greatest interest was the pre-recorded TV papal message shown to the 20,000 faithful gathered in the grounds of a local university as part of the live global coverage of the event. Pope Francis urged those in attendance to join 'from the heart' in the celebration to proclaim the beatified martyrs. The Pope said those martyrs were 'Christians won over by Christ, disciples who have understood fully the path to that "love to the extreme limit" that led Jesus to the Cross'. He noted that popes always tell people, 'Imitate the martyrs.' The core of his message came next. 'It is always necessary to die a little in order to come out of ourselves, to leave behind our selfishness, our comfort, our laziness, our sadness, and to open ourselves to God, and to others, especially those most in need,' he said.

Pope Francis's statement was carefully worded to avoid any subjective political judgement on the Civil War, not least given the fact that Tarragona, although traditionally Catholic and conservative, was in Catalonia, where political sensitivities were running high because of Madrid's refusal to allow a referendum on independence. But the Pope appeared to be talking beyond territorial or indeed religious boundaries, with its interpretation of martyrdom not in the sense of violent death in the cause of fundamentalist religious or political belief, but as an act of selfless humanity based on love. In contrast to the triumphalist air that pervaded the ceremony in 2007, this had a conciliatory as well as redemptive feel about it, with the personal histories of each case emphasizing that those who had died hadn't aggressively sought their death, but had been innocent victims of intolerance and bigotry.

In the months that followed Pope Francis would return to this concept as he spoke out against the contemporary persecution of Christians in areas such as the Middle East, Pakistan and parts of Africa. In late December 2013 Pope Francis spoke on the day after attacks on two Christian churches in Baghdad left at least thirty-eight dead. Coincidentally he spoke on the feast of St Stephen, an early Christian martyr. 'Today, we pray in a particular way for Christians who suffer discrimination because of the witness they offer to Christ and to the Gospel,' he said. 'We are close to these brothers and sisters who, like St Stephen, are unjustly accused and made the object of violence of various kinds. Unfortunately, I'm sure they're more numerous today than in the time of the early Church. They're so many!

This happens especially wherever religious freedom isn't guaranteed or fully realized,' Francis said. 'However, it also happens in countries and environments where freedom and human rights are protected on paper, but where in fact believers, especially Christians, find limitations and discrimination.'

The 'underreported catastrophe of our times', as described by John Allen in the *Spectator* in October 2013, was the persecution of Christian churchgoers, and this was perhaps destined to become one of the great tests of Pope Francis's spiritual standing and also of the Vatican's effective role as a global power-broker and diplomat. A sense of the scale of this challenge was underlined by separate independent research examined by Allen who wrote a detailed book on the subject. According to the International Society for Human Rights, a secular observatory based in Frankfurt, 80 per cent of all acts of religious discrimination in the world in 2013–14 were directed at Christians. Statistically speaking, that made Christians by far the most persecuted religious body on the planet. According to the Pew Forum, between 2006 and 2010 Christians faced some form of discrimination, either de jure or de facto, in a staggering total of 139 nations, which is almost three-quarters of all the countries on earth. And according to the Centre for the Study of Global Christianity at Gordon-Conwell Theological Seminary in Massachusetts, an average of 100,000 Christians have been killed in what the centre calls a 'situation of witness' each year for the past decade. 'That works out to be 11 Christians killed somewhere in the world every hour, seven days a week and 365 days a year, for reasons related to their faith,' wrote Allen.

Allen noted that both John Paul II and Benedict XVI raised the issue, and their rhetoric made little practical impact:

> On the other hand, it was also once fashionable to ask what any pope could do about Communist persecution of Christians, until John Paul II played a key role in the collapse of the Soviet system across Eastern Europe. Maybe Francis can be to the early 21st century what John Paul was to the late 20th, meaning a pope who genuinely changes history.

A hopeful thought, but premature and perhaps wishful thinking. Not only did Pope John Paul II's papacy last longer that one can believe Pope Francis's will, but the final years of the cold war, with the Soviet Union imploding from within, and the ascendancy of a strong transatlantic alliance personified by the Reagan/Thatcher axis, provided the papacy then with a simpler run of options. Moreover Pope John Paul II was an anti-communist Pole, and Poland, a Catholic country with a well-organized, anti-regime trade union movement, proved fertile political ground to demolish the iron curtain. By contrast, Pope Francis inhabits a world long ago made more complex due to the absence of clear-cut geopolitical ideological divisions and a crisis of leadership that has left the stability of the political class in long-established democracies severely undermined.

Pope Francis spoke out against political corruption and the social injustice and marginalization provoked by a globalized free market economy. This may have struck a chord in the grass-roots movements proposing a radical political and economic alternative to long-established systems of governance, but it was not a theme that pacified those bent on restoring a caliphate from Baghdad to Córdoba. Moreover questions such as that posed to Pope Francis in August 2014 as to whether he approved of US military actions against ISIS placed him in a moral and diplomatic quandary given his condemnation of war and violence. And here it is worth registering the convoluted answer Pope Francis gave to what was a clear question: 'In these cases where there is an unjust aggression, I can only say this: it is licit to stop the unjust aggressor. I underline the verb: stop. I do not say bomb, make war, I say stop by some means. With what means can they be stopped? These have to be evaluated. To stop the unjust aggressor is licit.' In other words, while military action against fundamentalists threatening Christian communities might be lawful, it was not necessarily desirable morally. Notably the emphasis of his statement was on the word 'stop' – which, as he clarified, need not be achieved by bombs or wars.

Evidently Pope Francis was not convinced that his papacy needed to, nor should, position itself as the leader of the twenty-first-century crusade. According to Joseph E. Capizzi, Associate Professor of Moral Theology at the Catholic University of America, the Crusades were 'fought to displace Muslim communities from their "occupation" of the Holy Land'. But the intervention for which Francis was calling 'is not to retake any land, nor is it limited to [the] protection of Christians', noted Capizzi. Rather, what Francis wanted was 'protection for all those threatened by ISIS' – a category that includes people of various faith traditions. As Francis said, 'there are many martyrs. But [in Iraq] there are men and women, religious minorities, not all of them Christian, and they are all equal before God.'

Pope Francis's comments, while capturing headlines because of the manner in which they were phrased, were not in themselves a major departure in Church teaching. Rather, they were consistent with the Catholic doctrine of 'just war', which lays down strict conditions for morally legitimate defence by military force. And yet after Pope Francis affirmed the Church's doctrine of just war, he also noted how that doctrine has been abused many times in the past and could be abused again. 'How many times under this excuse of stopping an unjust aggressor the powers [that intervened] have taken control of peoples, and have made a true war of conquest?' Pope Francis's belief that 'One nation alone cannot judge how to stop an unjust aggressor' appeared aimed at facilitating rather than obstructing President Barack Obama's policy of securing as wide a coalition as possible in his war on ISIS. It was the clearest indication in public of some diplomatic coordination behind the scenes between the Vatican and Washington.

Obama, conscious of the Pope's popularity as a spiritual leader, was just one of a number of heads of state that lined up to visit Francis in the months following his election, landing in Rome in late March 2014. Given the feverish nature of the information highway of instant mass communication, it was perhaps inevitable that his meeting with Pope Francis should lend itself to a plethora of comment, not always conceived or delivered in a spirit of generosity. Leading the cynical charge was the hawkish Fox TV, the

American channel, whose panel of commentators suggested that the meeting had exposed a huge political and ethical gap between the two men on issues like abortion and contraception while failing to find common ground on anything of substance. One of the Fox commentators drew a comparison between the lack of a clear ideological and ethical bonding and the meeting of minds to 'bring down the Berlin wall' when Reagan met John Paul II. Another lamented that Obama and the Pope had not taken the opportunity to issue a joint statement against 'the terrorism of Islam'.

In fairness the TV images of the initial encounter suggested that Obama's charm offensive – all smiles, lingering handshake and a litany of effusive thank-yous – were not exactly reciprocated. The relaxed smile that has characterized this papacy on major public occasions seemed to have momentarily abandoned Pope Francis. He looked sullen and awkward as well as exhausted against a background of flashing camera lights and the general razzmatazz that accompanies any US president in the modern age. Earlier Pope Francis's new cult of ecclesiastical austerity seemed under assault when Obama came through the Vatican gates with an imperial cavalcade of more than fifty vehicles.

'Several were packed with men dressed in black and, disconcertingly, wearing masks,' noted the *Guardian*'s John Hooper, before adding, 'It was not immediately clear if they were Italian Special Forces attempting to confuse potential terrorists or American secret agents trying to hide the effects of a more than usually gruesome hangover.'

Only later did both men seem more relaxed as they emerged from the meeting, suggesting that the encounter behind closed doors had found more common ground than points of division. The Vatican officially devoted just five lines in its subsequent communiqué, stating broadly that the meeting had covered international conflict and the problems facing migrants. But Obama at a press conference seemed happy to share enough detail to suggest a broad convergence of interests on issues like the wish to find a peaceful solution in the Middle East, and a concern for the glaring inequalities of modern society.

Both Pope Francis and Obama kept from the worldwide media the fact that the meeting had also given fresh impetus to secret diplomatic initiatives to try to bring the US and Cuba closer together after more than fifty years of frozen relations. As one Obama official confessed after the news broke at the end of 2014, 'Cuba got as much attention as anything discussed' at the Rome meeting.

Similar briefings of Washington-based journalists suggested that the diplomatic thaw between the US and Cuba entered a critical stage in June 2013 when the first face-to-face talks in five decades took place between senior Cuban and US officials at a neutral location in Canada.

As I had discovered during a trip to Cuba in March 2008, the Vatican's process of discreet bridge-building with the Castro regime had preceded the election of both Francis and Obama by well over a decade. As I subsequently related in a diary published in the *Tablet*, according to local Jesuit and diplomatic sources the turning point in Church–State relations came with the visit of Pope John Paul II in 1998 when the two Castro brothers – Fidel and Raúl – attended Mass. Suddenly Cubans who had backed the revolution while wanting to keep their faith saw the reconciliation for which they had been praying. 'It allowed people to come out of themselves, to express their religiosity,' Fr Alberto, a priest from Havana's main Jesuit Church of the Sacred Heart, told me. Although he did not accompany Pope John Paul II on the trip, Bergoglio closely studied the historic pilgrimage and edited a book *Diálogos Entre Juan Pablo II y Fidel Castro* (*Dialogues Between John Paul II and Fidel Castro*) in Spanish in 1998.

While on the island, one of John Paul II's prayers was, 'Let Cuba open itself to the world, and let the world open itself to Cuba.' The

Vatican later entered a protracted phase of diplomacy, which under Benedict XVI focused on allowing the Catholic Church not only freedom of worship but also to regain some of the access it had to the media and the education system before both were brought under strict state control in the early 1960s.

Even before the Vatican had secured any major concessions, it was not set on a course of confrontation. Indeed, some hardline opponents to the Castro regime considered the Catholic Church in Cuba to be collaborationist – by the time of my visit in 2008, there were no priests or bishops in Cuban jails. What was clear then was that the Vatican was positioning itself as a key player in whatever reform process lay ahead, with Western diplomats widely in agreement that Raúl Castro, who effectively replaced Fidel as president in 2006, was a pragmatic Marxist who saw the need to steer the island through some kind of economic and political renewal.

Benedict XVI visited Cuba in March 2012, which helped pave the way for the celebrations by mass crowds of enthusiastic islanders around the 400th anniversary of Cuba's patron saint, Our Lady of Charity, depicted in a small statue of the Virgin found floating in a bay in 1612. In 2011, the Catholic Church's efforts to alleviate poverty and human rights abuses on the island produced a widely publicized result when Cuba's Cardinal Jaime Ortega secured the release of over 150 political prisoners and permission for the Ladies in White, a local campaign group, to continue their weekly peaceful protest against the unjust imprisonment of other male relatives.

In a long-standing position shared by the Vatican and the US Conference of Catholic Bishops, the Catholic Church in Cuba has advocated that the US embargo in Cuba be lifted on the assumption that dialogue and exchange would improve human rights. Months of talks, in which Pope Francis emerged as a key player, produced an announcement on 17 December 2014 that Cuba and the US intended to normalize relations and, as part of the deal, there would be an exchange between the two countries of prisoners held on spying charges.

In the light of the Cuban deal, the meeting between Obama and Pope Francis in Rome in March 2014 deserves a place in history, but it needs to be looked at in a broader context. As noted by Roberto Guareschi in an article published in *Project Syndicate* soon after Pope Francis's election, the start of the Francis papacy found the populist governments of Argentina, Venezuela, Bolivia, Nicaragua, Ecuador and Cuba hit hard by the recent death of their great continental mentor, Venezuelan President Hugo Chávez. Guareschi, a long-term executive editor of Argentina's *Clarín* newspaper, predicted:

> They all, of course, have their own identities and strengths, but they will miss the protection of Chávez's global influence, as well as his subsidies. Moreover, they rule countries in which Catholics are an overwhelming majority. Although the degree of their religious commitment varies, they share a strong emotional attachment to the faith, which will provide Francis I with considerable political leverage.

Just as John Paul II, a Pole, was one of the decisive forces in eroding the hold of communism on Europe, Francis, an Argentine Jesuit and Latin America's first pope, set his sights on trying to influence greater political stability and social justice in the continent where he was born. In the first months of his papacy, the political vacuum left by the death of Chávez set the scene for constructive engagement between the Vatican and several Latin American countries, helping to calm the turbulent waters of the populist tide.

At the end of his two years, Pope Francis's vision seemed clearly stated: the creation of a better, more just and faith-based society – his theology of the people, with God and liberation minus the conflict. And yet the challenge South America faced was how to bring about economic and social reform with political stability on a continent characterized by huge inequalities, but also where redistributive populism faced resistance by the aspiring but frustrated middle class. In Cuba, the Church walked a tightrope, as a mediator, engaging with Castro's regime and the US, with the endgame far from clear.

Despite his willingness to engage diplomatically with the US, Pope Francis, who learnt his humility and concern for social justice from the shanty neighbourhoods of Buenos Aires, was instinctively cautious when it came to claims of ethical conduct emanating from the great capitalist imperial superpower. After all, this was a pope born to Italian immigrants who had grown up in a time when Argentina's populist leader, General Perón, turned the US into the convenient whipping boy for his country's failed political culture. Francis still has some *Peronismo* flowing in his veins.

In a similar manner, he would castigate the European Community in a speech to MEPs in Strasbourg on 25 November 2014 for producing a 'general impression of weariness and ageing', a Europe which was now a 'grandmother . . . no longer fertile and vibrant'. In so doing, the Pope intended to issue a wake-up call, in solidarity with the plight of the unemployed in the age of austerity and critical of the way contemporary society pushed individuals towards an 'uncontrolled consumerism'.

Of a rather different nature was Queen Elizabeth II's meeting with Pope Francis, days after Obama's visit. It may have lacked the razzmatazz or political status of that of the US President but it was no less charged with potent symbolism. This was the first trip abroad in over two years by the reigning British monarch, who despite her enduring physical and mental good health, wisely opted for a less hectic official diary befitting her age (eighty-eight).

A rescheduled day trip to Italy, at the invitation of the anglophile Italian President Giorgio Napolitano, afforded an opportunity for a short courtesy visit to the Vatican that was happily seized on by Buckingham Palace (advised by the Foreign Office and Britain's intelligent ambassador to the Holy See, Nigel Baker, an experienced career diplomat who had done a stint in London as an adviser to the royals). The Vatican for its part gave the nod within days of the papal election when Pope Francis asked his friend, the retired Archbishop of Westminster Cardinal Cormac Murphy-O'Connor, to pass on his 'warmest greetings' to Her Majesty, a thinly veiled message that the Queen would be well received.

At one level such mutual diplomatic respect was to be expected. Queen Elizabeth as not only a popular monarch of one of the oldest and most influential democracies in the world (and the head of fifty-three Commonwealth countries), but also a very committed Christian who had supported narrowing the historic rift between the Church of England, of which she was supreme Governor, and the Catholic Church. Her meeting with Pope Francis was thus consistent with a record of cordial encounters with the Vatican dating back to 1951 when, as heiress to the throne, she met Pope Pius XII. As Queen she has met Pope John XXIII (1961), Pope John Paul II (1982 and 2000) and Pope Benedict XVI (2010).

The current pontiff – a man who had made humility and poverty a touchstone of his reign – could be excused for momentarily looking a little baffled by the gifts of various food products and whisky from the House of Windsor's various estates. However, he ended up receiving them with a graceful smile. The ecumenical spirit of the encounter was meanwhile underlined in the papal gifts to the Queen, commemorating one of the last Anglo-Saxon kings, the medieval Edward the Confessor, who was canonized in 1161 by Pope Alexander III. His devout personality continues to command the respect of English Protestants and English Catholics alike.

Such a cordial encounter no doubt came as a disappointment to those in Argentina, not least President Cristina Fernández who once tried to fuel the illusion among her countrymen that an Argentine Pope would aid her efforts to transfer the sovereignty of the Falklands. The fact that Las Malvinas – as the islands were called in Spanish – was not even mentioned by Francis was an important reminder that, whatever his roots and understandable love of his country, the office of a modern pope is a universal one and cannot be influenced by narrow nationalist interests.

As for Queen Elizabeth, her silence on the controversial issue showed admirable tact as well as realism, knowing that the bond between her and Pope Francis transcended politics. Lest we forget, the coins of her realm still mentioned the title bestowed on King Henry VIII by Pope Leo X in 1521 before the break with Rome: *Fidei Defensor*, or Defender of the Faith. The Pope had no reason to doubt that the current monarch was a spiritual ally. He was wise to consider that the Falklands/Malvinas was not an issue in which Vatican diplomacy should waste its time meddling.

And yet the Holy Land was another matter in terms of its ripeness for papal involvement. Pope Francis drew on his experience of extending hands of friendship to the many Argentines of Jewish and Arab dependency, and made a politically risky pilgrimage to Israel in May 2014. Pope Francis seemed to walk straight into a political minefield, getting himself embroiled in a propaganda war between Israelis and Palestinians competing to claim him for their side. On the second day of his visit, the pontiff made an unscheduled stop to pray at the wall that divides Jerusalem from Bethlehem, which is in the West Bank; then the following day, Israeli Prime Minister Benjamin Netanyahu accompanied him on yet another unscheduled visit, this time to an Israeli memorial for victims of terrorism. As Emma Green of the *Atlantic* reported, it seemed 'like a competition to capture the pope's most politically poignant moment: praying at the Western Wall, praying on the banks of the Jordan River, praying before a Palestinian security checkpoint covered with Arabic graffiti'.

Francis met with Netanyahu and Palestinian Authority President Mahmoud Abbas, and days later they were sharing a prayer and extending a hand to each other in Rome. Barely a month later, the latest round of bloodshed in Gaza began. Even hardened veteran Middle East commentators found it difficult to blame Pope Francis for what they argued was a pointless PR exercise.

'If he had invited the sheikhs and rabbis who are the real movers in the wars of hate they would have turned him down,' wrote Anshel Pferr, a correspondent on the Israeli daily newspaper, *Haaretz*. But, as Green argued, his trip wasn't about solving the Arab–Israeli conflict – that was not in the Pope's gift. It was, however, about Christians, the forgotten stakeholders of Jerusalem, as Green put it: 'People like the nuns who live on the Via Dolorosa, the road Jesus walked to his crucifixion; the Franciscan priests who maintain the Garden of Gethsemane, where Jesus prayed before his death; and, perhaps most importantly, the shrinking number of Arab Christians who live in Israel, the Palestinian Territories, and surrounding countries.'

On the Vatican website dedicated to the Pope's trip there were several sections about the persecution of Palestinian Christians, emphasizing that they were 'faced by an exclusivist Islamic movement that often refuses to recognize Christians as co-citizens with equal rights, equal obligations, and equal opportunities'. In a meeting with local Muslims, including Muhammad Hussein, the grand mufti of Jerusalem, Francis spoke of the role of Abraham in Christianity and Islam and the 'fraternal dialogue' between the two faiths, but he closed with a rallying cry for solidarity between men and women of goodwill against the violence of fundamentalism: 'May we respect and love one another as brothers and sisters! May we learn to understand the sufferings of others! May no one abuse the name of God through violence!' Thus did the world's most important spiritual leader appeal for peace in a city – sacred to three monotheistic Abraham faiths of Judaism, Christianity and Islam

– which had been a tinderbox for more than two millennia. And yet his words and presence seemed to fail to avert an increasingly bitter confrontation over territory in the Holy Land turning into a visceral religious war.

Pope Francis had followed in the footsteps of St Ignatius, the founder of the Jesuit order, who saw a pilgrimage to the Holy Land as one of his key missions. The Pope's interview with fellow Jesuit Antonio Spadaro in *Civiltà Cattolica*, syndicated in Jesuit magazines around the world, was not only a clear statement of Ignatian principles but also a conscious act of reconciliation with the Jesuit order, several of whose members had been critical of his leadership in the past. He held up as an example not the rigidity and conformity to the establishment that the order had fallen into at different stages of its history, but the mystical and missionary spirit of the founding fathers, and of Jesuits who had moved boldly into the modern age, 'searching, creative, generous, going to the frontiers . . . looking at the horizon'.

Looking back at the 1960s and early 1970s during his years as a young Jesuit priest, Pope Francis reflected that those were tough times, 'especially when it came to the issue of . . . obedience to the pope'. Bergoglio had dealt with it by imposing his authority as Jesuit provincial and distancing himself from the political activism of other priests and the progressive theology emanating from Father Arrupe – the superior general of the Jesuits at the time. And yet Pope Francis now paid tribute to Arrupe, the one-time General Provincial of the Jesuits, as a man of prayer. 'I remember him when he prayed sitting on the ground in the Japanese style. For this he had the right attitude and made the right decisions,' Pope Francis recalled.

As a historian of the Jesuits, Jonathan Wright has noted, 'the papacy and the Jesuits have had their share of squabbles' during the 500 years of the order's history. Squabbles in recent times included some Jesuits struggling to abide by the centralized rule and dogmatic teaching under Pope John Paul II and Benedict XVI. For his part Bergoglio as Archbishop of Buenos Aires had tended to keep his distance from fellow Jesuits on his periodical visits to Rome, developing a closer relationship with papal nuncios and cardinals than with the Jesuits' Roman headquarters.

And yet it was during his time as archbishop that Bergoglio came to act more as a progressive Jesuit on his home ground, even if his theology was neither original nor radical given its focus on the transformative action of faith and the importance of popular religion as opposed to reason, ideology and structural change. He did not actively promote political action, still less revolution. He was, however, reminded of a good Ignatian principle by his shanty-town priests, the *curas villeros*: that one had to go out to the *periferia*, the margins of society, to develop a social conscience. In his interview with *Civiltà Cattolica*, Pope Francis quoted 'a brilliant letter' on the theme of poverty Fr Arrupe had sent to CIAS, the Jesuit social research think-tanks spread out across the developing world. Arrupe had stated clearly that 'one cannot speak of poverty if one does not experience poverty, with a direct connection to the places in which there is poverty'. Long forgotten was the clash Bergoglio had encountered with Arrupe's emissary in 1977 over the Buenos Aires CIAS's refusal to speak out against the military regime on social justice issues.

But while the interview with *Civiltà Cattolica* was important for marking out the identity of the Pope, it was also significant in underlining the important role the Jesuits could play as Francis's promoters. Spadaro not only syndicated his interview with the Pope across the global Jesuit network, but the interview also came to play an important role in broadening the Pope's engagement generally with the secular world. Few phrases seemed as applicable to the modern Church than the subsequently widely quoted comparison Pope Francis made between the Catholic Church and a 'field hospital after a battle, in need of forgiveness and healing'.

Within the Vatican, where they retained their cardinals, priests, theologians and other experts, the Jesuits were an influential force not least in the media, and Fr Lombardi, a Jesuit, served as a loyal and highly disciplined press spokesman to Francis as he did under Benedict. *Civiltà Cattolica*, under the hugely energetic Jesuit Antonio Spadaro, also saw to it that the Pope's best promotion was through his own words and gestures. Lombardi and Spadaro saw their role as simply ensuring the message was transmitted accurately, with full use of TV, print and social networks.

And yet to see the Francis pontificate as an exclusively Jesuit papacy, to the detriment of other influential Catholic organizations like Opus Dei, would be an oversimplification, just as it would be to suggest a major shift from orthodoxy to radical liberalism. While removing or demoting some awkward intransigents and plotters within the Curia, such as Cardinal Tarcisio Bertone and the reactionary Cardinal Raymond Burke, Pope Francis also aimed at building on established theological common ground that could heal divisions, not accentuate them. Opus Dei, along with the Jesuits, retained an important secular and clerical presence in Rome, including the media. One of the slickest TV operations linked to the Vatican was that of the Opus Dei-financed multinational Rome Reports TV news agency. Its discreet but strategically placed offices were based in the Via della Conciliazione, north of the Tiber. They were a short walk from St Peter's Square, and the agency's mainly Spanish and Latin American staff had a clear view from their outside studio of Castel Sant'Angelo, where Pope Clement VII sought refuge during the sack of Rome by anti-papal forces in 1527.

While ensuring that the beatification in September 2014 of a former general president of Opus Dei, the Spanish Bishop Álvaro del Portillo, got top billing in its weekly news programme, the agency was careful not be seen as a propaganda or voracious recruiting machine for its own order. Instead, its reporting and documentaries portrayed the Catholic Church under Pope Francis as open to accepting criticism about its past failings on issues like sex abuse while also pursuing a path of spiritual renewal and communication in a more transparent and less judgemental way. One of its bestselling DVDs was *Rotten Apples*, a documentary on the Church handling of sex abuse cases in the John Paul II and Benedict XVI eras. An even bigger seller was called *Francis, The People's Pope*, an uncritical account of Bergoglio in Argentina, focusing on his work with the poor as a bishop and describing him as a world leader who had 'changed forever' the direction of the Catholic Church.

Mgr Lluis Clavell, a clergyman of Opus Dei and a professor of Metaphysics at the Pontifical University of the Holy Cross, told me that while the *Civiltà Cattolica* interview had left him with no doubt that Francis was a Jesuit 'from top to toe' in the way he approached his faith, the Pope's social conscience and spirituality was not an exclusive preserve of any Catholic order. Contrary to the fictionalized version of Opus Dei as a secretive, scheming and politically reactionary force, this priest seemed to be open about emphasizing that, like Pope Francis, they had no partisan 'line' on secular politics (although some members did not share in his respect for General Perón), and had no other agenda for Catholicism than loyalty to the Pope and defending Church teaching.

Mgr Clavell along with other influential Opus Dei members in Rome interviewed for this book saw, as they believed did Pope Francis, sanctification of work, contemplation in the midst of the secular world, and divine and Marian reverence as elements of sound spirituality. They were becalmed by the fact that nothing in Pope Francis's history as priest, bishop or pope had suggested any radical break with Church teaching on issues like gay marriage and abortion, while what he had to say about divorce was not abandoning the indissolubility of marriage, just as he was not about to condemn priestly celibacy or authorize women priests.

Mgr Mariano Fazio, the Argentine-born former rector of the order's Pontifical University of the Holy Cross, and currently the vicar (or head) of Opus Dei in Argentina, was probably the person in Opus Dei who knew Pope Francis best, having been personally appointed by Pope Benedict XVI as an expert theological adviser to work alongside Bergoglio at the CELAM conference in Aparecida in 2007.

Under the somewhat unwieldy title 'Disciples and missionaries of Jesus Christ, so that people may have life in him', the bishops in 2007 had formed a consensus around ideas with which many Jesuits and Opus Dei members would have been comfortable and which Pope Francis would integrate into his papal mission statement. This included opting for a more hands-on evangelizing effort as opposed to a passive clericalism, in a 'grand continental mission'. It contained a commitment to social justice in a modern context. The 'new faces of the poor', with which the Church should concern itself, included refugees, victims of human trafficking, the 'disappeared', those living with HIV/Aids, drug addicts, abused women and children, the disabled, the unemployed, street people, landless peasants, indigenous groups, miners and the 'technologically illiterate'. The document made no mention of liberation theology, ratifying instead a consensus on a 'preferential and evangelical option for the poor', without Marxism, with the Church's hierarchical structure maintained, along with the acceptance of the importance of popular religion, not least devotion to the Virgin Mary.

Fazio, the author of several books warning of the dangers of relativism and the challenges faced by Catholicism in the secular world, marked his friend Bergoglio's election to the papacy by publishing a small volume, *Pope Francis: The Key to His Thoughts*, based on their personal correspondence and conversations. In it Fazio sums up the Pope's spirituality as the 'central union with Christ and the primacy of prayer', the 'mission of each Christian to look for the existentialist frontier', the 'trust in God's mercy', 'the value of popular devotion', and the 'unyielding search for a dialogue capable of reaching consensus'.

It was not just Opus Dei stalwarts who seemed content with the consensual, non-revolutionary aspects of the Francis papacy. As a former member of the Curia, and currently the rector of one of Rome's historic seminaries, the Venerable English College, Mgr Philip Whitmore thought the Catholic priesthood was being asked to change by Pope Francis, but not in a manner that necessarily paved the way for Catholic priests to get married and remain priests.

Whitmore said: 'Pope Francis is full of surprises but I have to say I would be very, very surprised if he went down that road. The reason I say is that again and again he has underlined his passionate belief that priests and religious should move away from anything that is, as he would say, worldly. He doesn't believe we priests should live in comfort, have smart cars, or expensive holidays or the latest gadgets. He believes that priests should have a radical simplicity and other-worldliness and this will sharpen them up spiritually. I cannot see how getting married, and having a family and having a home would coincide with that image. It seems to me he is moving in the opposite direction to a very radical commitment. Also, he is of course a Jesuit so he lives very radically his vows to poverty and chastity and obedience, and that is the model from which he is calling us. He also puts great value on family life so, who knows, he might want to find ways of combining these two vocations. But I would be very surprised.'

And yet the expectations that Francis, the first pope to hail from outside Europe for thirteen centuries, would set in motion change not just of style but also of substance were high among Catholic liberals. Few Catholic theologians had attacked the legitimacy and credibility of previous popes and suffered for it as much as Hans Küng. When I visited Küng in January 2014 the most telling evidence that he had come in from the cold were three cordial letters he had received from Pope Francis. Küng shows me the latest in which Francis said he had read an article by the Swiss theologian '*determinadamente*' ('very carefully') and that he welcomed the ongoing correspondence: '*La carta y el articulo me hicieron bien*' ('The letter and the article made me feel good').

In the article he sent to the Pope, Küng enthused over Francis's apostolic exhortation, *Evangelii Gaudium*, while criticizing the prefect of the then Congregation of the Doctrine of the Faith (CDF), Cardinal Designate Gerhard Müller, for his insistence that remarried divorced Catholics be barred from Communion.

'*Determinadamente.*' Küng repeated the word after I had read out the full letter in Spanish. 'This is important,' he said with similar emphasis. In that moment the old man seemed to have the look of a rebellious student who after years of feeling unfairly reprimanded by a bullying teacher had finally earned his brownie points.

I was talking to Küng in a medium-sized house on a hill above the centre of the German University of Tübingen that doubled up as his home and the offices of the Global Ethics Foundation, which he helped run. The figure that greeted me with a warm handshake and engaging smile on this, our first meeting, was frailer than the Küng of official photographs printed in his foundation's leaflets or the sculptured bust on his lawn. Küng was then approaching eighty-six, just a year younger than the retired Pope Benedict XVI, whom he has known from when they were fellow professors at Tübingen, then a hub of revolutionary student activity. Benedict would later reflect how upset he was by the violence and intolerance of radical youth and how this shifted him to the conservative right.

As I passed along the corridor and up the staircase leading to Hans Küng's study, I noticed bound copies of *Concilium*, the international review of theology – my late father, the Catholic publisher and one-time editor of the *Tablet* Tom Burns, had helped give birth to the publication of over five decades ago. Küng had been one of its founders, along with the German Karl Rahner and the Frenchman Henri de Lubac, both Jesuit priests, who together with the French Dominican Yves Marie-Joseph Congar were considered among the most influential Catholic theologians during Bergoglio's time as a priest. All four were active participants in the Second Vatican Council back in the mid-1960s, contributing to the reforming spirit within the Catholic Church, which subsequently met with resistance.

I asked Küng if he was now more hopeful about the future of the Church.

He replied: 'This Argentinian Pope started immediately with a new style. With his direct language, with his simplicity. He showed himself human by asking people to pray for him.'

The Pope's decision to shift his lodgings and main meeting place to the residence of Domus Sanctae Marthae was consciously strategic as well as symbolic, Küng believed. Some things have changed, more than others, he continued. He noted, disapprovingly, that Archbishop Georg Gänswein, Prefect of the Papal Household, was still former Pope Benedict's private secretary, and that the current prefect of the CDF was Cardinal Gerhard Ludwig Müller, who he called a 'professor of old dogmatics'.

Küng told me: 'Of course there are people in the Vatican now who are in a state of fear, of silent opposition. The question is whether the Pope will be able to overcome this opposition. A lot of things are going on in Rome which for me are indications that Francis wants to shake things up.'

He was heartened by moves towards greater accountability in the Vatican bank, and other well-publicized changes – such as the replacement of Bertone as Secretary of State – showed Pope Francis's potential to be decisive and reformist. He was also hopeful that the Synod of Bishops would lead to changes he has long called for in Church teaching on issues ranging from contraception to access to Communion for remarried divorced Catholics.

But for Küng the most pertinent sign of the Pope's 'theological openness' was the personal correspondence he had exchanged with Francis in the early months of his papacy. This began when, within weeks of the papal election, Küng sent Francis a copy of his new book *Can We Save the Catholic Church?* and a letter congratulating him on his appointment of a group of eight cardinals from all continents with the mandate to initiate reform of the Roman Curia. Küng recounted in the preface to the English edition that he received, within days, a 'personal fraternal handwritten letter in which he promised to read the book'. And so began the correspondence that gave Küng cause for so much hope. 'The first thing is that he is writing to me, a person that the CDF has declared is not a Catholic theologian. They tried to eliminate me spiritually. But now I have written to the Pope and I have received an answer immediately.'

In 1978 Küng locked horns with John Paul II over his criticism of the growing authoritarianism in Rome. In 1975, the CDF had asked Küng not to repeat his questioning of papal infallibility. But in 1978 he did so, in an introduction he wrote to a book by August Bernhard Hasler, *How the Pope Became Infallible*. Then in October 1979, he drew up a highly critical balance sheet assessing the first year of John Paul II's papacy which was published internationally as an article. In December 1979, the Vatican and the German bishops conference withdrew his mandate to teach as a Catholic theologian. And yet despite this attempt to silence him, Küng was allowed by the German university authorities to retain his chair of theology at the University of Tübingen, although the institute he presided over was separated from the Catholic theological faculty.

So did he want to be brought in from the cold after all these years? I asked him.

'Well it would be nice. But they will have to do it very soon because I will not live very long anymore,' he replied. As he revealed in his memoirs, Küng had been diagnosed with Parkinson's disease, and separately with macular degeneration that can lead eventually to blindness. He also suffered from polyarthritis in his hands which made writing by hand increasingly difficult. Küng made no secret either of the fact that he was contemplating assisted dying in neighbouring Switzerland.

I recalled a book I had just read called *On Heaven and Earth*, which contained a lengthy dialogue Pope Francis had with his friend, the Argentine rabbi Abraham Skorka. In it, Pope Francis supports Catholic teaching against euthanasia and assisted suicide, calling it a 'culture of discarding' the elderly. 'In Argentina there is clandestine euthanasia. Social services pay up to a certain point; if you pass it, "die, you are very old". Today, elderly people are discarded when, in reality, they are the seat of wisdom of the society,' Pope Francis says. 'The right to life means allowing people to live and not killing, allowing them to grow, to eat, to be educated, to be healed, and to be permitted to die with dignity.'

So I asked Küng how, as a Catholic, he could contemplate assisted dying. Surely life was a gift from God?

'Yes, my life is a gift. But God also gave me responsibility for this gift. And I am myself responsible for what happens with me,' he argued back.

Küng went on, with what seemed a last burst of lucid mental effort at the end of a long day. 'There are thousands and thousands of people who have dementia. One of my closest colleagues who lived round the corner died after suffering it for six years. I observed him. I don't want to go through the same experience, and spend the last decade of my life like our great poet Johann Christian Friedrich Hölderlin walking through this city being ridiculed by children . . . It doesn't have to be injected. I can drink it; I can do it like Socrates.'

After a long pause, I pressed the question, more as a desperate plea: But it is suicide – is it not?

'Yes, it is suicide. But it is not murder. It's giving back my life to my creator . . . My position is very different from people who do not believe in eternal life and who think only of nothingness. I hope to come back to God, back to my origins . . . I am in his hands.'

Küng was not alone in believing that modern demographics and the advance of medical research had opened up a necessary new area of theological debate about assisted dying.

'It's like the problem of birth and the origin of the human being. The Church's official teaching is that it is the will of God that you are not to have contraception. Now they are saying it's against the will of God to help you die. The fact is that birth and dying are our own responsibility.'

Küng acknowledged that this was a position that was difficult for me 'as a friend', and a Catholic, to understand. I told him that it was not the only difficulty I faced. His latest book dismissed the Counter-Reformation as a dark age. It also made no concessions to mysticism and questioned the validity of forms of popular religion of which Pope Francis has spoken favourably.

He replied that Anglicanism has 'done a few things very well' including a vernacular language and having elected bishops (except in England itself), that he was against superstition and complete decentralization, and wanted priests as well as laity in parish life. He supported the papacy as a pastoral Petrine office within the Catholic Church, but took the Gospel as his yardstick for reform. 'I think Pope Francis is a Pope of the Gospel.'

And so we ended where we began. However, I remained saddened by some of the things I had read and we had talked about. Küng, respected by his followers as a courageous prophet, seemed once again to be pushing the boundaries of his theology to a position that many Catholics would see as an attack on their faith. And yet his lifelong dedication to the cause of reform and renovation within the structures and for changes of some of the other teachings of the Catholic Church seemed to resonate with the hopes of many believers and non-believers for the Francis papacy.

Before I left, I told Küng that, even if some of his critics now had more reason than ever to see him as a heretic, I still considered him a Catholic priest (he had not been officially defrocked or 'laicized' by the Vatican, so Pope Francis still considered him to be one too). I asked for his blessing. He gave it to me in Latin, his fingers pressed against my forehead as he made the sign of the cross, before we bid each other farewell with a 'God Bless'. I felt we both wanted to belong to that 'Church after battle' Pope Francis had proclaimed needed healing.

Epilogue
Pilgrim at Large

Among the petitions circulating the worldwide web in August 2014 was one calling for a Hail Mary to be recited for the Pope's health. Weeks earlier, suffering a severe headache and nausea, Pope Francis had been forced to cancel an appointment and returned to his room in the Domus Sanctae Marthae. Exhaustion, physical and mental, appeared to be the cause. I remember, early on in the papacy, halfway through Pope Francis's frenetically paced trip to Rio in July 2013, the veteran Vatican press spokesman Fr Lombardi admitting that at the pace his boss was going, the whole staff would struggle to still be on their feet by the weekend.

As well as having had part of a lung removed when he was young, in later years Pope Francis developed sciatica, which brought periodical crippling backache. Despite the intervention of physiotherapists, exercises and painkillers, and having his shoes reinforced, Pope Francis still had to endure regular pain.

In August 2014, as he flew back from a tiring five-day trip to South Korea, where he had urged reconciliation with the North and sent a telegram of prayers and greetings to China's President Xi Jinping, Pope Francis was asked about his popular appeal. 'I try to think of my sins, my mistakes, not to become proud, because I know it will only last a short time,' he said, before adding, 'Two or three years and then I'll be off to the Father's House.'

This last remark gave leading newspapers around the world a most-read item online, underlining the interest readers had in the Pope's survival. How serious were reports that the Mafia and Islamist fundamentalists were among those plotting to kill Pope Francis? Would he end up throwing in the towel, paving the way for a young, physically stronger cardinal? Such scenarios did not seem so implausible given the precedent set by Pope Francis's predecessors. John Paul II, on 13 May 1981, was shot by the Turkish national Mehmet Ali Ağca as he rode in an open car in St Peter's Square. The pontiff narrowly survived the assassination attempt. He was hit in the abdomen, left hand and right arm, but the bullets narrowly missed vital organs. His successor Pope Benedict XVI, a year older than Pope Francis, quit after five years in post. Other popes in modern times provided contrasting points of reference. Pope John Paul II had been elected at a much younger age, fifty-eight, and ruled for twenty-seven years. Paul VI and Pope John Paul I were both sixty-six when elected. The first died after fifteen years as pope; the second after only thirty-three days.

In the immediate aftermath of their respective elections to the papacy, there were some striking parallels between the former Archbishop of Venice, Albino Luciani (John Paul I) and Jorge Bergoglio – not only in how they were initially perceived by a majority of people who knew little about them, but by the cardinals who had taken part in their election.

Basil Hume, the Archbishop of Westminster at the time, called Luciani 'God's candidate'. And added: 'Once it had happened it seemed totally and entirely right. The feeling that he was just what we wanted was so general . . . We felt as if our hands were being guided as we wrote his name on the paper.' In 2013 similar enthusiasm was voiced by Hume's successor Cormac Murphy-O'Connor who had gained a favourable impression of Bergoglio in the previous conclave of 2005. Eight years later Murphy-O'Connor described Bergoglio as 'a humble, gentle and very intelligent and spiritual man' that the Church needed in its time of crisis. 'I think that Pope Francis is going to be a blessing for the Catholic Church and for the world,' he said. Although Murphy-O'Connor, having retired, did not vote at the 2013 conclave, he was an influential lobbyist behind the scenes in pushing for Bergoglio's candidacy.

Luciani, as his biographer John Cornwell reminds us, announced no sooner than he had been elected that he was dispensing with the traditional pomp of the papal coronation and the gestatorial chair, and declared that he wished to be known as 'pastor' of the Church rather than 'pontiff'. 'He was universally dubbed the "smiling Pope". Seldom had a papacy begun with such popular appeal,' noted Cornwell. Yet thirty-three days after his election, Papa Luciani, as the Italians called him, unexpectedly died in his private apartments. It was the shortest papacy in nearly 400 years. Conspiracy theorists suspected foul play. Cornwell, on the basis of a diligent investigation, concluded he had almost certainly died of a 'pulmonary embolus due to a condition of abnormal coagulability of the blood'. Rest and monitoring might have ensured his survival even if his papacy may have proved disastrous. For Luciani, while remembered as a holy and humble pastor, was unprepared for the challenges that faced him from within the Vatican and wider world. 'The Holy Spirit did a good job: relieving us of him before he did too much damage,' Cornwell was told by one Vatican official, a comment typical of many he heard.

If Luciani's place in history was to be confined to that of a terrible mistake that fate rectified, that of Bergoglio can be seen as a papacy foretold. There was much talk, in Luciani's long-serving successor John Paul II's final years, that the next pope should be a Latin American; the feeling was widespread that the continent's hour was near. As things turned out, the cardinals at the 2005 conclave voted for what they considered a stabilizing set of hands, electing Ratzinger, the German theologian who had loyally served as Pope John Paul II's chief doctrinal enforcer. Ratzinger owed the strength of his final vote to Bergoglio who, for the sake of unity, transferred his backers. It sealed an important and enduring bond between the German and the Argentine based on mutual trust and respect.

Bergoglio's not insignificant support at the 2005 conclave reflected the fact that within the international Church hierarchy he was not the unknown figure he seemed to be in the secular world outside Argentina. His star had first shone in Rome back in September 2001 when the terrorist attack on the US had American Cardinal Edward Egan dashing back to New York, and Bergoglio replaced him as relator for the Synod of Bishops. Among those who knew Bergoglio well in those days was the Argentine Catholic journalist José María Poirie. He recalled, in a profile published in 2005 in the English *Catholic Herald*, that Bergoglio, 'moved easily [in the role] and with great confidence, leaving a favourable impression as a man open to communion and dialogue'. But as Poirie also said there was little else in public view, 'the modest glimpses of Bergoglio only serving to heighten his enigmatic profile'.

During the decades of revolution and military dictatorships in Latin America – the 1960s and 1970s – Bergoglio had kept his distance from the radicalism of the Third World Movement priests and the vocal group of Latin American bishops for whom there could be no social justice true to the Gospel without revolutionary activism. This was to tarnish his reputation as head of the Jesuits. His discreet actions to help some of those who suffered human rights abuses during the military repression distinguished him from those sectors of the Argentine Catholic Church that collaborated with the torture and the killings or turned a blind eye to both. His discretion – or ambiguity – when it came to the human rights issue conformed to the official strategy taken by the papal nuncio and a majority of Argentine bishops, who as a body were politically conservative. But it failed to match up to the courage and self-sacrifice of the Catholic martyrs that took pride of place in the history of the Jesuit order from the early days of the Reformation, through to the Nazi concentration camps and, later in the twentieth century, in El Salvador.

Bergoglio had survived, leaving himself exposed to his critics. Only when he became an archbishop did he adopt a more outspoken attitude on the issue of human rights and social justice. But he did so in a country that for all its political and social failings had been ruled since 1984 by democratically elected civilian governments and where the violence of the state and paramilitary organizations had dissipated since the Dirty War. His stand suggested that like Archbishop Óscar Romero, his appointment to high office had brought with it paradoxically a new humility as well as courage in facing up to a range of issues, even if his reactions to some sexual abuse allegations proved belated. The difference, of course, was that Romero, in defence of his faith, faced up to right-wing death squads and their military allies knowing that he would end up being martyred. Romero, Archbishop of El Salvador, was shot dead on 24 March 1980 while celebrating Mass, one day after calling on the country's military to stop carrying out the right-wing government's repression.

Just months after his election, Pope Francis sent the case of Archbishop Romero to the Vatican's saint-making office, thereby speeding up the beatification process. This overturned decades of resistance inside the Vatican and from conservative Latin American bishops who regarded Romero as an advocate of liberation theology and neo-Marxism. Bergoglio's own instincts early on in his Church career made him suspicious of radical theology, preferring priests and bishops to steer away from political analysis and secular psychology. And yet, following a process of conversion, Pope Francis seemed to recognize that a man killed for standing up for the poor could no longer be ignored by a papacy that claimed to speak for them. Pope Francis had not become a Marxist. He had simply acknowledged that for many Catholics Romero was already a saint, in practice if not in name, and an example for future generations.

Once elected, Pope Francis reflected publicly on his failings as a Jesuit provincial, but not because of his ambiguous record on human rights; rather, he was questioning his authoritarian style of leadership. As he told Spadaro, 'In my experience as superior of the Society, to be honest, I have not always behaved in that way – that is, I did not always do the necessary consultation. And this was not a good thing. My style of government as a Jesuit at the beginning had many faults. That was a difficult time for the Society.'

Judging by the comments made to me by numerous Jesuits affected by Bergoglio's rule, this was an understatement. 'He exercised his authority with an iron fist as if he was the sole interpreter of St Ignatius Loyola,' was how one put it. Such was the distress he caused within the order that a negative perception of him politically and theologically endured right up to the moment of his election as pope. Several of his former colleagues in Spain and America greeted the news with a sense of profound shock, fearing the worst for the order and the Church at large.

Bergoglio by his own admission was attracted to join the Jesuits because of their character as 'an advance force of the Church, speaking military language, developed with obedience and discipline', according to *El Jesuita*, the book of interviews by Sergio Rubin and Francesca Ambrogetti. St Ignatius of Loyola used military metaphors because he had been a soldier in his young years but Bergoglio as a young Jesuit provincial seemed unable to transmit that Ignatian spirituality as marked by a discernment of a personal vocation, rather than the conformity of standing in line. And yet for Bergoglio, as for Ignatius, discernment was an instrument of struggle as much as resolution – finding the true path and following the Lord more closely was not easy, and it was full of potential setbacks and deviations.

We do not know for sure what prompted Bergoglio to enter the 'dark night' of doubt and remorse after being replaced as head of the Jesuits and being sent, eventually, to semi-exile in Córdoba. But it seems likely that the criticism he received about not having done more than he did during the Dirty War may have weighed on his conscience. His outspoken defence of the poor and the victims of injustice became a key part of his biographical narrative only once he had been promoted up the clerical ladder.

I am not suggesting, as I have found no evidence to support this, that Bergoglio was hypocritical or opportunistic in his pursuit of power, thinking only of his own protection − but rather that a combination of circumstances and the inner working of his own conscience contributed to his conversion to a person more deserving of being elected pope. His replacement as Jesuit provincial was a 'dark night' but it set him on a path to spiritual transformation. A lifeline was thrown to him not by fellow Jesuits but by the papal nuncio and the Argentine Archbishop Quarracino when they brought him out of obscurity and appointed him.

Promotion in the Argentine hierarchy gave Bergoglio power again, but the circumstances had changed and so had he. He now exercised his authority and gave witness to his Catholic faith in a different way. Like the English Catholic saint Thomas More, when he became King Henry VIII's Chancellor, Bergoglio came to show courage in the face of a State which had lost its soul, and he did not betray the truth or compromise it on the altar of power.

As Archbishop of Buenos Aires, he showed sincere modesty, dressing mostly as a simple cleric, travelling by public transport and telling his priests to 'be out on the frontiers', as he put it, just like the first Jesuit missionaries. Bergoglio himself went into the *villas* to show his support for priests, religious workers and development organizations; he was committed to an effective New Evangelization, with the poor, for the poor. He showed he had become a leader keen on listening sympathetically, and who took care in his judgement of people and in handling their lives, never rushing into personal condemnation. He stood by and spoke out in defence of his priests when they were threatened by drug traffickers, or struggled with their vocation or illness. His lay followers included migrants, young drug addicts, battered wives and prostitutes, and others struggling to survive on the fringes of society. He also engaged in dialogue with other faith groups, which was to help him venture forth on the global stage.

Archbishop Bergoglio was admired as seemingly being pre-occupied by the future of society, and as a man looking always for new forms of social solidarity and justice – this, in a country that had squandered its food and energy resources and left thousands trying to scrape a living by rummaging through bins and recycling garbage.

Bergoglio's ideology was homespun, opposed to Marxism on the left, and fascism on the right, but influenced from an early age by what he perceived were the similarities between traditional Catholic social doctrine and that strand of popular Peronism that was as hostile to liberal capitalism as it was to socialism. His politics were framed against the background of a long history of social conflict but also of accommodation and complicity between the Catholic Church and government, whether military or civilian, and occasional confrontation.

His experience was also of the endemic corruption of Argentina, a failed State in which his own governance proved an exception in terms of the quality and ability of its leadership, along with its evident social consciousness and spirituality. And although Bergoglio as Jesuit and bishop scrupulously avoided siding publicly with any political party or movement (despite evidence of his sympathies for Peronism), he was a pragmatic political player. As one commentator put it, he was skilled at 'moving pieces along with the best chess player'.

Once elected, Pope Francis reflected publicly on discernment as the pillar of his spirituality in greater detail than ever, revealing at the same time the extent to which he had changed since his days as a Jesuit provincial. Talking about how Ignatian spirituality shaped his attitude towards Church governance, he told fellow Jesuit Antonio Spadaro: 'I was always struck by a saying that describes the vision of Ignatius: *non coerceri a maximo, sed contoneri a minimo divivo est* [not to be limited by the greatest and yet to be contained in the tiniest – this is the divine]. Thus it was important not to be restricted by a larger space, while it could be equally important to stay in restricted spaces. The virtue of the large and small is magnanimity thanks to which we can always look at the horizon from the position of where we are. That means being able to do the little things of everyday with a big heart open to God and to others. That means being able to appreciate the small things inside large horizons, those of the kingdom of God.'

While Pope Francis's spirituality is not in doubt, the life of Jorge Bergoglio, as Jesuit priest and bishop, was far from flawless, and deeply human in its vulnerability and complexity. The cardinals who elected him claimed to have had God on their side, choosing a bishop they thought capable of facing up to the challenges of a world in desperate need of sound leadership and moral guidance – but a safe pair of hands nonetheless that would protect papal authority and Church teaching.

On his election, Pope Francis showed himself visibly renewed in spirit, far from daunted by his appointment, positively uplifted by it, and bent on giving a Church in crisis a new sense of purpose and legitimacy. Those who had known Bergoglio over many years remarked they could not remember him with such a smile, not a nervous one like Luciani's, but a relaxed, generous one, exuding inner peace.

A film released months before Pope Francis's election, called *Habemus Papam*, directed by Italian filmmaker Nanni Moretti, lampooned the arrival of an outsider to Peter's throne in a fictionalized account of a modern papal election. Melville, the non-Italian cardinal elected as pope has a crisis of self-doubt and mini-breakdown on his way to the balcony overlooking St Peter's Square. He refuses to continue, claiming the challenge is simply too great. It proved, in part, prophetic. Pope Benedict XVI resigned, believing that the task of dealing with the Church's problems would be better undertaken by someone with the energy, vision and necessary support within the Church at large. The election as pope of Jorge Bergoglio, Jesuit and Argentine, took the Vatican and the world into uncharted territory.

As Pope Francis later told Spadaro, during the lunch period when he began to realize that he might be elected on Wednesday, 13 March 2013, he felt 'a deep and inexplicable peace and interior consolation come over him, along with a great darkness, a deep obscurity about everything else. And those feelings accompanied him until his election later that day'. Spadaro does not elaborate because nor did Bergoglio. But the reflection brought to my mind a comment in *Dark Nights of the Soul* by the contemporary US spiritual writer Thomas More (no relation to the saint):

> The dark night of the soul is not restricted to holy people. It can happen to anyone. I believe that in some ways it happens to everyone. Yet it is much more significant than simple misfortune. It is a deep transformation, a movement toward indescribable freedom and joy. And in truth it doesn't have to be unpleasant! The dark night of the soul is a profoundly good thing. It is an ongoing spiritual process in which we are liberated from attachments and compulsions and empowered to live and love more freely. Sometimes this letting go of old ways is painful, occasionally even devastating. But this is not why the night is called 'dark'. The darkness of the night implies nothing sinister, only that the liberation takes place in hidden

ways, beneath our knowledge and understanding. It happens mysteriously, in secret, and beyond our conscious control. For that reason it can be disturbing or even scary, but in the end it always works to our benefit.

Not for the first time in his life, Jorge Bergoglio was at a spiritual crossroads, discerning which was the true path he believed God had marked out for him as Pope Francis, a journey without maps, but not without hope.

Bibliography

Ackroyd, Peter, *The Life of Thomas More* (London: Vintage, 1999).

Allen, John L. Jr, *Conclave* (New York: Doubleday, 2002).

——, *Opus Dei* (London: Penguin, 2006).

Armstrong, Karen, *Fields of Blood: Religion and the History of Violence* (London: Bodley Head, 2014).

Basco, Francesc, *Beatifican 522 Mártires* (Tarragona: Basco, 2013).

Bayer, Osvaldo, *Fútbol Argentino* (Buenos Aires: Sudamericana, 1990).

Bergoglio, Jorge Mario, *Dialogos entre Juan Pablo II y Fidel Castro* (Buenos Aires: Ciencia y Cultura, 1998).

——, *Evangelii Gaudium, The Joy of the Gospel* (Vatican City: Editrice Vaticana, 2013).

——, *In Him Alone is Our Hope* (San Francisco: Ignatius Press, 2013).

——, *Las Homilías de la Mañana* (Vatican City: Editrice Vaticana, 2013).

——, *Meditaciones Para Religiosos* (Buenos Aires: Diego de Torres, 1982).

——, *Nuesta fe es Revolucionaria*, ed. Virginia Bonard (Buenos Aires: Planeta, 2013).

——, *Reflexiones en Esperanza* (Buenos Aires: Universidad del Salvador, 1992).

——, *Reflexiones Espirituales sobre la Vida* (Buenos Aires: Diego de Torres, 1987).

Bergoglio, Jorge Mario and Abraham Skorka, *Sobre el Cielo y La Tierra* (Barcelona: Debate, 2013).

Borges, Jorge Luis, *Obras Completas* (Buenos Aires: Emece, 1979).

Burns, Jimmy, *Beyond the Silver River* (London: Bloomsbury, 1989).

——, *The Land that Lost Its Heroes: How Argentina Lost the Falklands War* (London: Bloomsbury, 2002).

——, *Maradona: The Hand of God* (London: Bloomsbury, 2010).

——, *La Roja* (London: Simon & Schuster, 2012).

Burns, Tom, *The Use of Memory* (London: Sheed & Ward, 1993).

Byrne, Lavinia, *The Journey Is My Home* (London: Hodder & Stoughton, 2000).

Caimari, Lila, *Perón y la Iglesia Católica* (Buenos Aires: Emece, 1994).

Camarasa, Jorge, *El Verdugo* (Buenos Aires: Planeta, 2009).

Camarotti, Gerson, *Segredos do Conclave* (São Paolo: Geração, 2013).

Campbell-Johnston, Michael, *Just Faith* (Oxford: Way Books, 2010).

Carril, Mario del, *La Vida de Emilio Mignone* (Buenos Aires: Emece, 2011).

Cornwell, John, *Breaking Faith* (New York: Viking Compass, 2001).

——, *Hitler's Pope* (New York: Viking, 1999).

——, *Newman's Unquiet Grave* (London: Continuum, 2010).

——, *A Pope in Winter* (London: Penguin 2005).

——, *A Thief in the Night* (New York: Viking, 1989).

Cornwell, Rupert, *God's Banker* (London: Victor Gollancz, 1983).

Dostoyevsky, Fyodor, *The Brothers Karamazov* (London: Penguin, 2003).

Ellis, Alice Thomas, *Serpent on the Rock* (London: Sceptre, 1995).

Elorriaga, Federico, *Pequenos Manantiales* (Bilbao: Mensajero, 2012).

Endean, Philip (ed.), *Writings on Jesuit Spirituality by Jorge Maria Bergoglio* (St Louis: Institute of Jesuit Resources, 2013).

Escrivá, Josemaría, *The Way* (New York: Doubleday, 2006).

Figueredo, Octavio (ed.), *365 Días con el Papa Francisco* (Madrid: San Pablo, 2013).

Gabetta, Carlos, *Todos Somos Subversivos* (Buenos Aires: Bruguera, 1984).

Gallagher, Charles, *Vatican Secret Diplomacy* (New Haven and London: Yale University Press, 2008).

Gallagher, Tom, *Divided Scotland* (Argyll: Argyll Publishing, 2013).

Graham-Yooll, Andrew, *A State of Fear* (London: Eland Books, 1986).

Hebblethwaite, Peter, *The New Inquisition?* (London: Fount, 1980).

Hebblethwaite, Peter and Margaret, *The Next Pope* (New York: HarperCollins, 2000).

Hernández, José, *Martín Fierro* (Buenos Aires: Terramar, 2009).

Himitian, Evangelina, *A Vida de Francisco* (Rio de Janeiro: Objetica, 2013).

Hodge, Alice, *God's Secret Agents* (London: Harper Perennial, 2006).

House, Adrian, *Francis of Assisi* (London: Pimlico, 2001).

Hughes, Gerard W., *God in All Things* (London: Hodder & Stoughton, 2003).

Ivereigh, Austen, *The Great Reformer* (London: Allen & Unwin, 2014).

King, Nicholas, *Jesuit Companions* (Cape Town: Southern Cross, 1997).

Küng, Hans, *Can We Save the Catholic Church?* (London: William Collins, 2013).

Lamet, Pedro Miguel, *Arrupe* (Bilbao: Mensajero, 2014).

——, *Esclavo de Esclavos: Pedro Claver* (Bilbao: Mensajero, 1996).

Larraquy, Marcelo, *Recen por Él* (Buenos Aires: Sudamericana, 2013).

Manzoni, Alessandro, *The Betrothed* (London: Everyman's Library, 1962).

Merton, Thomas, *The Literary Essays* (New York: New Directions, 1981).

Methol Ferré, Alberto, *El Papa y El Filósofo* (Buenos Aires: Biblos, 2013).

Mignone, Emilio F., *Iglesia y Dictadura* (Buenos Aires: Pensamiento, 1986).

Miroff, Nick, 'Pope Francis Was Often Quiet on Argentine Sex Abuse Cases as Archbishop', *Washington Post* (18 March 2013), www.washingtonpost.com/world/the_americas/pope-francis-was-often-quiet-on-argentine-sex-abuse-cases-as-archbishop/2013/03/18/26e7eca4-8ff6-11e2-9cfd-36d6c9b5d7ad_story.html.

Monedero, Juan Carlos, *Curso Urgente de Politica Para Gente Decente* (Barcelona: Seix Barral, 2014).

Mugica, Carlos, *Peronismo y Cristianismo* (Buenos Aires: Punto de Encuentro, 2012).

Murphy-O'Connor, Cormac, *An English Spring: Memoirs* (London: Bloomsbury, 2015).

National Commission on Disappeared People, *Nunca Más: A Report by Argentina's National Commission on Disappeared People* (London: Faber & Faber, 1986).

Nichols, Peter, *The Pope's Divisions* (London: Faber & Faber, 1981).

Noel, Gerard, *The Hound of Hitler* (London: Continuum, 2008).

Norwich, John Julius, *The Popes* (London: Vintage, 2012).

O'Donnell, Santiago, *ArgenLeaks* (Buenos Aires: Sudamericana, 2011).

O'Mahoney, Gerald, *The Other Side of the Mountain* (London: Geoffrey Chapman, 1989).

Pierron, Yvonne, *Misionera Durante La Dictadura* (Buenos Aires: Planeta, 2009).

Piqué, Elisabetta, *Francisco: Vida y Revolución* (Buenos Aires: El Ateneo, 2014).

Posner, Gerald, *God's Bankers: A History of Money and Power at the Vatican* (London: Simon & Schuster, 2015).

Premat, Silvina, *Curas Villeros* (Buenos Aires: Sudamericana, 2012).

——, *Pepe: El Cura de La Villa* (Buenos Aires: Sudamericana, 2013).

Puente, Armando Rubén, *La Vida Oculta de Bergoglio* (Madrid: Libros Libres, 2014).

Rahner, Karl, *Ignatius of Loyola* (London: Collins, 1979).

Romero, Óscar, *Memories in Mosaic* (London, CAFOD, 2000).

Rubin, Sergio and Francesca Ambrogetti, *El Papa Francisco* (Barcelona: Ediciones B, 2013).

Sarmiento, Domingo F., *Facundo* (Buenos Aires: Kapelusz, 1971).

Scavo, Nello, *La Lista de Bergoglio* (Bologna: Emi, 2013).

Sebreli, Juan José, *Comediantes y Mártires* (Buenos Aires: Sudamericana, 2008).

——, *La Era del Fútbol* (Buenos Aires: Sudamericana, 1998).

Shortt, Rupert, *Benedict XVI* (London: Hodder & Stoughton, 2005).

Spadaro, Antonio, 'A Big Heart Open to God: The Exclusive Interview with Pope Francis', *America: The National Catholic Review* (30 September 2013), www.americamagazine.org/pope-interview.

——, 'Wake Up the World: Conversation with Pope Francis about the Religious Life)', *Civiltà Cattolica*, I (2014), 13–17.

Tanner, Norman, *New Short History of the Catholic Church* (London: Burns & Oates, 2011).

Tenenbaum, Ernesto, *Kirchner es Peronista* (Buenos Aires: Catálogos, 2003).

Tetlow, Joseph A., *Ignatius Loyola* (New York: Crossroad, 1992).

Thavis, John, *The Vatican Diaries* (London: Penguin, 2013).

Tornielli, Andrea, *I Fioretti di Papa Francesco* (Milan: Piemme, 2013).

Vallely, Paul, *Untying the Knots* (London: Bloomsbury, 2013).

Vedia, Mariano de, *Francisco el Papa del Pueblo* (Buenos Aires: Planeta, 2013).

Verbitsky, Horacio, *El Silencio* (Buenos Aires: Sudamericana, 2005).

——, *Vigilia de Armas* (Buenos Aires: Sudamericana, 2009).

Von Kempis, Stefan and Philip F. Lawler, *A Call to Serve* (London: Wall Street Journal (staff of), *Pope Francis: From the End of the Earth to Rome* (Kindle Edition, 2013). SPCK, 2013).

Walsh, Michael, *Opus Dei* (London: Grafton Books, 1989).

Walsh, Rodolfo, *Operation Massacre* (Brecon: Old Street Publishing, 2013).

Woodrow, Alain, *The Jesuits: A Story of Power* (London: Geoffrey Chapman 1995).

Acknowledgements

This book would not have been possible without the generous support of many friends in several countries and across continents, as well as the enduring patience of my family. To all I owe huge thanks.

While I have mentioned many characters who participated in this project, my thanks go to many others, including those not identified. (Note: SJ signifies Society of Jesus – a member of the Jesuit order.)

In Buenos Aires: Claudia Acuna, Luis Ampuero, María Luara Avignolo, Carolina Barros, José Benegas, Rafael Braun, Santiago del Carril, Alicia Castro, Gabriela Cerruti, Bob Cox, Andres Federman, John Fernandes, Juan Eduardo Fleming, Fernando González, Monica González, Andrew Graham-Yooll, Roberto Guareschi, Ricardo Kirchbaum, José Ignacio Lopez, Fr Guillermo Marco, Silvia Mercado, Marcela Mora y Araujo, Ricardo Murtagh, Ernesto A. O'Connor, Nacho Puente Olivera, Fr Pepe di Paola, Fr Ignacio Peréz del Viso SJ, Francisco Piñón, José María Poirier, Julian Randle, Sebastián Randle, Sergio Rubin, Romina Ryan, Ricardo Sabanes, Abraham Skorka, Eduardo Suarez, Rupert Sword, Ernesto Tenenbaum, Josefina Tizado, Miguel Ángel Toma, Claudia Touris, Washington Uranga, Eduardo Valdes, Greg Venables, Horacio Verbitsky, Jude Webber.

In Rio de Janeiro: Fellipe Awai, Gerson Camarotti, Fr Francisco Ivern SJ, Oscar and Gaby Porto.

In La Paz: Ramón Alaix SJ, Elizabeth Coloma, Felipe Hartman, Roberto Laserna.

In the UK: Tina Beattie, Paul Betts, Des Brogan, Tom Callagher, Michael Campbell- Johnston SJ, John Cornwell, Vicky Costick, Ted Coyle SJ, Elena Curti, Mark Dowd, Philip Endean SJ, Abigail Frymann, James Harding SJ, David Hurst, Christopher Lamb, Liz Leydon, Brendan McCarthy, Stephen McGinty, Jack Mahoney SJ, Cardinal Cormac Murphy-O'Connor, Michael O'Halloran SJ, Fr William Pearsall SJ, Catherine Pepinster, Robert Powell, Hugh Purcell, Moira Reid, James Roberts, Tony Robinson, Jack Valero, Fr Rocco Viviano, Brendan Walsh, Peter Wintgens, Augusto Zampini.

In Rome: John Allen, Fr Jacquineau Azetsop SJ, Nigel Baker, Cardinal Antonio Cañizares, Marco Carroggio, Guy Dinmore, John Hooper, Armando Matteo, Dario Menor, Robert Mickens, Mgr Antonio Miralles, Rachel Sanderson, Manuel Sánchez, Nick Squires, Mons Roderick Strange, Fr Norman Tanner SJ, Fr Paul Tighe, Mgr Philip Whitmore.

In Spain: David Baxter, Dominic Begg, Tom Burns, Robert Graham, Pedro Miguel Lamet SJ, Gregorio Marañón y Bertran de Lis, Jose Luis Melendez, Juan Carlos Monedero, Maite Nicholson, Peter Nicholson, José María Martín Patino SJ, Fr Josep Pausas, Juan Antonio Rubio, Federico Trillo.

In Munich: Andreas Batlogg SJ, Christa Pongratz-Lippitt and Rupert Bell.

I am much indebted to John Wilkins, Fr Nick King SJ, Michael Walsh, Juan Eduardo Fleming, Martin Andersen and Isabel Gómez-Acebo for their useful commentaries on a rough early manuscript.

With thanks also to Andreas Campomar, my editor, and Clive Hebard, Howard Watson and the rest of the team at Constable in London, and my agents Annabel Merullo and Laura Williams and their team at Peters Fraser & Dunlop – for their diligence, forbearance and good humour.

My interview with Hans Küng and my recollections of Stonyhurst College are based on articles I wrote in the *Tablet*. Other media consulted include: *National Catholic Reporter, Civiltà Cattolica, Financial Times, Daily Telegraph, El Pais, Catholic Herald, Washington Post, Vida Nueva, Economist, Guardian, Clarín, La Nación, Página/12, South China Morning News, Religion News Service, The Times* and *Observer*.

I have identified in the text where possible those who I interviewed and agreed to be quoted openly. There are others whom I met on this journey but who asked not to be named.

Index